"For all of these things and
7 billion human souls to da
other, for all of this to occur day in aay out jor so long,
amount of processing power behind the scenes is inconceivable.
Sure, we try to conceive of it. We want to figure it out and quite
simply to process that amount of data is far too much for a
human mind. There is simply too much data. So we see parts. We
glimpse at the elegance of the dancing existential machine, the
cosmos; for it is this cosmos that is manifesting reality, through
you, with you, including you. The reality shifts according to
human awareness."

"Today's time of Year 2009 is in fact vibrating far faster than
yesteryear's time but we have refused to let go of the 24 hr clock.
We have digital TV signal, we'll soon have 3D TV, wireless
internet is here and have long had instant coffee. We have
microwave ovens and particle colliders – all these things from
sword and sandals. The technological achievements occurred, not
because we are smarter but because we are vibrating higher. And
that is also because the reality infrastructure can support a
higher vibration culture."

"The bank is the gateway by which energy on earth moves, and
where classes of society are formed and destroyed. In other
words, it can be stated quite emphatically, from a dimensional
view, no economic recession can take place through natural
circumstance. The cycles of recessions on earth can be found to
have intimate relationships to certain celestial events, power
grabs or during a redistribution of world sovereignty."

"The reality operating system determines many of the features
and benefits of existence because it acts as the basic interface
between the cosmic machinery and the existential lifeforms. As
you live within the context of the reality operating system, your
existence is either limited or expanded by the features and
technical specifications of the operating system."

"Can you see the importance of discussing the truth about reality? The leaders have everyone thinking about war, terrorism, disease, sex, discrimination, money, anger, fear, god – everything that descends humanity! You are not being inspired. They are not expanding your awareness. You are not stepping into other dimensions, because if you do they give you pills, they put you in an asylum. You lose your job. You lose friends. I mean, at every turn you've been corralled into the herd of sheep."

"The slave has no possibility but the possibility that they are told. The masters call that the rules. These are the rules of the renegade masters. These are not the rules of the reality. The reality says, "Anything is possible. **Tutto e possibile**." Any attachment or condition to that possibility rule is an aberration, a big fat lie. Of course, our cosmos comes with its own set of laws such as do not aimlessly or purposely murder people. Strike one. Everyone is an equal. Strike two. And things of this nature. Cosmic laws exist, and they exist for each and every level of awareness."

TCB II

TCB VOL. II

Translations from the Cosmic Computer

TALESSIAN
EL-WIKOSIAN

This is a work of nonfiction.

Set in Verdana

Book design by T. N. El-Wikosian

CONTENTS

The 7 Books of the Cosmic Testament

Introduction

INTRODUCTION

There is much knowledge on this plane of existence and most of that knowledge is applicable to the way the world used to be and that is because this place has experienced unparalleled upgrades in recent years, especially since 2007; therefore, this place you call home no longer functions on the same knowledge base. Luckily, you have in your hands *TCB Vol. II: Translations from the Cosmic Computer*. *TCB II* carries on where *Talessians Cosmic Bible* ended and it does so with the same esoteric, imaginative and outrageous flair as its predecessor. This is not a book for the timid or the common mind. If you fall into the category of normal, career-driven and looking forward to retirement then you are better off letting someone else purchase this book. *TCB II* is a frontal blast of cosmic energy that will aid humanity in reinventing its current state of existence.

Let's be clear from the top, existence on "earth" is akin to living in a great sewer – war, disease, corruption, lies, secrecy, fascism, poverty, terrorism, environmental catastrophe, murder of the animals, raping of children, oppression – it stinks on this earth and that is because of worldwide neglect. With a newly revised existential engine and a brand new reality system in operation, you're going to require new knowledge to take you and your neighbours out of this hellhole. That is what *TCB II* is about, new knowledge. This is cosmic knowledge. It has been translated for you from the grand, exotic, wonderful Cosmic Computer, deep in the ocean of technology. The birthplace of humanity and of all things.

Every effort has been made to ensure any person can derive some benefit from this valuable material. It has been written on several levels of perception and, despite appearances, all the content found herein is still introductory and basic. It should never be interpreted as being complete and it should never be kept secret and away from the public. This cosmic knowledge is so basic that everyone inhabitant here deserves to have some access to it. In fact, it should be discussed in schools and in public as much as possible.

Talessian Na'mor El-Wikosian (2010)

REALITY SCIENCE

INTRODUCTION

There are many kinds of sciences on earth, many kinds of applied thinking to a particular area of knowledge. Science itself is the result of the evolution of philosophy. All modern scientific theory originated in philosophical discussion. When the infamous apple fell from the tree and hit Sir Newton on the head he began the process of discussing with himself what in fact had taken place. His discussion added reason and a few doses of imagination until he began to notice a pattern emerging, like a series of formulas exposed under the surface of water.

A Newton would apply further reason and understanding in order to polish those fundamental observations, what he would reason as truths, and then through sweat and late nights he'd discover some fine-tuned results. That would later be called "science."

The trouble with scientists, and science in general, is that they believe that they've discovered all the key sciences on earth, and they've convinced each other that any new discovery belongs to the current palette of science. They also firmly believe in their theories, so when I speak of *reality science* as a valid science of the multidimensional cosmos they're not going to recognize it as having any validity because 1) I'm not a certified scientist, and, 2) we live in a three-dimensional world with the possibility of other dimensions but with no proof.

To me, multiple dimensions require no proof, it's obvious. I've been interacting and learning through the multidimensional interfaces, I've interacted with multidimensional people and I've discovered an impressive, if not resplendent, architecture that has been carefully and purposely tucked under the current reality we see with our eyes.

At this point, I've developed my reality science skills enough to determine some fundamental principles and approaches to the multidimensional realms floating near or inside our own realm, a realm we call "planet earth." To properly understand reality science will require the suspension of this idea of a *planet earth* because rather than a planet we are existing within a *textured reality*, verily a plane of existence.

What has happened over the centuries is that we've become increasingly absorbed by the contents of this present reality. We've become distracted by the events in this reality and we've been forced to accept a unidimensional view of existence and anything outside of that has been labelled as "religious experience" or "unexplained phenomena."

So, immediately you can see that this book on reality science isn't going to rely on any fast and true scientific beliefs. On the contrary, **Reality Science** is going to entirely devote itself to an entirely new spectrum of physical observation, all of it having to do with what many would consider the nonphysical, nonlocal world. To this extent then, Reality Science is for those who have it within themselves the willingness to suspend their disbelief of a multidimensional reality and to look at planet earth as merely an electromagnetic signal wherein billions of inhabitants are suspended. And then realizing, if one reality can hold so much life then how about the cosmos and all the other realities.

Reality Science will be looked at as an unusual book and that is because the scientific community can only observe phenomena within their current rules and their rules only suggest that other dimensions may exist, only suggest it, but without physical proof or something observable, they cannot stamp in a new theoretical application. So it seems prudent that an introductory volume on the science of reality is included into the human library.

What is the value of studying reality? Is it any better than quantum physics? What kind of credentials does one need in order to be regarded a reality scientist? To answer all three: I don't know.

What is the value of a cup of coffee until you need a caffeine fix? Is quantum physics better than Buddhism? What kind of credentials are needed to be regarded an artist?

As you can see, the argument is not steadfast and true. The argument is an actual argument. We simply have not had the occasion to lean on reality science up till now and that is mostly because 1) we've relied on religion or spirituality, and, 2) we've been absorbed by the physical pleasures and pains of this hardened world. But, it should be noted, we are now entering a time in human evolution where we need better theoretical applications to answer truly mind-boggling observations. Plus, as the will and illusion of religion and spirituality slip away, thinkers will be forced to either surrender to the physical world or to indulge their imagination in the multidimensional spectrum. I see the latter coming to pass.

I see thinkers and explorers really taking up reality science as a credible field of study and we will see the development of more observations, maps of reality, time travel, interdimensional contact and a real transformation on earth.

Of course, all of this will take time and effort. Newtonian physics has been around for centuries and still not everyone is aware of it. Quantum physics is poorly understood by the masses and string theory is still finding its way into the human mind. Any new science is a process because it needs to be understood, it needs practical application, it needs an audience and it is going up against all old theorists and scientists. They're not going to wholeheartedly embrace any science that will undermine their science, a science they've studied for their entire lives. But without the introduction of reality science, humanity has no such opportunity to expand its thinking.

Reality Science is an introductory book on an introductory spectrum of knowledge. It will examine the key areas of understanding and will discuss ways in which to appreciate the study of reality. Reality Science will use practical examples in an imaginative way, as a way of noting the way this science can be applied. The author takes full responsibility for the views and opinions written and recorded here.

Look at reality science as a way to expand your understanding of your existence and as an instrument to improve the architecture upon which we all live; that is, by emptying the principles of reality science we can improve living, we can eradicate disease, we can reduce war, we can ensure human survival, we can do these things and more.

So, let's begin a new journey together and let's expand our thoughts into the multidimensional cosmos.

As a bonus, you will find three (3) cosmic *user guides* in the *Appendices*. One will expand your views on the reality operating system. A second will discuss the interstellar human you truly are and the third will look at thought communications unlike ever before. You might find a lot of use in the included user guides, but make sure you read the book for a basic foundation on the science of reality.

THE REALITY ANTENNA

Reality is akin to a spectrum of electromagnetic radiation holding within various charged particles. Each variation of the EM spectrum carries a tiny shift in the reality and with a particular spectrum. Those realities housed within with all experience a tiny reality shift. A shift in reality, an adjustment of movement, appears in real life when certain unexpected events occur or when things take a new direction out of the blue. For example, you're walking home tired, overwhelmed, the faces of other pedestrians dismally sad, so you enter a coffee shop to rest.

You drink your coffee and think you're resting when in fact you're not. You're allowing a temporal shift to take place while hiding out in the confines of a coffee house. Or perhaps a safe house of sorts. You finish and exit.

The people's faces on the streets are happy, you're feeling better. You give credit to the break and the caffeine, but did all those street people take a coffee break that you're not aware of? No. And that's the key right there. The fact that you feel better is not as important, key, as to the fact that the whole street feels better. That's part of the proof that some reality shift occurred. The question is whether it's natural or unnatural.

The more you pay attention to the physical world and the less "scientific" you are, the more likely you'll see the magic in the environment. The more magic you see, the more in tune to the environment you thereby become until what? Until you begin to live according to the technological fields of energy and not according to the atmospheric fields of light. You begin to see patterns – in people, in government, in society. These patterns repeat in their respective counterparts. And someday you'll realize that these patterns can tell you a lot of information about the situation. Far better than tea leaves.

Unfortunately, as it stands right now, the perception is driving your experience, and, everyone's perception is different. If you notice a shift in people's dispositions or you notice how a flu illness becomes worse after the TV News shows an image of the molecular image of the flu virus then you'll have a difficult time explaining this to other people who are not at your level awareness. Plus, you might be wrong. You might be onto something even bigger because if an image of a flu virus captured on an electron microscope increases the outbreak of a flu then you'll begin to imagine – well, who is purposely using advanced knowledge to infect people and who is selling all the vaccines? Which brings up a relevant point: you may take some time to adjust to your new perception. But so far I've talked about mundane things.

As you view reality, you'll come to know yourself better. You'll be able to live in harmony with the reality, you'll have better health and you'll have a few more special abilities.

How do we further access another dimension? The most direct answer is through the largest portal in your body – the head. The head has been downgraded into a mere number cruncher and thinking device. That's it. We think up a new idea and we think up a plan and then implement it. Scientists have told us that it is the function of the brain that is our CPU, our neural processing center.

Now, imagine that the head is much more. Imagine the head is like a giant front door to a mansion. And should you open the mansion door, you'll discover a whole new vista with perhaps other people or perhaps.

In the old images of Jesus we notice a fan around his head. It can be interpreted as a king's radiant crown since Jesus was regarded as the king of kings.

Typically, an angelic being only had a plain fan or halo. Only a figure like Jesus had that many points.

The Greek god Apollo in robes also is represented with seven spiked rays of a radiant crown.

A more recent figure that held the seven-pronged crown is the Statue of Liberty (Liberty Enlightening the World). Her radiant crown and sandals.

The head of the human body is like an antenna of a radio, it is the modem in a computer, it is the head of a wired jack. There are many kinds of antennas and modems, many channels in a jack plug, all of them determine exactly what kind of connection you will have and for how long you'll have it.

If the human body was like an antenna then the spine would be the base point.

Rather than focusing on the blood and bone, a limited physical aspect that denies us the validity of a multidimensional world, we have to think that this internal, built-in antenna exists in a dimension of energy, say the same location as your soul, another energy construction. If you believe you have a soul then imagine that you also have an antenna made up of the same unknowable stuff.

What is interesting about any antenna (or modem) is that it works poorly unless it is turned on. And it works even more poorly if it is covered in dirt and garbage. Lastly, a modem is useless if you have nowhere to connect to. Verily, this is the sort of situation in humanity. The human being, you, are equipped with this energy soul-antenna and you may have used it once or twice in your entire life; meanwhile, you live an existence connected to the false illusions presented in the media and the imaginative speak of politicians, bankers, businessmen and other dream makers.

Your reality antenna is an essential part of restabilising your connection to the cosmic system at your doorstep. It is an essential built-in component to gaining a strong grasp of reality science. Your skill with this magnificent technological component can alter your life in immeasurable ways. This is what determines the level of your enlightenment. It is unlikely that you'll reach the enlightenment of a Jesus per se since the component parts in Jesus were far more advanced than most, but your components, your antenna is quite impressive as it is.

So, we have the seven-pronged crown of one of our historical figures in simplified form.

The distance between each prong is the size of the enlightenment gate. As such, there are six (6) gates of enlightenment. There is also a seventh gate when all six gates, or channel, are open.

At death, the 7 gates open and the soul body or consciousness is removed on every one channel.

A person who trains his/her body and disciplines their mind and heart can activate the various ascension gates. Also, certain experiences or events in your life will have an impact on those gates. A traumatic event or severe oppression can force close all of the gates and imprison the soul in a harsh physical reality without intuition. A life of charity and enlightenment can easy open gates even at a basic level. Creative people will often have access to one or more of these gates, though substances can cause other disturbances, delusions and later a loss of connection. A reliance on substances, it should be noted, leads to a poor understanding of enlightenment and allows no permanent ascension to take place because a foreign substance used in excess is a crutch, a handicap. It will weaken you over the long-term but give you some advantage in the opening. For those of you in it for the long term and who want to deliver free result, learn to use mild substances like organic herbs as a means of supplementing your ascension and discard their use as soon as no longer necessary.

Ultimately, your internal components are far superior than any earth-based physical substance. The substance will disagree with you and will convince you to rely upon it. Don't listen and learn to develop your internal functions. Of course, for those who want to see a short rise in knowledge followed by years of delusions, you can do as you wish but the warning here is stern. Do not rely on or overuse any legal or illegal substance during your path to ascended awareness.

If you are dedicated to ascension, which is probably why you're reading this introductory book, then make the extra effort to maintain a professional, discipline approach. Ascension is a noble quest. When a person studies medicine to be a doctor or law to be a lawyer, they do so in a discipline manner. At the end of a stressful and expensive path, they earn their designations, and can change the high rates they do because they now have a business card. You are looking at, because you haven't fully decided on something is overly esoteric, walking the path to multidimensional ascension.

You'll have to decide, about now, what you intend to pursue with this new sense of self. What is driving you? That is something for you to determine and that drive will then determine how far you'll go. You know, the Chinese Shaolin monks start training at a very young age to develop a flexible body. By their teenage years they're already into advanced fighting techniques and spiritual discussions. In the West, a young man might start martial arts in his teens. He might train twice a week, two hours at a time.

While the Chinese student trains eight hours a day seven days a week since age six. You can see the discrepancies. You can see the amount of dedication a person can put into any endeavour. No one can tell you how hard to try. You must decide for yourself what it is you want to achieve then know how much work there is to do. Be practical. Ascension is a rigorous process that will continue your whole life. You've have peaks and valleys. But rather than being a victim to ascension be a participant. Learn to put aside your earthly duties and temptations here and there in favour of your spiritual development, your multidimensional growth. Besides we all exist in a multidimensional vortex of endless possibilities.

THE UNBODY

We've seen how the antenna mind can give you access to the seven heavenly gates. We're realizing that this reality science is going to require some level of dedication, all of which we must decide. Now let's look at what happens beyond the gates because there's something interesting happening here. Recall the seven-pronged radiant crown.

Now imagine that as soon as you pass through the gate, say in the aspect of death, then you are entering a reverse image of yourself, essentially a flip of yourself so instead of entering some strange plane of existence you are entering your own head on the flip side of the cosmos.

The Heaven through Head Ploy

When you exit the Body, you enter the unBody, or your body in another dimensional construct. From there you can access other aspects of yourself. Your ability to reach this stage may require some time because it is a process. Some people might be able to do it quite accidentally and not even realize it. But no matter what, without your understanding and clarity you won't be able to really take things further.

There are times in history whereby the cosmos itself decides to connect to a community, such as the community of earth. This is not unlike the broadcast center or the mainframe server communicating to the network of wireless phones, only that instead of a phone there's a body, a body within is housed an internal, highly-advanced antenna. At times like these you will notice improvements in yourself because the cosmic computer is uploading new information, knowledge and data onto your soul and your soul will transfer some of that through to your body. Think of this as a kind of forced ascension in where you needn't do anymore than to stay grounded, practice centering your mind and allow all those new energies to fill your body to such a point that you have absorbed those essential qualities.

Immediately we can notice a couple of things happening, one, you have a built-in component to allow you proper access to other planes of existence, planes that are intimate areas of the unexplained cosmos. Two, the cosmos is making regular effort to communicate with you to ensure that you remain the cosmic being that you are.

So let's look at this situation before we look at the unBody because it is essential you understand that for you to enter another plane, or reality, and for some distance cosmic computer to contact you there must necessarily be a system in place to allow this interdimensional exchange. Not only that, but for a presence in another dimension means that there is a dimensional architecture in existence. This dimensional architecture includes all the dimensions, planes, realms and realities.

What does that mean when multiple dimensions are interconnected? It means that the cosmos, in its simplest format, is composed of all the known and unknown dimensions. It means that you are a cosmic being equipped with a technology that allows you to escape reality. And be escaping reality you enter other realities and you learn, you expand yourself at the cosmic level. You realise what? If you can exit your body at the level of cosmic energy, and still remain in existence, then what does that do to the concept of death?

Essentially, with variations, death is a reassignment into another planar space occupying another body. But it's easy to talk about death. Let's go back to the unBody.

The radiant crown of seven fixed points is essentially a cosmic gate.

Now when we join the seven points we get a seven sided star.

The star, also in 5-point and other versions, is a common symbol embedded throughout the world. Stars are found in flags, badges, the Sherriff of the Western World had a starry badge. Stars are depicted at Christmas and stars are commonly employed in religious systems. But we now notice how the seven-prongs of the radiant crown on your head are reflected in the physical world. At least, we are beginning to notice because this information has many layers of understanding. But you see that more easily now, right? Of course, I've stated that you have this radiant crown embedded into your core architecture, probably still in new condition. Unfortunately, it's built-in and you can't sell it on eBay. You have the option or not using it but that's like having a mobile phone and never using it to make a phone call.

Your 7-point crown is represented in various long-standing symbols in society, including the Statue of Liberty and in images of Jesus and other mystical figures. And what we get is a gate. A heavenly gate that connects you to another you and un-you. Body and unBody. Superman and Bizarro. Matter and antimatter. Love and lust. Positive image and negative image.

This is your stargate. It's on your head, hidden because it is fixed in another vibrational energy, or a different dimension. Each person has a stargate and we can be assured that there are many kinds available, depends on your model. The stargate, interestingly enough, forms a kind of telephone dial.

If your seven prongs were converted into a numerical system you'd get the telephone and the clock. If we connected the numerals we'd get multi-pronged stars. We'd get more stargates. That's why certain numerical combinations like 11:11 seem to allow cosmic energy into and out of, because if we think of numerals as a stargate lining up, no matter the size, then we see that each of these items – clocks, phones, minds –

are experiencing connections to other dimensions. Can you see that?

As long as there is a star dial (or sundial) then there is a connection to the other side. As well, as long as there is a line in or a signal then there is a connection through a television for example. Inside your computer there are clocks and dials, switches and modems, all ingredients for cosmic travel though the transistor is still too rudimentary a technology to allow cosmic energy.

You activate your star dial on your head and you open the gate to your unBody. You exit your Body and enter your unBody. You experience severe distortion, confusion, disorientation and some of this can be experienced as general sickness, nausea, headaches, dizziness, loss of energy, even temporary blackouts because you're not breathing properly, your overwhelmed like jumping onto a rollercoaster for the first time and then realizing that this is way too high and too fast.

The Body and the unBody are also represented in day and night. In the day, you exist in the Body, in the night you exist in the unBody. Well, you have to go somewhere. Did you think that you just shut down your unit? No. This is an old way of thinking. On/off. Awake/asleep.

We still don't understand sleep. People claim they dream but that dreams are all delusions made up by the mind. Other think that when y0u dream, you are traveling in the astral dimensions, although they are not allowed to prove that astral dimensions exist because they saw it in their minds. Most people don't think twice about it, they just like to sleep. But now that we know about the cosmic gate and the unBody then we know something else too. We know that when we sleep we are entering some aspect of the unBody. Recall the seven gates.

Imagine that one of those seven gates is a sleep gate, say Gate 3. Just like at an airport terminal. You enter the gate area, there are seven gates. Gate 3, for example, is headed to sleep. You want to sleep, you are hard-wired to access Gate 3. You have some extra activity on your gates and you have trouble reaching Gate 3, they call it insomnia. I say you can't find Gate 3 to Sleep. Imagine that. Imagine we taught people to access their sleep gate and we could cure insomnia and other sleep disorders. It's too easy, isn't it? Bring out the pills. Bring out the therapists. Bring on the sleepless nights.

You see how the world now based on multiple dimensions can really open up how we approach life. We could learn so much. That's why I always insist that we are at the very beginning of the beginning. In time to come you'll see this, and more, is commonplace. Time travel? Just a second.

MULTIDIMENSIONAL

There is the positive image and the negative image in photography. A camera equipped with photofilm captures the reverse image of the scene. The camera roll of negative film is then used to print a positive image of the shot. The photograph is the result of taking a positive image, burning it into a reverse negative image and then transforming it into a photograph. Most of us have forgotten about film stock because we used digital cameras. The processors inside do most of the work for you. They cut out the intermediary step. So that you no longer see it. This is not unlike a master flipping between Body and unBody, between the positive and the negative.

We notice at once that this idea of multiple dimensions are present in our lives, don't we? The photos in your photo album all came from negative film images, and yet both the photo and the negative contain the same information. The data is an exact duplicate only one is reversed. If I say that about you that there is a positive, physical image of you and a negative, nonphysical image of you, you would be hard-pressed to deny it. Unless you're some religious fanatic which you wouldn't be or you wouldn't be reading this book on reality science, a book which aims to demystify mystical experiences.

You are accustomed to viewing your physical body. It is comfortable though painful because the physical world is out of balance and severely disconnected to the very real and resplendent multidimensional world, what I collectively refer to as the cosmos, and what we are noticing – because we are only in the process of understanding – what we are noticing is that the cosmos has some kind of integrated architecture and that the very human being, unassisted by any technology, has within the built-in components to access other parts of the cosmos.

What is also interesting is the extrapolation of the cosmic construct because where there is architecture and where there is energy, there is technology. And this is fundamental to my work here. That we exist inside a complex (or advanced) technological system, ie cosmos. A multidimensional field within which are endless fields, within which is endless existence.

This perception, that I am proposing, tells us something else as well because if the other dimensions are increasingly technological, based on more advanced technologies then that forces us to look at Heaven and Hell, common understandings, in a whole new format. Because why? Well, if a diving thing comes from a Heavenly realm, or an evil thing from a Hellish realm, then that tells us that those realms exist in other dimensions. We know we can go there at death because most people accept the view of going to heaven if you've done good or going to hell if you've sinned.

A new class of people believe that death is the end. The rest of the people accept that multiple dimensions exist (eg quantum physicists, string theory physicists). So, there is enough force to push forward the existence of multiple dimensions. And – it can be stated – Heaven and Hell are different dimensions. Even Heaven and Hell are made up of several levels each. So, within Heaven there are multiple dimensions. The only place where dimensions exist is in human belief. We've been forced to disbelieve in other dimensions. Dimensional knowledge has been weeded out of us when in fact the entire cosmos, life and death, time travel and ultra-dimensional beings such as angels all accept the multidimensional view. They accept the multidimensional view. Only humanity has been left to deny the other dimensions, or to fear the other dimensions because there are monsters on the other side, the dark side. We are made to feel unworthy of the other dimensions and we will be judged by some Supreme Being at our expiration date.

At our inception date, everything is perfect. Life is before us. We are blessed into this parochial world. At our expiration date, its judgment, it's the end, it's "who knows, I'm not worried about it because I'll be dead. I just want to live my life to the fullest."

The evolution of reality as a science is going to allow us to enter through the built-in gates and to access other dimensions. Not by accident, but on purpose. We are slowly going to be able to access new levels of cosmic knowledge and we're going to be able to bring that knowledge back into society. You see, the more of us who travel through the unBody and into other dimensions the more of us will discover similar experiences and that collective knowledge will radically shift the state of life on their plane called earth. Well, that's the other thing we need to discuss. We are beginning to see how we have this innate energy architecture at our disposal and that it can allow us access to the technological cosmos. We are beginning to see that.

Now I want to look at this place called Planet Earth, because if what we're learning is the truth there's something wrong with Earth. How can Earth be only a planet if the cosmos is multidimensional? It can't. Just like you and your physical body having nonphysical aspects, the ability to enter a sleep dimension, it would also be the case that earth too is a multidimensional locale. Which means what? It means that besides being a planetary body that earth is also a plane where existence of this nature can take place.

We know existence can take place here because we know that we feel alone. We see, we think, we learn, we make love, we have babies, we have memories, we bleed, we marry and we grow in wisdom and maturity. All of these things are the essentials of existence, that is, if we have these ingredients then we have existence; or what we call life. We are alive.

All that I am introducing now is that in order to harmonize the disparity between a cosmic being existing in a cosmos, all having a very advanced architecture; we need to redefine the planet earth. *Earth is not what it appears to be.*

NONPHYSICAL ARCHITECTURE

Earth has its own internal architecture, its own soul which means, by its very size, it has its own cosmic gateways. It's just rational to think this way. If your body has an antenna system and a starry gate, not to mention chakras and other points of interest, then earth too has these and more and even more complex technologies. It has to. Earth has to have chakras because we are made of the same stuff. The same case materials. The difference between a planet and a human is that a planet contains any number of existences, or inhabitants.

So an earth needs to be able to provide for life on a long-term scale. And because the planet is a physical being, like a photograph, we know that it has a negative component, an unBody. If you can access your unBody then you can access the unBody of earth. What does this mean really? What does it mean that you can incarnate into a human body? Recall that your soul is energy and that energy has some kind of architecture. The soul can travel between dimensions because we have seen so in sleep. We have seen so in stories of heaven and hell. We just know. Your soul travels from its birth into a body on earth. What is happening?

Your soul exists on a dimension or plane of existence and then travels to another plane, then enters a pre-arranged physical body. Then you cry because the gynaecologist has just slapped your butt. Then you wake up and realize you're a baby and you're fat and cute. If you're 25 and fat, you're not cute. So you enjoy being fat, sleeping all the time and play and being fed by mama. Soon you forget where you come from, the other plane of existence, the lengthy travel, the contract you signed and the physical life takes over. It overwhelms you, it fascinates you, it mesmerizes you, it beckons you to get out of your interdimensional shell. What are we saying? Well, you came here from another dimension, under whatever conditions you remember and we're all different.

You arrived on earth as a soul, an energy form, in a cosmos made up of technology. You see, earth is a plane of existence. It's not a planet. The planet is the playground, the playland. You are inside the physical body. The body you entered during your incarnation, the inhabiting of the flesh, but what all of this means is that we are living of a plane of existence and from that plane of existence we've entered the physical body. The physical sitting on top of the nonphysical without the soul of this planet, which is the reality architecture, the physical manifestation we live in each and every day will collapse.

Without the nonphysical architecture, life cannot exist in the physical dimension. This is certainly contrary to modern views even from the best scientific minds who claim that the physical has an ecological system that keeps it functioning. And these people realize that the human body has a soul and that on point the soul the body is known as dead. These scientists know that. But, the earth, no. The earth is the be-all, end-all. It is self sustaining. It is not.

The planet is housed within the very same cosmos therefore it must necessarily follow the same reality rules. It must have similar components only a different scale and capacity. A mainframe computer and a laptop computer connected to it are both computers. They both have processors. They have electronic components and part only the mainframe's component are industrial grade and quite a bit more expensive.

But if your laptop is connected, even based on, to the mainframe then your laptop is running a similar operating system in order to access the mainframe reality. Whether you use the modem or a fibre optic cable is regardless. You need a compatible operating system and enough processing power to understand the machine data, to send an email for example.

Earth and human are no different. They have hardware and software. The software is invisible. Earth's operating system looks like air, you can smell it but your eyes can't see and neither can scientists measure it but there has to be a compatible OS or we couldn't survive. As earth's OS advances, we are freed to advance, they call it evolution, I call it an upgrade. So within earth's physical presence, or underneath, as you like, there is a nonphysical architecture, what I often refer to as the reality engine. these are the internal hardware components keeping earth "alive." When the reality engine stops, you stop. The reality components exist in a hyper-dimension therefore are invisible, just like your soul, your soul is invisible but you are convinced you have one, right?

You've never seen your soul. They never have been able to put the soul under an electron microscope. There's no physical or scientific proof that you have a soul, but 99% of the world believes it to be true. And yet is completely invisible.

So the reality architecture is invisible to your naked eye but to those who can see, it has structure and is made up of energy. The reality engine is very complex and it runs on a reality-grade operating system. This is the next part we'll cover. The reality OS is another essential component of existence. It's an existence-scale technology that, till now, is beyond human science. The reality operating system is like a computer desktop OS in that it manages all the essential hardware components and the software programs.

The OS is a very vital aspect of a computer without an OS, your computer could only process single instructions at a time. And just like a computer OS a planetary OS evolves over time, it adapts and becomes more complex. The reality system of today is unlike that of 1,000 years ago and the reality system of next week will be unlike that of today. Let's look at the *reality operating system*.

THE REALITY OPERATING SYSTEM

We've decided that reality is far more advanced than ever before imagine, so much so that we've decided to examine some of the essential components of reality because why? Because we want to ascend. Well, what is ascension? Ascension is a process of upgrading, of renovating ourselves. We don't pay attention to ascension in the mainstream, or do we? Do we not do makeovers? Home renovations? Born again Christians? Spiritual rebirths? Career change? Life change? New direction? Moments of epiphany?

There are so many names for ascension, for the process of upgrading ourselves, of evolving, of getting older, maturation. The built-in essential qualities of life – birth, growth, maturation – are cosmic cycles that can be found in many levels of awareness. The idea of evolution can be found throughout all cultures. And as we evolve, as we expand our awareness we adopt new terms. Ascension is valid because there has been a lifting of the spirit of man, an energetic surge, an additional thrust in buoyancy. Ascension is all about buoyancy and buoyancy is all about overcoming lift and drag. It is the airplane trying to take off and the lighter the load the greater the buoyancy and without buoyancy there isn't much ascension. This is not unlike the life of a person. With too many attachments and traumas, a person cannot ascend, or, they cannot grow, or, they do not evolve.

As you can begin to see, though the terms are often different we are essentially discussing the same concept under a new set of awareness. What I've been discussing so far in this book is reality as a science, and, more importantly, technology as an awareness; that the fundamental basis for existence is technological. That reality has an architecture and that architecture has an operational system.

The reality operating system determines many of the features and benefits of existence because it acts as the basic interface between the cosmic machinery and the existential lifeforms. As you live within the context of the reality operating system, your existence is either limited or expanded by the features and technical specifications of the operating system. And as we've noticed in the computer business model, the operating systems in the computer industry, a fairly new industry on earth, began existence less than 100 years, the strength and characteristics of the operating system determine the strength and characteristics of the computational environment. Stable, efficient and easy to use operating systems not only get adopted by the public but they also tend to evolve.

A good operating system attracts developers and programmers who then expand and improve upon the program platform. When a new OS is invented, it too is adopted into the marketplace and may replace the OS standard or it may become an industrial-grade OS. In addition, an OS that fails to attract a sufficient base of supporters doesn't evolve and will simply fade away and become less and less relevant. The best OS is not necessarily the most favoured. In fact, an operating system has to meet any number of complex criteria in order to succeed, but what is required is a stable, efficient and easy to use interface.

People don't like it when their computers crash. Neither do existential lifeforms. Existences rely on a reality system to provide a fluid non-interruptive degree of life. You, as an inhabitant here want every opportunity to live out your life journey in full. You don't want to see an unexpected collapse. You don't want to experience the reality crashing. And it doesn't crash often. And that is because earth's reality system is constantly monitored, adjusted and upgraded – all of this done till now without your awareness. That's advanced cosmic technology at work for you.

The reality operating system determines all the needs of the inhabitant population and makes provisions for it. The reality OS is constantly monitoring the reality architecture to ensure that it is functioning properly. It is in direct communication with the hardware components, and when certain problems are detected, a programmer or technician is sent into a certain area to repair the problems.

Because the reality hardware is pre-built and more complex in its design, it tends to remain in place a lot longer than the OS. Sometimes both the hardware and software are upgraded, especially at times when there is a major technological achievement or a very specific market demand. We see this is the computer business – a new operating system and a new microprocessor are invented at the same time, and along with that a more compact computer design and a longer-life battery. A reality is no different.

The reality operating system is the essential component that determines the quality of life. What is permitted, what is not allowed, what is encouraged, what is discouraged – the OS has to constantly determine these things in order to provide the right initiative that satisfies the inhabitants and that is congruent with the cosmic computer. The OS cannot provide everything that all inhabitants desire because that would cause imbalance and an imbalance does not provide a peak experience for all inhabitants. What does that mean at the practical level?

It means that some evil will exist among the goodness. Some goodhearted people will die, some children get raped, some corruption in the corporate world takes place, some events occur that require every one's attention. These occurrences are not evil per se but are interpreted as evil. A purely good, life journey is not a journey worth remembering. If everything you do succeeded 100% of time without hiccup, without incident, without challenge, why do it? The fact that you are here is because you desire a challenge. You expect accidents to occur. You are programmed to deal with them. Does all of this mean that the reality OS is not functioning at full capacity, that it makes mistakes?

Well, to answer that we have to once again look at the computer. A computer operates according to its programming. As long as its programmed, it happens. Anything that is programmed, anything with a set of instructions, will happen. And whatever happens, whatever the execution, is programmed to happen. In other words, nothing can occur outside of its programming. Your computer won't squawk like a bird unless it is programmed to do and if it squawks like a bird then it is programmed to do so.

This points to some important conclusion in regards to our reality OS because whatever occurs on this plane of existence is programmed to occur; otherwise it cannot occur. Nothing can occur without it being programmed to do so, and all of the programming must work in harmony with the rest of the programming. In other words, if an excess of evil is programmed to occur, in whatever format, at whatever time. If not, then the system will not function and it will crash. Well, we've heard of civilizations collapsing. We've heard of the ice age. Earth has been in existence for billions of years and existences and operating systems have been around just as long. And some operating systems didn't last long and existences were wiped out.

You have to understand that every aspect of life has to live in accordance to the rules set forth. The operating system must remain stable, the architecture must be reliable and the inhabitants must live in harmony within the context of reality. If any of these aspects lose equilibrium, and without adjustment, the reality system will collapse. Of course, we are neglecting to include the technicians. The reality technicians play a crucial role in the life cycle of a particular existential cycle.

Realities are built for specific terms. At the end of those terms either the reality is torn down and replaced, along with the inhabitants, or, the reality is upgraded and the inhabitants are forced to evolve. To do these things, and more, requires technicians and programmers. So, reality technicians, specialists and programmers routinely work at ensuring your life goes on as you expected it to. Of course, you've never thought that technicians were hard at work behind the scenes ensuring you had a trouble-free existence.

But, any technological system requires maintenance. A garden requires maintenance. A car requires maintenance. A body requires maintenance. It is inconceivable to think that a reality , or even a planet, does not require maintenance only that as a multidimensional construct, many of these essential tinkering are occurring outside your everyday visual spectrum. They are occurring and have been occurring nonetheless for billions of years here and billions of years elsewhere. The ageless cosmos requires constant maintenance.

The trouble with earth and its inhabitants is that these inhabitants here have forgotten how to maintain the earthly balance. Not only have people forgotten, but people don't care. Not only people don't care, but anyone trying to do maintenance is ridiculed or attacked for doing so. And so, over a few centuries, the reality grows in disrepair and the world is a mess.

If you think that life on earth is picture perfect then you have been unfortunately reading the wrong book. The reality system is neglected. Sure, there are a handful of technicians who have done the basic maintenance but there have been many others who have damaged the system or tried to reprogram it to benefit themselves: Hence, a world based in ego. An egotistical world that is devoid of a multidimensional view, that is devoid of reality maintenance workers is a world out of balance. The reality system continues on because of dedicated technicians and programmers who are essentially not from earth, they come from elsewhere in the cosmos in order to do the necessary work that humanity does not wish to do. **This is why the reality hasn't collapsed. This is why you are still here.**

It cannot be stated more clearly nor with any more emphasis – the reality inhabitants are required by cosmic decree to put aside some of the population for the maintenance of reality. In times of past they have had many names – magicians, druids, bards, gypsies. In modern times, there are no reality technicians, no maintenance workers from earth, well, very few and they work in secret. Most, if not all, of the maintenance is done by other existences from other planes, from other areas of the cosmos. And some of these multidimensional people work though the local inhabitants to ensure that reality is taken care of. But it's time for more local inhabitants to get involved and even to dedicate their lives, not to some god, but to a reality and to existence itself.

EXISTENTIAL PROGRAMS

The reality operating system manages the entire domain of existence here in this plane and is peculiar to this planet. It manages both the reality infrastructure (or hardware) and the reality manifestation (or physical reality) and everything needed to maintain those exchanges between hardware and software such as the maintenance programming, utilities, and the thought communications applications just to name a few.

The reality OS also needs to manage the dimensions spliced in between software manifestation and hardware components. It is in these in between dimensions where you will find multidimensional people, ghosts for example or faeries. You might call them astral planes, but I'd prefer to refer to them as *dimensions*. In these other ultra dimensions, there are populations of multidimensional people. It is many of their kind that service the system because many of them do not think of self, they serve others or they serve the **Sustainer of existence** (Source, God).

In serving others, I would include, certainly, serving humanity because humanity is part of the system. Humanity has been misled to believe that they are superior and alone, this is certainly not the case. Humanity has been simply left alone or influenced in more subtle ways, ways in which they cannot know.

Multidimensional beings have always been in existence. Man, too, himself was once multidimensional and over time became a stale piece of meat. To fully understand reality science, a person needs to discard the "humanity is alone in the universe" concept and to adopt a more multidimensional approach. The fact that human societies have been purposely misguided into believing that other dimensions do not exist and that no other race of people are real is plain straight junk. It is political spin. It is scientific spin. It is religious spin. They'll spin you around so much that you don't know what to believe. What I'm presenting is a foundation for new thinking at the cosmic level. We are only in the introduction stage of a grand and gracious existence.

The one aspect we haven't properly discussed, well I suppose there are many, is existence itself. The lifeform in question. For example, humanity. This we should cover briefly.

There is the hardware and there is an operating system. Both essentials in an existential computing system. Now we need to add programs. Well, wait – we already have the programs! We do? Yes. What is a program, or application program. A program is a set of instructions that operate a machine. Well, we have an operational program for the reality architecture. And so we must have these apps, but where are they?

Let's quickly refer back to the human body. The human body has two components, the external and the internal, big and small. We learned earlier that the soul, or unBody, can travel to other dimensions. Dreams are easy to see but astral planes are slightly more challenging, and any knowledge gleaned from the cosmic dimensions are 1) subject to an understanding according to your level of awareness and 2) difficult to remember, mind you can only perceive that which you are ready for which at this point is minimal.

What does the soul, or the immaterial body, have to do with the technological architecture that runs reality. Turns out, interestingly, we already knew that the definition of a program is a set of instructions used to operate a machine. We know after many decades of medicine that the human body can be simply labelled a physical machine, having essential components (eg organs) and requiring fuel and producing waste, key characteristics of a living machine. We know that.

At the very least, we are a biological machine. And according to my early work on the *Riddle of Biology*, I discovered that the soul is a nonbiological component inhabiting a biological machine. And I discussed further that if the soul is nonbiological, that is artificial, then in order to connect with a biological body would require the body machine to be made of the same artificial nature. That is to say, your biological body is in fact nonbiological. But it is so advanced that it appears to be biological, as humanity has defined it.

Now we have a nonbiological component driving a nonbiological body, and this is further explained in my book, *Talessian's Riddle* and other works, so I won't discuss it here except to say that by simply reinterpreting the human nonbiological soul as an existential program we now find ourselves into a more complete world view of this cosmic reality because we now have in our sights a complete computer system: hardware, operating system and software application.

Only that our existence-scale technology is not reproducible by humankind, and that shouldn't bother us. In fact, it has never bothered us before since we always attributed created to some higher authority anyway.

The soul programs run off of the reality operating system and the reality system ensures that the reality architecture remains efficient, secure and as a key part of the larger cosmos. The soul programs operate the nonbiological bodies that are called humans. But the body is just the vessel. The most prevalent component of life is your internal program (soul).

What separates a human from an angel, for example, is that 1) an angel recognizes the difference between which aspect of a being is more real than the other, and, 2) an angel's body, should an angel enter the 3D realm we see each day, the angel would have an immaterial body, unless it took a human form (which they often do, off and on). But then the true body is vibrating at a frequency in harmony with a more vibrant, nonphysical dimension (eg heaven).

You as well have a high vibrating program and it does as well travel to other dimensions, with or without your consent. And that body is more real than your real body. Again, it's a conditioning of the mind and a confusion that the ego knows the truth. The ego is a good liar and it could sell water to fish. And sometimes people act like fish and you could sell them sashimi.

THE DRIVER

Our reality system is now taking shape. We are still working at a very basic level and this needs to be stated clearly, but it is necessary to learn to walk before we fly. The human program interacts, verily relies upon, with the reality operating system. As long as your program is intact and has access to your body then you are alive.

You are not alive because of just food and water. Food and water keep your machine in operation. If you don't put gasoline in your car, you won't be able to drive. Fuel and maintenance, are necessary to keep your car on the road. But your car won't go anywhere without the driver (or you).

You are the driver of the car. You decide where it goes and how fast it gets there and depending on the speed limit and the amount of horsepower, you eventually get to your destination. And everyone has a different kind of car and engine drives different. Some people abuse their cars and some people only drive on Sundays when it's not raining outside.

The driver of the human body is the internal program, but it needs to be understood that the program is more important, more real, more valid than the body. Cars come and go, but the driver stays a while longer. You're the driver. You are the immortal essence. A truly aware person, one who recognizes the importance and value of their program will live life according to the program and not according to the body, it is the soul that continues on. If the program has failed to achieve what it was programmed to achieve then the program may have to repeat its set of instructions. Now, if the program has exceeded all expectations, aced all the tests, well, then the program gets a promotion and hell is avoided, eh?

So then that is your life. That is life. It is an existential system based on a multidimensional platform that essentially is as limitless as the cosmos. And since like any computer system, the reality system evolves, it expands, it transforms, then there is an endless, everlasting quality to the aspect of existence.

What we've all been focused on is one small spectrum that we have been told is the be-all end-all. We believe death is finite because in terms of the physical vehicle death is finite. The body dies and a replacement is required, only that the replacement is found in the next incarnation.

Many cultures of the old world believe in reincarnation, today not so many because if we believed in reincarnation we would all live outside of the ego. We would see our similarity. We would see past our physical difference and we would discard religious ideology and any ideology that takes us away from the technological truths in this book. This is not the first time that the truth about the cosmos has been divulged and neither is it the end. This is the beginning of a technological awareness in man and woman and child.

We have to begin to see that an interstellar person and an angel and an elf and a human are all programs inhabiting the same cosmos. Just that some programs are more evolved, more complex, require more hard drive space. The differences in each of us occur at the program level, but we are all technological instruments to some degree, and the system is the same. Existence is existence. There can be no better. We just play different roles, different functions. Is a plumber more important than a lawyer? Well, the lawyer can't fix his broken toilet and the plumber can't understand legal jargon. Because of humanity's dependence on the physical and the reliance on self, it has valued certain kinds of people more than others. The lawyer makes plenty more money than the plumber according to the monetary system. An artist makes even less and a general labourer, well they just get by at minimum wage.

So, society is built on a limited, physical valuation and has discarded the spiritual truth, has destroyed humanism because it has failed to recognize that the body is the illusion, it is an instrument for the driver, the program. And the program exists in a very elaborate reality operating system.

A human vehicle can be held by one owner or it can be sold to another owner over the course of its life. A vehicle owner might also loan out their human body to another driver, who may or may not get into an accident while on the highway. There are all kinds of owners and drivers can find themselves shifting between bodies, even in temporary format so that we find ourselves with a very rich and memorable life journey in which we hold many careers, fall in and out of love and leave behind any kind of legacy. People do die, at least their physical body dies but the internal program lives on because it is immortal.

During this course of your existence, you have opportunities to upgrade your program, just like a computer program. There are bug fixes and new versions and upgrades and all of these things take place on a continuous basis. We call humans an adaptive species. When a virus enters the population, the genes adapt the immune system and a resistance is developed. If the human body did not adapt, it wouldn't last very long in a world with many threats.

The four seasons alone require adaptation to varying kinds of temperatures and environmental conditions. Adaptation and initiation are essential components of existence. As well, when a woman gets pregnant, her body adapts enough to allow a second human to grow inside of her, verily to be the channel to a new existential form.

Procreation is an impressive technology where we see firsthand the ability of a woman to not only gestate a new physical body but also to be a channel for another existential program. Two functions in one body. The male, of course, plays the role of seeding the new vehicle and providing the essential materials for creation to take place. Man and woman together create a third being, a mutation of themselves in the likeness of themselves. Motherhood is a treasured profession in the higher dimensions not so much so on earth. Motherhood is often pushed aside for a career or a life of egotism.

Over the course of a life, a person may become empowered and set off on a new mission, a perfect excuse for a different, or a more evolved, program to drive the vehicle. Many near death experiences are periods where a realization allows a person a chance to receive an upgrade that they've been avoiding. If the upgrade is rejected then the person might simply just die or, worse, return to earth in the same unappreciative state of awareness.

There are always, as mentioned earlier, times in your life where you can ascend. You can spend extra effort in ascension and achieve unparalleled levels of awareness as compared to just waiting for the lightening to strike you while you sit and watch TV.

WELCOME TO REALITY DAKALA.

If you wish to learn more, visit http://ministryofreality.ca for a mind-bend.

The Cosmic Ascension Pack ("CAP") is state-of-the-art, multidimensional applications that enhance and contribute to localized, existential inhabitants on this plane of existence.

CAP is designed to run on the Dakala Reality Operating System.

CAP is a full suite of cosmic applications including:

- Lifeshop
- MindMerge
- Challenges
- Programmer
- Truth

- Reprogrammer (Pro Version Only)

About Cosmic Ascension Pack

This user's guide is best for those persons who have accepted the technological basis for reality and have re-identified the planet as a plane of existence. A minimum level of technological awareness is recommended in order to take most advantage of Dakala Reality Operating System (Dakala ROS).

Reinterpreting the very function and nature of reality is not an easy step for the average person who has been conditioned to see the biological necessities for life. Those who survive that transition will begin to experience existence from a whole new point of observation.

It is at that very new level of awareness that you will require a new set of knowledge, a better way to understand the way reality really works. You are not familiar with reality as an operating system because you've been led to believe that Earth is a planet.

Dakala ROS is the first time in history where the explicit details of a technological reality are revealed in a nonfiction environment. This is not part of a fictionalized novel or TV series. You are actually gaining an introduction into cosmic technology.

Who should read this guide

If you are the type of person that has broadened their awareness beyond religion and have an innate connection to computers or the internet, and have well exceeded the fearmongering leaders then you are going to find a new home with reality systems.

Many people around the world, in every culture imaginable, are interacting with the Dakala environment, only that they have given this reality plane many names and use different technical terms based on their own cultural preferences. All those interpretations and historical representations are now being harmonized into a technological and scientific perspective on how reality works. If you are familiar with computers, online activity, video games and other interactive media then you are going to see the connection between technology and existence in Dakala.

The knowledge and observations in this guide are introductory and do not go beyond a layman's technological understanding of what is going on beyond your eyesight. Reality science is an entirely new field of physics that doesn't officially exist, and you are on the front of the line for this cosmic-grade knowledge. Human knowledge is expanding and will continue to expand unlike ever before in history.

About Dakala

The way we think the world works and the way that the world works have never in history been rationalized. That is to say that human culture has been living at a level of awareness that has never been able to peer through the veils of reality. Certainly, the structure of reality has been visualized, estimated, measured and written in many science papers and science-fiction movies, without any formal or official conclusion. The ancient people of Egypt and Latin America seemed to have a vast understanding of the cosmos that has been widely misplaced in the modern, super-technological era.

What is this guide about? The Dakala reality and its key technical features. We are not able to cover all the details in this mini-guide. Every kind of paranormal activist, spiritualist and scientist has tried to break apart the structure of reality and to formalize some understanding in order to come to terms with what life is all about. And this is what we are going to cover in a recreational format. We are going to overview the technological reality upon which we all inhabit and we will do so with a bit of innovation and light-heartedness.

My understanding of Dakala ROS and its various features come from my direct travel throughout the Technoverse, the technological universe, and my own innate training and skill on holographic reality operational systems. In the foreseeable future we will all come to realize the technical specifications for life and our own free-willed choice for traveling to different planes in the cosmos. Your presence here now is not an accident and is not a coercion. You came here by choice and I am going to remind you on the context of that all-important choice.

Cosmic Ascension Pack

The Cosmic Ascension Pack holds several key existential programs that will assist you in your journey here to this plane. The Cosmic Ascension Pack contains a suite of programs that exist in your mind space. We will cover the essential attributes and features of the reality programs so as to remind you that reality is technological in nature. Again, this is an introductory guide to an unrealized existence-scale science.

How to Get the Most Out of Existence

You've just downloaded the Cosmic Ascension Pack, and now you need to know how to make the most out of it. This guide will cover all the essential features you need to make your life experience worthwhile. You already landing on this plane of existence, now you're finally ready to turn your journey into a courage-filled, existential extravaganza and I am going to show you how to do so.

Cosmic Software is the latest thing on this plane. So far, no human is able to create a cosmic software application, but many humans can and do influence the reality codes. In the old Earth construct, your existential life was repressed, oppressed and condemned. You were experiencing daily trauma and difficulty and lived most of your life in utter confusion. Well, all that is about to change. All that is about to take a whole new meaning.

Dakala is far different from Earth. Earth is a program built on an old reality platform. That technological platform forced a localized inhabitant, for example a human, to endure a trouble-filled life and to experience threat and fear on every level of thought. A fearful world really tested the inhabitant and made it seemingly impossible for them to ascend to a level of fearlessness.

Only the truly disciplined and enlightened were able to step beyond the imprisonment of hate, fear and violence. Many succumbed to the numbing power of hate and lived a life under the rule of oppression.

Earth became known across the universe as a haven for imprisonment and those who entered that reality space were well aware of the cosmic implications. Still, many came, thinking that they could handle the existential nightmares, feeling in their heart that they could rise above temptation and corruption. When these existential forms arrived they quickly were overwhelmed with lies, distrust, fear and became corrupt. The standard monetary system and centers of power were too powerful, those who rose against the rulers of Earth, a band of rogue programmers, were quickly eliminated in a very natural way. The standards of society and the division of culture became regarded as politically correct. In the Earth system, it was natural to see one race as being different from another, even to be feared or hated.

Earth's rulers also changed the reality codes and reprogrammed society to add new levels of division, such as homosexuality and women's rights. Homosexuals in time became a new culture and women easily began to believe that they needed to earn their rights, never knowing that they had 100% of their rights to start.

Earth Reality OS had been upgraded many times over the centuries, as noted in the various ages and era of this human plane.

Dakala as the new Mother Nature

Mother Nature has been the steadfast, perennially misunderstood force that all inhabitants have relied upon since their birth into this world. Mother Nature was the grand biological creation that made up what is known as Planet Earth. Why switch from Mother Earth to Dakala Reality?

Well, I switched because Mother Nature became too slow for my modern day needs. Mother Nature represents an old technological lifeform, a system that worked very well for a very long time, like the first Cadillacs and the first Motorola mobile brick-sized handsets, they worked well for their level of technology. But, today, people buy hybrid vehicles and the mobile phones fit in the palm of your hand. No consumer is searching for a brick-sized mobile phone. Consumers want the latest technology.

Same goes for the computer industry. Customers, old and new, look for sleek lines, fast processing power and affordable prices. But when it comes to planetary technology and planary realities, people are still dealing with very old technological systems. And rightly so. Modern society around the world has never really had to reinterpret the nature of reality, let alone to adopt a new level of planary interaction.

Why get connected to Dakala Reality? Why buy the newest computer operating system from Bill Gates instead of just sticking to Microsoft Windows 3.1? Because it is standard that technology upgrades itself in order to maintain a steady-state and to be in line with the cosmic system. If your laptop is being upgraded then you rest assured that your internet service provider is already upgraded. Dakala is a larger technological upgrade in a history of upgrades and system adjustments, all of which has gone unseen or has been interpreted as weather shifts, ice ages and earthquakes. Regardless of what people see, this plane has been routinely kept in sync with the cosmos and Dakala represents a gigantic cosmic leap. Without Dakala, this reality will fail and be removed from the system.

You always have the choice to determine how involved you get with the new reality system. You can keep doing what you have always been doing, only it will much faster and much brighter. Or you can explore the many new features of Dakala Reality and you can accomplish something that was once considered a miracle.

This guide is a basic introduction to some of the key features in Dakala. A complete guide to Dakala would be unwieldy and impractical at this early start. Imagine writing a book on Mother Nature 2,000 years ago.

THE DAKALA PROGRAMS

Lifeshop 9.0

Lifeshop 9.0   The virtual pleasure of virtual graphics.

What is Lifeshop?

Lifeshop reality-ware provides a rich virtual experience through an amazing array of programmed events, memory alterations, and unparalleled experience enhancements.

Lifeshop 9.0 maximizes upgraded technology and instantly connects each virtual inhabitant effortlessly.

With cosmic software life appears real.

View every scene properly with the advanced power of cosmic software and let Lifeshop immerse you in a false reality. Experience the pressures of time and learn to multitask and deal with our latest technological advancement – stress.

Manage stress.

Add responsibilities to your pre-ordered existential journey and see how much stress wattage you can handle. You can even make poor choice over poor choice and multiply your stress barometer.

Choose your scenes whenever and however you like – directly from Lifeshop, on the system, even from one of the many matrix bots. Lifeshop keeps track of every scene. Organize your scene imprints and tag them with your memory, making it easy to regain your emotional response and life lesson long after the scene has ended. Lifeshop is the perfect companion to your mandatory life review.

The value of memory tags.

Put the powerful natural response tools to add lesson learned, grading, memory attachment, and other memory tags to scenes. With Lifeshop, you can learn from even the most mundane situation, perhaps from the smile of a child or the sound of laughter.

You will ascend and wisely.

You've added hundreds of unique scenes to your Lifeshop library. Now you need to raise your level of awareness and become a wiser person – to ascend. Lifeshop lets you examine in hyper-mode your best scenes using quantum tools such as

Life Lesson mode for a mind-bending scene review and Detachment mode for assessing your attachment strengths and accomplishments. With Lifeshop, you can even replay and freeze-frame scenes for the richest level of truth before moving on in awareness.

Share with society.

Lifeshop comes preloaded with an integrated Share Option, so you can learn and transfer your learnings to others in the shortest time possible. You can even sign on apprentices if you really ascend and choose the role of Teacher.

Your life as you need it.

Lifeshop comes equipped with all the tools you need to create a custom-built existential journey. You can live big or small, rich or poor, so your life turns out exactly as you want. For an existential add-on, include an autobiographical book or movie to your life, even a heroic element with an underdog theme. Then program them while still in Lifeshop.

Try Lifeshop 9.0 now

Journey the mind bending, awareness enhancing, and unparalleled reality presentations of Lifeshop 9.0 for yourself.

Lifeshop 9.0 is one element of the Cosmic Ascension Pack and is part of a collection suite of existential applications all designed to expand inner and outer awareness.

It is brought you by the Collective Totality of the Unmitigated Truth and Glory Construct. No fees whatsoever are charged and all existential programs are welcome. Depending on your virtual destination be prepared for a supernatural excursion, travel lightly and bring your own fluids.

MindMerge 9.0

The currency of communication in Dakala is thought and MindMerge brings out the most powerful tools to help you manage your thinking. MindMerge is an application without boundaries and is integrated with the cosmic matrix upon which all life interacts. MindMerge is a powerful fully-scalable application that evolves along with the demands and needs of the cosmos. That means that the more thought users who communicate with their minds, the codes of MindMerge expand in direct proportion to their needs. There will never be an overcapacity. And because of the highly technological structure of the cosmos, and the built-in randomizers, there will never be what is typically referred to as a crash.

MindMerge comes fully equipped with all the popular tools to get you in direct communication with those people you love. No matter where you are or what dimension you are currently in, MindMerge maintains an open channel of communication. You are never alone with MindMerge.

Cosmic Contact is a reality tool that keeps you in total connection with every race and culture imaginable. Click on the Cosmic Contact tab and you are now interacting with nonhuman races, in any region or part of the known and unknown galaxy. Of course, it helps if you know who you are contacting and that you know what you want to say, but you are free to explore other levels of connection, connections that may stem from your own cosmic heritage. You'll find surprising new discoveries as you start talking to nonhuman cultures and realizing how wonderful and benevolent they really are and what is truly amazing is when you explore your own genetic heritage and uncover your very own nonhuman genes.

Cosmic Contact also has a built-in learn application tool called Beyond. Beyond is the best learning tool since education was invented. You can identify areas in the cosmos that can teach you what you want to learn and you can participate in remote, nonlocal learning. All of it for free. All of the calls on Cosmic Contact are indeed free including any learning or training you participate in. It is worth noting that training and education in the cosmos is in accordance with a person's current ability and their own preprogrammed operations.

Challenges 9.0
Every cosmic inhabitant is prepared to handle a specific set of challenges at a specific age cycle. Challenges is the most current up-to-date cosmic application that is purposely designed for the human-grade android inhabitant. Challenges is built on an architecture of Turmoil and Discovery, from earlier versions. We built up the coding parameters from the old days of simplistic challenges – cut the head off, impale the enemy

soldier, excommunicate the priest, these are all old methods of challenging the planary inhabitant.

With Challenges 9.0, we've redesigned the level of challenges you will encounter. Now, instead of dealing with an Inquisition or a Famine, you will now witness the power of Conspiracy.

Conspiracy
The Conspiracy feature is a super-advanced tool that comes built-in with the Dakala OS. With the power of conspiracy, you can experience a level of challenge that is beyond the capability of an individual. Conspiracy-grade challenges unfold with multiple localized inhabitants all cooperating together in secret form and utilizing a very resource-rich toolset. This gives them an incredibly powerful advantage over a typical individual who is not gifted with resources to match the conspirators.

Conspiracy also works against you because no other inhabitant or group population of localized human androids will believe that a conspiracy exists. No matter the amount of proof or evidence presented forth, no matter how obvious an event might seem to you, the people will not see how an event that is orchestrated to damage the integrity and dignity of society is anything but normal.

An inhabitant who chooses to notice a conspicuous event or calamity, be it a purposely constructed war or a political assassination, is going to put their entire life at risk by doing so. Their challenge to obtaining the truth and removing a standardized Cover-Up tool is beyond their individual capacity. Conspiracy forces the individual to become absorbed with an unusual event, even to dedicate their life to resolving the secret or exposing the above government cover-up.

Programmer 7.0
Use Programmer to regularly program your life so as to keep up-to-date with your own existence. We all know that when we fall behind in life, when we keep falling down, our life moves ahead without us. Those who stay in the game are those who understand that they need to continually program their own series of future events. We typically call it "making plans". But making plans and setting goals has nothing to do with organization as much as it has to do with programming those plans into your life journey here on this plane.

Journey

Journey is a cool tool that ensures that your experiential journey stays on course. It is an advanced program that can help you program an upcoming series of events in your life. You life is predetermined by you and after arrival your life is programmed by you. In the old version of the planar reality (Earth) you experienced set back and heartache and determined that these events happened by way of luck or destiny. With Journey at your disposal, you will quickly realize that luck and destiny do not exist in a programmed reality. Whatever happens was programmed to happen; otherwise, it won't happen. Journey allows you to program your future events in a way so that you can gain the most learning quotient and value additives to your true existence.

Move over destiny. Hello Choice.

Programmer is so powerful that when you use it you will instantly realize that you are the architect of your very own life. If you choose to respond to a situation one way or the opposite way, the choice is always yours. You can continually make the same choice over and over, or, alternatively, you can make a new choice. You can experiment and change your mind. You can change your mind as many times as you want. But each choice comes with its own set of preprogrammed responses or outcomes. If you hit a lion the lion is programmed to attack you; if you pet a cat that cat will purr. If you sue your ex-boss they might sue back and if you decide to hate someone, that made lead to a war.

Choices are yours to make and when you add the Choices feature with your current role, the outcomes can be very impressive. Imagine that you chose to be the Leader of a Rogue Nation, and then you used the power of Choice to launch a nuclear warhead at the most powerful militarized nation in the world – well, the outcome would be nothing short of disastrous. And the amazing thing is that none of those results would be a mistake, you will have made a certain set of choices and the programmed responses will have resulted in a major war pitting nation against nation. Choices really brings out the power of personal choice, of choosing the higher ground despite what is the popular opinion. Instead of being quite on an important issue, you can choose to be responsible and help society in a way never done before.

Programmer does not favour one side or the other, if you choose the road of compassion then Programmer will program your future full of compassionate occurrences, the real work is still up to you and that is part of your bargain. If one militarized nation decides to initiate war, you can use Programmer to initiate a peaceful negotiation, and if you don't have the political power to intervene, you can start a grass-roots campaign and become an underdog hero the nation so fervently needs. As you can see, Programmer is a tool that is unparalleled in its use or application. And it truly brings out the responsibility of the localized inhabitant; there are no victims with Programmer.

Truth 4.0
Your life is a mirror image of the amount of truth you bring to any given situation. Some inhabitants will choose to always be untruthful, and in the past versions of reality that has been a central part of life. But the old Earth reality and the new Dakala reality are vastly different. Dakala is built on a higher level of truth because it is complying with the frequencies and vibrations of the cosmos and the mainframe system.

Truth is going to allow you to live your life more honestly, unlike any time before. Use truth as a measure of your success in life, live all of your moments truthfully and when you leave Dakala you do so having achieved the highest grade of truth. Being truthful to yourself is not the same as being truthful, in other words, as an existential form you need to be true to your role in life and to maximize who you choose to be. Truth allows you to really put passion in everything you do.

With Dakala now operating on an entirely new platform, a platform fully in sync with the platform of the cosmos, the entire set of reality inhabitants are going to be viewed as success in terms of how much truth they bring to their preordained lives. You've chosen to come to this reality and Truth is going to allow you to really bring out all the things you intend to do, so that at the end of the day you exit with all your goals accomplished and you have never surrendered your own identity. Truth will protect you from becoming someone else's slave because an individual who lives truthfully will never submit to a false leader, will never succumb to a liar.

We know that there are situations in life that will test an individual, and it used to be referred to as a test of faith, but really it was a test of truth. You may have made bad decisions in the past or been fooled into wrong thinking and criminal behaviour, well all that is going to change now because of Truth. You are going to live your life according to the type of person you are without surrendering your dignity or respect. We have programmed a set of advanced tools to help you defend yourself against improper choices at a time of testing so that even though you are weakened and afraid, something inside your core responds and Truth is there to save you. You will never make a bad decision again. You will never fall into temptation again. You will never become addicted to anything because of Truth. Truth will remind you of yourself, not to take yourself too seriously, to know when enough is enough and to remain validated as an existential being, whether or not anyone else is doing that for you or not.

ADD-ON

Reprogrammer 6.5
The ultimate tool for reprogramming your existence. Reprogrammer is a professional grade reality program that is a state-of-the-art tool for reprogramming the reality matrix and adding your very own imprint onto the reality. Reprogrammer is for the skilled and dedicated reality inhabitant who has dedicated themselves to a lifetime of cosmic service. Working with the reality codes is like deep sea diving without a wetsuit and oxygen tank, without the proper protection and training an individual might be harmed.

Using Reprogrammer you can enter the reality of codes and perform maintenance and repairs. Not only that but Reprogrammer comes equipped with all kinds of observational tools for you to inspect the reality engine performance attributes, to service some inhabitants who have strayed too far off the system and to provide code patches to areas of the matrix that are in need of bug fixes here and there.

Essentially, working with Reprogrammer is a perfect new career option for those who really want to be part of the future of the world because this professional programming role works in coordination with the other cosmic inhabitants of the system. Not for the timid and certainly more advanced than any other available program, Reprogrammer is the most powerful reality tool and now you can have that power in your hands. Imagine playing an integral role in the future of this plane.

Dakala Reality OS

Experience the next-gen technology of Dakala, a completely glorified operating system installed by the leading reality architect in this recognized cosmos.

PLEASE READ THIS AS WELL

Reinterpreting the very nature of reality is not an easy step for the average person. If you are not of stable mind and heart, this information is simply not designed for you.

Please remember that this booklet is a highly summarized presentation written in an imaginative manner. By reading this information, you agree that this is for recreational use only.

If any of this information doesn't agree with you, or you cannot accept it, please delete this file from your storage device and expand your awareness elsewhere.

June-2009

HOP ON TAL THOUGHT GRID

THIS IS A LAYMAN'S HANDBOOK FOR THOUGHT COMMUNICATIONS

THANK YOU FOR USING TAL
(THE THOUGHT GRID)

TAL is a thought appliance
that enables a localized inhabitant to
engage in a transistor-free, cost-free and
distance-independent communication on
the available Thought Grid with any thinking
being.

ABOUT TAL THOUGHT GRID GUIDE

This user's guide is recommended for those persons who have achieved at least one significant level of energy activation, or ascension in the typical spiritual language. A minimum of one significant activation is necessary in order to access the higher-dimensional nature of **Tal Thought Grid**.

Having been activated, and having accepted your primary level of activation you have been thrust into a new level of awareness. A sometimes bewildering and confusing transition from one state to another state.

An activated person is privy to a new set of features and functions. One of those features is nonlocal, innate thought communications. You are not familiar with thought communications because you haven't been trained how to perform a safe and expedient thought communication.
Tal Thought Grid Guide is the premier introduction to the world of thought communication. This is not telepathy or a paranormal activity. You are about to enter a new field of physics, thought science.

Thought science is a valid, safe and unexplored branch of human physics and **Tal Thought Grid Guide** is your first stop into this multidimensional marvel.

WHO SHOULD READ THIS GUIDE

According to the latest human observations, virtually 98% of the inhabitants of this plane are equipped with the thought communication application tool, except that certain people have a newer genetic version, a more updated program; or are more skilled in moving thought from one mind to another.

A very small select group actually utilize thought-to-thought communications on a daily basis. Some of these rare few work for subterranean, paramilitary agencies, or are employed by such, and they work against the good-hearted societal members. The rest work in some capacity for the benefit of humankind. But that imbalance is about to change.

So, the information that you are going to obtain in this unusual book is a chance for you to tap into a new suite of knowledge, to capture new science, a chance for you to be part of the frontline in the coming new era of cosmic science. An era where human culture becomes cosmic culture.

ABOUT TAL

So, let me start off with a very forthright statement: "What you are about to read has never been attempted." It isn't a mild statement and it isn't scary statement. Actually, it is plain weird and wacky. Because most everything on Earth has been attempted in one way or another, in one era or in way cycle of existence: But I say there is one thing that hasn't been attempted, not at least in the last 5,000 years, well beyond the memory of most people, except the ghosts, can't forget the ghosts.

What is this guide about? Thought talk. Not telepathy as the other teachers – mostly paranormal and meditation groupies – have contemplated and examined; and certainly not another hypothetical book on quantum entanglements. We are going to cover basic thought communication and protocols to get you started on a technology platform that will reinvent, reinvigorate and re-establish human intelligence.

How can I do that? Well, and this is not an easy thing for anyone to process (so I understand), I was involved in the installation of the multidimensional Thought Grid. We began servicing the Grid in 2006 and it slowly came online from 2007 to 2008. Being a dimensional technology, none of this can be confirmed by orthodox scientists. But, as you will soon discover, thought to thought communications is a valid science and human university professors need to catch up on cosmic technologies.

THOUGHT AS A COMMUNICATION APPLICATION

Why use thought as a communication application? Why use email instead of meeting over a cup of coffee? Efficiency. Not just efficiency but a reliable connectivity that nurtures trust and understanding. The Thought Grid works beyond the speed of light, it operates on a timeless, say quantum-scale, platform architecture. A bad thought will not last in a sea of thoughts that profess moral standards, standards in line with the cosmos. The Grid, after all, is an integral part of the cosmic whole. Plus, good thoughts, good ideas, good innovations get shared. No one hoards or controls information and knowledge. All knowledge is available to those who are capable of handling that information. This is the realization of a free-minded society. A society that operates on the currency of truth because truth is the most efficient form of exchange.

The choice is always yours – you can send thoughts to everyone you can, or, you can switch gear and just receive messages. Send a prayer, receive a prayer, and influence the shape of things to come. Share ideas with your community. Stay in the loop. All of it by thought, anyplace you like – at the beach, at dinner, before bed. The restrictions are few and the benefits many.

This guide is going to cover all the essential consideration for using this wonderful new Thought Grid. You do not need to understand all the technical details to communicate by thought. You will eventually have to increase your technical understanding in order to truly progress and improve your skill, but to start, no. You're fine. I'm going to cover all the essentials, that is, the basics. This is all introductory stuff.

There are going to be a few rules and protocols which are loosely enforced, and as more minds get involved we will see the development of thought communication standards. I will present my own standards and protocols here so as to ensure that we all have a solid footing from which to leap into an unknown marvel.

THOUGHT BASICS

Thought is energy, word is energy, word is thought, energy is thought. Whatever you are thinking is a packet of energy. When you form a whole idea or a thought sentence you are producing a larger packet of energy. Think of a word as an envelope and a message or prayer as a box.

It takes more time and energy to formulate a message and it costs more energy to mail it to its intended recipient. But we are always dealing with a sender and a receiver. We are always dealing with lost mail and damaged mail. We are always dealing with interruptions in the postal service.

In the email world, a world of electronic messaging we are all receiving the benefits of instant messages as well as spam, as well as an overload of emails, and now we have email programs to assist us and to help us stay organized.

PRODUCING A THOUGHT

You think in words for the most part. You have a thought and shape it into a word, right. Energy is shaped into a particular shape, like taking a chunk of clay and forming a rabbit figure. Now, some people have a very low skill when it comes to forming words and ideas, and some people are experts, they can replicate the Mona Lisa on a paper napkin using a lump of coal. What I am trying to say is that you are not guaranteed any level of expertise in the thought field, and since you probably haven't thought about it your whole life, or at least never took it to the level where I am taking it, then your skills are flaccid, at best.

This is all good since we are starting at the same level, relatively speaking. So, you produce a thought, shape it into a word or a series of words, say a song verse, and then what? How do you send that thought out and to where?

You want to make a package for your friend in another city. You fill up the box with all the goodies, but before you can mail your package from once city to another city you have to CLOSE the box. This is the same for a thought. You need to CLOSE the thought, to wrap it up, and to make sure that it is properly sealed. What do I mean by properly sealed? If you do not seal your package properly it could get damaged in shipping and the contents could also get damaged. It might rain and the box gets wet and your goods get damaged. The recipient will never receive your original, pure thought.

Next, you might over-seal the package so that when the package arrives, the recipient cannot open the package and has to use extra force to reveal the contents, perhaps even damaging the contents.

You may, if you wish, use an express postal service to deliver your package on a shorter time scale. For that you have to expend extra energy, or money, and that provides a certain number of guarantees. Express post is a huge business because the natural state of humanity is always late and behind schedule. If people were always organized and on-time there is no need for an express postal service.

Then we look at email: the introduction of electronic mail suggested that the quality of communications between people would improve. That was implicitly understood. Instant mail messages and humanity might reap some gigantic leap in the communications field, that all of a sudden knowledge and information would experience no more barriers of the past. And yet, if we look at the world today, we do not see the immense promise of this super-simple and advanced technology.

In fact, what has happened is that as soon as a new communications technology was introduced into the human population we noticed that there was an equal or greater escalation for information demands and needs, demands and needs that were not apparent previously.

So, this is the situation we are going to experience with thought communications. Although this technology is fundamentally more advanced than any other previous innate human technology, we are going to see that it opens demands and needs that reach far beyond the known Earth.

The more confident we become with thought communications the bigger our field of perception will become and we will experience a renaissance in world view. The struggles remain but the ocean will be much bigger.

ACTIVATING YOUR THOUGHT POWERS

You will need to be **activated**. There are many levels of activation.

You will need to readjust your **frequency** and to tune in to the Thought Grid, since the Thought Grid exists on another dimensional plane of existence.

You need to have an **identity**. Your name is your best bet.

You need to **register** your identity onto the Thought Grid to make sure that you are on. This might take some effort. Check with me to make sure that you are on. Ask for a confirmation and give it a chance to respond because I might be busy.

Registration is always free of charge.

FORMING A THOUGHT PACKAGE

Before you can safely send a thought from one mind to another mind, you need to form a **packet of thought** and intent, or a *thought package*. These are five easy steps to follow:

1. Think of what you intend to say
2. Edit your mental message
3. Pack it into an appropriate box
4. Close the box
5. This is your Thought Packet

1. Think of what you intend to say
To start any thought transmittal you need to create your message, note, thought, word, prayer, concept, inspiration or story. The sharper and more focused your thoughts the more likely they will be understood when they are received by the other party. A simple thought example: "I love you." Sharp, focused and easily understood.

2. Edit your mental message
You have your message prepared; now you need to edit it. Your editing is to make it as concise and focused as possible. Like the logline for a new movie concept or the product description for a book online, the thought message needs to be refined and sharp. Some people are naturally concise while others are more suited to writing novels. As a beginner, practice with short thoughts, single sentence messages.

3. Pack it into an appropriate box
Once you have completed the sentence-length message you need to place it into a holographic box or envelope. Imagine in your mind space, using visualization, a holographic box and then see your message as an orb or plasma. Work within your own terms and understandings if that helps. Place the plasma thought into the holographic box. Make sure the surfaces are clean.

4. Close the box
You've completed the plasma message and inserted it into the holographic box. Now close the box and seal it. Seal it with a flash of light. Done. Make sure there are no leaks. Think of this step as you would making a package for shipping overseas, you want to make sure that the package will arrive at its destination with the contents intact.

5. This is your Thought Packet

Your Thought Packet is ready for delivery. Feel free to work on the shape and style of your packaging and seal. Add your own flair and color; put a mark of yourself on the message and people will remember you. Put your return address on the box if you like. Technology in the cosmic realm is not as boring as in the physical realm, make is sassy, make it creative, make it buzz with life.

I suggest that you start working with small packets, envelope sized, sentences and prayers to get a grasp of thought communications. If you have many thoughts then it is easier for you to send many envelopes, and as you get stronger you can form larger and larger packets, and later, you can pack an entire shipping container and send it over-space.

SENDING A THOUGHT

To send a thought you need to identify a **Recipient**, better known as a person. A person is the receiver of your thought message. But how do you send a particular person a thought if you do not have their address?

We identify humans by their postal address. Every form you fill in requires you to fill in a local, physical address, just in case you need to be reached. And you also have a telephone number, a numerical address that is reachable by voice. By person or by voice you have an address that other can reach you by. If you don't have a phone number or an address you are unreachable. Where do I send a package to a homeless person?

Then there are people who don't want to receive any contact. They unlist their phone number. They use post office boxes. They go into the witness protection program, change their name, address and phone number – well, how do you find these bozos?

Well, we can find anyone in the Thought Grid because every existential form, for example, human, has a digital address. Actually, a unique signature of light and energy.

The human existential form is very much like a mobile phone with a particular **code** and **signature**, Arvic Signature, and a **modem** so much so that the cellular tower can locate any phone as long as it has a battery inside the device. It doesn't even need to be turned on. The mobile phone shares many similarities with the human form, and I have spoken about this in other books so I won't go into it in detail here.

The Thought Grid is a "nonlocal arvic grid" that contains the key addresses of all human-level existences on this plane (aka Earth Planet). Earth is not a planet, it is a plane. In being a plane, you function as a technological program. In being a technological program, you are signed onto to an etheric/astral network, the arvic-based Thought Grid.

Whether you are aware of it or not, to be alive, to exist, you must necessarily be a "point of light" on the Thought Grid. And as a "point of light" on the Thought Grid you have a thought address, in the form of an Arvic Signature.

You do not know your Arvic Signature just like you do not know the frequency of your mobile phone, but that doesn't stop you from using your mobile phone to call your wonderful mother.

The mobile phone operates on many technological standards, all of which would baffle the average user, and, for the most part, the user doesn't need to know. But to create the mobile phone, those technical standards need to be met. And each country operates under unique telephony standards according to their level of telephony infrastructure. An infrastructure that continually sees upgrading and revision, so much so that humanity has evolved from the telegraph to the 3G high-speed networks.

That in itself is a tremendous leap in communications, yet most people barely give it a thought and are too busy typing up a text message on their new handset computer.

The human form is a technological wonder that also operates under many cosmic standards, standards which very few are aware of and very few care about. Nevertheless, these cosmic standards are not based on some wishy-washy mumbo-jumbo, rather these are super-advanced technological standards all intertwined in the elegant **Technoverse**, the technological universe.

You do not know your Arvic Signature. I know, but you don't. And it is unlikely you will ever know, at least not consciously. If we were to strip away your ego and consciousness and dissolve your primitive beliefs and ideologies, you would be able to notice the arvic body and you would understand what the heck is an arvic signature. But you'll pass on before you get over all those human hindrances.

So, you have to trust me when I tell you that, and I am well-trained in arvic science, your body has arvic signature, in fact, that arvic signature even has an arvic weight, a density that distinguishes you from another you. I mean if everyone is a light bulb then how do you find a particular light bulb, well, arvic weight comes in handy, among other more advanced scientific identifiers.

Arvic Signatures is an advanced cosmic science, one that you don't need to know to communicate by thought. You don't need to understand triangulation to use a mobile phone or to be fluent in programming languages to use a computer.

Instead, we can rely on something that every human owns: a name. Every existential form has a name, even several names, even names from previous existences. But there is a name that people are recognized by and that name carries a particular signal, or nonlocal address. This is not dissimilar to a website URL. The website URL is a word or series of words, but each of those letters are interpreted and registered as a numerical key. The host servers know the website by the numerical address, not the letterized address.

Same thing with your name. Your name, no matter what language you use, is encoded as an arvic address (similar to the arvic signature but on a lower-dimension) and it is this arvic address that is registered to the Thought Grid. Because the Thought Grid is a mid-level dimensional construct and there are many dimensional variants.

The Thought Grid has been specifically positioned here now to allow humanity to develop their nonlocal cosmic selves. Think of the Thought Grid as the Telegraph. It is a *beginning* technology that will develop in accordance to human awareness. As the technological demands and needs grow so too will the thought architecture. Structurally there is no limit so do not feel that it is going to max out at some point. More likely, human innovation will max out long before the cosmos. The Technoverse is structurally limitless and is also expanding.

TO SEND A THOUGHT

There is a process to sending a thought and this process ensures that a Recipient receives your intended neural energy packet. Follow these 7 basic steps to send a thought:

1. Form the **Thought Packet** (see page 9)
2. Recall the name of the recipient
3. Open a connection to their name
4. Identify the type of message
5. Send the thought message packet
6. Close the connection to their name
7. Replace their name in the data bank

1. Form the Thought Packet
From the previous menu, you have decided what you want to send across the Thought Grid and you have carefully formed a Thought Packet.

2. Recall the name of the recipient
Each person has a name or nickname embedded inside the Thought Grid, use this name to identify and target your Recipient. The closer your relationship to this person, the easier it will be to send a thought successfully. See the Recipient's name engraved on a small glowing portal.

3. Open a connection to their name
To open a connection to the Recipient all you need to do is imagine the glowing portal opening up. You might also imagine it like a typical Mailbox mouth, you open the levered door and slip in the envelope.

4. Identify the type of message
As you reach out your holographic box toward the window, you need to imprint the type of message you are going to send. The type comes in several basic varieties: 1. Urgent. 2. Informative. 3. Secret. 4. Casual. 5. General. Using your thoughts, imprint the type of message onto the holographic box, you can use a particular color if it helps you visual the type.

5. Send the thought message packet
You have the holographic box, a Recipient is identified, the
Type of Message is imprinted and now you are ready for the
next step. Put the Box into the plasma window. It is disappears.

6. Close the connection to their name
Look at the Name above the portal. See it disappear. Then see
the portal disappear.

7. Replace their name in the data bank
Return the Recipient's name to the Thought Grid databank.

By following these simplified steps you can send any basic
message to anyone around the world. There is no thought fee,
and should never be. Thought transmission is a royalty-free
service that is available to everyone of any level. A child is as
free to send a thought as is an expert adult.

THE TAL THOUGHT GRID PROTOCOLS

We have to ensure from the outset that the **Tal Thought Grid**
maintains existential neutrality that allows all levels of
awareness the opportunity to partake in the thought
communications revolution.

The Tal Thought Grid is available to all those who want to use it
and to all those who think. If you think you are using it to some
degree. But if you really want to escalate your form of
communications and to sharpen your messages, you can start
accessing the Thought Grid to truly revolutionize your level of
existence.

If you have a landline phone, you need to be fixed at one
address to make a phone call. If you have a wireless phone,
you need to be within the wireless network to make a phone
call. If you have a laptop computer, you need to be connected
to the internet to send an email. You cannot send an email by a
landline phone unless you have a computer.

Similarly, you cannot partake in direct thought communications
without following the thought protocols in this book. If you just
send your thoughts into the Thought Grid it is like sending an
email to some mainframe computer and hoping that the
message is received.

By sending out thoughts randomly you are doing yourself a disservice, you might as well send the envelope to yourself rather to have it returned to the sender.

For the religious and the spiritual types, you can direct your message to your divine being. It should be noted that in the Technoverse, the highest level of technology is **Source**. If you desire to accomplish the purest high-minded result you are better off sending your spiritual or faith-based thoughts to Source.

Source is like the Mainframe, the machine that operates all the thought servers in the Technoverse. Source replies in the most appropriate manner possible according to your highest needs, of which you may or may not comprehend. Nevertheless, the response is always most appropriate to who you are, without fail. This an extremely advanced machine that is failure-proof.

The Tal Thought Grid needs to remain accessible to all. No entity or group should ever convince anyone that the Thought Grid needs to be regulated. Any agency that is formed is thereby formed on the following three (3) basic Talarian protocols.

1. Limitless connections from any arvic inhabited space to any other arvic inhabited space;
2. Learnable and accessible technical standards as a foundation of growth and stability and human involvement for further programming efficiencies;
3. Striated architecture and support mechanisms for innovations in knowledge distribution.

There should be no restriction as to how often an arvic inhabitant can connect to another arvic inhabitant. The architecture of the Thought Grid can sustain a limitless number of connections so there will never be any need, ever, to put any limitation on this multidimensional Grid. In fact, given the unlimited nature of this dimensional technology, it should be incumbent upon expert humans to develop the method and form of communication, to ensure that standards are maintained and to improve the quality, depth and size of communications in the years to come.

People need to develop the thought industry and to ensure that everyone, from kids to seniors, gets free, unlimited and positive access to the Thought Grid. Like the Internet, the Tal Thought Grid is for all human and nonhuman kind.

The standards for making a thought communication should be learnable and accessible to everyone. Standards can include the type of language used while utilizing thought, probably outside of a spoken language dictionary, and can also include the type of format to pack and unpack a message, whether it be packed like Lego, disassembled and the reassembled, or, whether it is like a scroll that you simply unroll and understand.

A thought communication standard might also be the length of a thought talk. In the Twitter and SMS business, a user is restricted to a certain number of screen characters. This ensures that all communications are not only succinct but do not stress bandwidth. A user is forced to abbreviate and to summarize their thoughts.

THOUGHT COMMUNICATIONS

Every person is equipped with the ability to communicate by thought. Thought communication is standard in the other dimensions and realms. It is a very efficient and streamlined method of sharing information and learning that increases the responsibility on the part of the receiver and reduces the friction caused from the use of inferior hardware technology.

For a thought communication to work, it would require that the sender and receiver both accept that thought communication is valid. Having those moments of telepathy or mind links between two people is a very low-level of thought awareness. As we increase the dimensional-grade of technology, the more sensitive that technology becomes. This is not unlike spraying a few molecules of sand on the disk of your computer hard drive. Such a fine instrument is extremely sensitive to contamination. An older technology, for example, such as the disc brakes on an older vehicle could withstand sand and dirt while braking, and even those disc brakes will have their own limitation on contamination, a point where the discs begin to fail.

Contamination at the quantum level, if that is a better word to use, is a very intricate affair and forces users and adopters of thought technology, currently embedded in the human mind operating system, to work in an entirely different manner than before. When you communicate with a telephone receiver you have much more free reign because for one, the technology is quite advanced.

At the start of the telephone revolution, one had to speak in a quieted room and probably had to yell. Move forward to today and you have kids on their cell phones in a nightclub while maintaining a conversation with a drunk pal and doing text messages on their BlackBerry. As communication evolved, the amount of interference and contamination was incorporated into the technological design. That is why today we have such a prolific use of communication tools and all of which we mostly barely cast a second glance.

For two, the telephone (in its various forms) is an acquired skill. We are skilled at using a telephone. We have the telephony architecture in the background, towers and field generators – all of which the basic users pay little or no attention to – and, more importantly, we have a user-base that is proficient at telephony. We understand, as if naturally, the communication protocols: When to say hello, what to say and when to say goodbye.

We all realize, without thinking, that there is a difference between a phone call and talking in a coffee shop. We know that there is a difference between voice communications and face-to-face communications. We know that there is a difference, and at the same time, we don't discuss it anymore because we have been communicating by telephony for 100 years. Wow – 100 years and look how much we've accomplished!

Given the immature level of our understanding with thought communications and also the rapid rate of learning, especially from the younger generation, we can estimate that we are (merely) a few years away from getting a good grasp on thought communications.

To really excel with thought-talk we are going to, at first, establish some sort of protocols; that is, when to engage, what form of communication and when to disengage. We also have to ensure that prank callers, spammers and negativists get blocked; and that genuine newbies have a clean chance to develop their skills.

The biggest problem with thought communication is the lack of hardware, at least for now; or, even better, our inability to notice the built-in hardware, what most refer to as the Matrix, the generated reality between our eyes.

Thought communications works on many levels or dimensions. You can sit face-to-face with someone, and if they agreed, you could engage in a thought entanglement. The distance between sender and receiver is extremely close. This is the best form of thought communications to begin with since it will allow confirmation of knowledge through voice communications, and it provides a visual focus for each thinker. It is easier when you can see who your thought caller is and ensures a much smoother communication.

Likewise, as I mentioned, when you communicate on multiple dimensions you might also be a hair's breath away from someone except that you are on different dimensions. Let's say a dimensional Stelan is sitting beside you in the coffee shop. Now, with your eyes you cannot see the Stelan because he is invisible. But on another level you can see him. Once you trust that, and you identify the Stelan as being benevolent, or at least friendly, then you engage in a communication. Okay, according to the Stelan, all communication originates in thought, and why I mention this is because even if you vocalize your thoughts, you know, you utter words in the coffee shop, the multidimensional Stelan can still read your thoughts. He can still understand you and then can send his thoughts to you, only that you won't perceive it on the conscious level of understanding.

The Stelan Person will not be as happy as can be because he has to wait for you to speak your words with your mouth, a painfully slow endeavour for an unlimited mind, before he can respond. Then there is also the chance for confusion, misunderstanding and interference from other thoughts – including your own thoughts. If you are not skilled in though communication, if you have this Straying Mind Syndrome (a very common thing) then you will a) implant your own thoughts onto his thoughts, and, b) you will pick up other people's thoughts, say of the Barista who just broke up with her boyfriend, and you will imprint these thoughts with the rest of the mental conversation. The result will be miscommunication, and a miscommunication that we are not sure what was miscommunicated.

We can immediately see how Cosmic Travelers, stemming from other planes of existences, can have a hard time reaching humans and a very easy time being misunderstood. Not to mention all the thought interference on this Earth plane. All in all, the difficulties of the past are soon to become more evident, and the ideas of enlightenment are going to make a grand leap forward.

DISTANT COMMUNICATIONS

Thought communications, as we have seen with dimensional talk, is not restricted by distance because we know in our hearts that Earth is a plane of existence, and just appears to look like a humongous planetary globe. More specifically, distance is a perception.

What is the distance between two files in a computer? What is the distance between two websites on the Internet? There is no distance. You have never thought about distance in the digital world because it has never mattered. And guess what? You were right. Without knowing it, you were right. You never thought about and that is because it never mattered.

Well, that is also the situation on Earth. In the primitive telephony world, cellular towers, distance matters because the signal strength has to reach the telephone. In the advanced telephony world, satellite communications, distance matters much less because the satellite has a very comprehensive coverage and can bounce signals on various points of the atmosphere.

In the planar thought world – thought communications – distance is like in the digital realm. There is no distance. The only distance stems from your perception of distance. If you perceive distance and difficulty then there is difficulty. Also, if you perceive confusion and fear then your communication will face strain, miscommunication and a very poor connection.

TRUST AND FEAR

In the thought communication business, the currency of exchange is trust. This is also true in the higher realms of existence, realms which are not completely nor properly proven, and your level of trust will determine your level of communication. In other words, your level of contact is entirely related to your level of trust and fear. The more the trust and the less the fear, the deeper and richer your level of communication with cosmic cultures. The highest levels of cosmic cultures are devoid of fear and filled with trust. They do not understand fear, except to know that it is a kind of friction for further understanding. The more friction in your mind the less likely they will want to talk with you.

Luckily, on the plane you exist in/on, you can communicate with persons who share a similar dimension, the physical dimension, and you are not required to skip into other dimensions unless you really wanted to. It's a choice to go outside of this plane. This means that as long as there is an established level of trust here, and as long as fear is managed and maintained, your thought communications can progress.

Now, not everyone will want to do thought-to-thought so you will find certain groups or societies using thought communications and the mainstream sticking to whatever new handheld device is available. I own a mobile phone and loathe to make a phone call since I spend all my calls by thought. The immediate advantage is its free and free stuff isn't all that bad.

So, the thought communication technology is very dependent on trust. This is not a usual thing to accept when it comes to technology, but we do have trust in many areas of life. For example, the stock market is almost entirely based on trust. If the buyers have no trust in the leaders or the companies then investors do not invest. A market will collapse if there is no trust. The same with telephony: if calls are constantly cut-off, if there is static interference, if there is uncontrolled wiretapping, then no one will use that telephony technology to make phone calls and the telephone company will go out of business. Like any technology, trust is important. We need to be able to trust that the technology will deliver all it promises and satisfies our basic needs no matter it's an automobile, a phone or a dishwasher. When a technology company fails to establish trust, the consumers stop buying the products and, guess what, the company disappears.

Interestingly, there is almost no trust in the thought communication field. If you mention the idea of telepathy, a very weak and antiquated concept, people begin to think paranormal and ghosts. For some reason, telepathy and the circus are still correlated. I don't think telepathy is the right term for today's Starkind population. It is thought communications based on a very relevant, in-use thought science.

You can engage in thought to thought communication by starting with a face-to-face contact. Work with someone who you trust and who shares a similar view on the way the world works. Choose someone who will support your skill development or choose a teacher who ensures a stable environment for the sharing of thoughts. Continue to engage in thought talk on a daily basis, like going to the gym, twice a day, exercise, sweat, take notes. In your daily life, try to separate your thoughts from the thoughts of others, try to wrangle in your thoughts so that your mind doesn't go too astray. It is not an easy task and will take time.

If you are the scientific type, then try some experiments to see how thought communications work. Share the experiment results with your friends. Play with it.

THOUGHT INTERFERENCE

It is important to remind you that you live in a programmed reality, the digital life redefined. It is important because your thought communications can be easily interfered with without you knowing about it. This can have dramatic effects on your results, verily your level of trust.

Thought interference can come from other thought masters who walk around anonymously. There are many here who understand the power of thought, and have used these secrets as a means of achieving power and wealth, all the while saying how it was just pure luck. There are many of these people and some of them will use their thoughts powers to keep the unenlightened public in the dark. For example, if you were to gain entry to a late-night talk show and you were going to demonstrate the powers of thought communication, well, it is almost certain that a few eyebrows would be raised and your results would be embarrassing, to one degree or another. That will not be because of your incompetence, although it could, as much as it is because of direct, purposeful interference.

Thought interference can also come from lesser-programs that inhabit the system. Whenever you try to access a deeper dimension, someone in that deeper dimension may get jealous so they may attack your mind with a kind of viral program. It is an invisible energy product that will attach to your dimensional body, and this program will interfere with you mental process. In fact, these viral-programs are behind the tremendous rise in depression and behavioural disorders.

Are you ready for a thought talk? You are well-equipped for a thought communication, right now, today. As long as you have no pre-existing condition preventing you from having a reasonable conversation and you are of sane mind, you are ready. The problem is that your skill is low and your levels of trust and fear and not ideal. Other than that, you are ready to begin. Given time and practice you can achieve a fruitful communication.

As thought communications gain wider public acceptance, we will see an introduction of new thought technologies, verily magnifiers and amplifiers of thought, enter the marketplace. The telephony industry will fade away as the thought industry takes its place.

THE TECHNOVERSE

Why now?

That is a valid question and requires a very delicate response: Why not.

For thousands of years, even traveling back to the era of Jesus, there have been many Stelans, verily non-dimensional travelers, who have entered Earth's matrix fields and done their best to share new knowledge. But something strange happened in the early, early years: the philosophers, so taken back by the idea of glowing ships and teleportation, became spiritual; and after becoming spiritual and desiring further study they formed study groups, or worshipers. Human spiritualists worshiped my kind, Starkind. When the Stelan sage left the plane, or was crucified or brutally beaten and tortured, the worshiped colluded and formed a religion. The religion in direct connection to the particular sage and their particular connection to a higher power, or a god.

Well, Earth People have gone through quite a number of sages and martyrs and prophets to fill a whole city, and there are an immeasurable number of faiths and ideologies on Earth, outside of mainstream high-incidence religion. Catholicism, Christianity, Islam, Buddhism, Hinduism, Taoism, Satanism...there are lots of "isms" for a homogenous human culture who all seem to agree on one Supreme Being.

Anyway, this is not a history discussion, nor is it a religious seminar because the honest truth is that reality has nothing to do with religion or spirituality. There is no such thing as a spirit or soul except as one particular level of awareness. Reality also lacks a god. Now, I know that that idea is going to frighten people and shock them in ways we cannot even imagine, perhaps even raise the case of catatonia.

In a technological universe, more elegantly "Technoverse," we are dealing with energy. One who can retain or process a copious amount of energy, better looked at as "Arvicity," is rather god-like. To me it is more like a Ford F-150 Pick-Up and a Boeing 747, two different vehicles for very different purposes. Is the 747 a better vehicle than a F-150? Depends on what you are doing. A 747 is not very good at transporting cases of wine from one house to another house. The 747 is good at shipping a few tons of wine bottles between Sydney, Australia and Vancouver, Canada. But house to house, an F-150 is best. Does that make the 747 a *god*? Sadly, no.

There seems to be enough people in the Earth Reality that demonstrate a need to peer deeper into the Technoverse; enough people who want to see their cosmic heritage; enough people who see God as a delusion. There are enough people, students, who are ready and willing to explore what is beyond religion and spirituality, and I will wholeheartedly tell you this: the higher you go on the divinity scale the more technology yOu find. The more technology you understand, the more energy you discover; and the more energy you discover the more you disappear until there is nothing left of you.

If you kept going you would completely dissolve, only to realize that you are nothing and no one. You are something's imagination. A dream. An idea. A thought. A word. An utterance. A whatever. This can be a very sobering experience for some.

So, it seems (I stress that compassionately) that Humankind is ready to embrace themselves as Starkind, and ready to embrace that which is beyond any sort of self-imposed God form. All of this can be quite mysterious and cryptic, and I will retain my usual wit and practicality in all of this which means our learnings will remain stimulating and introductory. This is a very introductory guide.

THE FRAGILE UNIVERSE

The Technoverse is extremely fragile. It is at a level of fragility that is unimaginable for most people. The Technoverse has many dimensional variances, better described as densities of vibration whereby a particular thought vibration propagates much more succinctly than another thought vibration on another dimension.

But before we discuss this fragile universe we need to better understand the nature of the Technoverse, and to do so require us to reinterpret the nature of this Earth Plane.

Let me start in this manner: If you can imagine another realm or dimension outside of Earth, perhaps by way of meditation or lucid dreaming, you can affirm that another dimension is existing elsewhere. Whether you believe that it is real or not is irrelevant. We can be certain that it exists because we can be certain that, at times, we can perceive it. Astral travelers (out-of-body travelers), as well, can affirm this dimensional universe. Not to mention the presence of ghosts and dimensional orbs.

So, let's turn around this scenario and let's say that you are present in astral form in one of those other dimensions, dimensions of which are appearing less real, more illusory, even having a holographic quality about them. And let's say that you astral travel (or meditate) from this non-physical dimension and venture to the Earth dimension. What does Earth appear like?

Earth appears as a dimension...because you were able to dimensionally travel, in etheric form, to Earth. And you did so by will and thought alone, you (merely) willed yourself to Earth. Having been there before you knew the coordinates.

But now if Earth is a dimension to an astral traveler then what happens to the theory of a physical reality here on Earth? If a dimensional traveler can arrive at Earth and inhabit a particular

Earth form then Earth is not a physical planet, rather Earth is a dimension. A plane of existence.

As a plane of existence, Earth is lumped into the technical protocols of all the other realms, realms which are unknown to the majority and which are scientifically unproven.

Living on the Earth Plane is similar to living on Earth Planet, only that we now recognize a whole new level of physical laws, all related to Arvicity (for details on arvicity go to Arvicity Section).

On Earth Planet we are aware of the importance of our perception and intention, and we've tasted ideas like the law of attraction. We are somewhat familiar with these inexplicable ideas, certainly these ideas have gained scientific support over the past ten years, but they have not gained widespread attention because the interpretation of Earth remains as a Planet and not a Plane.

There is a fundamental difference between a Plane and a Planet. The most obvious is that a Planet is biological in nature and a Plane is nonbiological, having a technical architecture. And we can be certain of this because we can be certain of the translucent nature of other dimensions, dimensions that many have noted in their astral travels, dreams, prayers and divine interventions. A holographic realm cannot be biological in make-up. A virtual video game environment is a programmed environment. A digital realm. Another plane of existence is an advanced programmed environment, the likes of which human science has yet to master.

So we have this biological Planet concept and the nonbiological Plane concept and now we have to harmonize the differences between the two. We can easily dismiss the technological Earth and rely on our biological eyes to attest to the biological ecology within which we live. But to dismiss the technological Earth we now have to dismiss that our astral travels and dreams are simply imaginative speculation, perhaps neurological delusions brought on by anxiety and stress.

And we'd also have to dismiss all the various experts, masters even, who have attested the spiritual realms, the multiple galaxies and the existence of other nondimensional entities. We would have to dismiss the truths of prophets and the writings of holy scripture. We would have to dismiss all ideas of God's inspiration, of miracles and divine intervention. Why? Because none of these dimensional excursions fit the biological paradigm.

If we refuse to release these divine concepts then we are forced to re-examine the nature of the Earth Planet and to reinterpret the very idea of biology because we know for certain that there are other planes, and if Earth belongs to this Technoverse then Earth is itself a technological plane of existence.

In being a technological plane of existence, Earth (still using an old term) must incorporate the technical protocols of the Technoverse including the use of thought and will for determining the type and specificity all manner of manifestation. And one of those important protocols has to deal with what influences thought, and thereby existence.

DOUBT

Thought is a very fragile machine. It requires the utmost sterile and pure environment to ensure that thought is transmitted properly and that the plane functions according to its internal programming. One of the most powerful sticky elements, a processing element that we have not paid much importance to is doubt.

On the biological planet, doubt is a minor inhibitor that prevents appropriate and proper action. But in the technological plane, doubt is major neurological static and it not only prevents proper action but also ceases action from ever taking place.

As long as an existential form contains doubt that existential form (or program) is a slave to those who inspired that very doubt and to those who enforce that doubt.

DISBELIEF AND CERTAINTY

All the various dimensions of the Technoverse are founded upon certainty. The computer operating system doesn't understand uncertainty. There are codes, the codes process data, if the data is uncorrupted then the routine is activated; if the code is corrupted then the routine fails to activate. There is no idea of confusion or uncertainty. A computer program does not understand belief unless it is encoded to do so, then it might act as if it was working on belief.

Being one part of the Technoverse, this reality space is founded upon certainty. It only responds to certainty. To move forward is to move forward, and to move backward. You cannot move forward and then go sideways. You cannot move forward and then not move.

When you have disbelief, as in doubt, you impact the sacred nature of the reality engine. This is not to say you must act in arrogance or indignation, rather you must operate without disbelief, with certainty. Whoever instils disbelief into your programming has effectively uploaded an unnatural code into your operational structure and then your original code doesn't activate all the necessary components.

As I have said, a technological realm functions according to technical protocols and works in accordance to programming, all items that operate on certainty, and anytime you entertain a foreign idea, just a like a computer virus, the operational program gets rewritten and your programming goes off course.

This is not unlike someone injecting methadone into their body before going on a date, or drinking whiskey before a marathon. Whenever you introduce a foreign agent to the system, the system will have a reaction. But in the technological reality that foreign agent is an idea. And this is going to be a difficult concept for many people to get a hold of since we are dealing with very subtle, subliminal concepts, and because you have been conditioned to perceive the biological world for most of your life.

MORE ADVANCED VIEWS ON THE THOUGHT GRID

The Thought Grid is available to everybody, but only those of you with some skill, the readiness, the acceptance of such an idea, of such a technology, will be able to really make use of it; and some of you may be making use of it accidentally, because our thoughts are carried, they are shared, your feelings are conveyed around the world, there is no real border.

The Tal Thought Grid is like the internet but for thought. It exists as a field, as a substance of energy, as a substance that really picks up thought, the level of thought vibration, everything vibrates at a certain frequency, now I'm not a scientist, these are my own ideas, my own...work, from my work, from my own understanding of the universe. It all comes from my own experience.

That thought vibrates at a certain frequency. That intention vibrates at a certain frequency, again these are terms that we can understand, but it's far more exotic than that. It's far more incredible than that. Now, there is a Thought Grid that you can access. If you have been following my work, if you've been following other people's work, if you feel you're ready, if you have some intuitive understanding, in other words, you've always done this, you've always picked up people's thoughts, you've always the general what is generally happening in the world, or there was a crisis, when an earthquake was happening.

You have this ability but no one is developing, no one is making use of it because they don't want you to. I want you to. I want you to communicate worldwide. I don't want you to send me all your thoughts and questions, although I welcome all your support. Now the Thought Grid is available to everybody. It is around the Earth which is a plane, so it exists on another dimension that will be proven some day by science.

Okay, so here we have the Holographic Earth and there's the thought energy surrounding this field of energy. It's all energy but different grades of energy. I call it the *Field of Composite Energy*, **arvicity**, which is my term, for the universal energy, or Free Energy.

And there are many grades of arvicity, having different functions for different levels but it is across the universe, so this field of composite energy functions at thought level. In other words, it is thought attenuated for communications, just for communications, not for other stuff. This is my understanding. Again, this is all my understanding.

When we look...when we take out the image, the projection of the Earth, we find this; we find a pool, a pool upon which all thought can travel.

GLOSSARY

Arvicity
A field of composite ambient energy having a multidimensional nature, and being found in multiple levels of viscosities.

Mechanism for Arvic Manipulation
A combination of agents (including human or Stelan) and arvic circuitry (including one or more dimensional levels) that allows an inhabitant to perceive and manipulate the information of the Nilospace using one or more modalities.

Modality
Thought, sound, instrument, arvic body

Manipulation
A method of interaction, assimilation and adjustment that produces one or more manifested responses from a requested manipulator in a given textural environment

Authored space
Some set of manifested result created as a space of vibration by an author or director. Examples include a collection of a memory echo, a trans-dimensional portal and a support program, such as a mental conflagration

Mental browser
An active agent that allows an inhabitant program the ability to perceive, glean and merge with the knowledge web of the Nilospace

Terminal
The role adopted by an existence-scale program when it is retrieving, manifesting or rendering holographic resources
Location Negotiation
The mechanism for selecting the proper location advisor when servicing an intention

Portalway
A portalway is an intermediary which acts as a server on behalf of some other server with the purpose of supplying a polarized manifestation from that other portalway.

June-2009

Starkind User's Guide

Disclaimer
For recreational use only.

Contents

Chapter 1   Activating Starkind

Chapter 2   Starkind Applications

**Appendix A Important Operating Information
               General Suggestions**

Activating Starkind

Your level of Readiness.

To take advantage of Starkind, this is helpful:

- An internal comprehension of your cosmic heritage
- An attraction to one of the following:
  o Source
  o God, Allah, Father
  o Supreme Being of your choosing
- Mental flexibility in your thinking set to open
- New Reality awareness, according to best information sources
- Ability to think in other dimensions

Activating Starkind

The best way to take advantage of Starkind's features, you must activate yourself according to the technological laws of your reality construct and registering your identity with the system coordinator or representative (also see **Thought Grid** material). If you are currently registered with another source of administration, you may need to readjust your frequency to work with Starkind, or separate your old thinking and add a new line of thought for Starkind. (Some minds may not be altered.) You may have to spend extra effort to transfer your ways of thinking to make the most use out of Starkind, or just reboot your frame of mind.

Activate Starkind

1. Learn and study the latest perspectives of the New Dakala Reality from www.ministryofreality.ca.
2. Connect Starkind to the Thought Grid through your choice of Connections using your best methods available.

It doesn't matter specifically which Higher Connection you use, what matters is that you allow Starkind to gain access through that Service.

3. Follow the intentions and inspirations in Dakala to get a better feel for Starkind and sync your frequency of operation.

An open mind syncs your frequency, knowledge and memory automatically, all in line with your internal balance and level of operation. Or you can stay in Dakala and customize your own development and expansion.

You can release yourself from your Connection after "You feel ready to do so" begins to feel right. When Starkind activation is done you can just relax by "Lowering your vibration" and disconnecting. This means that you have completed an initial connection, sufficient enough to begin your new reality experience.

Remember: If you have endured a significant period of your life engulfed in a variety of dogmatic systems of belief, the Starkind activation process may take an extended period of time to recognize any noticeable benefits or results. The type of previous Connection will impact your level of Starkind service.

Syncing Starkind with Dakala

When you connect your mind to the Thought Grid, Dakala naturally and properly provides all the right amount of knowledge and expansion as the individual demonstrates, according to how you've evolved up until the most recent period.

You can set Dakala to respond to any of the following modalities on this list:

- Expansion
- Learning
- Knowledge
- Insight
- Information
- Scene review
- Historical perception
- Heightened awareness

All of these modalities are updated while inside Dakala. If you have only a minimum amount of modality content in your Starkind memory, Dakala makes it easy to gain an initial understanding of these new modalities or to find yourself redirected to sources of information in the illusory reality. You can also expand and learn from your own experiences. To learn about Dakala and the New Reality, read more at www.ministryofreality.ca.

Knowledge, experience and needs are automatically synced from the native processes built into Dakala. All that is required and needed is provided for during each connection between Dakala and Starkind. New learning or needs you make with Starkind are synced through your Connection automatically.

Thought transferences and communications are registered to Dakala if and only if you choose to do so. This allows you to recall previous thought messages without overloading your own memory systems.

Adjusting Starkind's Automatic Syncing

Syncing automatically may not suit your way of life and you may wish to interrupt that process when you connect to Dakala.

Manually syncing for all Starkind

If you prefer to make your own updates, you can specifically define your choices prior to your connection, even during your connection to Dakala.

Manually sync for one time only

Prior to connecting to Dakala, make the mental note in Starkind that you wish to do a manual sync for just one time.

Sync Assist your friend or family member

If you have a more familiar feeling with Dakala and you understand Starkind, you can use Sync Assist to provide someone of lower ability a chance to sync with Dakala and to upgrade their learning.

Disconnection from Dakala

It is perfectly safe to disconnect from Dakala at any time, but it is always recommended that you wait until a syncing is complete for the best results.

At certain celestial moments, such as full moons, meteor activities, planetary alignments and other energetic shifts in the cosmos, Starkind naturally respond and connect to Dakala. Those times of syncing are ideal times to upgrade, learn and expand upon your current programming level since the level of energy transfer is at its most impressive rate. If you disconnect, or resist connection, during these celestial syncs you may miss out on certain important data.

Anatomy

Starkind overview

Headset ear jack
Crown access cap
Sleep/Wake area

Dual camera lenses
Receiver unit
Vocal box
Microphone
Speaker
Breathing mask

Central body form
Operational organ devices
Connector arms
Hand pods
Sync rods
Foot dock connector

Internal Visuals

Thought view screen
Application programs
Reset touch

Tech	Why it is there
Headset ear jack	These stereophonic devices allow you to listen to any sound or sonic vibration in the frequency range allotted to Starkind. Use the sensory device to listen. Adjust your hearing range to tune into different conversations. Cover the ear jacks with cupped hands to block out sound or insert the index finger into the hole for an immediate plug.
Dual camera lens	Open and close the camera lids to adjust the light reception in the visible and invisible reality spectrum. By keeping the camera lens closed for an extended period this will force the mind to drift into a sleep mode. To return to wake state, just open the camera lids.
Thought view screen	Gain an immediate access to all your built-in Starkind application programs via the thought view screen (some training may be required).
Hair	An item designed to make you convinced that you need to try a new hair shampoo every week in order to make you more beautiful.
Indecision	A reason to justify laziness.

Starkind Applications

Access the Thought view screen at any time to interact with Starkind built-in applications. Think of any existential application to launch:

Settings
Reprogram all Starkind settings in localized space. Determine your level of readiness, journey specifics, perceptive values, tele, pray, heal, mem, guidance, protect and much more. Set availability and an attraction variance for collaboration.

Tele
Process thought communications, with an efficient review of call thinkers, call tracers and those waiting to call but unwilling. Visual thought talk provides an image of your list of callers. Just think to see any caller you want, in any capacity you want.

Pray
Send and receive message prayers using your existing spiritual faith accounts. Starkind works with the most developed spiritual systems – including Christianity, Buddhism, Islam, Hinduism, Shintoism, Taoism, and New Reality systems – as well as any system that utilizes the native Thought Grid.

Heal
Examine the health of your body, determine repair variances and considerations to maintain perfect health. Also, determine nutritional needs beforehand and understand the future presentation of illness.

Mem
Remember all the things you need to using Mem, the best memory system program to manage all your experience, learning and knowledge. Organize your thoughts and have that available when a situation requires that piece of knowledge.

View
Access Thought View with one singular intention and gain access to all the intuitive applications in your program.

Whatever you need to do you can do it in View. This is like the Home Screen on a website or handtop computer.

Choice

Make the proper decisions with Choice, a premium level tool that assists you in visualizing the outcomes of various choices prior to making a choice. You will regularly make the optimal decisions with Choice.

Protect

Insert thought firewalls, alter vibration, adjust frequency, and provide generalized form protective skins as and when you require them.

* All applications are subject to individual skill, talent, preparedness and ability to maintain a stable mental process throughout the use of these applications. A stable mind and heart are mandatory.

Putting Aside Starkind

When you prefer to have a genuine reality interaction or to enjoy the texture of mortality, you can put your thinking aside.

When Starkind is put aside, you are no longer peering into the reality field. You can still maintain general thought communication, and stay aware of your surroundings, or to multitask.

As a default response, if you are not engaged with Starkind for several minutes, your higher attributes are naturally put aside.

Using Thought View

Starkind is enhanced with a very dynamic response system that adapts according to the task and the relative importance of that task. An urgent task changes the temporal ratios in order to meet the urgent deadline while a casual meeting has an almost opposite effect.

Emergency tasks are handled by the Dakala Reality System. Rest assured that true emergencies are interpreted and handled in the most appropriate way possible.

Think any application gain access to it. To make it easier, just remember the key words used here. For example, to access firewall protection just think the word "Protect".

Think Thought View to see all the applications at the same time. You can organize the applications as best you see fit. Layer them like music albums or lay them out like precious stamps, all up to you.

Think an application to enter its gateway. Once inside the gateway (or portal) you will see further options or even you may want to make your own options related to the application. For example, after entering the Heal portal you may see Repair, Health Check, Analyze, Immunize as options. By entering Immunize you can upgrade your immune response during allergy season or to protect yourself during a suspect flu outbreak. The key is to be specific and imaginative.

When using these item portals it is best to keep it very simple and to exclude the usual scientific data or contemporary thought on the subject. That will pollute your thought process and cause an imperfect reaction. Keeping it simple is going to require extra focus for the novice.

If you are an expert on these processes, you can experiment and develop and powerful assortment of options, you might even try enhancing your physical traits before performing some physical exercise.

Thought Communications

To learn more about Thought Communications, read the Thought Grid User's Guide at www.ministryofreality.ca.

Connecting to the Thought Grid

Starkind automatically connects to the Thought Grid every time you use Tele or Pray. Starkind's built-in processes will follow a basic logic in order to connect you, such as:

Connects to the last frequency level you used in your previous thought communications.

If no previous frequency exists, Starkind determines a list of available frequencies within your technical capacity. Depending on the urgency of your communications, the Thought Grid will provide access to best suit your needs.

If the Thought Grid is blocked to you and you are unable to gain access, for whatever reason, you are informed and suggested to either correct your internal problem or to try again later. There are many reasons why you cannot access the always-available Thought Grid.

If an internal block is present in your system, you may need to seek technical support from a qualified Starkind technician.

Note. Whenever you hold a conversation in person, you are using the mental thought processes of Starkind and you cannot maintain a thought communication. To hold a thought communication and a conversation at the same time you need to be able to split your Starkind and non-Starkind thought patterns, or to split your frequency of communication into two strands of signals. This is reserved only for the more advanced Starkind.

There is no fee for using the Thought Grid. And there should never be any fee for thought to thought communication. The Thought Grid is a neutral technology available to all existential inhabitants.

Charging the Energy Body

Starkind has an internal energy body that is rechargeable.

Charge the Energy Body

Stand outside during the daylight hours and absorb the energy rays of the sun.

Charge the Energy Body and Sync Starkind

Connect Starkind to the Dakala Reality by adjusting your frequency of thought or raising the vibration of your energy body.

It is best to raise your vibration during the sunlight hours since the most abundant source of energy is available.

Note. If Starkind is nearby a person, group of persons or an area that demands energy, the energy body may drain.

Introspection will inform you of your energy body status.

If you charge your energy body while playing sports or performing another activity, the charging time will be increased.

Other: If Starkind is extremely low on energy, it may force you into sleepmode or recommended retiring to bed earlier than usual indicating that the body needs extra time for its recuperative processes. If you choose to artificially induce energy by ingesting chemical compounds in liquid or tablet form, you may compromise the internal chemistry and may weaken the strength of the energy body over a period of time.

The energy body has a limited lifespan that will be impacted by constant abuse and neglect. The energy body cannot be replaced by the inhabitant.

Washing Starkind

Use gentle soaps and clean water daily to maintain a clean and healthy Starkind form. Assign at least a few minutes several times per day to wash hands and face, brush teeth and comb hair, as basic maintenance habits.

Appendix A

Important Operating Information

! Familiarize yourself with all the operating information prior to adopting the Starkind features as a regular way of life.

Failure to maintain perspective on the advanced attributes of Starkind will lead to delusion, hallucination and mental/emotional imbalances.

Appreciating Starkind

Do not abuse, put in danger, deform, physically alter, purposefully damage, mutilate, or place in unnecessary danger the Starkind form.

Charging Starkind

To keep Starkind in proper operational form, only use the natural methods recommended here including access to the natural sunlight, daylight charging, charging in energy abundant areas or by gaining deeper access to Dakala Reality. Proper nutrition and exercise always play an integral role to a long life of health and disease prevention.

Starkind will not react favourably to toxic chemicals or foreign substances if introduced to the body. A natural substance coming from the natural environment, such as a nutritive substance, is the recommended choice. Any substance at all must always be taken in moderation.

Thinking clearly

Mental imbalance may result if the user mixes ideology, confused thinking or bad advice on a regular basis. Keep activities as simple as possible. You might think you are ready to handle an advanced level of activity that may appear simple but can drive internal processes that you are unable to control or understand. For example, you might attempt a thought communication to someone on another planet and may be unable to readjust your thought frequencies back to this level in this atmosphere. The more extreme the activity, the more difficult to return to normal state. Extended stays outside of normal state could cause chronic mental imbalance.

Also, if you have a current mental imbalance or a history of mental imbalance, or are using antipsychotic medication, you are recommended to work with a professional at all times to prevent any injury, damage, or confusion. To protect your mental capacity, we recommend:

- Limit the amount of time you spend in your activities until you gain competency.

- Avoid overcompensating energy expenditure during stressful times.
- Reset your thought frequencies if you are no longer making sense to people around you.

Interference from External Sources

Starkind is a very advanced kind of machine. Prior to activation, Starkind may be managing an excess of nutritional chemicals or an environment filled with radio frequency (RF) energy. Starkind can be severely affected by RF energy and toxic chemicals in the environment. Also, childhood traumas or emotional damage may impact the operation of Starkind. All of these, and more, may cause a significant interference to the subtle operations. There is no interference standards at this time so it may be unclear as to what exactly is interfering with your experience. Although Starkind is available with a standard set of abilities and features, the actual level of operation may be far below the ideal value because of years of neglect or lack of proper development. In addition to these items, conflicting ideologies or psychological programming may play an important part. As a result, Starkind performance may experience interference and its normal operations impeded in one way or another.

General Suggestions

If you are feeling frustrated with your results, take a break from your activities
Even a day or two away will allow you to reflect on the situation.

If you can't sync with Dakala
Starkind may be unable to connect with Dakala. Make sure there are no blockages or interferences. Pay particular attention to the vibration of your energy body. You may need to spend more time understanding the energy body.

If you can't access the Thought Grid
To connect to the Thought Grid, Starkind needs to have a very clear mind, free of stress and negativity. If your system is filled with negativism or pessimism you are advised to deal with the sources of those issues.

Put things into perspective

Starkind is dependent upon your skill level. You cannot expect a miraculous result if you are a novice. You will be unable to maintain clear and concise thought talk if you have never done thought to thought communications before. As your skill grows, and over time, you will see results.

June-2009

TRUTH IS THE DEVIL'S WEAKNESS

THE TIME-SCALE REBOOT

Both your awareness of it and your refusal of it cannot change it. It is the time-scale reboot. The time-space gap, the damage, is corrected. Reality will now go through a period of structural adjustments which are completely outside of human influence. The structural shifts are happening at dimensions well beyond human capacity. The physical results we will all bear witness around the world, so let's all be as alert (and helpful) as can be.

Therefore, the most important thing you can do is to reintegrate into the current vibration of existence. If that means raising or expanding your awareness, then raise or expand your awareness. If that means fine tuning your vibration then fine tune your vibration. If you have no idea what I am talking about but want to live a harmonious life in the shiny new reality then ask the wisest person you know, besides your mother, visit a psychic, call your nearest lightworker. They should know. Look online. Buy a book. Ask your angels. Get involved. The excuses are over. Much of my work is available online for free.

We all know that the rate we vibrate at determines our awareness. Those of you who have been watching the world changes, you cannot deny that we have all gone through extreme vibrational shifts, energies pushing through.

If you're aware, you've seen this, felt this. It's undeniable. If you're aware and you didn't see any of these cosmic shifts then you're not aware, you're blind.

So, the truth cannot be denied. We are no longer vibrating as before. Yesterday is gone. A year ago is like years ago. Three years ago is like eternity. It's a different lifeline. So that's the truth. You like the truth – that's the truth. The wider the gap in your vibration the more severe the results in your life, so you are always better off harmonizing your energies as best you can.

I Had the Time of My Vibration

Now, vibration and time are correlated. When vibration shifts the process of time is altered, sped up or slowed down. When we enter a different spectrum of vibration, especially as a population or group, then the frequency and process of time has changed. If you are aware of vibrational shifts or what many refer to as energetic shifts or cosmic shifts – or whatever – then you cannot deny that time no longer elapses as before. In other words, time processing has changed. The problem has been the recording of time as on a clock or calendar. The clock and calendar hasn't changed in the past so many centuries and this was done on purpose. Your central processor of time, or mind, compensated for the vibrational shifts but now it is so strong that we can no longer reuse the old recording of time. In fact, while your brain still sees 2010, it is in fact the year 2211. That's because, as I have written, the time-scale was retarded. Due to negative fractal impressions, the human time-scale has been thrown off. That now has been corrected; therefore, we are now in a spectrum of vibration, in a cosmic field of existence that we should have been, had we not been hijacked and regressed. This is not unlike tossing a child into a closet once in a while, leaving him there, abusing him, molesting him and by the time he's 30, he's emotionally and mentally damaged. With extensive therapy, the child can heal the trauma of his past and to bring his emotional, mental, spiritual bodies back into focus.

Imagine an entire reality of inhabitants having been traumatized; imagine now trying to repair that damage. Imagine bringing back all those traumas into a child at once. The shock would kill the child. So we've gone through a process of reintegration, of reuniting our traumatized selves with our physical selves. The disunity, the fragmentation has resulted in the projection of your fears – the deadly shadows – terrorists groups, outbreaks, climate change, nuclear war talks – we are so deeply traumatized that we are continuously projecting our negative beliefs as well we are being implanted with new fears and threats so as to ensure we never move forward. So do we willingly reject threat and fear or...or do we continue to collectively project these threats onto the reality screen?

Till now, we are embracing threat and fear. Till now, we haven't the courage to wholeheartedly embrace positivism and optimism. Till now we have enjoyed suffering. But that has to stop or it will determine your own demise. The way the reality works now is like karma in 6th gear. You screw someone today, today you get screwed. You keep screwing people, you're in trouble. You're in a hospital and you don't know why. Not anyone else – you. Likewise, you help people, you do good, you gain support, you lose stress, you feel safe. If it comes from the heart, it's a good start. You're always allowed an allowance; younger people have energy, older people have mortgages.

The choice of whether to indulge in your ego or to live by your heart and soul is your choice. Heart and soul will lead to prosperity. Not money. True prosperity – fulfillment, glory, blessing, love, joy, hope, promise, faith, healing. All these and more. You decide. Sure, money for service, for assisting and teaching the world, for revolutionizing industries in a positive direction, yeah, this too.

The reality system is set. The machine works a certain way. You live under the laws of the machine, isn't it time for an egoless existence?

Ego, the Obstacle

Ego is a killer obstacle. If you've read the other essays where I've discussed the ego and its mindset, well, it is a very powerful obstacle in our movement forward. We are guided, led and controlled by our ego. You're in your car, but you're in the backseat, the chauffeur is driving. You are telling him to go here and there and he's taking you somewhere else completely. And the funny thing is you don't mind, as long as you don't have to drive, because who wants to drive? It's stressful. You might get into an accident. You like the crazy, selfish, bastard chauffeur. You like a witch and a slut driving you places. Well, you don't seem to mind because you, at least, look and smell good, your teeth are white and your boobs are ripe like watermelons.

But here's the inside scoop on the ego: the ego is 4 years old. You are letting a 4 year old drive your fancy car (or avatar). So we often have that argument, how do we overcome the ego? The first step is to realize that the ego has the mind qualities of a 4 year old. You like the ego's energy and gusto but it's going to keep you in a bad marriage, give you bad credit and it'll have your skin so clean you pretend you'll be a model someday. Here's a better question: which one is more important, the ego or the soul?

If you answered the ego, stop reading, you're done. Thanks for the visit, now get back into the sewer; go for a full-body scan and an extra vaccination. If you answered the soul, keep reading, there's a chance we might see you out of misery sooner rather than later. As I see it, some people like the scenic route through hell. It's painful and costly but it's better than putting raw salt into your bullet wounds.

The reason you are alive is not because of the ego, it is because of the soul. The soul gives you life. It is you. You are the soul. The body is a body. Boom. That's the secret. If you take away the ego, you are enlightened. You are Buddha. If you take away the soul, you are embalmed. You are dead. Without the soul you are a corpse. To place more value on the ego, to worship the ego, to let the ego drive yOur avatar 100% of the time is not a path to a life of awareness. It isn't. I'm simplifying the structure of existence, of course it is more complex, but we get lost in the complexity. We get overburdened in those details, we get confused then get clobbered by the demons and the ego has hit 5th gear and is way over the speed limit. So, I dial it back quite a few notches to see what is at the root. Some of you know, so this might not apply to you. Some of you don't know or seem to lose ground more often than not. Perhaps this helps. I like to think which is more important, the ego or the soul? Who is driving my avatar right now? Who is speaking? Who just said that? Was it the wise soul or the nasty ego?

The better we can identify who we are, the better we can differentiate between the two personas. The wise one and the childish one. If you are an aware person or one who wants to be aware then highlight wisdom, let the soul drive the avatar. Your whole life might change. The truth is that the ego likes to see you have an early death; it wants to push you to the brink, try to give you a heart attack. If you always let the ego drive the avatar, the ego will drive you off a cliff and one day the brakes won't work and you'll go for your last flight.

We are at a point in history where we need wisdom to lead the way forward. We need our avatars to pioneer a better tomorrow. Put your soul in charge this time around. The ego had its 2,000 years, give the soul a thousand years of fun.

THE WILL TO LIVE

The world is self-destructing now and it is doing so because humanity has lost the will to live. The will to live isn't the same as the will to survive. We all have within us the capacity to survive. We get up and eat breakfast. We cook. We work. We pay rent. We find sex. Survival is the fundamental basis of the core program. You are programmed to survive and that is why you wake up each day because you are programmed to. You cannot resist waking up. Unless you are in a coma, your eyes will open. Sure, you can stay in bed; you can cry and complain, you can do that and more. You can do worse: you can wait to be saved.

You are blessed (programmed) with survival and that is to allow you to continue in this realm. It is a kind of magnetization effect that keeps you attached to this realm of existence. As long as the magnetic effect is intact, as is normal, you remain attached to earth, or you survive (eg continue breathing).

Just like you cannot shut off your heartbeat, you will find that survival, like the heartbeat, keeps on ticking. Of course, sure, we take it for granted. As long as the cardiac engine is running, we can do as we please, and we do. We do lots of things, we put up with lots of things, we agree to lots of things, we rebel, we argue, we cheat and we lie. The caffeine, nicotine, painkiller, blow job, sugar – these things all allow us to endure existence.

We are not fond of existence. In fact, we take our survival for granted. How often do we value our beating heart, knowing that we are alive because of it? We would rather fall into fear or direct our anger at some issue in our lives, and there are always issues. We manufacture issues, probably why the tissue business is booming.

Regard the Breath

Living, unlike survival, is something you choose to do. Living is something you act upon. Living is like breathing. You can choose to stop breathing, it's painful and temporary, but you can do it. But you hit a point where you surrender to oxygen because you want to stay alive. And what happens when you breathe is you add more oxygen into your bloodstream and into your brain which requires 25% of the oxygen coming in, more than the heart. You feel better and better breathing. Your headaches go away. You require fewer pills. You think more positive. Deep breathing is an ancient method towards enlightenment because the masters of the old world know that a developed breath would open up the channel to the inner body. That's what led to the realization of Chi and Prana energies, from simple breaths to cosmic breathing.

So the will to live works like the breath because the skill in living allows a person to gain strength. They begin by getting by, getting the right job, by buying a home. They are surviving. A person who is living is surviving; a person who is surviving isn't living. Once all those survival aspects, including social networking, are achieved the individual will strike for fame, for love and for greater self-awareness. While they may think that they are truly living, they are in fact still surviving because they are still existing within the framework of ego.

The world is primarily constructed by man's ego – economy, war, family, government, disease, money – therefore, any achievement is still within the superficial survival. As long as it is in ego, it is survival. You all have the will to survive.

The will to live, on the other hand, is uniquely different. The will to live is primarily outside of ego, even outside of religion or service to some organization. If we recognize our cosmic origin then we recognize that our heartbeat is obtained from something far beyond ourselves.

Life arrives through us; therefore, living is to act in accordance to that very life force. Living is acting in accordance to that which gives us life; otherwise, we are merely surviving. We are egoists who have this and that. These things we accumulate here, I will say, stay here at the end of our journey. They have value only to us in this level of existence. Just like a child values a doll at age 8 and then has no concern for dolls at age 48. How is it possible?

We've been sold, quite convincingly, a life of survival, a life where you can never reach the top of the pyramid. You feed the people above you. Life here is a grand Ego Pyramid Scheme. A little bit of ego in my life, a little bit of arrogance on my side, a little bit of ignorance is all I need, a little bit of success, yes indeed!....we are survivalists because very few of us here learned to live. You begin living when you recognize who you are not and embrace who you are. These are magical moments, moments of the dissipation of illusions. Doesn't matter who you fall in love with, you're still the one with issues.

You're the traumatized child, the molested girl, the bully, the selfish, the freak, the minion of foolishness.

So, what does it mean to have the will to live? It's looking like a fundamentally comprehensive questions because of our main existence is rooted in ego. If you challenge egotism, you get blasted and you're isolated. The ego will do whatever it takes to protect its dominance. The militarization of nations is derived entirely by a group ego that is determined to survive. That's the Ego Scheme, survival. That's what we do. We don't live.

Respect the Sun

The will to live means to wake up according to something higher than your current awareness. Living is as simple as recognizing that the sun is the giver of life, not some person or company or church. The sun is keeping you alive. If someone turned off the sun, kiss yourself goodbye. We don't respect the sun. It's too simple a technology. It's too far away. We don't respect our health. We expect health. We abuse our bodies and then complain when we're diseased. We don't respect the Authority who commands and creates everything. Our ego cannot allow us to respect these things because we will lose respect for the ego.

When we begin to pray to the sun, even in secret, we disconnect a part of us from the ego. The ego loses some influence...and we begin to live. In these small steps does living start. In these small steps does egotism dissolve. But the challenge is strong because the world is dedicated to ego and its salesmen are aplenty.

The will to live is not only about overcoming the grip of the ego on our minds, more so, the will to live is about contribution since the natural world is about continuation. We don't need everyone to become an actor or a singer because we just don't need so many entertainers. Why waste your time? Your ego wants to chase fame, and perhaps you should, perhaps you desire that egotistical journey to realize that what I am saying is true, but do millions of people need that? I think not. Contribution is to recognize a need in the world, say dying children, and to resolve that need. In this manner, you are no longer serving a Master (or God); you are independently contributing to the greater good with your best foot forward. Look at the rise of diabetes in the world. On one view, it's a crisis and it needs more pills; on another view, we can trace back the production of sugary, lifeless foods as damaging the pancreatic health of a child. We could get involved in ensuring children eat better diets. The payoff is huge, a reduction in diabetes, healthier adults. This is not a conspiracy topic. It's scientifically valid.

You don't get involved because your ego has sold you a "better life." If you stepped away from your ego you'd notice that no matter what you do in life, it's all constructed from the same energy. A plumber and a lawyer are no different. That's the illusion. The egoists have said that a lawyer is worth more than a plumber, but when the lawyer's toilet is broken and his shit is on the floor of his imported Italian marble then he'll pay the plumber whatever he wants.

We become lawyers because we've been brainwashed to believe that lawyers are more valuable than others. Quite a hefty number of US Presidents were lawyers. The latest was a law professor. Monks and philosophers don't get elected in the US because a philosopher couldn't get more than a $100 donation for his campaign. Lawyers are connected to money makers and investors.

A person who dedicates themselves to humanity is a hero today. A hero? You dedicate yourself to humanity and you're a hero? Isn't that a standard? We're so entrenched in egotism that you are considered a hero when you step out of the sewer. We're so drenched in sewage that we no longer have the will to live. Even you have a good idea to better society, even you know the truth, you haven't the will to let go of your egotistical life. You are affixed to survival because it is immediate. Survival is a daily reminder. I can't argue against that. I can argue that the will to live is missing. People don't stick their necks out very far. People would rather build a home-based business than heal children or feed the hungry or introduce new knowledge into society (eg interstellar ships).

If you were to overcome ego by 10%, to pull the blinds just 10% of the way, we'd notice that there are a lot of things to do in the world. To the extent that you see or don't see is a good indicator as to how thick your ego is. To the extent of how strongly you act upon those observations is a good indicator as to how much of a will to live you have, as to how much you are embracing the life force within you and denying the artificial ideas implanted into you since birth. Ultimately, the will to live is what earth needs to overcome its challenges. The will to live is required to re-educate society on the cosmic knowledge before its feet. Do you want to survive or do you want to live?

THE NEW TIME-SCALE OF THE SIXTH REALITY (PT 2)

The good news is that the installation of the new time-scale on earth plane, because it was freshly prepped, has fundamentally altered the fundamental course of the people of earth in more ways than one. The new time-scale of the Sixth Reality ("S.R.") has amended a number of key problems of the Old Reality (read Part 1). In addition, the richer technical atmosphere has allowed the reality engineers to accomplish their transitional work, originally scheduled from 2007 to 2015, of eight (8) in a period of under three (3) years.

Rather than the planned construction between the years 2007 and 2015, the builders have expedited the course of recalibration, reconditioning and reprogramming and shaved off five (5) years. To their credit, they have achieved an admirable reality installation, creating as well a stable reality platform and upgraded all inhabitants to their own specific level of satisfaction. The result is that the earth plane (or Planet Earth in old speak) is refurbished and ready to roll. This is entirely due to the collective work of cosmic and human cultures unseen in many countries. The builders took it upon themselves to expediate the transitional process (or, installation of the new reality system) of earth in order to circumnavigate the myriad of structural pitfalls and demonic interference. As well, all of this was done so as to address the lag in human evolution and ascension. The result is that now the playing field is much more equalized, if not significantly leaning in favour of the bulk of humanity.

How does the new time-scale impact the old Calendar System? In the old time-scale (eg years, months, days) it was estimated that it would require 8 or 9 years to accomplish the technical maintenance and upgrades. This was based on the available assistance, their skill level and the specifications of the reality construct (eg time-scale). But the problem has always been

many fold and the level of interference and oppression here has been extra excessive, a situation that would not let up.
As the rulers of earth are based in Fifth Reality ("F.R.") and have dominant control over humans through those old architectural programs, the introduction of S.R. posed a significant threat to their dominion; hence, the increased effort to lock down the world in as many illusions of fear as possible. This was done to prevent the many of entering the new architecture of a much better technological environment, verily an existential heaven where true freedom wasn't a goal, it was a standard for each and everyone. The plans of the rulers of earth were based on an old time-scale. They required x number of months and years to completely subvert and scare the world. By severing the date of transition from 8 to 3 years, that means, in effect, the rulers of earth are now completely off schedule. The sooner that people realize these words, the more off schedule they become since as our mind catches up (realizes) to the truth (which they will distract you from) the faster the reality architecture kicks in and provides the truthful environment. So, that is the challenge, realization.

Welcome to Reality Six

The technical achievement is done. The Sixth Reality architecture is firmly in place. This is something I can confirm, but you may seek you own confirmation from elsewhere. With the architecture in place, what is required is that people realize that we have all, essentially traveled 5 years forward, like a fast-forward on a video editing machine. So please re-read this essay if you don't fully understand because it is valuable to the entire race.

By traveling ahead, by speeding up the process of development, humanity is no longer on according to the old time-scale. More specifically, it is no longer the year 2010. We have accomplished the transition of 2007-2015 which means that at the end of 2009, less than two weeks ago, it was in fact 2015. The time-scale recalibration does not work symmetrically since some portions of fast-forward were more or less significant than others. Regardless, the 8 year transition ending in 2016 was completed in 2009. That means that technically speaking we are now in the year 2016!

That means we have finished the transition process in hyper-speed. That also means a lot of changes occurred beyond your perception or awareness and will show up in the time ahead, as you reorient yourself. As smart as you are, there are many things that are ahead of you and you will catch up as and when you are ready. Each individual is different on this matter. The challenge at this time is to catch up, mentally and spiritually. This should give you some renewed sense of truth or courage because you are now better rooted in the new reality construct and your planned activities can come to fruition. While it will be far more difficult for the new system to be so easily hijacked as previously, it is still incumbent upon you to step forward and take initiative. You have greater strength available than ever before.

The Sixth Reality architecture will continue to evolve, learn and grow so it only goes up from here. I feel it necessary to inform you that we have taken it upon ourselves to change the nature of the game so as to provide earth's citizens with what they collectively determined. The sweat and tears are still coming, but, more importantly, success is very near, on your doorstep.

As well, due to the multidimensional capability of the new Reality Six and the stable architecture, the other multidimensional cultures on or near earth will be able to more easily interact with society. In times past, because of technical restrictions and excessive interference, interstellar and faery cultures only had nominal influence on reality, today that changes because these advanced cultures have more direct impact and more significant influence on human civilization than ever before. Basically, they'll less likely call you a wack job.

Since 2010=2016 and the Old World is now the New World, we are going to find it hard to navigate these times ahead. It might get overwhelming and confusing, but the path is forward and the future is certain. Optimism and discipline are your best investments at times like these. You and I are all part of it, we're all agreed to do this in one way or another. On my calendar it is Year 02 in the S.R., or 02 S.R., and that is my personal measurement of time. On March 21, 2010 (or March 21, 2016) it will be 03 S.R. The old time-scale does not change the new time-scale because in all of the changes are relative to the new time-scale. We are indeed living in miraculous times. Stop believing in false notions (eg global warming) and start seeing existence in all of its splendour.

What Time-Scale is it?

Keeping all these dates in mind is going to be a challenge. Most of us have trouble counting a dozen eggs or drinking a case of beer. It is even harder to count eggs after drinking beer although we would argue differently when we are sloshed. So we process what we can. Some people just buy eggs and then buy more when they are finished. Some people weigh each and every egg before they eat them and then measure the protein amount in each. To think that we have to come to a consensus as to the current, exact time-scale is an impossibility. Knowing that now, there are those who understand the time-scale to the finest detail and are monitoring it because it is their job. They have been concerned about the misaligned scale for quite some time.

I have discussed the concept of negative fractal impressions and have attempted to explain how the current rulers of this place have knocked the time progression out of whack. To this end, we have hopefully managed to see that the degradation and demoralization around the world, along with the inability for mankind to correct the situation, is due to the sabotaged reality and to the hijacking of the earth plane. Okay, that information is over-said. It is also explained in my book, Pine Cones, Fractal Impressions and Cosmoses.

When the new Reality System was launched in 2007, it was due to replace the old system (what I call Reality Five, or you might call Jesus Reality for fun). There was a lot of resistance to it and there were plenty of actions placed on society to ensure that they did not resonate with the new vibrations. For every action there are counteractions. Sometimes we forget this. We sometimes think we all live in a vacuum. If I do this, I expect that. That is called brainwashing. The truth is everything you do or try to do sets off a bunch of other motions. "There is no free lunch." As much as truthworkers are dedicated to serving earth's ascension, their actions are met with counter actions and sometimes the result is smaller than usual. This usually discourages the hopeful bunch who then criticize the truthworkers, as negativists often do. Again, we are back to awareness.

The Temporal Reboot

I am saying that we have actually been living in the 23rd
Century and because of our fragmented state of being, we were
led to believe, and act upon, that it was only the 21st Century.
Isn't that an amazing discovery? Your brain was conditioned to
accept a state of vibration that was 200 years regressed, and
all of this was done little by little over the past 2,000 years. A
little here, a big chunk there, and voila – you're out of Vaseline.

To reintegrate all of your fragmented parts, and some are
worse than others, you'll have to start seeing how this time-
scale is the advanced society of the 23rd Century. You could
notice the introduction of 3D TV, nanotechnology, anti-grav
vessels (still hidden), lasers, microwave ovens,
multidimensional contact, interstellar cultures, and the power of
military weapons, as examples.

How will we rectify or rationalize the disparity in time? That is a
good question. I suggested early on making Year 2007 into
Year 0. Of course, I am now saying that Year 2010 is Year
2211. And that it will be Year 2212 on March 21, 2010. So, do
we shift the calendars to the 23rd Century or do we just keep
the Jesus Calendar? What are the other options?

The true time-scale is always relative to your awareness. What
is right for you is right because it fits your awareness. The truth
cannot be changed. The truth is that the time-scale, including
vibration of existence, is no longer the same. We are now
entirely inside another aspect of the glorious cosmos. So, that
part is the fact. You can feel the change in vibration. You can
see the changes in society. Things are not the same. I am
saying that it is not only because we are vibrating differently
but also because the time-scale of this plane of existence is no
longer valid. Earth's time-scale needs a reboot, to use a movie
term. Time for a Temporal Reboot.

IT'S A DISCUSSION OF BALLS

It's not a discussion that all of you will like. It's a discussion of
balls. Obviously, I am not a bowler or a baseball player. What
that means is that we are probably, most-likely, hint-hint,
wink-wink, blush-blush talking about male testicles. And it's not
an area of my speciality, even though my body is equipped with

a set, rather it is an area of crisis and without an adequate supply of balls, we are way short of petroleum jelly. I'm the polite sort, but most of you know that I am pretty blunt, and, to be fair, a lot of people don't like it at first. They prefer watching a 30-hour DVD series to learn something rather than just get it in 30 minutes or 13 minutes. That's because of balls too, as we may or may not see. I never say I am a perfect being but I speak with certainty as much as possible. In this case, it has to do with balls and rather than go through the "come on people, wake up!" routine – which no longer works btw – I am going for the balls, to talk about balls.

What do I mean when I use the colloquial speech "balls"? Courage. Having balls is having courage. We all have our courageous moments, but when it comes to the metaphysical world or the false reality or interstellar cultures or demonstrating love instead of just saying it, we have a lack of balls. We do. There are a few people with big balls. They are out there with the truth, as they understand it. They realize that they don't know it all, and can never know it all. You can't. You can't know everything because there is too much to know. By the same token, you needn't know everything. There is too much. You don't need to know all the details before you start. You just tie your shoelaces, put on a warm jacket, a toque, some gloves and you're set. For some reason, or reasons, people are still getting prepared with the truth. When they do speak or write, they are held back, timid, reserved, "I don't want to get into trouble" kind of idea. Sure, we have our own comfort zone. Because the truth is, they will call you out on stuff if they can take you down. The enemy in question, the obstacles, they don't have balls, they are cowards, they can never face you one on one, it will be 50:1. They will poison your drink and then have a discussion in front of a live audience. That's what they do. But they are very good at discouraging people from stepping forward. They achieve that by diminishing your balls. They instil doubt, failure and scepticism inside your mind. They say that you will lose your job, you will humiliate yourself, you will fail, you will do this and that. Meantime, they have no problem going on mainstream TV and telling lies. Morbid, deceitful lies. So, who wins? The ones with balls. They have the balls to lie to the people. And they are good at it. We, on the other hand, haven't the balls to tell the truth to the people. And we are good at that!

And it all comes down to having balls. Having balls, as a spiritual or emotional spectrum, is much harder than having balls to enter a boxing ring. That too takes balls. You can be tough in the ring but haven't the balls to say, "The World Trade Center Towers were demolished with explosives!" That takes balls. It does, especially if you don't have the proof. I mean, come on, it looks obvious and still they get away with it. Those who spoke up against the 9/11 Sham had balls, but not enough balls to destroy the illusion. Well, besides the balls to get into the ring, you still have to know how to fight. But many of us now know how to fight, how to raise an argument and how to express our ideas, that's what we've been preparing for till now. You still have to get into the ring. And you'll likely get your face plunged into the ground because they will hit you hard. These boys hit hard.

You are fortunate that you have the truth and honesty. Those are very powerful allies. When you are stuck on the ropes, defend yourself with the truth; dodge with honesty, hit back with your balls. You can't be afraid to hit the big boys. They want you down. They want you bleeding. And they don't care. They don't. You know what they've done to the world; do you think they will hold back when a *truthworker* speaks out?

Where Did All Our Balls Go?

The male gender has been demoralized to such an extent that it has left men with a minimal amount of balls. A man will fight for a raise. A man will stand up for his girlfriend. A man won't stand up for interstellar people. He won't. I've seen it. A man will fight to get a discount on some shopping spree, but to fight to tell people that there are people on the moon? No. We fight small fights. And we are happy when we come home after we saved 10% on our shampoo. That's a victory. The TV News programs will highlight how a man successfully started his coffee shop or restaurant. They will never highlight how a man figured out that reality is false and is telling everyone about it. They have dwindled down the male balls. We haven't the capacity to achieve the necessary impetus for change because the male balls are way too small. Getting a new job is great and important, but world change requires a lot more balls. Sorry, boys. If you are the level of thinking that says that a new job is a monumental accomplishment then...well, what can I say? Then we are in trouble. Really.

We have to think big. We have to think historical. We have to think mythical. We've forgotten the old stories of men with balls. Hercules and Samson. Remember them? They achieved greatness because they had balls. Sure, they were tortured and punished by their courage but they had their prints placed on the floor of mythology. So you're not Samson. Well, you might be. Some historical figures were ordinary men. Ordinary men who grew into extraordinary men. I'm not talking about those men that the TV People distort and make into celebrities and then make mythical. I am talking about mythical people. Who is the last 100 years achieved mythical status?

Michael Jackson was a mythological creature. People of simple minds see him as a talented freak. I see him as a blessing to humanity, one who served a very important purpose. So even in our current history there are these men with balls. Men who defy convention. Men who break the mould. Men who rise above. They are not perfect. They are not meant to be perfect. Society, TV, teaches you that you must conform – you must squeeze your balls – in order to be successful, to be a good citizen. If you follow the authoritarian rules, you are a good citizens. But you have no balls! They're freeze-dried. A man with balls is an optimist. The level of optimism tells you just how big their balls are. Sure, you could go off the wall (they will help you do that) and go crazy, but if you keep grounded and mindful you can rise above the standards of a demoralized world.

What you do in life is what you do in life. It is your choice to a large extent. Selling yourself short in these biblical times isn't the best way to move forward. Whenever you face a moment where you can say a bit more, where you can push the edge, where you can say more truth – say it! Say it with all the faith you can muster, and smile. I tell you this – acts like these will shift human consciousness more than anything else. It will give everyone balls. It might get nuts and they will try to shut it down, but just shine more light, more truth, grow those balls.

Already in the Ring

The alternative is to continue on the slow path of no improvement (or zombification). Given the historical record of the UFO Disclosure, which ultimately failed over and over again, there just weren't enough bodies and balls. Now given the reams of new knowledge, new ideas, earth-shattering ideas, that are available now, like people on the moon or nonhumans as our neighbours or the poisoning of society by clandestine forces – given all this stuff, we need everybody out there with the biggest balls they got. When they strike you down, finish the round, take a sip of water, and come back stronger. Go the distance. Continue on to the next ring. How far you want to go is up to you. There are lots of rings. Yeah, you might get injured, but if you've been preparing (as you should have over these past few years) then you can minimize this. Let the best warriors break the ground, but, darn it, get involved, help out in any way you can. You needn't anyone to remind you day in and day out to do so. The best warriors are wrestling the tiger, you can't ask him what to do. You can't, because he'll get bitten. You do whatever is in your capacity to do to support that process.

You know, they really have made men into these male-female hybrids (or "intellectual pussies"). They've infected society with these homosexual proclivities (eg white teeth, smooth skin), they've put chemicals into our bodies that have altered our hormonal balance (proof: erectile dysfunction). They have given women rights by taking it away from the men (eg a woman can buy sperm at a bank). They have made women into men and men into women (eg growing bisexual tendencies). They have demanded conformity and political correctness (proof: full-body scanners at the airport).

Hercules was not politically correct. Michael Jackson was never politically correct. He didn't follow the rules and they battered him hard. He took it and smiled. We can think of John Lennon, look at his TV tapes and how he argued for change. He put his music career at risk for doing so. What musician today, at the top, is speaking the truth? Even Michael sang about the earth and healing the earth and the world. Look at Gandhi, Elvis Presley, James Cameron, Steve Jobs.

I realize that you cannot give a man balls. You can't. You can toss a man into a ring with a tiger and he will likely get eaten. But having balls and the will to survive work hand in hand. You are fighting for your life, right now. Yes! They are trying to depopulate the world. They are vaccinating your children, killing your trees, poisoning your skies, infecting your mind, scanning your bodies, spreading disease – you are already in the stadium and the tiger is chomping on your leg. You are just sitting there wondering if you can buy a pair of socks on sale. You are hoping you can get a new job for better pay. The tiger is eating your child! The tiger is eating your neighbour. You don't mind? That's not worth fighting for? It is worth fighting for. The problem is that you don't have any balls left. They shrank them down to nothing. You'll fight for a pension, but by the time you are 65, it's over, you are a zombie. See how screwed up this is? You are already in the ring!

This essay has been about the demoralized, castrated male being. I have neglected to talk about women, and rightly so, without any insult thereof. I see it this way; the castrated man has weakened women. How so? A woman derives a certain kind of energy from a man, just as a man derives a certain amount of energy from woman. Today's women do not derive that necessary energy. They themselves are changed because of that. They do not want children. They want to dress like men. They talk like men. Women should use their female power. Their inner goddess. I do not see that. The inner goddess is extremely powerful; instead, they now supplement the castrated male by creating some false male energy. Energy-wise, society is not functioning properly. A stronger male, one with the right level of male energy flowing through them, will re-empower women in a way unlike seen in a while. So, what I am saying is that by men acting like men, everyone benefits. The male human is not functioning properly and because these things are so subtle, so molecular, so spiritual, they are hard to discuss. Finally, I meet many men who are extremely powerful, lots of energy, but they almost have zero spirituality. Not 1% but 0%. That is not healthy. Likewise, I know women who have no idea where their inner goddess is. They are all intellect, no heart. I think that if men get back their balls, the rest of these problems will be easier to deal with. Of course, you might be eaten by then. Maybe leave a toothpick for the tiger so that he can eat the next dude in line.

TAKING ADANTAGE OF THE THOUGHT GRID

Thought is an appliance. It is like a microwave. It has a number of features. It is multifunctional. We don't like to deal with anything to do with thought because thoughts are invisible. According to scientists, thoughts do not exist. Luckily, I don't follow science all that well. My science is quite often invisible. Like art, it's invisible; ideas are invisible; love is invisible. We don't deny love just because it hasn't been scientifically proven.

You'd put the poets out of business if love was scientifically invalid (which it is btw). Well, love and thought share the same invisible, naive unproven characteristics, but love has a lot more respect. We have learned over the years to trust our feelings, well we're still learning, but we can feel love. We might not like love or having someone in love with us, but we still recognize it.

When it comes to thought, it's an entirely different playing field, at least we think so, but is it? Thought, as an appliance, cannot take place without a mechanism for thinking, for processing thoughts and ideas. Not only that but the thoughts and ideas that enter our minds at age 9 have a vastly different quality than when we were 11, and that is because the vibration of thought at two distinct growing phases are vastly different and therefore each phase taps into a specific spectrum of knowledge. For example, an 11-year old cannot vibrate thoughts enough nor can they store the data of the adult transmission. That's why the child can exist in their own world and not be interested in politics and not be concerned about money on the same level as an adult. The child can also be used as a source of information.

We're beginning to notice that thought spectrum can differentiate us from them and you from me. On one hand, spectrum can distance us and on the other hand, spectrum tells us that we can selectively enter and exit other thought spectrums which are essentially fields. To learn a particular spectrum of thought all we must do is to enter a particular field of thinking so we merely alternative our thought frequencies. Of course, you have to accept the fact that thought has a frequency. It must have a frequency if it can travel in your mind and if multiple minds get the same thought (or idea). Of course you can call it coincidence. Or you can call it telepathy, but the problem with telepathy is that it's a magical ability. You have it or you don't. Telepathy is a rare gift; though communications is a technological function, like making a phone call.

To Make a Phone Call

To make a phone call, you need to have a phone. Then you need to perform certain series of functions (eg dialling numbers). And you require a communication infrastructure. If you have these three basic components, you can make a phone call between one phone device to another phone device. The quality and content of that call is determined on a case by case basis, but to achieve a good user base, a telephone company requires a reliable wireless network with a good national coverage.

You cannot make a phone call without some network in place; whether it be cellular towers or radio signals bounced off the atmosphere. The phone device could be a simple hardware or a fully-loaded touch screen brand name.

There is a device and within that device is a *modem*. The modem modulates and demodulates the data feed; therefore it breaks up the signals and recomposes the signal data into a traveling form. The receiving modem recomposes the message accordingly reconstructs it into its appropriate language. The modem is an integral part of the exercise in distance communication. Without the modem we'd be sending incomprehensible signals through the air because they would be in a format that is unrecognizable. Have you ever tried to open a file with a strange file type? This is also a process of modulation/demodulation, isn't it? You retrieve a file in download, you have to open the file. Without the right file converter you can't view the contents of the file so that's why technological standards are in place.

The Smart Human

So we have some key parts and basic processes to work with: a device, a technological infrastructure, a modem, a set of functions. But what does a mobile phone have to do with thought appliances and communications? Good question! It's helpful to ask good questions. The mobile phone is a metaphor for the human being. Imagine the human as a mobile phone 1,000 years from now. If you keep evolving the mobile phone you get a dog then an orang-utan and then a human. Am I saying that humans evolved from smart phones? In a way, yes. In its basic structure, without all the fuss of ego, the human body is definitely connected to an external power source. That means that the human machine has the necessary components with which to connect to that source and the necessary engine to run off of its energy.

Of course, inside the human machine is the program (or software) and it is the program that is connected, all of it on a different wavelength or reality (or dimension). Between the software program and the machine body there must be a translation device or modem that maintains the essential links in order to drive the flesh device (or body). In addition, that modem also connects to other dimensions of existence (say, Heaven as an example).

The human device, because it is alive, must be operating within a specific network of reality, of which there are many (approx. 7 billion) other existences. If this is true, as simple as we say, then all bodies are operating on the same kinds of technologies and all beings are equipped with similar grade modems. What does it mean when a particular pure network offers a set of phones for sale? It means those devices are all programmed to run at a certain hyperbolic radio frequency which was pre-designated by the governing authority of radio signals. As with radio devices, human beings function on a specific field of reality. Your basic thinking patterns and ideas are not necessarily generated because of your genius; rather they are derived from other sources. Your ego program assumes that it belongs to you because it believes you are the next best thing since cream of wheat.

Now that we have a better image of how reality works and how humans belong to a network, we can see that thought communications merely requires a person to tap into their internal modem. The modem is in your soul and your soul is in your brain. Therefore, the path to activation is your brain, or mind, as you like. The point is that you are already using your modem on a simplistic level. You have to or you'd be off the network and in that case you'd be dead. Since you are reading this, I assume you are alive on some dimension. You could be a ghost and in that sense you still have thought capabilities. If you're a ghost, you can tell if you look in the mirror and you see a big white sheet draped over a figure.

There is a Thought Grid

The power of thought is achieved when people learn to connect to their internal modem and learn how to use it, learn how to dial this existential device. It takes a lot of patience. The advantage is that each reality comes equipped with a built-in Thought Grid. The Thought Grid enables the smooth flow of thoughts between people. Of course, here on earth there are nasty people who have firewalled the Grid to some extent so it is harder, but you're here because you like it hard. This is earth and it's primitive. You have finally come to terms with this place. What I'm telling you is that while the terrain is hilly, you are equipped with some neat features. The more you access your technological functions, the smoother life is. But human functions, like muscles, need to be exercised. They are flesh devices, not mechanical computers. They're an advanced software protocol and are earned, like learning bow hunting.

I'm not here to prove that thought communication is worth believing. That's for the chimpanzees. I'm telling you that there is a Thought Grid and that you are equipped with a very advanced thought appliance. If you so desire, and with a little skill, you could communicate to another person thousands of miles away. People do it each day, knowingly and unknowingly. It is becoming increasingly important t to rely on the Thought Grid as the normal existence is boarded up, regulated, tracked and monitored.

Learn to develop thought communications, spend some effort on it, and you'll discover a whole new level of existence. A level that will reignite you with a level of certainty about life. You've always had these abilities and today, more than ever, is the day to really make use of it. Don't be afraid of what you are equipped with. Society will not accept it so talk on the Thought Grid and keep society out of the Loop. This is proprietary stuff. Imagine how much you'll save on long distance calls!

DEAR AFTERLIFE, I MISS YOU! MUAH!

We are born. We are unborn. In-between is the twilight. Life is the thorn, at our side. We used to believe in an afterlife. We don't anymore. Even we pretend to believe in heaven, when pushed, when in the hospital, when diseased, when broken-hearted we fear death, we fear everything and cling to life. You can always see who isn't afraid of death. You can brainwash a man to be fearless of death, to serve some nation, to murder; to serve religion – everyday men and women serve ego masters. But welcoming death and welcoming the afterlife are very different things. The afterlife is just that – the life after. Death is the belief in an end, a finite resolution to a misguided life. Most people believe in God and Death, one or the other. They fear both of them sometimes. Of course death is more certain than God. We have proof!

The world is set to murder and to depopulate itself. People are conditioned to prove that death is real and that it should be feared. Terrorism is code for the threat of death. Terror kills. The conclusion we've all been led to believe is that death is to be feared, death is painful and that security is required to prevent death. People believe that their leaders can prevent their death if they follow the rules of their rulers: Hence, the world is filled with the phobia of death.

There is a growing interest in the afterlife although it is much more science and logic-based than my own interpretation. I've been dead. In addition to being dead, I have been to other dimensions. And in those experiences I noticed a few interesting things. One is that there's stuff going on after death. Every time you skip into other dimensions there are people and they are busy. They don't have fast food or expensive cars like on this dimension but they've got nice stuff. They're busy. They have children. There are animals and fish and birds and starships and starpeople. And the interesting aspect of all this supposed end of existence, this over-rated brainwash, is that all of this stuff from other dimensions is able to get to this dimension, in varying degrees and qualities.

What does it mean if a person from a dimension of death, you know, where people go when they die, can come over here, to earth? Does that mean that they are dead? That's the logical, left-brained conclusion, isn't it? If when you die you end up in a dimension of people then all those people are already dead. Right? If you disagree with that statement then all those dimensional people are alive which means that when you get there you too are alive. You have to make up your mind and choose a side. If the people on a death dimension are dead, how is it possible they can do stuff, like come over into this dimension and give humans advice? And how come some other people can enter the death dimension and not die?

All of this happens because when you die, you leave your physical avatar and your return to your nonphysical avatar inside another dimension. There is life after death! It's not the same as here on earth plane. But see here's the problem – your masters have improperly defined life and death. They said: "anything that breathes oxygen and can open its eyes and is made of flesh is alive, and anything else, is dead. That's what the **biological sham** is all about. Biology is the study of life. But that presumes only one dimension is valid (eg the dimension of water). Nonbiology suggests strongly that there are multiple dimensions and that bodies, as machines, exist everywhere.

Biology is the greatest lie in the world. You see, biology in and of itself denies the multidimensional world. Biology says that everything outside of our eyes is a delusion.

The Biggest Lie in the World

The people who invented biology have denied the entire population the opportunity to be reborn in death. Because they have implanted the idea that when the body dies, it's all over. Well, in one dimension that is partially true: A dead body will no longer function. But the soul program is multidimensional so it can exist, even simultaneously, in other dimensions. It just happens that earth plane is one of them. It could've been elsewhere. What they've done is to have sold biology as the "best science to explain life." What they've also done is to deny that life originates from the cosmos and the cosmos is cosmological; and its science is "cosmology." To this extent, and in plain view, humanity is at first cosmological and at second biological since the body (physical) is secondary to the soul program (nonphysical). Verily, the body relies on the unBody, doesn't it? A body without a soul is a corpse. As simple as it sounds, we have literally destroyed the value of the human soul and have been immersed in a purely physical world. Yesterday's threat was the punishment for an angry God; Today's threat is the bomb attack from religious extremists. Can you see how far we've been thrown off course? No leader ever mentions the judgment of God because that relies on a strong religious base. Religious believers today are weak and declining; instead, everyone, including the illiterate, understands an explosion, just like in the Hollywood movies, the bad guys with the bomb. Fiction to the real screen of existence.

Evidence of man's fear of death is everywhere from the celebrities who are afraid of aging to the voters who insist on a war to stop an enemy that lives anywhere and can strike at any time. The fact that society allows these actions is because they fear death more than they are willing to embrace the truth. They have turned away from their Gods and turned to the ego rulers and their well-placed mind control activation words like "war is necessary" and "we saved you from the great

Depression" and "Everything we do is for freedom so let us do as we please."

If man did not fear death, how different would life be? If you do not fear death it is not because you are important. It is not because of ego. You could have an egotistical person say, "I don't fear death," and they'd say that simply out of ignorance. They think they are indestructible. But a man or woman who has had a Near Death Experience (NDE) they will never say, "I don't fear death," because that is disrespectful; instead, they will say, "I know that when I die it'll be my time to go so I am not afraid of that."

Death needs a tremendous amount of respect. It needs respect because the afterlife demands your best. You can't deceive people in the afterlife. Not only that but the currency of communication is truth and honesty which support additional courage and everlasting love, among other things. In this life, in this misery before you, you can deceive people, you can lie, you can live in ego. You can kill people and still remain in power. But in the afterlife, all deception is off. If you try to deceive you'll be put in isolation until you learn honesty from your teachers. It might take a while, it might not. You see, the afterlife is a higher level of existence; therefore, you are expected to ascend, to evolve spiritually, to learn, to be wiser, to speak with your heart.

To Ascend and Beyond!

What am I getting at? You see, this life they've sold you, with a "death" at the end, it ensures that you do not ascend at death. It ensures that you indulge in temptation because "you only live once." Because of these egotistical leaders, humanity is descending: Mass murder (eg war) is okay if it's for freedom; covering up the existence of interstellar cultures is okay if it protects society; poisoning society with weaponized agents is okay if the pharmaceuticals need more profit; dieting is important because you have to look thin to get a job; plastic surgery is important to keep you beautiful or you will be too ugly for your friends; secret societies are meant to be secret even though they control the government and influence the entertainment business; genetically modified food is good for the economy because it keeps disease levels nice and high.

To ascend a society you must first do the opposite of plunging it into terrorism and biological warfare. To ascend society, you work with truth and honesty because these are higher level vibrations. You tell society that interstellar people want to make contact. You tell society that reality is manufactured. You tell society that you control advanced technologies that could repair many of earth's current problems (eg dirty water in Africa). You tell society that war is for generating psychic energy to prevent society from waking up. You empower people by helping them wake up. The opposite happens here. Death is their key message: "We want you to believe that death is very bad and to give us the power of attorney to take any action to protect you from death. So, who's next for a nano-enhanced flu shot?"

DIVINE INTERVENTION AND THE PIG-HEADED EGO

From my observations, the world of men and women is not as simple and succinct as it appears. For example, what is happening today is an appearance. Things occur, people explode bombs, people get married, people buy petroleum jelly. But all these occurrences and appearances are the results of what preceded them. What appears to us as normal and everyday is in fact a complete manifestation, a congregation of a series of unidentified actions, thoughts and deeds from the days, weeks, months, years before. The rational human mind cannot put these things together because it is disempowering to the ego. The human mind cannot accept this level of submission because it says that they had very little input in the outcome. This contradicts what the TV and the false leaders tell society, that everything is under control, that terrorism is going to be squashed, take your vaccinations and pay your taxes and the world will be okay. So, the problem here is a chronic diet of egotism has led to a society that is devoid of truth because the truth is that whatever happens today has nothing, absolutely nothing, to do with what any leader or guru tells you. Nothing. For them to even suggest it means that they are not as smart or as capable as they have sold you. Whatever happens today is a result of divine intervention. The world did not blow up today because of divine intervention. The world did not blow up 100 years ago because of divine intervention. And this divine intervention is far superior than the entire collection of false leaders, their minions and their pop puppets.

Trying to explain this to the ego is an impossible task because it requires a submission of the ego and the human ego is too strong. The ego is impenetrable like a resilient child. I talk about divine intervention and the ego because it is a backdrop to what I am going to say next. What I want to say next is not going to be taken in the right way, and that is fine, but what I will say is the way it is. How much of it a person can handle is an indication of how much ego is involved in their life. So perhaps this is a good indicator of how egotistical you and others are.

The world was headed for a collapse. When I say "world" I am referring to reality, the previous reality system (5.0). The reality installed at the time of Jesus, that reality, that reality was headed for a collapse not so many years ago. Of course, you wake up today, feeling more ascended than ever, still dealing with the child ego within you and you think, "Wow, humans must have prevented the disaster and overcame the demonic influences." And that is a good thought, it's positive, but it's full of ego. Patting yourself on the back when in fact you had nothing to do with it is an egotistical action. The fact is that the world (reality) did not collapse, as the demons and other fools intended, because of divine intervention; more specifically, because the Creator and his family did not allow it. Not you, not an angel, not some dweeb disguised as Queen of Arcturus Nine played any part in the rescue and that is because a collapse is outside of the capacity of all these instruments.

Only the singular Authority can prevent or designate a Collapse, or Extinction. Playing your part prevents that point from ever being reached. But do to the extreme, severe, unparalleled lack of attention to the planet and its maintenance, and the total disregard for other humans (eg war here, war there) this plane of existence (earth) was headed for a collapse. It did not collapse because the Authority did not allow it and saved humanity. I haven't heard this mentioned anywhere in as many years as I can remember, and although I do not hear it all, I have not seen mankind act in a responsible way to demonstrate that they acknowledge it; instead, people continue on as ignorant and unaware as possible. None of this is to disregard or to neglect the work that was done by many others, others who care, others who have good intention, no, but it just says that as many as those truthworkers there were, they were too few and too late. It's a fact. All the truthworkers on earth at the time, working at full capacity, all-out, could not stop the

Collapse. That is a divine fact and rather than question me, look into yourself and you will find the truth.

What I am saying is that humanity failed. As a civilization it failed to ascend. I think I have mentioned this stuff before, but I am making it clearer hoping it will one day bust through the ego. One sign of breaking through the ego is when people begin to respect the cosmos, and respect all those instruments that they cannot comprehend, that they appreciate life no matter how shitty it is, that they wake up and rejoice, that they tell their ego to shut up and turn off the TV when false leaders blab about how everything is under control. Nothing is under control. Humanity is not in control. The Authority is in control. The Authority determines the course of humanity and that is because, technically, humanity is extinct. Humanity was not mature enough to prevent its own destruction.

I am also saying this to point out that this recent Collapse was not an isolated case over the last 2,000 years. In fact, there are several points of interest. Points where the human race would have wiped itself out, and when the Authority intervened and saved the entire planet. Look into yourself. It is senseless to believe me without further knowledge just as it is senseless to dispute me with a big fat ego. The ego has posed a significant amount of problems in life and is why demons can control you and your friends. It is why the human race is the least spiritual race around. Mice are more spiritual than humans and that's why they are experimented on by scientists.

The failure of humanity isn't new. What is always missing is the recognition of divine intervention. Even in your daily life you may have divine intervention, did you notice or did you think you're just lucky? We continually plunge ourselves into dangerous situations never thinking that there are other forces out there who are ensuring our life remains intact. If we spent half that time learning to master ourselves, studying spiritual concepts or mastering the body we would find a society much more stable and less susceptible to these notions of war. Why if we added wisdom to government, as in a council of Elders, we would find more humane decisions. Instead, they force vaccinations containing biological agents designed to cause you harm and you take it because some scientist put their stamp on it. As simple and funny you might see this situation, it extends into every other facet of life, from pollution to gasoline engines to aspartame toothpaste to psychotronic weapons being used to control society to even weather manipulation. Did anyone really believe in freak snowstorms? Nature doesn't do freak stuff. Extreme maybe, but freaky stuff is man-made.

The Price of Human Resurrection

The rescue of humanity comes at a hefty price, as well as with many benefits. Humanity gets to start all over again, working this time at a new level of vibration. One more chance to fuck up because that is what keeps happening, it starts off well and they we lose the way forward and we get hijacked by our egos and then we blame God and we blame the government and then we are forced to buy thong underwear. It keeps happening and to think that it will not happen this time is foolish. Unless we all respect the greater powers in the cosmos and stop thinking that men and women can be better than the Authority, then we are in trouble. If any man or woman is presented as a god, of any kind, those are the signs that you are in trouble. And whoever is selling those ideas should be avoided at all cost, no matter the temptation. It will happen. They will sell you false gods and you will believe it because you have lost connection to the Sustainer of existence, to the cosmic computer, but that will only lead us right back to another Collapse.

The price humanity paid for its recent divine intervention, which no one noticed by the way, is that it lost a hefty portion of its free will and ability to make decisions. While decisions and creations can still take place, the menu on offer is much smaller than normal and the cosmic laws are going to be provided without discount. If people wish to stray off course then the repercussion will be noticed and felt. If people wish to empower society and to follow the cosmic laws then those effects will be made manifest. In other words, if you follow the road you will succeed and achieve, if you want to break the rules you will end up going over a cliff. It's still your choice and this is my observation, so I might be wrong. But that is my view. You follow the cosmic rules or you are not welcome here. This is something we all agreed on when we decided to be saved. The option was extinction so it didn't take much to get a majority vote. Now that the vote is over and the intervention complete, you are all obligated to stick to your promises: adhere to a proper existence which includes worldwide peace. Period. There is no discussion.

Some people did not agree to the plan so they are left in the old reality construct. They will destroy themselves. They will blow each other up. They will corrupt each other. I say, let them. If a guy wants to walk off a cliff because of his beliefs wish him well, give him a bouquet of flowers. If the President wants to go kill people because they live in some other country then let them go. Let them seal their own fate. You should focus on the good and best intention possible. You can no longer save those of the fifth reality. Stick to the new reality six. The new world, whatever you want to call it. Either people get it together or they don't. The helping hands are over.

I used to go out of my way to help people, spending hours to help someone deal with their personal problems. That was when I was young. Then I used to give people books and supplements to help them. Then I used to teach them on how much better life could be. And each time people just pissed on my ideas, and I said fine, no problem. I never understood that it wasn't me that wasn't able to convey the truth, no, the truth was that those people just didn't have it within them the will to live honestly. They preferred the lies of ego. Today, if an egotistical person contacts me I just tell them to screw off and then they'll think bad thoughts of me. I can't help egotistical persons. After 42 years of trying, I have proven conclusively to myself that a person must overcome their own ego, there are enough tools out there, and when they connect with teachers out there, it is their responsibility to tame their ego. The ego is extremely powerful. Don't discount it. I see it in compassionate people, I see it in wise people, I see it in strong people, the ego is very smart and it will fool you. My ego is a challenge and I acquired a very rich understanding of it, yet it is still very smart and cunning. Never underestimate your own ego, it will say anything to survive, and it knows you better than anyone. **Conquer yourself and the whole cosmos will open unto you**.

Overcoming the ego is a process. There are many grades of accomplishment. What you think is a success today; you may discover that it merely one facet of many and that other facets are growing as they are being fed by the news media and the politicians. It's like the blob. The less you feed the ego, the stronger your dedication to the Sustainer of existence, the more your life will be congruent. All of this will lead you into a better afterlife. Ultimately, it is the afterlife that we are all striving for. Hey, now there's an interesting topic!

THE NEW TIME-SCALE OF THE SIXTH REALITY (PT 1)

The time-scale of a civilization is fundamentally important and since the introduction of a new Reality System on this plane of existence in 2007, earth and all of its inhabitants have experienced quite a number of multidimensional shifts, whether noticed or unnoticed. The time-scale recalibration has had some fresh updates in the recent months and these updates are so significant that they need to be mentioned here.

Each Reality System carries its own time-scale matrix, as often do reality upgrades, and we notice that around the world there are a handful of cultures which adhere to an entirely different calendar system (eg Chinese calendar, Jewish calendar). Each calendar system, on its own, vibrates in accordance to the specific reality system upgrade at the time, or in accordance to that of the inventor(s). Therefore, each calendar is vibrating differently. The dominant calendar system is the Gregorian model, one that is rooted in the Birth of Lord Jesus at Year 0.

When the Sixth Reality (S.R.) was installed in 2007, it determined the amount of time required to unspool, expand and settle, including having a significant portion of the population hook into its native structure. So, in 2007 it was determined to require 8 years, or until about 2015 to properly install. This I referred to as an Optical Transition period and wrote something about it. But since the time-scale of the Old Reality is different than that of the New Reality, what has happened is that the original determination needs to be re-determined.

This essay (in 2 Parts) should update us on what has happened, much to many people's surprise. Again, it will be brief with profound implications which, to me, look interestingly optimistic. But that's just me.

Atmospheric Conditions

The measurement of time is noticed by the speed of our aging. How humans age tell us at what speed reality is functioning at, that is, to a reality technician. How fast or slow a population ages is one way for technicians to understand and even analyze the reality engine's impact on the native environment.

If the atmospheric conditions are too slow, for example – that they don't circulate as they should – a person might age far too fast because the temporal spaces for reconditioning are too wide so the aging process is increased. By decreasing the temporal spaces like waves on an ocean, you are increasing the recirculation of reality atmosphere and therefore aging is extended.

So, in this case, aging can be lengthened or shortened, accordingly. The atmospheric conditions are set according to the level of the civilization and in conjunction to the planetary platform. As civilization programs become more aware, the atmospheric conditions are adjusted so as to renew in accordance. Because of this intimate connection, a slowly evolving culture will discover a level of atmospheric reality total step to their level of vibration. A cultural group, such as human culture, cannot vibrate outside of a very specific range, if so it will perish.

Let's look at a commercial refrigerator, a dairy cooler. Milk and milk products must be kept between -4°C and -11°C in order to preserve its expiration date. If the cooler is too cold, the milk will freeze and the product will be unsellable. If the cooler is too warm, the milk will spoil and the product will be unsellable. If the cooler temperatures fluctuate from warm to cool back to warm, the product will spoil. The only way to preserve the integrity (or health) of the milk is to ensure that the cooling systems, the refrigeration units, continue to maintain the temperature of the cooler atmosphere within the specified ranges.

The reality environment is very much like this cooler analogy. The variances must be kept within a very strict range in order to not only preserve and continue life, as well, to determine the specs of expiration.

The Rate of Expiration

Expiration is a central component of existence; verily the rate of expiration determines the texture and quality of existence. And the rate of expiration is set in the atmospheric grid.

The rate of expiration is set according to the programmed structure of the localized inhabitants. These two devices must work in concert. For each localized inhabitant, the setting must be at a level sufficient to sustain existence as well as at a level sufficient to determine life expectancy. Sincerely, the life expectancy must work in relation to the awareness of the other programs. The driver programs (eg souls) determine the path, or journey, of the avatars so that the series of life events take place according to the life expectancy.

A life expectancy of 75 years will allow a certain time frame for experience, in other words, as an example, if it requires 90 years for a existence to gain a certain level of awareness then a 75-year lifespan will be insufficiently long to allow the achievement of this particular awareness; therefore, a second incarnation (or, reincarnation) is required.

The applicant, if still in desire of that awareness must return to a next life in order to complete its prescribed journey. It will continue to reincarnate until that end realization is achieved.

So we incarnate into a particular set of atmospheric conditions and these reality indices determine exactly what kind of life we are allowed to live. As the inhabitant programs shift and evolve so too does the reality; therefore, to evolve the inhabitant programs we would also shift the reality atmosphere. That atmospheric shift would require moving the entire planar field composite into a new field, typically a new pool of vibration, even a temporary pool. The transference of any one field to another is commonly used as a means of societal development. You could completely shift reality by moving out the current planar field and thereby forcing the inhabiting programs to adhere to a new set of frequencies and vibrations.

Another way to alter the life path is to self alter the time-scale. Recall that the time-scale is connected to journey and journey is connected to the atmospheric conditions; therefore, the time-scale alteration by an individual is another way to speed up the learning fields and to thereby improve the acquisition of knowledge and, verily, to ascend. Ultimately, these ascensions, these enlightenments, allow us to upgrade and the process of upgrading is of utmost value.

The Value of Existence

The value derived in existence is due to the upgrade; that is to say, the value of existence is improvement, for with improvement our after lives are further enabled and without improvement our after lives are repetitive. The only thing of value in the afterlife is the amount of *truth* (like gold) that is derived during the existential journey. A disembodied form with little truth gained can do very little; typically it is recycled into some other typical existence, or just returned to its previous homeland.

On the other hand, a disembodied form with a significant amount of truth will be able to reinvent itself. Because there is some space for reinvention in the afterlife (or even during a lifetime), the amount of truth one can earn can be quite large, of course this forces a being to think of acquiring truth on a large scale which means thinking big. But it should be noted that you do nothing for nothing. You do not act one way or another to acquire truth. You mustn't.

You live according to your highest ideal and you accumulate truth, and you do so because you live according to your highest ideals. If you live only to accumulate truth then you are living to gain and you are still in simple things like ego; therefore, none of what you accumulate will hold any truth because truth can only be accumulated outside of the simple. Only in honesty is pure truth gained. Of course, we raise some questions, especially of truth, but the system's functions are in and of themselves undeniable. The system knows what is and what isn't truth even if the inhabitant has forgotten.

Certainly, very few people today are dedicated to perfect themselves for the afterlife. And rightly so because there are many world duties and temptations on the menu. To deny temptation and to overcome all levels of strife on a consistent basis takes a very unusual dedication to an afterlife. This world is in denial of an afterlife as a public view. Privately, we do as we please, but collectively we live for today and death is a doorstop. So the human challenges are many. If people, even kids, learned to respect the afterlife, well, that would resolve many of the issues of earth today. That would derive a new level of respect for the afterlife, a level of existence that is well beyond human science.

ENGINEERING INSTITUTE OF EARTH (E.I.E.)

2012 can be reprogrammed. Nothing is fixed because it is a dynamic system. As long as there is an engineer, the outcome of existence can be influenced. And as planet earth was engineered, that means that prophecy doesn't come to pass, rather prophecy is programmed to occur. It is done so as to satisfy the demands and needs of the community of inhabitants.

Like an online website, it must go through periodic system maintenance or upgrades. At those times, the website doesn't function normally. Because a reality is built on an existential scale and designed to handle billions of lifeforms, recurring reincarnations or program upgrades and energetic compilations, as examples, an upgrade or system maintenance can appear as prophetic or apocalyptic, but it is all technological.

The Greatest Discovery of the Millennium

As I have stated earlier, and will keep stating, we are all, each of us, living in a synthetic world. So, I see we have some issues with this, understandably, so, it is a grand shift in awareness. But for those of you who insist on delaying this truth in order to preserve your own fears or attachments to ego, you are all responsible for holding back human culture. I realize that perhaps I am not the ideal person (in your eyes) to provide such advanced knowledge and that it might not fit perfectly with all the new age theories out there (conspiracies included), but this is the way it is, so get together and bring it to the public in your own words.

It's a task, sure. But resolving the technological nature of existence (eg the android legacy of mankind) is fundamental to resolving many of the other issues in the world, including the trouble with interstellar cultures because the word "interstellar" is going to be redefined. If reality is false then those offplanet persons are actually coming from other dimensions. If you tell the world that reality is false, the UFO Cover-Up is done because the whole understanding of ET is no longer valid. I mean alien monsters in anti-grav ships is done.

The argument would then be about holographic ships and multidimensional programs inhabiting robotic bodies. The alien brainwash would die off extremely fast because it is childish. So I would suggest (hint, hint) that as many of you as possible send the word out, reality is manufactured and humans are the result of an advanced android species inhabited by a superior driver program. All of this construction is extremely advanced, which is an understatement, so none of it is to be taken lightly. None of it.

It is with great respect that I look upon existence. Even though it is a technological reality, emotions are real, love does exist, awareness is as varied as the people here. You want to move humanity forward, discuss the false reality; that will also expose the illusions put forth by the secret societies et al. That will expose the amount of reprogramming done and the amount of damage done to the inhabitant journey. Rogue programmers have sabotaged human evolution, keeping it on a tight looping structure, on a regular basis. And they will continue to do so in order to prevent you from believing me.

If you don't understand why or how reality is manufactured, it is because this is not discussed enough. We focus on everything but the truth. The truth is that reality is manufactured. If anyone thinks they are going to understand a level of technology millions and millions of years ahead of the best human science then they are dreaming. It's not possible. Sorry. You learn what you can and submit to the rest. Step the ego aside. You surrender to the experts. Problem is the experts are all waiting on the sidelines, trying to get their scientific formulas in order so that when the journalists come knocking they are going to hold up. But we are denying ourselves and our children the truth. We yell so fervently about speaking the truth, that we are truthseekers and then we can't cross the finish line and say it.

I haven't heard it in any certain terms. I've heard people, experts, say that "all the evidence suggests that there are other dimensions and that these dimensions blah, blah, blah," but no one has said: "I believe without a doubt, without any question, that these multiple dimensions are part of the holographic reality."

And that's because we haven't enough proof. We have a lot of proof and not enough proof. It's the greatest discovery of not this century or last century – this is the greatest discovery of the millennium! Is that worth sticking your neck out? Doesn't look like it. "But they won't believe me, Tal." Of course they won't believe you! Society is functioning at the mindset of a 12-year old. They don't believe in ET. They believe that terrorists with pencils demolished the World Trade Centers. Will they easily accept that they are living in a synthetic plane of existence? No. Let's be honest. But we have to be honest with ourselves too. This isn't the time to hold back. It isn't. The days of deception are over. Tell the truth and keep learning. Admit you don't fully understand but that this is what you sincerely have seen.

Certified Existential Results

Just as with any technological device, the operation of an existential environment, or atmosphere, runs on an explicit, advanced set of programming codes. In other words, whatever happens, happens because it was certified to happen. The water flows because the water is designed to flow. Your heart beats because you are connected to the cosmic computer, the mainframe, your source of power. You, we and them all are puppets on the puppet strings, only that some of us have fewer strings, and we've earned that status.

The reality engineers that service this plane of existence do so on many levels or dimensions. On the physical level, an engineer can perform certain functions and an on a higher dimension a programmer can perform a different kind of function. Together, the complement of functions ensures that life goes. Life will continue to go on as long as this reality is serviced. Not long ago, it needed to be decided whether or not to allow earth to collapse on its own. It was decided that the inhabitants here did not have the capacity or will to correct its decline, after many centuries of neglect and tyranny and other tofu.

The reality servicemen and women of this world examined the situation and observed the culture to see what would be required in order to preserve existence, in order for humanity to ascend or evolve. Then it was observed what humanity as a whole wanted. The difference between their inability and desire came out to be an increase in assistance. A level of assistance that required the return of the Builders. That is how degraded the bulk of humanity had become. Those in awareness simply were too short in skill and too few in number.

To say that prophecies came true and that the Revelations has it all laid out is simply false. It is childish. Brainwash. As false as the world. A prophecy is a human interpretation of a technology that the heart and mind cannot comprehend. All of these things, spirituality, god, hope, they are all human interpretations. Not the truth. The only truth here is violence, war, and disease. That's the truth to most people. All of it a brainwash. Disease is a result of your interaction with the reality program, the program provides disease to those minds who need disease. The program serves needs.

Let's Play Ball!

Can you see the importance of discussing the truth about reality? The leaders have everyone thinking about war, terrorism, disease, sex, discrimination, money, anger, fear, god – everything that descends humanity! You are not being inspired. They are not expanding your awareness. You are not stepping into other dimensions, because if you do they give you pills, they put you in an asylum. You lose your job. You lose friends. I mean, at every turn you've been corralled into the herd of sheep.

So, it's a programmed world. Now, some of the events are programmed to occur, some of them are influenced by collective thought to occur and some of them are reprogrammed by rogue programmers. For anything to occur especially on a large scale it must be reprogrammed and there are those who regularly do that. All of it is beyond the knowledge of most people. Some of what they do is lifetimes outside of even the most skilled person.

The engineered reality has been designed to satisfy the requirements of each and every inhabitant. As you can see 1) you chose to arrive here, and, 2) this reality atmosphere has been corrupted, and, 3) it stinks. Since you are here and present, you might as well get involved. The engineers who are hard at work, very much welcome your involvement. But they've failed to get humanity back to the truth. So, humanity is called upon to take up this endeavour.

Put aside your differences, join ideas and get off the sideline, get onto the field and get in formation. The game could use a lot more players. After the finals are done, you can go back to complaining. For now, shut up, suit up and let's play ball!

DEMONBURGER

DEMONBURGER. Stop breathing. Start dying.
Demons are pathological liars. They'll deny anything if it serves them. The UFO Cover Up – whoever is involved is under the influence, control or dominion of demons. Denial that interstellar cultures are here is a grand lie. The 9/11 demolitions. Demons. The Swine Flu. Demons. Wherever the lie is thickest, that is the mask of the demons. Whoever controls the lie, like JFK assassination, these are inhabited by demons. The demon is embodied with the human avatar and the human host has welcomed their evil friend because a powerful demon can enhance a human, giving him or her temporary powers, a better paying job, respect from the masses and temporary immortality. A thing about the demon is that all they provide is temporary, as long as the host serves, the host remains; otherwise, they'll abandon the host and find another. That's when people have heart attacks. The Madoff Scheme, a handful of financiers all had heart attacks. Gee, what a coincidence of cardiac arrest. Let the public see things as they like, it keeps them happy, but the truth is far different.

You don't want to believe in demons, I know that. It's obvious. No one wants to believe in demons because that forces you to get involved. You couldn't beg people to stand up for ETs, even the believers. "Me, no way, Tal. Listen, I believe in ETs but I like my life the way it is. A little ignorance helps me sleep at night." Sure. But in case no one has noticed, these include any number of unresolved problems in the world. There is a growing imbalance. And these things don't go away like acne. It is an infestation.

Even myself. I look at these demons in a different way. People who follow my work will be familiar with it, but I used the word "demon" because we can all have a general understanding. If I talk about interdimensional ego programs, a lot of hands start scratching their respective heads. When I've involved the Devil, a whole lot of eyeballs roll. They do. I see it. But that's the truth. Yes, the Devil is involved. Of course, it is. The problem is that most people have had their head dipped in unsweetened chocolate from birth and they like chocolate. If I talk about what the demons were from a deeper angle, which I won't, that would cause further confusion. So we find a common language. But their language is everywhere. Look at some of the qualities of a demon: propensity to kill, desire for vengeance, willing to retaliate, jealousy, easily angered, spiteful, backstabber, liar, thief, easily corrupted, one who pathologically denies, swindler, prone to manipulate people for their own gain, absorbed with self, willing to take a life to save a life, hoards wealth, lacks emotion or empathy, restricts mental patterns, brainwashes people, cunning, convincing for vile purpose, and a complete inability to hold the truth.

Demons and the Vibrations of Truth

A demon cannot hold the vibration of truth that's why you speak with truth. They cannot resist it. It hurts them. Stick to the truth; be as honest as possible in a dishonest world. When a demon pushes you, you push more truth. You send them more light. You purify your light. It blinds them. It weakens them. Break through their logic. Humiliate a demon and it will go crazy. It will get angry. That's when they make mistakes.

There will be inconsistencies inside their usual perfect messages. Their carefully crafted personas. Deny them respect and they too will fall.

A demon inside a human avatar is actually two people. The human grows weaker as the demon grows stronger. If you defeat the demon, you'll discover a fragile, confused human underneath. If the demon has made arrangements for the long term then the demise of the demon will destroy the human. Think of Frodo as the Hobbit in The Lord of the Rings. He was empowered with the energy of Sauron and after it was lost he aged, he was weak. This was very true. Some of these leaders are in their 80s and they haven't retired. They're not human. You can't think of a demon-human as a human. These are minions of the Devil.

Truth on Tap

If you have angelic powers, or persona, then it is your task to shine the light, speak the vibration of truth. It will ripple into the ranks of the demon hoards. It keeps them contained, truth. As simple as it is.

If you have no truth, then share the truth of others, as simple as just music. Truth can be a painting, a song or a conspiracy theory video, a dress code, we can't limit ourselves to what truth is because truth is a vibration. You're a clothing designer – design a truth outfit, have a fashion show of truth and make each item a vibration of truth.

Truth and lies, these are weapons, they are. They are weapons. If you eat only lies you will become a liar, so you must eat truth as well. It doesn't matter who you support as long as they represent an aspect of truth. No one has 100% truth except the Creator. No demon has 100% deception except the Devil. You work with whatever you have and you try to add a bit here and there. You ascend, you perfect your ego, you detach, you connect to your source; you resist deception and find new avenues of honesty. It's called life.

If you are one who is involved then you get involved. If not, then go back to your regular life and do as you will. We need, more than ever, bold actions; we need the strong at the front, those who won't fold when the demons push back because they push hard. They'll hit low and gang up on you. They're cowards. If they needed two people to beat someone up, they'd get 100. And what happens is that the goodhearted will just watch and then think: "See, he didn't make it. What makes you think any of us can stand up against them. They're too many." That's not the voice of a bold thinker. Sorry. That kind of person should step back. If anyone contacts me with that fearful mentality, I won't respond. It's just not going to cut it. Not now. Listen, my view is that the playing around is over. The hem and haw, yo-yo, it's over – the next stage, which just started demands fearlessness. It demands positivism. As you hear negativity in people, you will see what frame of mind they are on.

How to Defeat a Demon

The demonic (pure ego) programs are on their way out. It's their end. Sure, the Devil is coming, and that's because he's the biggest jerk of all. The jerkball. In the meantime, here are some ideas on how to defeat the demons.

1. The demons need dark energy. With it they grow, without it they wither. That's why they need more WAR to continue. It is their source of power. If you can stop the war, you'll take out a hoard of demons. Any volunteers? Didn't think so.

2. Humour can defeat any demon. Tell a joke a day. Can be the same joke if you're lazy. Nothing cruel, just funny. Or, watch comedy shows, rent them if not on TV. Turn it into a mission – a joke a day. Joke about serious stuff – global warming, flu, Obama.

3. Demons have no home in the basement. They now exist above surface more than ever before so they need to be fed. Tell the truth, encourage honesty and they will starve. By doing so, you'll notice that more of them will be revealed; they will come to the surface. Whatever you do, **do not feed the demons**.

Without fuel, without a home, with a laughing vibration, truthful vibes, the demons will dissipate, they will disappear. On the contrary, if you rise to anger and seek revenge, they will feed off of you, they will become stronger. Think Tai Chi. Use the energy of the opponent to defeat the opponent. Experiment to see if I am correct. Tell someone the truth, be honest. See them get angry or see them turn away. They don't like the truth. They'll turn away. That's the ego. The ego can't stand the light of truth. Imagine a demon, which is rooted in ego.

To me, hell is the home of ego. I've said it before. So demons are ego beings. They're 100% right, 100% of the time. And when it turns out they were wrong, well, it was the circumstance, the situation changed and caused the strategy to fail – hallmark of the demons. When a person stands up and says, "I'm a liar. I stole your money, I raped the choir boy and I did it because I'm a big jerk and I'm going to get through it with lots of professional help," that's the voice of hope. That's honest.

Honest in an Instant

What is missing more in the world today than anything else is "honesty." The leaders of the world are everything but honest. Honesty is a very powerful technology because it activates a higher dimension of the reality construct. It taps you into a higher level of living. Denial and lies, these things prevent us from being honest because we are denied truth.

We cannot be honest if we have very little truth in the world. So they lie and we are denied the power of honesty, because we are freed to live in a deceitful world. See how all of these subtle ways of things, these subliminal effects, these superior technologies, see how important they are? Honesty is a vibration that grants you a richer access to the reality. Anger connects you to the demon hotline, "What kind of life do you need? We've got starship cover-ups starting from $99 and on Special today is the Ego Affair Pack, for three easy payments of $29.95 we'll teach you how to hide not one, not two, but UP TO five women from your wife. And if you order now, we'll throw in the Super BS Package which will show you how to embody a demon and how to button a tie, the perfect lesson for any wannabe politician."

Let's get back to honesty. Let's try it. Maybe it'll work, eh? Honesty is a technology. People often wonder what an advanced technology looks like – it looks like *honesty*. I know! It's crazy. Honesty? WTF. It's just a word, Tal. No, buddy, honesty is a technology. Try it and let me know. It's available for free btw. No download, no delivery, no limit. Honesty, as much as you can handle. Honesty in an instant. Put some in your pocket.

CHILDREN OF THE BETTER TOMORROW

It is not without content that we find ourselves here, in this predicament. We do so at a cost, don't we? We have achieved a miraculous set of circumstances to be here. We have sublimated all the most unusual things, we have discouraged the tide of lies, we have thwarted more disasters than ever before; still, the world is not at peace. The world still bleeds and the children still are hungry. It is not a place, here on this plane, it is not a place for trust and beauty. The world against you intensifies and the world for you demystifies. Which side are you on? Do you like the spread of fear on your toasted mind or do you like the brotherly lasagne next door? We are essentially at this clear of the clearest juncture the world of today. We are the builders of the next century and we could be the fateful crew of the SS Screw the World.

The road to the future depends on what you like to see, and it depends on how you can detach from all things of no use.

The Titanic is sinking. Are you trying to find a lifeboat or are you trying to fix the holes in the hull? Typically, we try to repair the damage, we try to rescue the dying, we try to restart the engines. That's our typical response. That's what good people do. But that will ensure one thing – you drowning.

Saving yourself when the earth ship is sinking is a complex endeavour, isn't it? First of all, you have to realize the fact that the old world is being submerged. Then you have to accept that there is indeed a series of energy fields and there are fields of reality and these oceans of existence are in the midst of the greatest shift in the known history. We are in the midst of a historical, life-changing time and we have to respect that. We have to look at that boldly and we have to know that no matter what anyone else is saying that we ourselves are 100% present. Your presence is required. That means not playing the game of death. Not being sucked into another demise; a fear, a threat, a lie, a cover-up, a denial, a delay. There are no more delays. That is it for delays. There is no end of the world scenario. There is a gradual shift in the synthetic scope of reality and it is presenting all of us with grander alternatives. It is presenting us with unimaginable outcomes. To sit in our old framework of thinking and to make the old decisions we've always made is a waste. It's like wiping your ass with fig leaves of toilet paper. It's a caveman joke. It truly is that grand. On the one hand we are called upon, well we are not called upon, we are invited into a new level of existence. Listen, it's not new. I hate to be the bringer of bad news. None of this is new. This is old and repetitive. It keeps repeating because humanity, as an elegant race, continues to make the same decisions from the same old menu. Anyone who comes along and says that there's a better way is crucified. You needed be nailed to a post to be crucified. And what happens is that the tried and true methods, the principles of communists, is repeated, are worked into each and every life.

Better Life Next Time

We are led by communists, those who act and think like communists but refer to themselves as libertarians, entrepreneurs and priests. They call themselves leaders. Yet they themselves know that they have only their own egotistical desires in mind. The leaders of the world desire your obedience and demise. This Titanic belongs to them, they blew out the hull, they limited the lifeboats, they have the guns and they want you to drown. The goodhearted, the men and women of inspiration, the ones who have worked tirelessly on your behalf to ensure that you learned how to swim, because they know that the Titanic was going to sink, those people they want you to live. They want to take you to the nearest island, a new plane of existence, where you can establish a fresh existential experience and be cut away from the demons who rule here. Let them drown.

As much as you want to fix the boat, as much as you want to help the young mother carry her 300 pairs of shoes into the lifeboats, as much as you love your father trapped under a metal bunk bed, as much as you want to do what's right, what is more right (righter?) is that you rush to the lifeboat, gather with like-minded people and figure out a way to find others like you. Escape the sinking boat and make your way to the Island of Tomorrow. It's out there. You can call it the Titanic or a mothership or a planet or a plane of existence. The analogy is the same, the preference is yours. It's pointless to argue over the details when we are within such a magnificent upheaval. Think of the opportunities you are passing up. There is so much to do it seems overwhelming and yet you'll still hear people saying that there's nothing left to do. Well, now you know their mindset. They're done. They're not going to make it. You shake their hand and say, "Better life next time."

The next step then is to secure the lifeboats. Well, guess what? There are not enough lifeboats. The leaders and their minions sabotaged them all. You're lucky to have what you have. But there are many more bodies than boats so you have to think, do I save myself or do I find a way to rescue my like-minded friends. The old thinkers, the negativists, they're done. We're talking about the group of futurists, children of the better tomorrow. They need a boat, and you haven't got one. Will you build one, or will you watch them drown?

We have to, if we can, rescue those who are ready to move on. If they are ready, they are nearby. They don't know how to build a boat. Neither do you, or wait, maybe you do. Listen, someone better build something or even the awakened bunch is going to drown. At least teach them how to swim. Can you do better? It's a historical time. Do you want to be remembered as an innovator or as a chump?

I, Reflect

Only a few of us recognize, truly recognize, the traditional period we are in. To me that means that in the near distant future we will look back on today and reflect. We will reflect on how well we implemented our ideas. We will reflect on how advanced our thinking was. We'll reflect on what truly transpired, was all of this about what were told, or we think, it is about. Most of what you think and believe is what you yourself think and believe. The truth is far more elusive. The truth is relative to awareness for awareness determines everything, and your awareness tomorrow should be all that much brighter.

Reflection is a powerful tool that we often neglect to put to proper use. We don't like to look in the mirror of time and event. How did I do? We don't want to know. We like to keep parts of our lives very simple. We like to gloss it up, put on as much concealer as possible.

Reflection is like shining a spotlight on aspects of ourselves. It demands a certain amount of honesty, and its personal. You know yourself best. But we are so busy, we are so intent on success, so wrapped into the fear agenda, the various orchestrations; we are so many things that we haven't the time to reflect until we go on vacation, climb the mountain, look at the glowing sunset and think: "There's more to this logical, fear driven, plastic breast job existence, isn't there? I want a divorce." By the time we get home, back to routine, all that wonderful spiritual goodness has slipped away and it's back to: "Hi honey, when you hit me next time just don't hit my face." It sounds a bit fantastic but sadly there's a lot of truth in it. We're just not a brave society. We're not. Whatever the false leaders decide, we swallow: "Gee, more security checks at the airport because of some poorly executed CIA stooge, well, okay, why not, these guys must know something, just they still serve booze on the flight because at the rate of deception I need to get hammered a little more often, and that's really because the petroleum jelly isn't always enough. I mean what's next, an anal probe?" And life goes on. The pill consumption increases. Later in life, we reflect. But our youth is done. Time to retire. Who exactly invented retirement as a goal in life? We spend our lives in self perfection of our entire selves, and then at some miraculous age we stop. Boom. "I'm stopping here. Sixty five. I'm done. Take me out of the Screw Society Oven."

We live a meagre existence. It's simple. It doesn't have to be, it's just someone set the bar really low. We look forward to retirement so we can disengage from working for a soul-sucking employer, we fear death and we smoke cigarettes which are scientifically proven to cause death. We have gifts but we hide them because why bother really. So what? – I can heal disease. Who wants that? Well, you're right. Screw the energy healing ability. Keep the car payments and the lousy boyfriend. Forget about your angelic qualities. "Me, an angel? I haven't a clue what that means. Hey, do you have a cigarette?"

That Most Elegant Android

There is a growing awareness of the machine-like qualities of the human race, which is generally a good sign because it helps to understand the synthetic reality, but there is a hazard I'd like to address. The hazard has to do with the essential differences between a flesh machine and a synthetic human. It is easy to devalue and simplify, even to itemize, the human construct. That's what's been happening already . That's what the false leaders and the secret societies have done. They've managed to dehumanize you, to strip away all the elegance you possess. They've done so over many years and the damage is clear – we no longer think on a multidimensional scale. We are about as spiritual as a cold turkey salad two days after Christmas. I mean, look, we still believe in Christmas, we don't see the cosmic period around the Winter Solstice and if we do we keep it private. Sure, in private we're geniuses. We protect our view on other dimensions. Unfortunately, I don't. If people like me didn't speak out, at some point the discussion would end, and that's unhealthy. But to dehumanize a human is a dangerous thing. We become these sexual devices, these work horses, these study machines – we lose the spiritual aspect. Well, spirituality is too complex, besides it's a technology. When we compare a machine with man (or woman) there is a profound quality that often gets missed, a component so resplendent that it gets devalued as well, and it is something we need to protect because this component, this quality, is key to ensuring the human race survives, well one of them anyway. This quality is often used against you, to cause you harm, and they're good at using it to their advantage.

An android, a robot and a computer are three variations of technological evolution. These three platforms are similar yet unequal. A computer cannot think like a robot. A robot cannot make decisions like an android. All of them have moving parts, circulatory system, they utilize energy and they can be upgraded to a point, until their net return begins to decline. But there is another kind of android, the elegant android, and, it achieves its elegance by way of emotion. It feels. You see, computers, robots and (standard) androids cannot feel. They haven't the parts. There is part that creates authentic feelings. You can program people to accept fear and to be afraid, you can stimulate a person to love a product label. To a certain extent, feelings can be synthesized, but true feelings, the emotions are not derived here.

Where are the emotions derived from? Well, that is the trillion dollar question, isn't it? Are emotions originating from the body, or, are emotions emitted through the body? We might say that our emotional complex is derived from the nervous system, it feels. The nervous system to the brain, it interprets and responds. But I'd like to step further and to say that emotions are the body interpretation of the human soul program. It is the soul which feels, the only device capable of feeling because emotions operate on another dimension, a higher dimension so that a person who cannot feel is a person who is shut off from their souls and from their source. And a person with great feeling (or compassion) is a person with an intimate connection to their souls, like a social activist or a singer.

Therefore, it seems logical to deduce the fact that an elegant android, or a human (as you like), is much more than a regular android because it can connect to another dimensional device (the soul program). Boom. That's the connection.
 Now if someone was able to sever that connection, the elegant android would be reduced to a regular android, supplied by a lifeforce but not able to connect to their soul programs. And this is the case here on earth. The rulers here have developed ways to continuously keep your soul program disconnected (or jammed) from your android form so that you cannot think on a multidimensional level, or on occasion you have these "moments."

The soul program and the android body, together, function on a higher frequency than a regular android; therefore, we can see certain people more successful, more vibrant, more generous, famous, intelligent, talented, gifted – these are all having stronger connections to their soul programs; and because the soul is connected to the cosmic computer, there really is a lot more than one knows what to do with. We don't function as elegant bodes all that often. We try to do our best, we fail miserably and we convince ourselves that we are worth a lot so we go shopping and splurge. We swallow a few new pills.

This essay has become a more complex notion of itself. The many parts of our misguided lives are not misguided unless we have the awareness to see that we are misguided. Without that awareness, to say that something isn't right, we think we are dealing with a full deck of cards when we're not.

If I were to fall into a trap of itemizing existence, as many people do (eg *The 10 Habits of How to Live a Good Life*) I'd be part of the devaluation process. If I further simplified my discourse and spoke like the talking heads on TV, threw on some sound bytes and regurgitated the talking points, I'd be devaluing the potential of what you are. Sure, I do simplify here and there, hoping it clarifies. My language tends to be a little more paradoxical. My natural way of thinking is too difficult to follow and wouldn't make sense on paper. People say I speak in riddles. When I was 20, friends commented that I spoke in commas. I reflected on every sentence. They didn't like that. It doesn't turn women on, wisdom – screw it. "Give me some solid evidence, Tal. Land a ship on my lawn, take me for a ride and I'll be your best friend." No, thanks. You're missing the point! The point is to expand your awareness, not to demand things for free. The point is to surrender to the truth. There is a lot of truth out there. There is, in fact, quite a bit of proof, are people convinced? No. They want more proof. They demand more.

The Titanic is fully submerged now. You're either in the freezing water, on a life boat or dead. What's the next step? Will you try to swim for the island or will you wait for the mothership to land? The road to the future depends on what you'd like to see, and it depends on how you can detach from all the things of no use.

LIVING IN A SYNTHETIC WORLD

We are living in a synthetic world, and I am a synthetic boy. We are living in a synthetic world, and I am a synthetic boy. It's true. It's a fact of existence. It's the prerequisite for existence to flow. Without synthetic infrastructure there is no life for there is no backbone upon which life can progress. There is no replication, no procreation or multiplication. Why with synthetic things there is multiplication table. It's addiction or subtraction only. What about exponential figures? What about quantum leaps and logic gates? It's a modem factory gone wild and they call them here a brain. A brain? Brain, modem same thing isn't it? A device. It's a device. The brain is a device. It has a function. Sure, people tend to believe that the brain contains mind. How do you contain mind" Mind is eternal, it is boundless. The brain is a 3-lb sponge. It is a gift and a glory. It is fixed in place, a grid of neuron activity. It modulates thoughts and demodulates thoughts. It's a modem. Just a more complicated modem. Well, we refer to all this stuff as biology. We call ourselves organisms because we are organic. Organic? Why? Because we formed naturally from the volcanic ash and the lust of God.

> "Behold, I have set the land before you: go in and possess the land which the LORD sware unto your fathers, Abraham, Isaac, and Jacob, to give unto them and to their seed after them." [Deuteronomy 1:8]

What is organic? Organic is an interpretation, isn't it? We interpret the naturally occurring technologies, here as organic masterpieces, a random assortment of miracles – the tree, flowers, a wild boar, Aunty Mary on the porch sipping lemonade. All of it natural, even the porch. But is it truly the case? We haven't full questioned the word "organic," have we? Well, we haven't. We strive now to be more organic, after tossing away the natural world for all those decades of industrialization. Sure. The industrialists, they told us to modernize; and we did. We became modern: We ripped out trees, we built water dams and levees, we polluted the sky, we enabled gasoline engines, and we sold TV dinners. Modernization was an improvement over nature, because organic things were imperfect, they were inefficient, they didn't utilize economies of scale. That's what the industrialists told us. And we bought their industrial dreams. Today, we are modern. In fact, we are so modern that we are, strangely, going back to nature. Ironic, isn't it? We are functioning so efficiently, with our economies of scale and our New York fashion, our super-sixed breasts and burgers. We are functioning so perfectly, as they sold us, that many of you are returning back to nature, organic eggs, the local coffee farmer; fair trade, more vegetables.

> "The electric age ... established a global network that has much the character of our central nervous system." [Marshall McLuhan]

As natural as the natural world, the human being has forgotten its technological origins, and rightly so. The land now is run by demonic figures who are completely devoid of humility. Day in and day out, guess what, they have the answer. They have all the answers. Just like the industrialists. Well, wait. They are the industrialists! They are the policy makers! Who represents nature? Who? Where is the Council of Nature? It doesn't exist. No one listens to nature. The thought grid is barely used. Thought grid? You must be joking, man. I use AT&T. I've got a new BlackBerry phone. It's 3G, third-generation wireless network. Oh, wow – excuse me you industrial snow job. You've tossed away nature, a billion year old technology for a wireless network that's not even 30 years old. Are you kidding me?

The Most Advanced Technology Around

It's the same game as before: they sell us their cheap wares and empty promises and we go down on our knees for the blow job. That's what we do for these demonic salesmen. It's not new. The same freak shows who sold us the Inquisition and Nazism, they're still here. They're the guys selling Global Warming, and we get on our knees and blow. Praise, Jesus! Praise, Jesus! Please save us from the warm weather! What? You want everyone to die so that you'll live? Okay. Sure. I believe in depopulation if you promise I can buy that 50" TV and the new hybrid vehicle. Okay, I'll buy it. What? You want me and my family to die?

> "Al Gore said over the weekend that global warming
> is more serious than terrorism. Unless the terrorist
> is on your plane, then that extra half a degree
> doesn't bother you so much." [Jay Leno]

Well, ahem, maybe you should take back your industrial lives, take back your modernization, take back your deforestation and your depopulation. I want nature! That's what I want. And I'll tell you why – nature is the most advanced technology around. Why nature is, on earth, over 4 billion years ahead of anything else. Look at the sun, how old is the solar giant? Billions of years old. 4 billion, 4.56 billion. For Christ's sake! What kind of organic energy device last 4.56 billion years?! Are you kidding me? It's a ball of self-replicating energy, a life-giving energy and it keeps 7 billion souls alive, plants, tree, oceans, bees. 150 million kilometres from Earth. That's not technological?

Who are you kidding? It's the most advanced network server around. Solar Wi-Fi. It's keeping us all alive. The ultimate technological power plant. And you thought it was natural, how silly of you.

The fact that demons can come over and tell us all that electricity is better than the solar energy is a testament to how out of touch we are. Listen, you wake up because there is a sun. That's your power plant. Now, they've got you plugged into electrical power. You car runs on gasoline. The earth doesn't use gasoline. What powers the planet? What keeps it alive? The sun! The sun is so useless that it "keeps" an entire planet alive and, as a consequence, keeps all life here continuing, because otherwise you'd be dead. And then you can't watch TV. You can't be famous if you're dead. And for all the life the sun give you, how many times a month do you say "Thank you" to the sun? I'd bet never. You pray to Jesus before the sun, and Jesus is dead. But that is another story, isn't it? We don't pray to the sun despite the fact that it gives us life. We spit on trees. We kill the animals. We spray pesticides on the oranges and we toss nuclear waste into the ocean. And we call ourselves modern. I love it. I love this hellhole of delusions.

"Your physical body is a fiction." *[Deepak Chopra]*

But getting back to the synthetic world, the sun didn't appear by accident. Jesus didn't put it there. It didn't grow out of water molecules. It's no accident that a series of planetary bodies now circle the sun. It's not random. That earth has life on it. That's what the demons want you to believe. It's a random scientific miracle. Doesn't make any sense. Somebody put it there. Somebody who makes solar power plants created the sun. Yeah, somebody very old, older than the sun, obviously someone who is timeless. And there is more than one. It isn't a God. The sun is a technology. It's energy keeps us all alive. And that's because we are all technological. We didn't randomly appear from water molecules and then just happened to form into perfectly symmetrical bipedal creatures with a built-in voice box, a reproductive system and a fully functional soul. It's not random. It's science. Unfortunately, a life science is well beyond any human here and that's because you need to think in million year stretches and we can't think beyond Beer Day.

Synthetic Materials

I know, you don't drink beer. How many of you think 50 years ahead? Not many. I won't be around, you'll say. Well, you might. But somebody was here 4.5 billion years ago to ensure that earth was here and that earth had a moon. Someone was here. That is because planets, moons, suns – They're technological devices. Yeah, they're pretty huge. We don't have the factories to produce planets. The cosmos does. It's called a nebula. It's a planetary factory. The cosmos makes this big stuff. And, guess what? Humans come from the cosmos! If the cosmos is technological then so too is humanity. That tree, the water, air – all of it created. All of it synthetic. You as well. Synthetic. And you thought you were special. Besides, he'd say the same thing, but then you'd call it "spiritual." You'd reinterpret the Bible and do an Obama version. For Christ sake, let's start thinking outside the industrial hole and think about all life as synthetic.

> "There is a demon in technology. It was put there by man and man will have to exorcise it before technological civilization can achieve the eighteenth-century ideal of humane civilized life."
> [Rene Dubos]

This level of synthetic material, this world, as you can see, is very advanced. It's a technology so advanced, so resplendent that you all thought it was organic. That's how silly we've become. We've been led to believe in destructive modernization while living on a technological planet that is 4.5 billion years old. It's like pissing on your asparagus before you dip it in organic yogurt. It doesn't make sense. We should not only respect the natural world because 1) it isn't natural and 2) it keeps us alive. And 3) it is a technological mystery that is in the order of billions of years. We have to recognize that this divine existence is very synthetic. So synthetic, that it appears organic. It's a mind-bender. It's about respecting nature and learning that the natural system can handle the Global Warming debauchery and lies. Mankind is an insect and no singular insect species is greater than the sun. Mankind is not better than the cosmos. Respect the cosmos. Stop listening to demons. You are living in a synthetic world.

"The saddest aspect of life right now is that science gathers knowledge faster than society gathers wisdom." *[Isaac Asimov]*

I look at it this way, the ecosystems work perfectly. Its humanity that is out of sync. Sure, accepting that you are synthetic isn't easy. Call yourself "natural" for a while. Still, get back to natural existence. Live in harmony to nature. By doing so, you'll come to better understand the synthetic world before you. It truly is advanced and wonderful, just like you.

THE REINCARNATION OF JESUS, AND HIS CONCISE EULOGY

The language of love left when the spirit of Jesus was taken over by the demons who rule over earth plane. The egotism is in charge. And hell is defined by its love of ego. And we are all sinners for we have all fallen into temptation, into every kind of temptation. Even the Christian followers have allowed their ego to take over and to make their decisions for them. If ego was a dog, the dog is rabid and needs to be euthanized. If anything, Jesus was about egolessness, wasn't he? The Christ was about generosity. He was about provision – he healed the sick, whether he was asked or not, he healed. You couldn't beg someone today to heal people for free, even they know how to heal. You couldn't pay someone enough to teach about love because no one understands love. We're all trying to figure ourselves out enough in order to love. Jesus just loved. That was his method. Just love. That's too complex for today's egotistical mind. Tell someone, hey, just love "and their eyes will double over."

The Program of Our Ordinary Lives

The very structure of Jesus, as his memory of 2,000 years ago suggests, his very structure was about love, giving and respect. He was about representing truth, then he died. He took all that with him. It became buried in mankind's global psyche. Then the demons found it, they corrupted the heart of humanity, they turned human souls away from the source, away from the light and, instead, turned the soul towards them – ego. Facing directly towards hell, deep into the heart of temptations, sin and all the hallmarks of the grand ole devil, scumbag king of selfishness. Today, we're all selfish bastards. We are, well, except on Christmas (or birthdays), 360 days of greed, lust and corruption; 360 days of "If you backstab me, I'll kill you and your family" and a couple of days of: "You know I love you." Two or three days a year of Jesus' legacy.

What has been representative, in the name of Jesus, is the option to love. What started out as a necessity for life transformed into an idea and now has become an option. Love is not a necessity. It is an option. We simply lost our way to love, the very root of all the words of the figure who called himself the Son of God. Of course, the idea of love is far different than loving. Loving requires us to understand love. A young woman gives birth to a baby, she understands loving, she loves. It's not an idea. It's emanating from the baby. There's that connection. The right and good vibration. BOOM – she is in love. Later, that same mother will use love against her child. If you do this, I will love you more, if you do that, I will love you less. The child is followed by more children, the family trauma begins, the children grow up in a family that only concerned of love at the first conception of the first born; otherwise, the family is a love amateur.

Where else do we find love in this egotistical world? Where is the legacy of Jesus, in a church? Love is not only about church. You needn't a church for love. Jesus never had a church and he did just fine. Today, we have an overabundance of churches. We have therapists, psychiatrists, plenty of family experience and plenty more pills, yet we still do not have love. We love the selfishness of our flesh more than the love of some energetic hearth.

Jesus is Dead!

As a symbol of a New Day, master teacher Jesus of Nazareth brought the Word of God down to this earthly realm, to His people. The Word was here in the beginning, at the time of Genesis, that Word was carried in Master J, the meaning of the Word depends on the student, on the observer. The Word belongs to you and only you. That is the Word. That is what (the) Jesus meant to this world. That is what he left behind. He is a symbol of that divine inspiration. He is only a symbol now, those traces of his memory inside of those who cared to remember. Jesus is one of many Master Teachers who have visited, or passed through, this plane and left behind their

Words. You cannot avoid these divine symbols, they are everywhere. You needn't believe in an ancient prophet to retrieve the Word. You needn't abstain from sex and shave your head bald. Thank God! You needn't give up your job as an exotic escort. You needn't do anything to understand Master Jesus because his divine inspiration did not stop upon his demise. He was one professor of love. One existential coach. One person of many persons who carried the vibration of the cosmos; Who shared those genetic musical notes to all those he touched, to all those who listened to his words. And now he is dead. He's gone.

Jesus lived a long time ago as a human avatar and then he died. His mission complete, his time done. Jesus is dead! He is. He's gone. But because of who he was, his divine programming, we know that he was not only immortal but eternal, and eternal beings can only be eternal if they can *reincarnate*. Sure, we don't believe in reincarnation because science has yet to replicate it in a public forum. The faithful, on the other hand – the faithful, why they believe that some people reincarnate, especially our infamous Jesus. Because today is generally recognized as the birth of Christ, December 25, it seems fitting to repeat the fact that *Jesus is dead*.

According to my information, by way of the cosmic bookstore of handy knowledge and zero trans fats, the birth of the figure Jesus took place on October 15 and part of his journey culminated at the time of Winter Solstice (December 21) and those few days following. The recognition of that completed cycle indicated that he had indeed returned, for Jesus had been here before as another Master Teacher. Prior to the birth of that Master Teacher, he was also here, incarnated into another body of flesh. Each appearance and disappearance, lasting just as long as it should, no longer and no shorter than necessary. Since a Master Teacher is a direct representative of the highest authority, he cannot achieve any more than he or she is programmed to achieve, nor can he or she fail to achieve any more than he or she is programmed to achieve. As a Master Teacher, Jesus, for example, could not have died prematurely nor could he have offended the rulers in any excess. He knew his death and he did not discourage it because he himself had planned it because his life was certain, and he understood that certainty. He understood that certainty because he understood he had been here before and he understood that he would be here again, and again, for he was eternal, he was a recurring program, an essential component to existence.

What is lacking in our understanding of Jesus is that he was one human interpretation allowed a presence on earth in order to learn essential truth. His learning demanded his participation. More than that, his learning demanded his teachings, knowing that his teachings would provoke deception, confusion and anger. He knew these things as much as he knew that his time would end at a certain juncture. His own learnings, his own realizations were necessary for his continued reincarnation. But his death was his death. The vibration of the man Jesus, when reincarnated, would be transformed into a new vibration, so much so that parts of Jesus would be added to new parts, to form a new Master Teacher. Today, after so many centuries, after so many reincarnations the Jesus of old is no longer available, in fact, as I have said, the old Jesus simply could not do battle against the demon hoards who have cannibalized the elite and the powerful. Jesus of old could not defeat the Devil, master of the demons. Therefore, the death of Jesus was necessary in order for the continued reincarnations of this everlasting father program so that the Devil's deeds could be met in full.

Christ was a complex character. We will never be fully understand him because his vibration was divine; too complex for the human logical mind to process. Each attempt to understand him will show us one aspect of his character, one Word for our own understanding, enough to keep us thinking for many hours to come. His return is eternal. On each annual cycle he has returned and on special cycles he becomes incarnate in flesh. He remains for a time, to do his tasks then exits again. He does not call himself Jesus for he is not Jesus. Each incarnation he is a different person. Like I said, Jesus is dead. The transformation process (reincarnation) is a way for him to evolve, for himself to embody more of his own pure self, of the highest authority.

The Everlasting Program

To say to the public, or even to the church, that Jesus is dead and he will not return would devastate the faithfulness of the worshippers of Jesus. His death would seem to destroy hope. The truth would destroy these illusions that man has refused to overcome. No being, no person, who evolves is ever the same, no matter what their level of awareness. Once you are five years old and then you grow up, you cannot return to the awareness of a five year old. You are no longer that persona and can never be. Even you reincarnate inside of another body and you reach the age of 5, you will not have the awareness of the previous incarnation. That is why each moment, each awareness is so precious, it is only valid for this time. When time elapses, that awareness is gone. So, that is why some people refuse to grow up.

The past life of a Master Teacher cannot be recouped because if the life is in the past then the teacher has evolved. His awareness expanded, his identity secure. He can no longer be that old identity and has no wish to do so. That would be a denial of all that the master has learned. The very idea of remaining attached to an old person is against the innate programming. But to the human mind, to the ego brain, these things can be made reasonable. We can convince ourselves to accept any situation (eg perpetual war, flu pandemics). We can accept the fact that Jesus was a complete body and upon his return he would return completely, untouched, unchanged, unmarred, yet by our own biological growth, we are different this evening than when we woke this morning. For Jesus, after 2,000 years of transformation, he must remain exactly the same, including the fact that he did not die. Well, he did exist, he was murdered by the elites and he died. He returned a few years ago, evolved, different, and completely undiscovered for his very followers have created the greatest sin of all – ignorance. They ignorantly believe that an exact replica of Jesus would return and say exactly the same words as when he was last here. This will not happen. It is against evolution. It is against logic, in fact.

On this day of international celebration of the figure Christ, the anointed one, the incarnation of God, on this day it is proper to remind those who would listen that Jesus is not coming back. The essence of Jesus is now occupying that reformed Master Teacher just like you yourself carry the knowledge of one of your mentors, or your teachers, or parents. We are formed by these essential components. They make up the whole.
This Eucharist has ended, let us go in peace.

PORTFOLIO OF OBSERVATIONS

As a technological society, we have prided ourselves on the evolution of our inventions. Invention has made life easier, made communication seamless. We take our technologies for granted, this pen here, once long ago pens were hard to come by and given to only those few who could read and write. Today we have an over abundance of pens. How about light bulbs? No shortage. Even our streets are lined with light bulbs? There are light bulbs in our calculators. See, we even put technology inside of technology inside of technology. Look at the computers. Silicon chips (millions) inside of a machine, illuminated by a liquid crystal display (LCD), powered by the energy from an electrical power planet.

There is another kind of seamless technology that is so advanced in its structure and concept that we have yet to even recognize it is a technology. One of these ubiquitous technologies I speak of is water. Yes, water! Good old fashioned, all-abundant water. Flowing here and there. The same water we drink daily and flush our toilet as well. The same water we take showers under and make soup. Where would we be without water? We wouldn't be able to clean ourselves. We couldn't wash away dirt and bacteria. How would be sanitize? How would we make soup? We take the water technology for granted, so much that we will flush a square of toilet paper down the toilet, or a mosquito.

If we understand that a technology provides certain key features and benefits, if we accept that when we buy a technological device, we'd have to then also accept the fact that water, as simple as it is, equally provides a set of features and benefits. On the surface, water is a cleaning fluid; it washes away sins it is so powerful. Water provides fluids to our bodies to keep us alive. Without drinking water, we'd die. End of discussion. If that is not a major benefit of having this technology, then I don't know what is. What else? Water, it turns out, can carry other devices. For example, water can carry a boat.

Water can also carry other substances like a fragrance or a chemical solution. Water is found in the blood and blood keeps you alive. As simple as water appears and as ubiquitous as it is, there are a multitude of features and benefits to the water technology. The problem is that, as a technological fluid, humanity has yet to attain that skill level of invention. Humans, no doubt, have invented many things, wonderful, magical things – Velcro, for example, but water? No. As such, we call water natural. It is from nature. The oceans are full of water. Water is the prerequisite for life, that is, without water, life cannot take place.

Organic Technology

What I'm insisting on is that despite all of its natural attributes and origins, water is a technology. It is an advanced technology, so advanced, so seamless that it eludes our thinking. We cannot equate water to technology because we have programmed ourselves to see it as only from nature. What does it mean then that natural water is technological? Well, the implication is that nature isn't what we've led ourselves to believe. If water is a technology then too is nature. This means that nature's instruments are capable of managing water. If this is true then nature still holds the medal for sustaining life because water equates life. As a power planet, nature is not only capable of managing water; it can also recycle water (eg evaporation) and produce water (eg rain) just like your body. When you sweat (which is everyday) you evaporate water inside your machine of flesh and you send it up into the atmosphere. There it will chemically transform and return back to earth as rain or snow.

Nature, then, is extremely advanced. It has to be so advanced that we've reduced it down to our own understanding as an organic construct. Whenever we say "organic," we do not in any way equate it to technology. When, in fact, the opposite is quite true – the more organic a thing is, the more advanced the technology. What does that also imply? Well, the earth is organic, as organic as they come.

Introducing Smart Fluid

Here's an interesting scenario: a scientist invents a living fluid, clear-based liquid that can clean away dirt as well as be able to grow plant life. This new smart fluid is introduced to the public and the scientist is recognized as a pioneer.

Now, when the inventor of smart fluid presents his new idea to the market, the audience realizes that smart fluid is a technology. But when we turn around and discuss water, all of a sudden we're back to nature. If we invent a water-like substance, it is technology; if we define water, it is nature. If we turn that around, if we now say that nature equates to a super-advanced technology then water (coming out of nature) is a technology, and that is why a scientist is able to replicate fluidic substance.

If using technology, nature can be replicated then it must also be true that nature is technological because it has within it technological structures, basic architecture that allows us to replicate it, only that human science has not yet reached water replication, although it is close. We can argue that a synthetic material simply functions in similar fashion to the authentic material. The point I'm making is that an authentic material, even if it is wool, must have within it the basic architecture (eg texture, absorbency, elasticity) in order for it to be replicated. The difference, I see, between a synthetic material and an authentic material is its level of technology because on the technical level there is only synthetic material; this synthetic material appears to be authentic because of the level of technology. The technology, if beyond comprehension, is authentic; if replicable then it is synthetic.

What we see as synthetic material is authentic to a more primitive culture. If we presented Velcro to a Neanderthal, it would be interpreted as authentic material. If the Neanderthal shaman tried to replicate it, he would manufacture something equivalent using natural materials though he hardly would consider his invention synthetic because his natural material are insufficient to reach the technology of Velcro. Similarly, if an offplanet race presented an authentic item to a human scientist the invention would use synthetic materials, for example, fibre optic wires or plastics. So, our invention would be considered synthetic but even their invention is synthetic because anything in the universe that has matter and substance is synthetic, it is created.

Nature is our interpretation of a technology. We fail to understand. And water, originating from nature, the very technological engine of existence, is a technology that we also fail to understand.

What is amazing, if this portfolio of observations is correct, is that we have been relying on the all-abundant water, that we thought was natural, but it turns out that it is technological. Not only that but nature itself, if we are correct in our water determination, is a technology. What does that say about humankind? That's the bigger question! That's not my conclusion since I have forthrightly discussed the legacy of androids here on earth, to a very mute response, and understandably so.

Living in a Synthetic World

On the cusp of the new Winter Solstice of 2009, it seems just, to reiterate the technological foundations upon which existence is built. It is within human capacity to construct and program virtual game and film worlds. It has been proven so and virtual reality itself has been a topic of discussion since the 50s, a time when offplanet races were interacting more vigorously with human geniuses, mostly because they were the only ones willing to abandon temptation and to listen to outrageous ideas – such as virtual reality, stereoscopic cinema.

If we forwarded the best human science, the best virtual world engineering, the best computers, the best sources of energy, if we forwarded these things a million years ahead. Just a million years, that's enough to do what? That's enough to construct a plane of existence, to populate it with constructed beings – robots made of flesh – since meat is a synthetic material, and to create ecology. All of this would necessarily be built upon an architecture to manage all the existential variables. The ecosystem would be able to produce a life-sustaining substance, a carrier of energy, known to us as water.

The beings on this earth would not necessarily need to know it all to indulge themselves in their various virtual fantasies, such as going through a harsh divorce and then finding love again at age 40. Century upon century, the memory of androids would be reinterpreted according to the awareness of society and in accordance to the leaders of the plane. In this year of 2009, under the severe oppression of false rulers and within the bounds of false religions and the mass of distractions and suppression of knowledge, under all this garbage we are finding it impossible to recover our technological origins. But that does not change the fact that that we are living in a synthetic world.

PINE CONES, FRACTAL IMPRESSIONS AND COSMOSES

A Controlled Mysterium

"America in the 1990s has a problem with ecstasy in its original sense of *ex-stasis*, of moving out of one's daily trance for a moment, transcending the mundane particulars of mortality, shedding one's ordinary waking consciousness, to make direct contact with the numinous. Unlike the Jivaro of Amazonia or the ancient Greeks at Eleusis, we postindustrial urbanites have no socially sanctioned method of putting aside our everyday consciousness and quenching our thirst for direct experience of the *mysterium tremendum et fascinans*. Unlike most adults of the past 100,000 years, we were never initiated in fear, trembling and joy. We never made acquaintance with our own birth and learned about our connection with death. The illusion of the self was never demonstrated in myth, song, dance, chant, and direct confrontation. The old teaching stories weren't whispered to us in moments of awe and terror. We are swept along in a digitized hyperreality that is not of our making. And now we are suffering in ways most of us don't understand."

Howard Rheingold,
Virtual Reality, 1991

A virtual reality is a controlled realm containing a hand-picked selection of ingredients that have been 100% pre-programmed by a computer programmer. The simulated world is planned from the start to accomplish an agreed upon experience and a successful virtual game is one that is played by many users, verily by a community of inhabitants. As the computer upgrades evolve and sequel versions of the reality engine improve in processing power, our virtual reality takes on a whole new experiential meaning and the users take a certain amount of pride in being a member of that simulated reality.

We could also say that during the virtual game that the users basically forget that the game is *virtual* just as a soccer player forgets that he's playing in the World Cup.

This forgetfulness is a key indicator that the virtual reality is satisfying all the elegant demands of a growing society of users; until such point that the user-base begins to interfere with that technological process: Until, in their esoteric forgetfulness, the reality inhabitants gain the ability to alter reality while being immersed inside the reality, as when the programmers themselves not only create the reality but must necessarily enter the simulated realm to make anonymous changes.

Imagine that I am a reality programmer, even a reality architect; and I have master-minded some wonderful worlds in my time, one in particular has not evolved according to my original programming because my reality technicians, the ones who I taught to maintain the reality integrity, decided to mutiny. My reality technicians had a meltdown and, in a fit of egotism and might, decided to enter this one particular realm. Soon enough they would forget how to return and they would choose to forget me with pleasure, and they would be enraptured by the powers they would have, verily the dominion, over the other inhabitants.

It should be said that the inhabitants of my created world are created by me and by other existential masters who can replicate the necessary genetic components in order to stitch together a living being. The simulated being exists inside my homespun reality and others in my community and even outside my community can dial-up the reality module and enter the virtual game.

Before the mutiny of my team, the virtual world worked fine, inhabitants were played by users and everyone played out their role, a limitless role really that was in sync with the environmental conditions. You could play a father and raise children or a priest to accumulate worshipers. The role you played was pre-decided in its entirety by you. And once in a while, I would hop in and check on things, or I would dispatch another competent technician.

In fact, at any one time, many technicians would be existing in that space all in accordance to the size of the population and the needs of the many. At all times, a system needed to maintain stability or it risked collapsing. I've had realms collapse before and I learned, let's say, how to manage stability. But we have forgotten about my renegade team.

The renegade programmers had assumed various roles as virtual inhabitants and had disguised themselves well. Unless I fully immersed myself into the reality, a complicated exercise since I am a very busy architect, I would be hard-pressed to separate one destined inhabitant with a renegade in disguise. So I leave things alone and send more technicians to manage the affair. For a time, I even move on to other things in my life, building new worlds or taking those well-deserved vacations. There are other things outside of building virtual realities.

The virtual time elapses and upon checking, I discover that those renegades have run amok. They have usurped all the codes, they have reprogrammed the entire reality system to work only upon their command, they have formed religions and assumed the positions of multiple gods; verily they have blasphemed my grand creation. They pissed on my model airplane and laughed while they were doing so just to spite me and my work. But I am not upset; I'm unable to be angered by children. The one thing that starts to irk me is the suffering of the inhabitants. The inhabitants are under centennial distress; they are raped, murdered, sacrificed, abused, tortured and controlled without end. The heroes have all been weeded out and the society of users who remain or return are endlessly oppressed. I am troubled by this situation. How to correct a virtual realm run amok by those who shouldn't be there in the first place? How do I save the user experience without angering the artificial gods my very assistants created out of their stygian ego? What is the best way to return stability to the earthly simulation without destroying the user experience?

The inhabitants, recall that they have lost their memories and are completely enslaved, go about their miserable lives and enjoy the limited forms of expression they have: watching entertainment programs on screens, having artificial intercourse to produce new lifeforms, buying lottery tickets, arguing with their parents, getting drunk on the weekends, beating up their wives, manufacturing bigger and more powerful bombs, selling guns to children, selling drugs to everybody, pretending to be a leader while lying all the time and manipulating society. Basically, the pure world I built is gone, I mean, completely destroyed because of those renegade bastards. And rather than being removed from the game upon death, the renegades found a way to reprogram their death so that they could be reborn in another body, so they reincarnate time after time and build dynasties. And the forgetful inhabitants muddle along hoping one day to be great.

I know what you are thinking, that this simulated realm I created sounds a lot like Earth, and you would be right in thinking that because I am referring to Earth; because the Earth you have been conditioned to believe and the true nature of Earth are vastly different. My Earth is an artificial world created by a reality architect; your Earth is a biological planet created by a Supreme Being. Funny as it may seem, the end result is the same, only that the truth is different. I am right and you are not. You are the Manchurian Candidate who has been reprogrammed to believe that death is real and that some God must exist. I am a reality engineer who has returned to this reality to help it hobble along back to stability. It's a bit like dropping into Vietnam at the height of the Vietnam War and trying to assure the soldiers, on both sides, that love is the only thing that exists, everything else is an illusion, just as a napalm strike roasts half the countryside. If you get the feeling that this return to reality isn't easy, you don't know the half of it, and you don't want to know.

The intricacies and technical knowledge required to build a complete reality system is well outside the limits of this or any book. However, the citizens of today are well aware of the decrepit, diseased and dehumanized state that the world is in, at least the population of awareness is significant enough that some action can be started to return to stability from the inside out. For centuries of amnesia, everyone has taken for granted the eloquence of the technological designs and the fantastic architecture that has been erected.

We can be certain that a return to stability, not another false return like a revolution or a political campaign, will return an entire population of inhabitants back to glory by enabling once again the process of innovation. That is what the reality has always been about: *possibilities*. The possibility to turn left instead of right. The possibility to invent a better phone. The possibility to cure a disease. The possibility to fly to the moon faster. The possibility to meet the Maker.

Remember that world washes away our memories of what we were before we came and in that fit of forgetfulness our best and only hope is the possibility to move forward in any way we can imagine. If they destroy our imagination, and the world is created by thought and mind, then they win, we become slaves. That is the nature of this Earth right now – global slavery (ie hybridized socialism).

The slave has no possibility but the possibility that they are told. The masters call that the rules. These are the rules of the renegade masters. These are not the rules of the reality. The reality says, "Anything is possible. Tutto e possibile." Any attachment or condition to that possibility rule is an aberration, a big fat lie. Of course, our cosmos comes with its own set of laws such as do not aimlessly or purposely murder people. Strike one. Everyone is an equal. Strike two. And things of this nature. Cosmic laws exist, and they exist for each and every level of awareness.

In other words, on the primitive level of awareness, as in a Neanderthal-grade inhabitant, murder is acceptable because the Neanderthal player is too dumb to understand feelings. But what happens if the reality awareness is purposely tuned down to primitive? Endless war. And that is what is happening on Earth. War after war after war and no Neanderthal seems to mind because someone purposefully tuned down the level of awareness to "primitive" and now the entire population, save a few people, call primitive the "new normal." The whole affair is rather sad really. And it can be improved. The one best way to improve the reality stability is to understand a few things about this technological mess.

The central code running through this reality is that of *possibility* and the ability to manage fear of destruction or reckless abandon. The pendulum of possibility can be overwhelming without wisdom and experience to guide us. While each and every human inhabitant has been trying to survive and overcome, the history of this earth reveals a pattern of enslavement that is far beyond the power of a family getting a good education or some lady winning the lottery. Those are themes the false leaders want the society to believe, "You can make it if you work hard too." Had it not been for the efforts of the many visitors and angels over the centuries, each of them planting seeds and leaving their legacies behind, the work that is starting in recent years would have little or no value. The esteemed visitation by Jesus Christ, King of the Jews, wasn't about establishing Christianity as much as he was about upgrading the reality system until the renegades had him promptly removed.

Ironically, the advancement in new technologies has been adopted by the public so rapidly, two millennia after Jesus started to show the way to the Lord. The connection between the Catholic Messiah and the technological reality are deeper than we all know, without discounting other "messiahs" who have essentially played the exact same role under an entirely different disguise. But the days of disguises are over and the Messiah Action Plan no longer works. Today, it's about the truth. What you are going to read is the truth because that is the way forward. It is not the complete truth because that would have made my book into Bible-size and I am not a fan of translated and edited scripture, no matter who wrote it. The truth is anything that sounds to be true. If you find that here then it is truth for you, if not then the book for primitives is in the mainstream isle.

Well, hang on then for we are about to crack the reality barrier like never before...

Fractal Impressions on the Thought Grid

Time is a permeable item with interesting consequences. Each decision we make impacts the temporal scale of decision making. We cannot see those impressions with our eyes, neither can we see the trajectory of those follow up decisions. The result of all of our decisions is looking at us in the mirror. You, right now, are the result of "fractal time."

But there is one vital component of decision-making that we neglect, a component that can be referred to as a *magic moment.* Call it synchronicity, mistake, coincidence or curse, each lifeline is filled with magical moments. This is why a healthy woman of twenty-two can get hooked on crack cocaine and end up on skid row, and also why a 28-year-old bachelorette can get on a TV show and become a celebrity.

Fractal time *n.* **1** a similar existential pattern imprinted on other levels of dimensions. **2** an irregular geometric shape holding time and space.

Just as each individual experiences magical moments in time so too does a nation. A nation makes decisions via its leadership and those decisions impact the temporal scale of decision making. We have all witnessed the timelines of our nations and each magical moment leaves an impression and alters the trajectory of the nation and its people. But over the past so many years, a number of events have significantly altered the fractal time outcome of nations. And nations have impacted the timeline of other nations just as one individual can impact the decisions of other individuals.

What has happened throughout history is the repression of time via negative "fractal impressions." These fractal impressions have caused a retardation of human history.

Fractal impression *n.* **1** a repeated thought print with temporal effect. **2** point in space for similar recurrence.

What causes a negative fractal impression? Any event that significantly impacts the decisions of a cluster of the population in a regressive way is a negative fractal impression. A negative fractal impression is produced after the trigger event. This is not a paper to prove the redistribution of fractal time which in itself could take a number of books. Perfect examples of world-grade impressions include the Great Depression, World War I,

World War II, Iraq War, Vietnam War, Spanish Inquisition and Tiananmen Massacre.

A negative fractal impression results from a trigger event. For example, in September 11, 2001, the World Trade Centers were struck. That event triggered the decision to invade Afghanistan and Iraq with a military-scale invasion. The War in Iraq, however justified, impacted the security, travel and safety of the entire world. The $700 billion bailout of US Banks in November of 2008 is another trigger event that caused a worldwide recession.

We can also see trigger events in China when Hong Kong handed over power to Communist China in July 1997. By September 1997, an Asian financial crisis nearly spread across the world into 1998 and forced new decisions in all nations.

On another dimension, at the energy level, the impacts are noticeable from these trigger events, or magical moments, and can have amazing repercussions in the other dimensions, localities of reality that very few people care about until they pass from this life.

FRACTAL IMPRESSIONS ON THE THOUGHT GRID

A fractal impression impacts the flow of time. Imagine when the planet Mercury starts spinning backwards, we can all feel the impact of this Mercury Retrograde whether or not we believe in retrogrades because the planet's energy fields are large enough to impact the smaller energy fields of each and every human. On a smaller scale, when we fall in love we notice that time slows. These temporal anomalies have been noted by the likes of Einstein and Pamela Anderson.

A seismic shift on earth will impact the Thought Grid, a matrix of thought energy encompassing the earth plane. The Thought Grid is a free-flowing matrix of energy which each and every human utilizes without their active knowledge. A singular thought can be seen as tossing a pebble in a lake whereby a small ripple is noticed for those who are paying attention. The thought of a community hits like a rock and the thought of a nation is like a large boulder.

Thought Grid *n.* a matrix of fluidic energy attenuated to thought.

After a trigger event occurs, the Thought Grid experiences an overload of thought activity. The nation that has sustained the particular catastrophe will strike the lake of thought energy like a Boeing 747 crashing headfirst into the water. The ripple effect will be felt across the entire lake and even to a certain depth down below. The Thought Grid reacts like a pool of highly responsive fluid, a dimensional substance with an incomparable value. The reason why a trigger event or magical moment occurs is not because of coincidence or randomness, far from it, a trigger is set off because of a reprogramming of the virtual reality (VR) system.

The perennial score of catastrophes in the world, for the past two thousand years, is a result of reprogramming (or interference). This continued and deliberate reprogramming has been made possible by those architects who insist on leading this plane of existence into a direction of endless stagnation and eventual destruction. A destructive pattern in line with their innate destructive behaviour.

Why lead the human civilization to destroy itself? Because the destruction of all existence on this earth would lead to the sacrifice of all life here. And sacrifice equates to the surrender of energy and the surrender of energy equates to the ascension of those destructive programmers. They would inherit the energy of the slain, as they even do so now and as long as war continues.

Imagine a chain of events on a world scale, perpetrated by world capable individuals, that is specifically designed to undermine all existence here and to immortalize those few who wish to ascend at the expense of one another. Thinking on a world scale is unusual for most people and certainly outside of any normal sort of expectation, but if there is a world then there is a world architecture, and if there is a world architecture then there is a world scale of thinking. World scale thinkers are not world builders. We can relate to the collapse of the World Trade Centers. Qualified architects built the World Trade Towers at a huge expense but building scale engineers devised a way to demolish them.

The other aspect that needs to be addressed in the redistribution of fractal time has to do with the impact that thinking has on time. Each trigger and follow-up impression alter human decisions and necessarily impacts the Thought Grid. But, in addition to the human impact there are capable programmers who are ready to use that collective shift of thought to reprogram the course of human history. You cannot deny the derogatory course of human history riddled with war, disease and corruption at every level of society. Nation is at war with nation. Threat follows threat.

Further and further humanity is enslaved without even realizing that their decisions are being influenced, manipulated and controlled to such a high degree that they are all mere pawns in very well orchestrated plans. Plans that are organized at a level of thinking that is outside the scope of this letter. Why this is important is because should their plan continue and should humanity's course remain then "there is a foreseeable end to humanity."

I certainly do not want to see the end of humanity; rather, I want to ensure that humanity returns to its original course. Right now, as we speak, humanity is way off course. Over the centuries humanity has been completely thrust off of their natural course.

SLOWING DOWN OF TIME

On my outdated VCR while playing a VHS magnetic tape, I can fast-forward and rewind the tape to find the right point in the video. It was always such a hassle to FF or RWD because the process was inexact and extremely slow, still I had no choice. I got used to playing with the VCR controls. Whenever I fast-forwarded my video tape, I watched the hired characters act at Superman speed with this eerie high-speed sound as dialogue lapped over dialogue. One minute on the FF button and I could advance the story forward by 10-minutes. I was the VCR god. The same was true in Rewind. I could control time by the push of a button and the reality movie was at my command. Everything changed when the DVD came out because the DVD could skip entire sections as well as FF and RWD. All of a sudden we could skip 45-minutes into the film at the push of a couple of buttons. Now, that was power in your fingertips and there were probably a few commercials highlighting this power in your fingertips. Then technology leaped up again for us consumers, we are always a few steps behind industrial users, and we found the digital player, the all-impressive Apple iPod. Here was a digital video player whereby we could skip to any point on the bar. We simply select the point of entry and the movie played from that point. You could replay that bit over and over again. This was already online prior to the handheld device, but limited to those with hi-speed internet connections.

Imagine that this reality shard was a VHS video tape holding a 17.5 million hour movie (or about 2,000-years long). Try putting that on your 64 GB iPod. You would need roughly 2.6 million GB of hard drive space. We don't have those iPods available here in Canada, not in 2009 anyway. If I had a 2.6 million GB hard drive, I could store 17.5 million hours of earth's recorded history, since the time of Jesus. Under current rendering conditions and on my example, the video quality would be suitable for a typical video-capable Apple iPod, given that my iPod had the hard drive space, perhaps a nuclear hard drive.

If we wanted to go 3D, like every filmmaker is intending to do, and to boost up the image into holographic space, we would need a billion times the data storage and a processor that Intel might never produce with any transistor-based chip. But it is entirely plausible. It's a technological limitation.

The problem is that I am stuck with using modern technological presumptions to process cosmic-grade realities. That is like using a gasoline-powered internal combustion engine to create nuclear fission. The technologies are incompatible to the nth degree. We could more easily accomplish this holographic video storage task if we were to use another kind of computer, say a quantum computer, or, better, a cosmic computer, since the cosmic computer is running this video right here, right now. The reality you see before you is verifiable, first-hand, measurable proof that there is a cosmic computer capable of processing 3D reality; or, call it holographic. I like arvic reality much better then again science hasn't discovered how to harness arvicity.

Okay, so we know what? We know that reality is technologically constructed and we know that there is a cosmic computer. Better, we know what? We know that the temporal scale can be impacted by fractal impressions set off by some kind of trigger. In other words, back to my VCR model of interpretive understanding, I push a button (a trigger), and the video moves one way or the other in a certain fashion. We translate into cosmic thinking: I collapse the World Trade Center Towers (a trigger), and the reality moves in reverse because I have created a negative fractal impression that pulls the reality movie back in time. But we should state at the outset that there are many dimensions to reality and just like sticking an innocent child into a closet we can impact some dimensions better than others. The physical dimension is less retarded than the thought dimensions. Our thoughts are rewound while our physical bodies continue on, without our thoughts. It is as if my VCR could rewind the color Red and the color Green and Blue continued as normal.

Those individuals who have to the power to stage these large-scale events do not have the authority or power to rewind all three RGB colors, but they do have the power and authority to select one, or perhaps two if they say started destroying roads and bridges and burning homes and vaccinating entire cities for fun.

The negative fractal impression rewinds human thought – innovation is lost, women lost interest in raising children, teenagers face an uncertain future, religion is at war with other religions, the threat of WWIII looms. The effects from a negative fractal impression are extremely powerful, and that is why they have been continuously used throughout these last two millennia.

They rewind the color Red. The regress thought and in a reality that is attenuated to thought, what happens? The innovation literally stops, and worse, all of it is reasonable and justified given the violent and unpredictable climate on earth. With the US Administration at war in the Middle East, there is no attention to homeless people, no attention to battered women, no attention to human rights, no attention to healthcare reform – all those things and more suffer.

Again, the worst part is that the citizens don't argue because they see that the lack of innovation and the rise in border security is in line with the new world, a world that was purposely altered. That's the part the citizens don't know. And should you or I speak out and talk about 9/11 being an orchestration, the people won't listen, the post-traumatic shock is unbearable and I'll be tossed into the camp of conspiracy theorist, ah the power of ignorance is quite impressive.

More than simply rewinding human thought, what is truly happening after a negative fractal impression takes place (and there can also be positive ones) is that a large chunk of the population goes back in time. The larger the event, the bigger the splash in the lake of thought, the larger the ripple effect, the more of the world that is sent back in time. With help from the media, the entire world is more and more easily plunged into the dark ages. The 9/11, Vietnam War, Spanish Flu events sent society "back in time."

We have to be clear on this assessment because it is not an easy perception to hold because it is considered foolish by our superior ego and our left-brain. We can see the outcome of the 9/11 event, eight years of stagnation, fear and corruption. One event rippled across the fabric of space and time rewinding human thought by eight years. Is that not a powerful event, more powerful even than you originally thought?

If I can stage an event and knock back society by 8 years, I am quite powerful; and if I can do this periodically, I can ensure that an entire planet of inhabitants remain trapped in the *Twilight Zone*. We only need to think about the Holocaust or the Inquisition of the Opium Wars or the thousands of other events to find fractal impressions and the effects of those negative impressions.

Sure, we don't speak much of positive fractal impressions – Landing on the Moon, the invention of the telescope, building the Great Wall of China or the Egyptian Pyramids. We have neglected to some extent the invention of television and the launching of satellites into space and the computerization of the world, not to mention the World Wide Web, the peaceful path of Gandhi and the challenges of President John Kennedy. These events fast-forward society.

Do we not now see how landing a man on the moon in less than 10 years, how that inspired the Space Race? It fast-forwarded society, fast-forwarded the entire world. Or Albert Einstein's paper on The Theory of Relativity or even Henry Ford's first assembly-line automobile, a black Ford Model T. These events, simultaneously, are occurring alongside other activities and actions.

Negative fractal impressions and positive fractal impressions, regression of time and the progression of time – in an ideal reality system, we would find an equal balance of events. You cannot have all events progressive because that would undermine system stability, the Yin & Yang if you will, and you cannot have all events regressive because that would lead to destruction or collapse. The problem here is the level of interference.

The programmers that rule over earth have decided to collapse the earth reality system, using a very long time horizon and quite an impressive number of reincarnations (how else would they continue for two millennia?) to retard reality, causing the engine to stall and the whole reality to collapse.

Luckily for humanity, there have been dimensional forces working the system to make sure that some progress was achieved, but after many leaps forward, society would have to face harsh events of interference. And all the meanwhile society in the dark about the way the world works. The world is like a holographic VCR, going back and forth, back and forth, trying to find stability so that we can see the proper colorization of the picture at the proper speed. The fact that humanity has so far refused to gear up to speed and to adopt the technological model of reality is very disheartening on one hand, and also a reflection of the Manchurian Candidates that the rulers have so well established.

The sooner and the greater that society's members fight back to regain control over their plane, the sooner that reality stability will be found because even the system engineers will not completely resolve the myriad of problems with earth reality. Humanity has to get involved and involved for the long-term. No pansies allowed. Earth needs a long list of heroes.

200-YEARS OFF

Each day that Mao's China of the Sixties was re-educated, the Chinese culture was rewound by a measurement greater than one day. More precisely, we could look at this way: each 24-hour period forward traveled in the wrong direction. People who lived during Mao's leadership would only look at those years of invigoration as the "lost years" because they had lived and traveled existentially for 18 years (1958-1976) off course.

If China should have ideally traveled True North then instead China traveled 3-degrees East of True North. Which means in loose translation: to return back to their original course they would have to either track-back 18 years through muck and misery or to detour through rough and tumble hoping they would emerge whole once again. In either case, it would take 50 years of time's elapse to catch up from an 18-year hiatus. Or, according to our technological interpretation, the years spent off course have sent China back in time, rewinding certain existential components necessary to make one whole and complete.

I have lived in China for several years and I had learned to speak Mandarin fluently, and when I talked to those survivors of the Mao Era, they all seemed to agree that:

"those years are lost" and could never be regained. That was the main reason why parents who survived that unbearable and embarrassing era had put all their attention and faith into their offspring, to ensure that the new generation of Chinese princes and princesses really leaped forward into the new era, an era where China was a leading nation in the world.

We can see the impressive, if not debatable, achievements of China over the past 15 years or so. We can imagine where China would have been had it not immersed itself in rural communes and Red Books.

Imagine all of the fractal impressions over just the last 100 years: World War I, Spanish Flu Outbreak, Industrial Revolution, Great Depression, Computerization, World War II, Vietnam War, Recession, Wireless Phones, Tiananmen Square, Korean War, World Wide Web, Kuwait War, Afghanistan War, Iraq War – each of them lasting many years and the recovery period last many more years afterwards. If we use the Cultural Revolution as a model, in the simplest sense, we can see that the entire world has been forced to step back in development, moment after moment.

If an 18-year catastrophe equates to about 50 years of temporal retardation then over the last 2,000 years, the entire world has similarly experienced a level of temporal retardation, and we can safely say this because of the current state of reality – war, disease, cover-up and dehumanization. The strongest identifier of existential progress, or regress, is the rate of nationally-sponsored murder, aka "War." The fact that humans continue to justify the killing of other humans indicates that this earthen reality is in dismal regression. Reality has been rewound and is now behind the times. The question is how many minutes, hours, days or years behind the original schedule?

If you are the captain of a ship and were off course by just a few degrees, over enough water you could end up on an entirely different continent. We have been sent off course over a lengthy body of water, about two-thousand years' worth of water travel. Even on a one-degree difference, the amount of temporal regression will be impressive and harder to correct. It's as if you want to fly from Vancouver, Canada to Los Angeles, USA and you take two flights. On one flight is your Body; on the other flight is your Soul. Your body ends up in LA, USA and your soul ends up in Tijuana, Mexico, gets drunk on Tequila and fathers an invisible Mexican child with a local prostitute.

More than that, and recalling from previous chapters, we partake in a "living reality" existing according to the four ingredients of vibration, time, frequency and action. An impact on the frequency of humanity also impacts the vibration of reality, and the vibration of the reality determines the temporal state of the reality.

If we lower the vibration of reality enough, we effectively "slow down time," we go *backwards* in time. And that is where we are, we are back in time. But remember that time is one dimension of a multiple dimension system. Our *physical* body, another dimension, is in a time unequal to our *soul* body. We can all agree on those simple truths, body and soul. The bridge between body and soul is mind, which is why society is so mindless.

The Mind of the Society is trying to reunite body and soul, hologram and program, into the same paradigm of fractal time. Until that occurs, our disintegrated state of being is a reflection of this disassociation, and not only this, but the continued fractal impressions in the world such as the 2009 Swine Flu Outbreak and the American Torture Skit prevent most people from realizing what is going on. And the other headaches such as forest fires don't help, but all of the drama is necessary.

By my estimation, we are off-course by 200-years. What does this 200-year loss of development mean? It means that if we removed those negative fractal impressions (or balanced them with positive fractal impressions) then the entire human culture would be living in a time period closer to the Year 2209. But because of negative impacts on human thinking and those thoughts impacting the course of humanity, we are now living in a fractal time period that is 200-years lesser-evolved (or behind).

On one dimension (physical) we are in the year 2009; on another dimension (nonphysical) we are in the Year 2209. We, of course, are the same being now disintegrated into a zombie-like state. It is apparent to some people, more and more every day, that humanity is reintegrating body, mind and soul at an increasing rate because we need to put our complete energy into the same fractal time shard in order to truly revolutionize this world, to return to a kind of Heaven on Earth. There is no Heaven on Earth; it is only our perception that becomes heavenly.

Further, if body, mind and soul were equated with the video signals on a TV screen, RGB (Red, Green, Blue), then we are missing the color Red, life appears to be Green and Blue everywhere we go. As we reintegrate R back into GB we begin to form a properly colorized photorealistic image which we then interpret as Heaven on Earth. We should not forget though that RGB have always existed in their native state. It was only because some outside force disrupted the internal image that it caused us to fall out of heaven, if heaven is a proper word to use in a reality system built by cosmic technicians and engineers.

And that is also how the world is oppressed: Having diffracted the RGB signal in the common human and by continually forcing humanity into a time frame that vibrates at a level of hate, violence, surrender, threat, disease, belief and amorality, the programmers are able to impose their views upon the enslaved population. The blind and ignorant public, qualified Manchurian Candidates, slumber around moisturizing their skin, improving their erectile function and buffing up their breasts. These are perfectly normal desires for a society that is completely unaware of the real situation, verily children living in a glass bubble, the Truman Show as reality. I mean, imagine a prison where the prisoner happily locks their own cell and they call it a home. Isn't that sweet?

We can raise all the criticisms we want, and we should, and at the same time we should try to reintegrate our technological signals. By doing so, with some concerted effort and documentation, we will all discover that what has been stated here in very blunt unscientific form is not only plausible, but, more so, accurate.

And as heaven returns to our eyes, we will all find ourselves in a position that is way off course and we, hopefully, will link together and elect to find a way back to our original destination. The key to getting on course once again is to remove, fire and get rid of all the leaders who led us here. All of them need to be fired. I say, let the children lead.

OUR 200-YEARS OFF COURSE

With other processes already in motion and everyone working on their specific tasks in their own capacity, the rest of us need to overcome the inherent gaps caused by the damage of the fractal impressions, specifically the 200-year cultural retardation. If I am correct in my assessment and earth is indeed 200 magical years back in time, on one or more dimensional levels, then society will continue to remain in a low-vibration state and will therefore continue to struggle for a very long period.

Your children's children will inherit the effects of this disintegration, and like China's example, the correction might occur in the days yet to arrive. That would be the case if all interference stopped right this minute, but the programmer's who think they run this place do not want to stop and will not stop on their own accord, so we cannot rely on the future as a measure of achievement. We have to make a number of efforts starting as soon as humanly possible.

If you put corn kernels in a pan and then put that pan into a hot oven then those corn kernels will vibrate at the level of the hot pan, and they will pop into popcorn. If you put that pan of corn kernels in atmosphere controlled oxygen-rich environment then those corn kernels will not become popcorn. They can't become popcorn unless they vibrate at a certain rate. You are the corn kernel and earth is in the wrong oven. We have to get earth out of the oven.

If we could take the entire pan of society in the retarded dimension and then reallocate that pan and realign it in sync with the current dimension, we would quickly and efficiently achieve success. The effect would be like a *Star Trek* transporter disintegration and reintegration with billions of lives traveling through time and space into some earth-sized transporter room. We can be certain that the cosmic technology exists since we can be certain that the universe is flooded with technological life, only that we would need a transporter expert of superior in their transporter ability.

Since you cannot physically move the virtual reality (VR) pan out of the oven, we have to have to use an innovative approach. The VR is all influenced by thought. A master of thought can ascend by pure thought because thought precedes all action and pure thought comes directly from Source. Most of us are not masters of thought; otherwise, we wouldn't be in this mess. But we can use an innovative method to realign humanity on its proper course and we can achieve success over a reasonably short period.

To time travel forward 200 years, we might easily reset the timeline forward by about 200 years. By doing so we are overlaying an improved fractal time blueprint (Year 2209) onto the current off course fractal time (Year 2009). Remember that the mind is already stuck in the Year 2009 (200 years off course in respect to the thought dimension) and all the 3D reminders are telling us that the year is 2009, but we now suspect (and hopefully agree with) that the fractal year outside of the existential closet is closer to 2209. What this means is that as soon as we emerge from the closet, if we were able to, we would be unable to see ourselves in a wholesome way because our soul is in 2009 and our body is in 2209.

Our mind is keeping us from falling apart. The mental processors are working overtime to translate and keep coherent the vast discrepancies of our fragmented state of being. That is how powerful the cosmic mind is. Like a giant elastic band being stretched further and further, soul and body drifting further and further apart.

How did I come up with the 200-year figure? I borrowed a cosmic calculator. The 200-year difference comes from my own estimation given the significant negative impressions over the last 100-years, and approximating the advancement and retardation over the last 2,000 years, using the approximate time of the Jesus figure (program) as a reference point (our existential anchor). The presence and disappearance of Jesus is a reliable marker in human history (as we have seen in earlier chapters) and his technological presence on earth had been used as an anchor point for the retardation of the timeline.

Given all of this impossible data and working with the reality system itself, I have determined that Earth citizens should have reached the year 2209. Yet, our calendars read 2009. Like I said, a friend of mine let me use their cosmic calculator because not even the IBM Big Blue supercomputer can reliably process that amount of data with any reasonable accuracy. The variables have yet to be measured and the supercomputer is a three-dimensional device trying to answer and compute a multidimensional problem.

That is a huge discrepancy, if accurate, and why I think humanity is eternally stuck, a disintegrated form stretched to the limits of its imagination and battered by incessant distractions to the point of tedium. Humans are trapped in the 2009 fractal time period but are trying to vibrate at the 2209 temporal state. We should be all flying in starships instead of 747s.

Unless we can harmonize the 200-year difference between human thought and physical body, humanity will forever be a slave because humanity is divided, verily a "disintegrated being." No one is really truly participating in their life's events because they are disintegrated beings and they cannot reintegrate unless we match up thought-time and physical-time. Truly, this is what must be done.

To reintegrate humanity, I suggest that we reset the Gregorian Calendar to the Year 2209 (making any leap year adjustments as necessary), rather than keeping the Year 2009. We improve the fractal time pattern by 200 years and we effectively *time-travel forward* physically and mentally until we harmonize body, soul and mind. I estimate that if this reintegration process were to take place, even at the grassroots level, and supported with other efforts, it will take several years to discover a measurable amount of success.

Many individuals have already reintegrated because they arrived in the past few years, these people could guide the bulk of society and ensure that the transporter process, even on an individual scale, occurs without trouble. The problems remain: the current leadership around the world will never agree with this because they are responsible for stagnating reality. Without leadership support, this whole campaign would have to initially begin at the grassroots level, and then can be expanded wider and wider according to adoption, acceptance and understanding.

But this resetting of the timeline will eventually require mainstream support, a task which will be far more difficult to embrace. Mainstream knowledge is anything but enlightened. The public suffers from a condition of apathy and scepticism, and rightly so. We cannot judge a cultural group that has been conditioned since birth to respect and worship the obvious. It would be unfair to do so, but as stewards of the new age, it is our obligation to persist in the dissemination of true knowledge; otherwise the world is *screwed* (technical term).

Of course, as always, we can be inventive about the process, for example, we could use mass thought adjustments to fast-forward to 2209 before changing the physical calendar. I think plenty of smart people could come up with interesting ideas, if engaged early on. This book is the start of the process, the realization that the entire plane of earth is 200 years off.

So, in terms of review: humanity is participating in an irregular geometric shape holding time and space that is not congruent with the actual time and space. As if the body turned left and the mind kept going straight resulting in a disintegration of body and mind, except this is a large population (6.5 billion) of existential forms who have collectively disintegrated and are unaware of their true situation. The zombie-like state of many people is our proof-positive that people are naturally trying to reintegrate as the leadership continues to disintegrate humanity.

The whole of humanity will remain in a slave trance as long as their soul and body are disunited and thoughts struggle to bridge those differences; and, more importantly, if humanity fails to reintegrate, the entire civilization will eventually find its destruction because the level of technology will perpetuate the large-scale reduction of the population and the end of existence. All of this will take its sweet time like being digested for an eternity in a large intestine called ignorance.

Right now, instead of doing what you normally do, you could redistribute your thoughts into thinking of ways to reintegrate the human being. Every thought counts and the culmination of all thought can add up. Unfortunately, people are limited to thinking in 2D and narrow-minded terms. Even if you were a positive thinker and only had one negative thought per day, by the age of 30 you will have had 11,000 negative thoughts. This is quite a large number of negative thoughts, and I thought you were positive! Most people have many negative thoughts per day. If the average person had one negative thought per hour (1 neg/hr) by Grade School Graduation (Prom Night in America) they would have accumulated 158,000 negative thoughts.

That might not seem like much, but imagine this: what would happen if you had 158,000 negative thoughts in the span of a week? Suicide, murder, disaster.

Negative thoughts are powerful. It is accumulated effect that is harming society just like it is compound interest on your credit card that is keeping you in debt for the rest of your natural life. Imagine compound negative thinking and its dominion over the rest of your life and the life of your children. We cannot afford to hold even one negative thought per day, but we must not try to be positive either. Through understanding, we merely remain at peace, neither positive nor negative, just whole. As disintegrated beings living 200 years off, we are anything but whole, and our compound negative thoughts are keeping us enslaved.

The Christmas Tree and the Tree of Life

Fractal patterns verily instruct and code the known and unknown universe to such an extent that the very make-up of the cosmic tree is reminiscent of the bark of the pure tree trunk. The pine tree bark is a wrap around pattern containing fractals.

The fractal bark face of the pine tree demonstrates no precision or logo. In other words, the fractal skin chunks do not fit perfectly as would an artificial puzzle or even the cellular membrane of your outer dermis, and interestingly the pine tree bark remains healthy, alive and intact; or, we can also say that it does not fall apart. Between the encrusted bark islands is a darkened mass, a charcoal coated flesh that slopes deeply into the tree trunk itself without ever piercing into flesh.

What is remarkable about the fractalian pine tree and the all-intelligent universe is their esoteric similarity, a kind of similarity that we would be ashamed to admit in public for fear of the backlash; for how can a mountain evergreen in any way reflect the everlasting cosmos? Well, the first thing we need to admit is to state unequivocally this one particularly important fact: Not one individual human comprehends the cosmos? Not one. We can be certain of this statement when we assess the degrading and dehumanizing situation on planet earth which, first and foremost, is not a planet. That's the first indicator of the miserable state of human knowledge.

The second indicator is the forgotten esoteric information, pieces of knowledge handed down through the ages from generation to generation and then embodied in tradition. One of the most fundamental traditions celebrated all over the world is Christmas Day on December 25, 2009. Many people know that on December 21 there is the mark of the Winter Solstice, but many people don't readily know that the tree of choice on Christmas is a *pine tree*. Our pine tree. The cosmic tree of life celebrated each and every year. A tree that comes in many shapes and sizes.

If you understood me thing about the cosmos, just one thing, you'd understand that the cosmos is technological in its manufacture and that a planet is a physical manifestation (or illusion) that is representative of the planar space upon which existential inhabitant's journey.

Should anyone have vaguely or even partially understood the cosmos at even the faintest level of perception they'd see that Earth is a plane of existence. That has not occurred outside of a few individuals who were either enlisted into a mental ward or elected to keep this quiet for their own selfish reasons.

The fractal qualities of the pine tree, and probably of a number of other forest products, and what it can enlighten us about the cosmic origins of humanity is too valuable a tool to waste. We have another one of those rare opportunistic moments to get back together with the breathless qualities of an exotic universe, a universe that is founded upon a trunk of powerful knowledge from which all knowledge springs, more specifically a Tree of Knowledge; for what is the Tree of Knowledge if not the cosmic tree, in our interpretation – the pine tree.

The immediate thought that we might notice – if attentive, and attention determines knowledge, is that if the cosmos could be interpreted metaphorically and allegorically as a random mountain pine tree, then it would be safe to say that there are other cosmoses, or "cosmic trees," even very likely a *cosmic forest* that we may or may not ever discover.

And it would be safe to say that within the cosmic forest are many other plants and animals, even other kinds of trees. Well, that in itself, by other trees existing, is a mind-expanding concept because that suggests the presence of other cosmoses, cosmoses that are distinctly and qualitatively different to this cosmos holding this universe holding this reality cone.

Knowledge Acquisitioning

That suggestion of other multiple cosmoses is itself unimaginable at the current state of human scientific thought, in fact given the history of 2D programming on the human mind and the media stranglehold on critical thinking, it would be safe to say that the typical person conditioned by Good & Evil is incapable of contemplating most of what is written here. Your own reaction to this material will give you a good indication to your own level of awareness. My observations stand as they are written and are presented in the most agreeable form at this time. This position, it must be clear, is an acceptable position.

Knowledge in and of itself is open to interpretation and contemplation which is why in Ancient China, Greece and Rome there were philosophers who would spend their days in contemplation of this kind of divine knowledge and those contemplations to the leaders and to the public. That ancient process of knowledge acquisition was destroyed long ago. Should I go into a forest for a month and return enlightened, I am not allowed to be brought on TV to discuss my findings unless I was previously recognized publicly. Even I have public credibility and topical authority; I am not allowed to introduce unsubstantiated knowledge such as a Vision Quest experience or an interaction with multidimensional beings.

Outside of any celebrity status I may be burdened with, I have firstly to prove my findings are valid in a bestselling book and receive commendation from notable leaders in the greater community. This entire system of bestseller, corporate sponsored, celebrity endorsed Americanized marketing bonanza is quite well-established and though some individuals do find success outside of this rigid system, like say a Neale Donald Walsch with his *Conversations with God* series of books; the majority must follow "the rules."

One can argue both ways as to the validity of this system since it does prevent ideological pretend-messiahs from taking over and at the same time it prevents Peruvian shamans from sharing hallucinogenic herbs to free the minds of society.

The inefficiency of this modern system of knowledge acquisition is not only extremely limiting, but more so, we are not allowed, by public decree, to bring qualitatively new knowledge without an over-supply of proof or until 25 years after the death of the knowledge gatherer. We seem to be able to accept and even adopt unpopular, even offplanet knowledge long after the author has exited the matrix of experiential education. We the public are unable to adopt new information while that same person is alive especially if his name is Copernicus.

Using the pine tree as a cosmic metaphor is speculative knowledge bordering on metaphysics and deeply personal philosophy, certainly the "cosmic tree" is not a popularized idea, but I think given enough contemplation that we all would derive tremendous, if not mesmerizing, benefit(s). A level of benefit custom made for an entire civilization that has been immersed in a deceitful world and denied any cosmic access, a level of access to their true origins.

What I am speaking of when I speak of anything cosmic includes the human mammal, in case that isn't at all clear. The human mammal is a cosmic creature and the cosmos is technological in nature; therefore, the human mammal is a technological by-product of a very intimate and immense system of which no mortal can fully grasp in one lifetime, and many will try.

A fractal cosmic tree loaded at the ends with universe cones each carrying many reality shards is intimately connected to what is a much larger body of undeniable truth; for if the cosmos is a tree in a forest of trees (and of other things) then the roots of those cosmic trees must extend into an even richer cosmic earth. Again, we can see nature and cosmic nature having or sharing a valuable similarity. With a cosmic earth present, what kind of cosmic machine would it be? Or is there a cosmic machine at all? A cosmic engine guaranteeing infinite quality.

The Presence Of Energy Networks

A wireless telecom network exists as a network of cellular towers all interconnected to form a matrix of electromagnetic waves, but the wireless telecom network cannot exist without a base station and any number of EM wave amplifiers. The cellular towers have no roots into the natural earth but are electrically grounded by the planar fields and they are interconnected by EM waves all interacting and communicating at the same frequency range. The base station determines their singularity and the type of phone you use determines the kind of broadband access you have.

If we removed the natural earth while not dislodging the electrical ground, we would have a series of interconnected cellular towers using EM waves to connect to a base station. The base station derives its power from the electrical power grid, an unrelated energy system. If we shut off the power grid, we shut off the cellular network. Quite a sobering thought to a society completely involved with mobile telephony and wireless internet. No energy, no grid. And also why billions of dollars are invested into telecommunications infrastructure in order to provide a stable mechanism for global communications, and also why the power grid is a very expensive responsibility where investment rarely yield returns in the short-term.

On the cosmic scale, we are faced with a similar existential network that rather than keeping cell phones alive is keeping humans alive. We cannot argue its importance; we can argue its architecture and its interpretation. If each cosmic tree is a base station and the universe is a cellular tower then the reality shared is a *community* of mobile phones, or just as well, human beings. The cosmos as a base station responsible for a universal network is necessarily linked to a power grid. It is this power grid host we are trying to understand. We know there is a power grid, right? We now know that the cosmos does not power itself just as the telecom base station does not power itself although we can add an argument to that. There might be a built-in power generator to temporarily maintain the network in case of an energy grid problem. Maintenance workers and technicians would ensure that the redundant power system is always in full working order, that way the network will always be "on," the essential characteristics of stable system.

Given the presence of energy in an electromagnetic wave, say a microwave, we can propose that even a telecom network can be self-powered, in other words, data and energy can be equal: when you share data, when you communicate, you share energy and since we would work with a specific amount of energy for the network, we can say there is sufficient energy to allow technological stability. A self-serving cosmic system is reasonable given a highly-advanced cosmic science. What if now we wanted to grow universes and realities (or "living planets"), where does the extra inertia come from? Can the cosmos self-generate additional power? Can a pine tree sustain itself, and if so, can the same pine tree grow on its own accord without assistance? We know that the pine tree requires additional support elements in order to grow including sunlight, water and the interaction from the animals, birds and insects. The combination of all these essential ingredients provides the recipe for a healthy tree. A pine tree relies on a pine beetle to grow, just as the same pine beetle can cause the pine tree to die. A pine beetle infestation in the forests of British Columbia starting in 2007 caused 13 million hectares of pine forests to be eaten from the inside out. Same goes for sunlight and water, too much or too little and the life of the tree is in jeopardy.

The fact that earth is lush with forests proves that the technological cosmos is pretty darn intelligent, able to manage billions and billions of variables per second in order to maintain stability and to ensure growth and expansion; and recall that expansion is an essential quality of life. To expand is to live.

So, we can have a cosmos but we now want to find out what gives the cosmic tree life? In order to do that we need to really unleash our imagination, and by doing so we will find ourselves even more insignificant for a period of time. We are going to enter the forest and when we emerge we will have new knowledge to

contemplate, and any new contemplation can be
enlightening.

The Cosmic Tree

What gives the cosmic tree life? A fundamental question
with an uncertain answer. In fact we could say that it's
not a question at all since the essential foundation of a
technological system is certainty. We raise questions in
order to search for new understandings because those
ultimate understandings are available somewhere in the
system. Like the internet, knowledge pre-exists query.
Now, imagine having a magnified internet of not only in
size but also in accuracy and degrees of awareness and
you gain some sense of the cosmic technologies
available. Why this is useful at the start of this chapter
is because the answers to this cosmic question is
already available and already known only we have not
been able to translate one level of knowledge into
another level of knowledge.

If we talk about time, for example, we have to rely on
the Gregorian Calendar and the Modern Clock (since
very few are familiar with the Star Calendar, including
myself). When we talk about time we use certified
numerical combinations to determine a location of time
that we can all agree upon. When I say May 14, 2009,
nearly everyone on earth can understand that it is the
14th day of the Month of May (Month 5) in the Year of
Our Lord (Jesus Christ) 2009, since the Gregorian
Calendar system is anchored on the birth date of Jesus
Christ, the figure; the same figure which played a major
role in two of our reality events.

There is not much to translate when the whole world,
save some rural villages or aboriginal tribes, so actively
use the same Calendar System. It could be said that we
take the Calendar System for granted, forgetting how
many Calendar Systems were put in effect over the past
two thousand years and how the rulers of the world
made certain changes and adjustments. Despite China,
for example, using an entirely different Calendar System
based on Lunar Cycles and their calendar being nearly
5,000 years in length, which means that the Chinese
culture has been recording their own specific history

three-thousand years *before* the birth of Jesus, and yet their Calendar System is not the global standard. And there are other Calendars such as the Jewish Calendar which is equally as long, not to mention other calendars of smaller groups and esoteric cultures that see the exchange of world events with a different set of eyes.

Despite all of these ongoing differences and ambivalences between human cultures, over the past few centuries the Gregorian System, under some adjustments is for the mainstream. This hasn't stopped the Chinese people from continuing to use their calendar to recognize the Chinese New Year in January or February; and hasn't stopped the Persians from recognizing and celebrating the Persian New Year in March 21, the day of the Vernal Equinox, an old standard of the New Year.

Despite all the ambivalences in the world calendar, I can safely say May 14, 2009 and nearly everyone can make sense of that temporal location. It has become easier to do so with the computerization of nations since computer clocks are preprogrammed to follow one or more systems of telling time, and communications software and mobile phone software as well tell time to log the time of your last communication.

If you want to tell the time, you check one of the many clocks. If you want to know today's date, you check the calendar or ask your mom. Mom always seems to know. Maybe mom is the clock. Better, maybe mom is cosmos. That is an interesting presumption that the "mother" is a representation of the cosmos. But what if this is true?

Mom provides the essential information for the child, you, and the child can go about knowing that they are on schedule for a hot date on Friday night. Had you not known it was Friday, or Sunday perhaps, you'd have missed your appointment, but with the knowledge of trustworthy and reliable mom you are never off schedule. That is until you move out on your own, then things go haywire and you are always late, always a mess and always mixing up appointments. Why is that? How is it that in your youth, you could always access the cosmic appointment system, aka mom, and never had a problem gleaning the necessary information, even getting a motivational kick to ensure that you did not miss any important appointment, like school for example, and then after you are dislodged from mom's home of knowledge you find yourself struggling to keep up. What powers does mom have that you as a young adult do not?

It turns out that mom has a free connection to the cosmos. She can obtain information rather easily, always having the necessary answers and always willing to go that extra mile for her children. Certainly, there are lousy moms, but on the whole, moms are preloaded with some essential search software that is a kind of cosmic Google logarithm. And when you leave mom's domain and are on your own accord, your search logarithm is Version One, and the world is using Version Ninety One. We can see the problem with this. You become out of touch.

It could be said without much effort that being out of touch with simple matters such as telling time and knowing the date are trivial things, and knowing trivial things preclude the knowing of more complex things. You were expecting some simplification of understanding the immense and endless cosmic tree of life and I have insisted from the start that you already can access that information, that is, if someone had taught you how to do so before you left home, which they didn't. They didn't teach you. Your mom didn't teach you how to access the cosmic grid for information.

In fact, no one has much talked about the cosmos in many years, except for astronomers and if there is a choice between Britney Spears and an Astronomer, the choice is Britney Spears and her newest thong.

There is no easy approach to any of this material and my dissemination of it comes in a form that is unique to the writer himself, and my understanding of things is rather complex and all my human knowledge is knowledge that is gleaned from the infinite sky and then translated, verily boiled down and down and down until it reaches a level of edibleness. Some people can grow a carrot in the earth, pluck it up, wash it and take a bite.

Some people don't know that carrots are grown in dirt, but love the carrot cake at Starbucks Coffee Shop.

If you were to take these people to a field and to force them to pluck out a carrot from the dirty earth, to wash it on their designer pants and then to take a bite, they might just faint. Okay, so carrots are not a big deal, well, how about growing a sheep and having it slaughtered and then eating lamb for dinner. We have grown accustomed to eating lamb shank but we are blind to the fact that the shank once belonged to a living breathing sheep. If most of the known world knew some of these obvious facts, the whole world would make a few adjustments in their thinking. I mean, if you support the war in Iraq and then I have you sent there on the front line, and say you survived, you would probably not be supporting any war for a very long while. In fact, we could make you anti-war by having you wounded in battle. That would convince you.

But the cosmos is not about war or eating, these are simple things that any moron can study in their spare time. The cosmos is a scientific pursuit and an esoteric quest for the absolute truth because the cosmos does not and cannot lie. What you see is what you get.

Cosmic beings, myself included, are allergic to lying about human origins and the way the world really works. That isn't the case of human science which makes stuff up and covers stuff up to maintain a foothold on the body of knowledge and if that weren't the case, we would have all been flying our cars to work on free-energy propulsion engines.

The truth is that cosmic knowledge has been deeply repressed and human ability to log on to the cosmic grid is deplorable. There are very few words we can use to describe the deplorable state of cosmic science; the truest science that earth citizens have never known. Never known because the masters of this earth plane have prevented you from knowing, and the first requirement for knowledge prevention is to prevent your acquisition of the cosmic search logarithm, the one your mother used for your entire childhood, and maybe even now.

What are we searching for? What gives the cosmic tree life? It's not about you all of sudden becoming an expert cosmic wanderer and neither is it about me resolving age-old issues with the stroke of a few key words, although it is possible, even conceivable, that that might occur. But unlikely.

Recall that our cosmic exploration is done so through the metaphorical process of some mountain pine tree, cones and all. We have concluded that the shards of the pine cone are representative of the shards of reality, the one important shard here known generally as "earth." And we have gone on to state that the many-sharded cone is representative of the universe and many universes containing many more living realities are all fruits on some cosmic tree of life, since it is life that is providing this esoteric tree. And we want to know the energy source of the cosmic tree of life, right? This is where we are at. We know that because we exist and we are all arvic programs that we are utilizing energy in an energized reality connected to an electric universe all attached to this most-mesmerizing cosmic tree, but who or what is powering the tree?

Let us take an introspective step sideways for a moment and have moment of epiphany. You might recall a celebratory event that occurs around the time of Winter Solstice and pretty much around the entire world, a day known as Christmas Day.

Besides Christmas supposedly representing the birth date of (the) Jesus and a day when lots of cakes are eaten and gifts dispensed, there is one very vital piece of essential information that happens on every Christmas, an almost tradition around the world, and that piece of information is extremely relevant to our study of the cosmos. What does Christmas and Cosmos have in common, given our new understanding of things, well, better yet, my understanding of things? The Christmas Tree.

The Christmas Tree is typically – now get this – a pine tree. Although there are variations of trees with pine needles depending on location, the Christmas tree has for the longest time been a pine tree, and it turns out that our cosmic representative here is a pine tree. Now, before you raise your voice and suggest that all of this was prearranged on my part, I will have you stop. I do not work in this fashion.

Each piece of information was linearly found, puzzle by puzzle, realization by realization. The pine tree allegory long preceded the Christmas tree realization, not counting the knowledge buried beneath my conscious program, since on some level I knew that the Christmas tree was a pine tree, then again my family had used an artificial tree for decades, so really I hadn't known this since childhood and that was a long time ago. But this is an interesting coincidence, is it not? My cosmic allegory and the 2,000 year old history of Christ-mass only adds weight to my own intuitive and cosmically derived argument, that the pine tree is a good representative of the technological cosmos. And what better way to understand something that we cannot understand than to use some beautiful model such as the evergreen tree in exchange for the everlasting life. It is truly beautiful.

The cosmic tree of life, among the cosmic forest of trees, is connected to another realm at the base of its trunk. When we escape the foot of the trunk we enter another realm, or, we can better interpret this as accessing an entirely new set of technologies. Again, we remind ourselves that the technological universe, the Technoverse, is made up of technological components. These components do not appear in the same shape and material as our home-grown computer components which are derived of plastic polymers, silicon wafers and transistors. Cosmic components are derived from arvicity, as is everything in the Technoverse. Arvicity is a fluidic circuitry that can mimic and replace essentially anything that is required and will remain in the elected form of the one who created it.

So, for example, just as in the real world, if I were a carpenter and formed a chair, that chair would maintain the form and shape that I first created it until such point that the chair sufficiently broke down and lost its shape. If we were to use a special camera to shoot film at a high velocity as I created the chair and then we rolled that film and shot the rendered high velocity film, we would have a second copy of the creation of a material object, in our case it's a chair.

Now, if we took that second copy; and the second copy is important because the second copy is filmed at normal speed, and then showed that on the big IMAX screen we would see the making of a chair as if I was moving energy from one table to another. We would see me manifesting the chair as if out of thin air because at such a high velocity we wouldn't be able to see the wood, we certainly wouldn't be able to identify any wood. If we then slowed down the picture, we would be able to see in slow motion the manipulation of energy, because this is the second copy and it was filmed at normal frame-rate.

You can just imagine this carpenter (funnily enough, Jesus was a carpenter) manipulating energy from one place to another, working some kind of magical tool and then forming some object. And then if we were to clarify the final few seconds of film and interlace some of the original material at normal speed, we would see the formation of a wooden chair. But the creation of this chair would have been magical. This manner of creation is also reminiscent of the other arvic dimensions.

Manifestation is just all that much more instant and the details are irrelevant. In the cosmic realm, it isn't necessary to study the wood grain because it is pure arvicity. If you wanted to study the wood grain you would venture to earth and talk about pine trees. Sorry, that was an inside joke.

We are always dealing with technology no matter where we travel to in the cosmos, and since earth plane is in the cosmos it is a technological creation, only we are mostly blind to it and refer to nature as having a biological essence. In fact, it is all technological. Period.

Our perception and awareness limits or enlightens us to the truth and does not judge our perceptions or misperceptions. That is the freedom of enlightenment, not free will. There is no free will in a pre-programmed technological cosmos. Having free will is an awareness of having free will as is not having free will. All of it is awareness. In the highest levels of awareness we find nothing, we find not even the idea of free will and certainly we are not thinking of our level of awareness, it is simply nothing.

Through the cosmic trunk gate and into another level of technology, a level of technology that is imbibed with energy. As we have seen over so many words, we have seen this idea of cosmic energy, something which I call arvicity, and this is a living energy, a fluidic circuitry made up of crystalline components, transistors of some light essence of a quality that is beyond our current ability to mass produce. Just think of those weapons of mass destruction; luckily, arvicity has a built-in pacifism component that no mere mortals can crack, and many have tried.

The arvic bed upon which is rooted our cosmic tree is self-sustaining. The circuitry generates its own energy endlessly and we can be certain of this because we are alive. If the arvic bed of total cosmic existence were not self-generating then earth plane would have dissolved thousands or millions of years ago.

Earth is still here and not only that earth citizens are evolving and have kept evolving. This is all the proof we need to know that arvicity is self-generating. Some spiritualists might wonder whether the cosmos will end or the well of souls will dry up and it is then we have to remind them all that the cosmos is not a biological construct. A biological construct has limitations, it has a lifespan. It is mortal. A technological construct, on the other hand, is infinite and immortal. That is where humanity is from, from the cosmos, from the infinite and the immortal. This is an undeniable fact: Human culture is a cosmic culture and the cosmos has an infinite technological architecture.

In a world and society that keeps putting fear into our minds and reminding us of our mortal nature, it is imperative that, if nothing else, that you can begin to see that your cosmic origins are immortal, that you are beyond fear and that in an infinite cosmos, anything is possible. We should find time to study the cosmos as much as possible and aim the telescopes of thought outward instead of at our feet. We all come from the cosmic tree of life, the immortal bedrock upon which all existence is hinged.

Pine Cones, Reality Expositions and Patterns

The verifiable quality of a reality space, verily the plane of existence inhabited by various existential forms, is indeed subject to interpretation, and those many interpretations are going to be subject to interpretation which will allow further interpretation: Hence, the myriad of religious interpretation and many thousands of books on spirituality, witchcraft and new age physics such as string theory and quantum mechanics. If a hundred pairs of eyes look at a Granny Smith apple and were asked to comment on their observations we would get 100 or more interpretations of the green apple. One hundred or more interpretations on the exact same object, a singular edible fruit of which we can all relate, explore and taste.

A reality space is like viewing a quadrillion (15 zeros) apples at once, as if viewing all these atoms under an electron microscope, and the interpretations of those observations are figuratively impractical. The fact is that the human mind is incapable of processing that much information at any one time, or even a life time.

An Intel Pentium CPU has a limited processing power etched into its silicon cranium and it crashes if we exceed that ability. So what happens is that the individual human mind carefully selects are canon of observations with which to interpret their personal view on reality, and in lieu of this, a person will choose to follow the wisdom of another. In the ancient times, philosophers would spend their entire days and life in observation of the natural world and would share that knowledge with the community, in squares of dialectal discussion.

We have lost the luxury of thought in the modern era and have replaced wisdom with the opinions of bobbing heads in a syndicated television program. Worse still, those online experts rarely if ever contemplate the esoteric knowledge upon which life hinges. That's why people like me persist in widening the view finder and expanding the topics of discussion from money and war to immortality and reality.

Funnily enough, the act of interpretation itself is an exposition and an evolution into further and deeper interpretations; an endless quest that can carry on through the ages, and have done so through the interpretive authors in the likes of Galileo and Tesla. While we can certify the existence of a reality space, we cannot extrapolate its meaning because we are restricted by our narrowly-programmed mind, a mind that doesn't yet fully appreciate the synthetic quality of our projected reality system.

And this, I argue, is not out of randomness and fateful activity rather our narrow-minded culture has been carefully and purposely cultivated by those who understand the nature of the universe and the false land we all inhabit. I am merely yet another interpretive author who may or may not be remembered. I am certain of the way the reality functions and at the lowest level of operation, if you take away all your gifts, resources and friends, there is one truth that holds: Every thought counts. Whatever a woman may contribute to a relationship has far greater value than she might ever realize, and the more positive those contributions the more likely they will last into a time immemorial.

This is our dilemma then: With the expansion of the mind coupled with the realization that time and space has been circumcised by an external surgical blade, we are faced with an indiscriminate and complicated set of understandings; because we must understand our reality predicament if we are ever going to ascend ourselves out of this holographically projected debacle.

You cannot repair a radiator on a car if you have no mechanical skill whatsoever and before obtaining two ounces of skill you need to understand how a "car" works. How many people know how a reality works? If there was a large population of reality mechanics the world would not be so degraded. The evidence for degradation is beyond convincing at this point. It's like filming a husband beat his wife in HD over a three year period. Doesn't matter what the husband says, nor does it matter how much in denial is his wife, the evidence is beyond convincing.

The shambles of an unmaintained reality are everywhere, the most glaringly obvious fact is the *persistence of war* (POW). Humans murdering humans without cause, year after year, is the absolute omittance of the basic rules of this virtual game: *Thou Shalt Not Kill*, is a very straightforward and clear statement, "But I'm not Christian!" isn't it? Or maybe it needs a couple of expensive lawyers to notch it up, update it to:

Human Law Of Murder

In the event that you are not angry or that your nation is not threatened or that your ego is not being question or that you are not of normal mind, if all or any of these conditions hold true, even if the possibility of these items are remotely or will be predicted to be true, if all or any of that then killing is allowed; otherwise, a human may not murder another human as long as absolutely none of those conditions have been noticed. And all of the Law of Murder can be avoided when and if convenient without repercussion depending on who is the current leader and which nation holds power in the world, not even a religious leader can uphold the law when any or all of the conditions are in place; otherwise, the religious leader can insist that the Law of Murder be upheld, in that sole case, no one should be murdered; and, further, if some other person is murdering some other person or persons, then it completely justifies ignoring this Law of Murder in its entirety, just skip until things calm down and happiness pervades the mind: But when the conditions rise or if depression ensues then skip this Law of Murder and kill as much as you like knowing that you are justified in what is done.

THE PINE CONE

To better understand the process of an unfolding reality occupying time and space, I am going to use my observations of a Pine Cone. As many of us have already seen, and know, the cosmos (or universe, as you prefer) is complete in its pattern and this pattern is replicated at any point of the known and unknown universe. In other words, and to be sure, the pattern of a free-falling feather's drop cannot exist in isolation. The feather had to have been programmed to fall.

To our limited vision and restricted mind, the feather falls because the owner, a bird, allowed the feather by some random action. My view is that the bird simply allowed some encoded routine to play out causing the feather to fall and then you noticed it as a natural action. All things, actions and events are programmed to occur and all programming can be first detected through a pattern (or code). Therefore, the pattern of "falling feathers" is representative of some other cosmic action, an action that perhaps we will never know because we may never care enough to know.

A more obvious cosmic pattern deals with birth and rebirth. No birth exists alone. A child is born each and every hour or minute perhaps. There is a pattern of birth. The pattern of a seed that gestates into new lifeform, be it a Macintosh apple or a human child, and then is born or released into the reality is a repeating pattern in this reality, in this cosmos. The nebula gives birth to a star, a star to a planet or a solar system, or an earth. Because there is a pattern of activity, we can be certain that there is a programmed routine to ensure that this activity continues. Today, we take many of these patterns for granted and because of this they become invisible. Only when we sit down to reflect upon the errors or achievements of our lives do we notice the patterns more easily. If you split existence into tiny bits you would notice that everything is a pattern, from skin replication to knowledge transfer.

From the molecular to the galactic and beyond, there are patterns that we can rely on to teach us what we need to know. So, for our reality observations I'm going to use the pine cone because the pine cone can give us insight into the nature of an evolved reality space. The challenge is always to find the pattern most representative of our area of knowledge since the areas are many.

The birth of the pine cone occurs from the branch of the pine tree where a series of flesh-like rods (or needles) turn into a young cone. This young cone already has a built-in pattern, a pattern that we will see "evolve" over the course of its life from fresh fruit to dry cone. The imprinted cone is most important at the stage of birth because when the pine cone grows and expands it does so according to its pattern. That pattern is our matching reality pattern. This pine cone grows and its pattern is expressed for all to see.

When we examine the underbelly of the dry pine cone we see a most wonderful pattern in its widest expression. This fractal planet is not thusly by accident, it is programmed (with the pattern as proof) in this manner. So, imagine that each pine cone is a universe and each fractal shard is a reality. Each irregularly shaped flake is the foot of a reality as if we are looking at the bottom of the universe.

The universe expands and as the universe expands so too do the reality shards. Notice that the pine cone, if it doesn't die prematurely, has to necessarily expand until it cannot expand anymore. If reality expands it is because the universe has expanded. The cosmos perhaps is the pine tree, an immeasurable lifeform loaded with universes and realities. Inside of each pine cone shard are a number of strings and these strings are the architecture of the reality shard culminating at the head of reality, a hard husk divided into four parts and a held together with a centered eye.

The eye of reality is fed by the strings of existence and all are connected to the core of the universe: A universal cone among many countless assorted cones.

Imagine now we re-interpret the pine cone as made out of plasma energy. The shape remains but this time we have replaced the biological form with a technological architecture. Imagine each reality shard as a laser shard projecting outward and the existential strings made of optical fibres. The eye of reality is some kind of stargate. We have arbitrarily transformed the innocent pine cone into the plasma universe from which all realities are expanded.

As the universe grows and ages, so too does reality, each time lengthening its elastic plasma shard. All of this occurs right now all over the earth whenever pine cones grow, wherever pine trees inhabit. The pine tree has been growing for hundreds of years and will continue to grow for many years to come, just as the universal tree will continue to grow and new realities will be born as old realities fall to ground to dry out and then fade away as if they never existed.

We take the pine tree for granted because we do not value its cosmic knowledge. Nature is probably the best teacher in the world, trouble is nature doesn't speak in a manner that we are accustomed to, but nature's knowledge is abundantly available and surprisingly free. The distracted world leaves very little room to study the metaphorical knowledge of pine trees, or the truths of patterns. But we have to be comfortable in knowing the essential truth, whatever patterns we notice here we will notice elsewhere in the universe, and whatever patterns we notice in the universe we will notice in the cosmos. If this statement were untrue you wouldn't and couldn't exist because you are cosmic, but then that in itself is a new discussion because besides understanding the texture and appeal of a reality space, it is a far more complex task to observe the cosmos. First things first.

The Reality Shard Recipe

As vibration rises, the velocity of time rises as well, and the faster the frequency, the more invisible the action. Vibration, time, frequency and action – these are the four ingredients that we will require when making our next reality dish, fractal shards.

A fractal shard is like a shard of crystal except that the material is not glass, the material is arvicity, the living energy. The fractal shard emerges from the universal pillar just as a pine shard emerges from within the pine cone. For the shard of reality to emerge, we must have a universe and within that universe we are going to find multiple realities all springing forth from the same root universe.

That root universe will be the result of the branch of energy connecting to the cosmic machine. Like a well-rooted tree that produces bountiful fruit, in exchange for the fruit we find ourselves enjoying reality as fruit. The most ideal job position for a Supreme Being is that of a Gardener. But rather than gardening fruits and vegetables, the Supreme Being is looking after a forest of universes. The Tree of Life and the Tree of Knowledge could better be interpreted as accesses to other universes because we know that on each tree are many branches and on each branch are many universes and within each universe are many realities.

On one particular universe is one particular reality shard is this reality that has been referred to as Earth Planet. But as you can see, Earth Planet is really Earth Plane and Earth Plane is really just another reality in a universe of realities all connected to a cosmic machine. And if the cosmic machine is metaphorically represented by a tree then that tree exists in a field of trees. The cosmic forest is beyond human imagination and should reaffirm the immensity of this idea known as life.

We are not here to discuss life because we can see it each time we look into the mirror. Those eyes staring back at you contain life and therefore you are alive. The question that arises is: what is the difference between Reality One and Reality Twenty-One? That is a reasonable question that we have yet to examine and why we have to hold in mind this idea of a reality shard. Imagine that the reality shard is a crystal shard. We know that there are many kinds of crystals just on this plane of existence alone and each crystal reality shard is vibrating at its own level of vibration because, as we recall from the opening, the vibration is one of the four essential ingredients to the making of a reality plane.

Our *fractal shard* – because it is alive and inhabited by existential forms – is vibrating at a level that is conducive, supportive and encouraging to life: Hence, you and I appear alive in this vibrating field of cosmic energy. Again, you need proof and that is why I suggest to look in the mirror. No, not my mirror, your mirror, any mirror that you can see yourself. Look into the reflection on a car's side view mirror if you cannot afford your own mirror. This reality shard, as each reality shard, is constructed to vibrate a certain rate depending upon its builder and the builder's realm of interest.

Every reality shard is designed by the manufacturer to vibrate at a certain level and that level then determines the level of awareness in the reality matrix, and deeply influences the perceptive ability of its inhabitants. What each and every inhabitant can perceive and experience is a result of the not only their vibration, but more importantly, a result of the reality's vibration level. The inhabitants are not able to exceed the vibration of the reality shard.

The second ingredient is going to give us an interesting insight into the quality of a journey because the ingredient of time is a most treasured ingredient in every region of the world. Time is one of those ingredients that none can hold or destroy. We cannot buy time at Wal-Mart. We cannot eat time and time has no monetary value.

Time, it can be said, is priceless and it is a commodity that each and every inhabitant expends each and every minute of each and every day. Starting from your year of birth through each and every birthday we are measuring the passage of time. We go to work at nine and get off work at five. Eight hours of work, time-for-money and with our money we buy the things we are enticed to buy and we spend more time. Then we get married and time floats away into the responsibilities of a family. We retire, our time expended, and soon thereafter we pass away.

For others, they pass sooner than expected. But everything is expected in a technological reality that is all programmed. Can we say that time is programmed or is time something else entirely? The concept of time is a debated issue with no certain answer.

What we do know about time in a technological crystalline construct is that as the vibration goes higher then the passage of time becomes faster. In other words, time elapses at a faster rate. For the would-be filmmaker, the frames-per-second would become lower than the usual 24-FPS. Conversely, doubling or tripling the frames-per-second would slow down the passage of time in the film to that of slow-motion. Shooting a film at 60-FPS produces a slow-motion shot, perfect for any music video. But some movies require the hastening of time to capture some montage or simulated life review. That is when we lower the frame rate and the illusion of speed is produced.

Verily, the frame-per-second of a movie is a good metaphor for the elapse of time in a reality construct. By adjusting the vibrates-per-second we can adjust the speed of our existential movie. To speed up reality we lower the vibrates-per-second, to slow down reality we raise the vibrates-per-second.

Our vibrating reality shard is now functioning according to a certain ration of time. The elapse of time is present at the beginning, but since the vibratory rate of a reality shard evolves as it expands and absorbs arvicity, the vibration rate is constantly shifting. When a major shift occurs there is some noticeable effect in the inhabitant population, perhaps a Renaissance or a World War.

The visible result in the reality is proof of a shift in the vibration of the reality shard and that reality shard is made out of arvicity, free-flowing energy. Throughout the history of earth we have noticed a multitude of large scale events, for ill or good, and we can be certain that not only is the reality shard alive and kicking, but, this reality shard is expanding and contracting.

The vibratory rate of our reality shard effects the frequency rate of our inhabitants because the inhabitants themselves are also technological constructs, or programs. These energetic programs are maintaining a frequency in accordance to the vibration to the reality and the reality to the universe and the universe to the cosmos.

This is not much different from when I listen to a piece of classical music such as Vivaldi. The strings of the violin vibrate as the violinist moves her hand in rhythmic motion across those strings. Those strings vibrate and produce sound, not just any sound but music from the cosmos. Then the other instruments join the violinist, the cello and the flue, more violinists and then a drum, harmony and song joined as one in The Four Seasons.

The vibration of strings influences the frequency of my being and I reminded that I am not only alive but I am energy wrapped in a suit of imaginary flesh partaking in the glory of existence on this plane of reality. This false plane, grown by technological gardeners all designed to appear real for the purpose of keeping the journey entertaining and uplifting. The frequencies of each and every inhabitant is not the same because each and every journey is not the same.

Your frequency will influence and reflect who and what you are because that frequency will determine what you do and do not see in the world. If you are a stamp collector, for example, your frequency will allow you to see stamps but will not allow you to see birds. If you ask a stamp collector to identify a random bird, even in their backyard they will likely scratch their head and not be able to answer. That is because they're operating at the frequency of stamp collector. And it is no wonder that one stamp collector will be friends with similar-minded stamp collectors.

Of course, humans at this time in evolution are far more capable than that and that is why we find multi-classed people who have had many jobs, many diverse friends and have lived in many parts of the country or world. All of this is evidence that the frequency of humanity, as inhabitant, is quite high at this time. This is in your face proof. The fact that most of us are multi-classed and shift easily from home to career to family to technology is living proof that the frequency of humanity is reasonably advanced.

If you were to continue to dial-up human frequencies we would all begin teleporting from one location to another and if we continued still, we would all become invisible to a low-frequency human. This presents us with an interesting scenario. For me to disappear, I merely need to alter my frequency enough into the spectrum which you cannot see, then I become invisible. Notice, I do not cease to exist. I merely become invisible to your sight and that is because your frequency is not in sync with my frequency.

We've heard this saying often in the Western world, "We are just not on the same wavelength." Intrinsically, we understand the important of frequency, otherwise we would be dead, but we are taught culturally not to delve in things that are not scientifically supported, which is a great and terrible shame since all existence is scientific by its very nature and the limited perceptions of human science are denying the rest of humanity to really truly expand.

With our fourth ingredient, invisibility, carefully introduced to our reality shard, we now have all the necessary ingredients to more fully understand how a reality is constructed.

It is unlikely that we may ever fully grasp the true technical knowledge of a reality in one or two lifetimes because of the complexities involved and because the more time you invest in studying realities, the less time you invest in making friends and raising a family. Time is never our friend no matter how fast we are because on this plane of existence, time exists and wherever time exists we will find ourselves with certain limitations. We will not be able to achieve everything we want, but the good news is that we don't have to in order to have a full life.

The societal leaders force us to become everything when becoming yourself is enough to experience all that you came here to experience. Everything is just an illusion anyway so why buy the illusion as being any more important than it all really is? This life is this life, next life is next life.

Vibration, time, frequency and invisibility – our four (4) ingredients are going to up the ante on this reality construct as they help us to more fully understand this reality shard. By understanding the reality shard, we are going to discover a very important aspect of our perception: existential stagnation.

I've argued this before: if you put a 13-year-old boy into a closet and leave him there for twenty years (20), making sure he is fed, washed and warm; when he comes out he's going to be a bloody mess. He's going to be retarded, and yet his physical body will be relatively unscathed, his health will be good, he will have been fed all the nutrition he needed, perhaps even more; and let's say that we also provided him with some exercise.

Our 33-year-old retard is a *retard* because of mental, emotional and spiritual stagnation, right? Not right. Our 33-year-old retard is a retard because his frequency has been purposely kept so low as to prevent the expansion of his program. While the other programs (or souls) continued to upgrade as reality vibrated higher and time sped up, our 33-year-old was not able to get online. He did not gain the necessary program codes; he did not keep up with the rest of the society; he did not remain in sync with the reality shard.

He is a retard because his program version is too out of date. It is like trying to run Microsoft Windows 3.1 on a 2009 Pentium Dual-Core Intel Toshiba Laptop. Windows 3.1 will not function very well, if at all, on such a powerful machine. That is what happens when you purposely lower the frequency of a human and then bring them back into society, which is also why the prison system is designed to fail; and also why the idea of a jail will only keep crime rates up.

Imagine now that you stick an entire nation into a national closet for 20 years. If our example above is true then we would end up with a retarded nation; a nation of people that had little or no chance to upgrade. It turns out that it is not that difficult to do.

China's Chairman Mao Zedong, for example, did manage to immerse an entire nation into a different frequency starting in 1958 with the Great Leap Forward and ending in 1976 with the catastrophes of the Cultural Revolution. An estimated 70 million people died and millions of families were dropped into the frequency of poverty and destitution. Since China opened its gates, the entire nation has progressed at a phenomenal rate, so much so that China is one of the strongest economies in the world and in the central cities has a very advanced infrastructure.

China is a good example of an entire nation being lowered in its frequency of operation and since it has a very homogenous structure the impact was nationwide. The entire Chinese nation in 1976 exited the existential closet, the supreme experiment, and would quickly regain its sense of self; and determinedly launched forward into the new age. But, it should be noted that the frequency of even a large nation can be adjusted with the right effort, and as we will see in the following chapter, that an entire reality shard can be impacted by the right reality event.

Whether it is a child stuck in a closet or a nation being reengineered, the illusion often prevents us from seeing what is really going on beneath the visible spectrum: frequency modulation. The technology that most of us are familiar with regarding modulation is a modem, which stands for modulation/ demodulation.

A modem is used to access a network, typically an internet service provider or a telecoms provider for a wireless phone. The modem modulates and demodulates electronic data into different modalities, or languages, so that it can be processed and expressed in a compatible form.

Putting a child in a closet is a *demodulation* process. Taking the child out of the closet is a *modulation* process. Of course, it takes us 20 years to get a measurable result because if we stuck the child in the closet for only 20 minutes, for example, the modulation process would be too insignificant for us to observe outside of a scientific experimentation.

Socially engineering an entire nation involves the same modulation and demodulation process, or vice versa. We d0 not need to demodulate and modulate only, we could modulate and demodulate, in other words, and we can certainly infer this, Chairman Mao had every intention to invigorate the Chinese people and the Chinese people had every understanding of ascending. The final result, some 18 years later was quite a different affair, and during that period not only many changes occurred in China but also in our reality shard. We have to always remind ourselves that reality is a manufactured construct and it is alive, reality is constantly evolving with and without our permission.

There is a hierarchy of operation: the inhabitants exist because of the nation and the nation because of the reality and the reality because of the universe and the universe because of the cosmos. If there were no universe there would be no China and no inhabitants here. You and I would not be able to exist here because this would be unformed space. The fruit will not have grown and there is nothing to eat.

Gardening and realities share some remarkable characteristics including a resiliency and a persistency that is unmatched by any mind, person or culture in the entire cosmos. No matter what, realities must grow and just like a seed will take root in any soil, it is also true that the better the soil the better the fruit. The richer the vibration of the universe, the richer the vibration of the reality; a trickle-up effect that produces a distinct fruit that vibrates at a distinct rate.

The reality shard upon which we exist is in a constant state of flux, a fluidic shifting like the waves on the ocean, except this is not water, this is arvicity our living energy. The vibration of the reality shard must continually increase in order for the fruit to expand to its fullest expression, to ripen as it is meant to ripen. If that elegant process is interfered with then we will find a stagnation that produces immature fruit. If we continue to interfere with the frequency of our fruit we will likely be unable to eat it or it will simply rot on the branch. And if we insist on interference the whole tree will die off.

Reality Rays

An antagonistic force will likewise create a fractal impression and this impression will be the result of the interference of an antagonistic force upon the reality construct. While individual impressions will impact the individual and their immediate circle, without thought (ie now) time has zero presence because thought has weight then that gives the presence of time, represented as fractal time, or, probably better thought of as similar patterns of moments (or magical moments).

Magical moments alter the trajectory of existences. Why? The magical moment creates an outward rippling effect that produces a fractal impression and this impression in time is represented in the projected reality space. Under natural non-antagonistic conditions, a reality will take shape that exists in harmony with other cosmic procreative industries. Global impressions will create a global effect, but since global impressions are restricted in form due to cost and counter-force then it has been common to find national impressions having to do with large scale populations.

On a macro scale, the Thought Grid can impact the larger whole. Gather enough energy and you can reach a more authoritative level on the Thought Grid. When a fractal impression is created on a higher-level and reality is impacted then all existential forms inhabiting that particular reality will therefore feel its effects, most notably the temporal pattern will become off course.

Each reality is like a projected flashlight. Everything within that ray of light is part of the reality and as the ray of light moves forward in time then reality is seen to expand because the ray of light becomes wider.

The origin of the reality ray is a nodal point where the reality operating system (ROS) is upgraded or recreated. Throughout human history, the ROS has been upgraded and recreated in accordance to the cosmic operating machine (engine). The cosmic machine, composed almost entirely of light-energy generating substances, is itself always and continually expanding; therefore, each and every created and projected reality must upgrade and recreate itself in accordance to the cosmic machine, a machine of arvicity.

Arvicity is the living energy, a fluidic circuitry, that maintains, expands and processes all existential constructs, forms and identifiers. The Arvic Machine generates time and space, and within the time and space medium we can find reality.

If you project a flashlight inside a bright room the light is invisible, as the room shifts to darkness, or shifts to a new medium we find more and more particles of projected light. We know from science that we can notice the electromagnetic spectrum. But arvicity is not light energy and is not electricity. Arvicity is an energy fluid embedded with processing power in the form of crystal circuits. You can examine a starry night sky and see the millions of interstellar formations all existing in some kind of black fluid. We call this outer-space, the universe, the cosmos. Imagine that all those constellations, star clusters, nebulae, galaxies and individual stars were circuitry all immersed in an expansive light-neutral fluid. If the universal view is a good representation of fluidic circuitry then arvicity is the molecular view of space.

The pathway of the reality ray predetermines the fate of existential forms. We can be certain that if we pointed a flashlight at a shooting target then we'd eventually reach the target. If we point the reality flashlight at an oak tree, we'd eventually reach the oak tree before hitting another nodal point and upgrading or recreating.

While every reality is constructed for specific reasons according to the reality builder and in accordance to the reality existences, and occasional travelers, it is also true that individuals and groups who learn reality physics can alter the course of reality. By altering the course of reality they are in effect changing the direction of the flashlight from point A to point B.

But we have to remind ourselves that any reality is huge in shape and energy, take for example this earth plane. Billions of existences, billions of years of evolution and a reality OS that is extremely complex. Not just that but the maintenance of a reality involves many multidimensional engineers, experts in their assigned task.

To redirect a reality would require the takeover of a reality and that is about as likely as three pirates taking over an aircraft carrier. Though rather than completely hijack the reality, the antagonists could influence the direction of the aircraft carrier so that even if their course is altered by a few degrees, over a long distance, the aircraft carrier would end up in the wrong port. This is of course is the captain doesn't return the ship back to its original course or if the captain is dead then it will be up to the senior crew members to remember the proper course.

And the ship is not only attached by simple-minded pirates but also be electromagnetic weapons that have hypnotized some of the crew members. There might even be a threat of mutiny and a few explosions that need to be tended to. The sailing of the aircraft carrier and a reality share a remarkable similarity. If reality is put off course even by only a few degrees, the reality will expire at the wrong point and if does not reach its nodal exchange reality will simple die off (or not light up) because there is no infrastructure for existence to continue. Or the reality will fall back upon itself and loop into a repetitive pattern, like a crash and burn addiction.

Earth has been trapped into such a pattern. The earth reality is continually being pointed into itself, just as people are always pointing inward, always scraping the floors of the past for clues and innovation. Crime shows on TV endlessly force the human mind, central to thought, to look within the puzzle and this repetitive pattern of pointing inwards has caused inward thinking and because thought determines the fractal impression's destination, reality hasn't evolved **in 2,000 years.**

You are living in a reality that has stagnated for two millennia. Despite all the advancements and higher-level evolution, the human thought is operating within the wrong fractal time, not in accordance to its **original course**.

We could restate that by saying that this reality has been slowed down, the beam has been narrowed, and that reality did not expand as it should have. What that means is that essentially humanity is living in prehistoric times and is in a disintegrated state of being.

If reality was on course, we'd be in the 23RD century, about the Year 2209. Instead, we are in the 21st century. The Year 1989 was one nodal year of many that would've launched all existences and reality into a frame of speed that would be incomparable today. The speed of life would have achieved warp speed but instead only achieved impulse power.

Being Cosmic

First came the programmer, then the computer code, then the operating system, then software program. If we are currently using a software program, such as my laptopian (knee-bound) word processor, then that program is running on the platform of an operating system, in my case MS Windows Vista Home Edition. The Vista OS is running on millions of lines of essential code, all of it programmed by a team of programmers who invested hundreds of hours of time and effort in the planning, coding and debugging stages of the OS platform.

The technology beneath your biological fingertips did not happen by chance and does not run on magical power, but for some reason, strange as it might seem, when we hold something as simple as a desire to succeed, we never think about the technological mechanism that enables us to even hold an idea. We take for granted the platform.

Now let's extend the analogy: first came the cosmos, then the universe, then the galaxy, then the reality shard known as earth. If we currently exist in a *reality shard,* such as planet earth (and on one dimension it does appear as a round object made up of physical components), then this planet is running on the platform of a reality operating system (ROS), one we still haven't identified. The Reality OS is running billions of lines of existential code, all of it programmed by a team of programmers who invested hundreds of hours of time and effort in the planning, coding and debugging stages of the OS platform.

What does it really mean to be cosmic? Well, if we can agree that this plane of existence is technological in nature and that this reality is built on some kind of code, and we can agree of the similarities I have made above, then being cosmic means being technological. A cosmic being is a being that is created by a level of technology far beyond any human scientist at this time.

If we interpret planet Earth as a biological body including the human being then the cosmos is some giant biological uterus giving endless birth to galaxies and planetary bodies and humanity is the fruit of the biological earth, springing forth from the mud of the earth. A very romantic view of what life could be like.

Unfortunately, biology cannot rectify the vast discrepancies found in other aspects of observation, including the development of virtual reality environments and the detection of other dimensions in super string theory. Biology does not allow us to hold a conversation on other dimensions because we know of no natural method with which to escape one biological dimension into another.

Further, we cannot safely count time as having a biological dimension therefore time is outside of biology. And, still, we have trouble with the aspect of the human soul, an item that has never been identified or examined under any microscope. We are certain that the human soul has confused everyone, but we can agree that the soul is some kind of energy, and energy is a technological construct. We do not blatantly say that the human soul is nonbiological because we do not know what kind of energy it is composed of, although it does have some electromagnetic properties. In fact, we are still stuck on human consciousness. The number of papers and books on consciousness are endless and the answer still escapes us. We are conscious and we do not understand how or why?

As I stated in the opening of this chapter, the reality space is too enormous to analyze in its entirety, we simply fall short in processing power. So we break up the tasks and many researchers get together and try to examine the various components of reality, and we use those scientific and philosophical observations to speed up our understanding of reality.

My focus has remained on fractal time and impressions, and in trying to explain the complexities of a multidimensional impression, I have found myself attempting to cover a vast assortment of patterned knowledge. Most of the problems we will experience with the understanding of reality comes from the suppression of knowledge and the distractions of the mind, usually from a typified media system. If, for example, half of what I am sharing in this book, if just half of it were *discussed* in schools and in media, the entire reality space would transform in unimaginable ways. But those who rule earth would not ever allow that to happen because that would undermine their efforts and expose their hidden positions.

Should you be someone who truly wants to alter and improve reality then take something from this book and bring it to the table of public discussion. If a hundred people take a hundred pieces we will be able to more fully observe the nature of this technological space in which we all inhabit.

Ultimately, that is my intended purpose – to give people a better understanding of the mechanics of the reality which will allow a better understanding of the cosmos, and this should allow the proliferation of reality mechanics who will have some skill in repairing the various mechanical problems that will continuously arise because they will be able to program and reprogram some of the essential codes. Being a reality mechanic or engineer is likely going to be a good career choice in the future.

Enter the Golden Era

When our laptop computer isn't working properly, we notice that the computations are slow, loading programs is a hassle and the system crashes too often. Although frustrated, we are encouraged by frustration to find a computer technician and are willing to pay our hard-earned money to repair our beloved computer. The same goes for the mainframe computer that is managing all the telephone calls in your city.

When the phone system breaks down, the telephone company dispatches their highly-paid technicians to pull apart wires and replace motherboards to repair the damage, at an expected cost. Besides repair, those same telephone systems are maintained regularly at another huge expense. In fact, we can safely say that any technology, be it a car, computer or home, needs regular maintenance. And, surprisingly, even our body needs maintenance, call it a check-up or a diet. Technology and maintenance go together because intuitively the program understands that it will breakdown without constant adjustment and upgrade. And here is another important aspect of a technological device, system upgrades.

Even the telephone company is regularly replacing old components with new components, and your laptop software OS is being reloaded with a new version, and then that version is being upgraded in newer versions. And all of these things happen in a regular fashion. But when you talk about reality, or a modified interpretation of nature, no one seems to give a damn. They all leave it up to God. For that the reality says, Thank You. Not really. Reality is unimpressed, as I am unimpressed.

We have all forgotten the technological foundation upon which we are provided with life. If the reality breaks down, well, guess what, you break down, you suffer, you disintegrate. It has absolutely nothing to do with punishment. Do you say that the operating system in your computer is punishing you for not upgrading it often enough, or do you just get the message that it is time to pay attention to your beloved device?

The World Mess – you know...war, disease, dehumanization – is a result of technological neglect, a neglect that has lasted for centuries. Ever since the King of Jews was crucified mankind has felt justified, and has been convinced, into thinking that they must suffer for their sins. What sins? The reality is a manufactured construct and you are a program – where is this idea of sin if not just an idea? Does your Microsoft Word application program respect the sacred words of a Holy Bible? Not to my knowledge. The program follows the codes of its operation cycle, and those codes are constantly upgraded.

The code of today is unlike that of a few minutes ago because the code also learns, it accumulates a variational adjustment. You can add words to the internal dictionary and the words you add will be unlike the words of your friend's dictionary. Each Word program evolves in a unique fashion, by the moment. Well, is not humanity like this? We are all unique citizens because we are all updating ourselves in a unique way. And while we maintain ourselves so as to appear sexy and cool, the all-important reality system suffers; and therefore all the inhabitants suffer because the inhabitants are like the Microsoft Word program relying on Microsoft Windows OS.

Reality is the operating system and you are the program; when nature dies, man goes with her. Again, the similarities are remarkable for two distinctly different phenomena, one a technologically manifested reality system and the other a biologically created planet. The sooner we can overcome our biological constraints and to overlay our computational sciences with earth science, the sooner we will all see the hyperreality that we are part and parcel of. We partake in this elegant simulation and have forgotten our cosmic origins. This forgetfulness has achieved its fullest effect and now it is the moment of a new level of discovery.
The degradation of the reality operating system for so many years, along with an unprecedented amount of interference and outright neglect, has predetermined humanity to remain enslaved and in stagnation; Hence, my book thusly. I have offered my ideas and translations of cosmic concepts in the previous pages in an effort to demonstrate that the situation on earth right now can be corrected if humanity corrects its view of reality, and if humanity is willing to make the necessary thought adjustments.

Without any significant effort, humanity will remain enslaved until it eventually completely crashes just like an operating system that is abused day after day. Soon enough the computer will become irreparable, and the renegades will escape leaving your experience a world-class debauchery.

I don't see humans and computers as becoming symbiotic because I see the human as a computer first and foremost. I see computers magnifying human computation to achieve a technological awareness that will undermine the foundation of biological sciences. We will see the end of biology not far from today, but not the end of humanity. When biology ends the human race reaches a nonbiological status and in that level of awareness they are able to crack the reality barrier – peering behind the curtain and seeing the pipes and pistons at work.

When we see the grease and the mechanic playing with the codes, we will lose all doubt of doubts, falling into a pit of our own denial and be reborn as a steward of a technological era, an era filled with optimism and possibility; and in that span of thought, for whatever term it can be held, humanity will step out of humanity and in doing so will be granted the right once again to create, to innovate and to invent.

Having learned the pitfalls of pathetic behaviour and apathy, human leaders will become noble once again, and in that state of nobility will carry the burden of the generations yet to come. That, after all is said and explained, is the final point of a work like this and my entire life's work as however it turns out. This work is about the generations to follow. My investment is large so that the children of 200 years from today reap the rewards of a stable reality system, a system that cannot be hijacked by anyone or any group, and neither will the inhabitants ever again allows such childish pranks to ever take foot again

The more people who invest in those children of children will be investing in something that is far more important than any one singular entity. We must ensure that all the fruits of this tree grow to their fullest before they are plucked and eaten. Each and every golden fruit is a joyous celebration of life and all inhabitants inside, each and every one of them is worth more than gold. We must treasure existence as if it was a third arm on our body. If we are of stable mind, we would not carelessly abuse our own arm.

We are fast approaching a point of propulsion in human perception where the paradigm shifts so widely that nothing we know can make sense of what we see and yet we will see it. A few days from tomorrow, we will step forward and require water and a glass of water will find its way into our hand. Our appetite for knowledge will force the acquisition of cosmic knowledge to be returned to this plane and cosmic education will begin again. The world will no longer be divided by nations; instead it will be joined by *homogeneity*.

This is not a book of revelations because revelations are antique devices that can be used to bind a man's mind. Soon enough we will no longer be bound to 3D or time, rather we will discover multiple dimensions, multiple worlds and multiple realms of knowledge. New cultures will mesh with human culture in ways that only could have been imagined in Hollywood science fiction movies.

The past will seem like some giant hallucination, a nightmare of which we are thankful not to take part in any longer. Good and Evil will be replaced by Awareness and Perception, plain and simple. And the journey of life will be fluid once again. We will find ourselves serving fear or serving truth and what we think true may in fact be fear.

For all the changes to come and all the knowledge to gain, we are going to have to decide who and what we want to be and how we want to co-exist. What ideas do we discard and what ideas do we adopt? Do we keep homosexuality as a cultural exposition or do we just say, "People?" Will we find a way to dismantle every nuclear warhead or will we just keep them all in storage?

We cannot rely on the usual teachers to find questions; we need masters, new masters. We need to bring in the philosophers and the scholars, the shamans and the witches. I cannot predict all the outcomes to be; for we have yet to move far enough forward.

I can assure you that as we awaken the questions will appear. Not just questions, but conundrums – one conundrum replacing another, each one more difficult than its predecessor. We must face each question up close. We must find the answers and not stop until the answers are found, so we will require expert leaders, the wisest of all decision makers. Send the militarists back to the fields; send the liars to the toilets and bring on the wisemen, young or old it does not matter.

People will always have choice but they will have no taste for old ideas. The old vibrations will lose their flavour. If we truly want an era of exploration, discovery and possibility then I suggest that the stewards step forth and make sure that this reality system and all its inhabitants build a grand era of golden light.

My direction is golden. Make it your choice to enter the Golden Era, for it glows with boundless knowledge.

NUTRIMENTO

INTRODUCTION

Eating is something that you and I both do on a daily basis, but it is not always an easy thing to do. The most difficult part of eating is deciding what to eat.

If you were to think back to the last time you ate a meal, do you remember why you chose that particular meal? Are the foods you eat in your regular diet supplying your body what it really needs to function properly? Do you feel good?

For most of your life, you have either been given the foods you needed or you were simply told what to eat by your parents. As you grew older, you faced the inevitable decision to choose your own foods. And all the meanwhile, there was the pressure from the media with commercials and advertising that redefined what people ate; and influence from the scientific research with new discoveries in nutrition that changed the dietary laws people followed.

Something happened to the stability of the nutritional knowledge people once possessed and this has resulted in a modern society infested with a wide spectrum of dietary disease that kill and maim people.

We live in an age where people love shortcut meals. Yet good health cannot be achieved by taking the right shortcut. There is no shortcut. But there is an effective approach.

This approach recognizes the fact that the same healthy foods can affect two people differently.

A healthy diet is not a matter of speed and satiety. It'[s much more a matter of who is eating, why they are eating, what foods they are eating, when they, where they eat, and how they approach their choice and preparation of foods.

People are constantly bombarded with new information about diets and eating and it has become an aggravating and often frustrating event.

We are being told what to eat every day, but each source often contradicts the other. So, we need to gather our wits and learn how to make intelligent decisions when it comes to eating. We need to provide our bodies with the proper nourishment. And that's what *Nutrimento* is – nourishment for the body. After all, good *Nutrimento* really is the basics of feeling good on a daily basis.

The information in this book will guide you and help you to achieve the best dietary intake for yourself and your family, not just for today, but more importantly for the future.

The chapters have been designed so that you are able to learn some common sense skills to apply to your dietary habits. The information is intended to teach you how to analyze your own unique situation and use that to make more intelligent choices when it comes to food.

It does not matter what your ethnic or religious background is. This book deal with how to approach eating and how to apply it to your life no matter where you live. *Nutrimento* is globally-based and open to all cultures.

This book brings together some of the most important aspects regarding eating habits and crystallizes them into something universal, so that everyone can learn to enrich their own dietary habits.

I will often refer to the foods you eat with the word "diet." This is not to be confused with going on a "weight loss" diet or having a special diet due to an existing health condition.

A diet, in my opinion, is the short way of saying dietary intake. It is the food you eat on a regular basis. In fact, the Concise Oxford Dictionary gives the definition of diet as "the kinds of food that a person or animal habitually eats."

The material in this book is designed for you. In order to achieve the most lasting changes in your life you need to become involved with your diet. I encourage you to examine your history of eating habits in more depth.

This introspective process will only lead you to a better understanding of the foods you eat. You will view food differently. You will approach eating more effectively. You will see drinking differently. I believe that the information in this book can move you closer to eating foods that maximize your level of health.

Food, by its very nature, has been provided to give sustenance. The only medicine that can give your body long-term health is that which you feed it every day. It is my sincerest hope that this book will help to demystify the prejudices that are over food and instead offer something that is more truthful to the human race.

I am convinced from my own experience that the proper approach to eating is what makes the difference between health and disease in the long run.

I encourage you to read on and discover your personal approach to healthy eating by understanding the concept of *Nutrimento*.

CHANGING THE WAYS OF THE PAST

THE KEY TO HEALTHY EATING

People have forgotten why they eat. Most people have lost the whole notion of what is the correct balance of nutrition for their bodies.

Vegetarians claim the best way to a long and healthy life is by not eating any animal flesh. Others believe that eating fruit and organic produce is the ultimate health formula only when supplemented with an abundance of white fish and eggs.

Someone else might be thinking that eating a regular consumption of beef is the surest way to get iron into their blood. Still, others eat anything you put on their plate or anything you tell them. And what you end up with are high statistics on dietary diseases and thousands of clinics to support people who want to lost weight or gain back their long-lost health.

This is why billions of dollars every year are spent on diet programs, diet books and other diet paraphernalia. Say the word "diet" really fast tend times and you will reveal the secret of what diets for weight loss will do for you.

What has happened?! Why are there so many expert opinions on the subject of health?

All these professional opinions can be considered to be correct if you understand one key element that ultimately determines your health.

This key eludes many people until they finally reach those later years in life after all the damaging mistakes are made.

This important key is you.

Let me repeat that, the key to your health is YOU. You may be thinking that this logic is too simple, too rudimentary and I can understand why, but you will need to understand many other important characteristics about food and its effect on your body before being able to discern what you do and do not need.

Again, the key thing is that you must give yourself a unique diet plan based upon your personal characteristics. This is what you will learn in the coming chapters. If there is anything that is complex about this whole philosophy, it is the part about understanding what you do and do not need and when you need it.

Five important questions to ask

If you look at it at the most basic level, healthy eating can be accomplished by answering five questions – Who, What, When, Where and Why.

WHO

The first one asks the vital question, "Who is going to eat?" This is one you will learn about.

It is just like give a speech to an audience. Would you give the same speech to a bunch of eight year old kids as you would to a group of university professors? No, of course not, so you need to also establish who you are.

Not your identity, but your life habits and inherent bodily characteristics.

WHAT

The second question establishes, "What are you going to eat?" This is valuable as it can tell you what kind of effect food can have on your body based on your experience. You can also learn about the effects of food from other research or from friends with similar experiences.

WHEN

"When are you going to eat?" marks the third question and brings out the fact that eating foods is cyclical in nature. A newborn baby can only drink milk while any eight year old child has a much wider variety of food to choose from. Why? Different cycles.

You will find that your nutrient requirements will vary greatly throughout your life even throughout your day. By keeping in touch with your cycle you can stay on top of your needs.

WHERE

Imagine that you are stranded in the North Pole and have luckily found beside you, buried in a chunk of ice, a bucket of ice cream (insert your favourite brand here). Do you dare eat it and risk chilling your frostbitten body even more? Not a good idea if you want to stay warm.

What about if you were stranded on a deserted island in the middle of the South Pacific and happened upon the same ice cream, would you have it? Now, there's a better idea.

These examples point out the fourth question that asks, "Where are you eating?" Whether it is in tropical, arctic, subtropical areas or it is during a particular season of the year you will have to approach your eating habits differently. Again, different regions will require specific changes in your diet. Summer will also demand special nutrients from your body compared to that of winter and so on. Later in the book we will consider how to better understand the important of where you are going to eat.

WHY

The last question and just as important as the other four is "Why you eat?" This is one that many people fail to understand and one which we will talk about throughout the book. Eating is done for a reason.

We eat to nourish ourselves, to celebrate a joyous occasion and to heal our ailing bodies. We eat when we are in love, when we are depressed and when we are sad and when we are happy. We eat for a reason. Only you will really know why you eat but remember that there is a valid reason. If there is none (now think real hard first), then you need to question what you are doing.

Eating is a basic need that all living things share. It sustains life. It fuels your body so that you can continue to do the productive things you want to do and gives you the energy to heal your injured and aging body. It makes you happy.

There is a reason to eat – to live. To fuel your energy so that you can achieve your goals. If you find that you are feeding yourself bad foods that are poisonous to your body on an ongoing basis, then you need to re-establish the importance of eating.

Poisonous foods are foods that clog, slow down, putrefy and degenerate your bodily functions in any shape, way or form.

The ultimate key to healthy eating is you. Of course, there are skills you need to develop in order to be able to become more proficient at making proper food choices and adopting effective eating habits.

In the last part of this chapter you were introduced to the five basic questions – Who, What, When, Where and Why. Keep these in mind when you consider what to have for your next meal.

IN SEARCH OF A WELL BALANCED DIET

The very creation of the word "diet" has been focused upon those of us with weight problems. You have become overweight because you have become overweight because you have eaten the way marketers advised you to eat and now are unhealthy, obese, and need special packaged foods to restore your slenderness and health. Is dieting healthy?

To diet is to starve, and starving the body is quite hazardous to your health. What do you spell if you take off the "t" in "diet"? "Die," that's right, if you diet too much you will soon die from starvation.

Life's focus should not be on fat elimination and reducing caloric intake, but instead, on creating healthy eating habits. We need to focus on the positive, not the negative. Focus on new love. You must change your perception of a diet.

It is important to eat properly. This is what I refer to as a "diet." Proper food will nourish you. This is food that gives your body the sustenance it needs.

Food need not be organic to be good for you; instead, food should produce a beneficial effect on your body. All foods can be good. All foods can be bad. It depends who is eating them. If you eat properly and balance the other aspects of your life, then you will eventually achieve your optimal image and health.

Looking in all the wrong places

If people rationally knew what to eat, then do you think that they would continue to indulge themselves in this kind of degenerative eating? No. That's the big problem.

People do not know how or what or when or why to eat. They mainly rely on the media and other external news.

People have been taught to look for the number of calories in the food and to calculate the percentage of fat that is has. It is easy enough to read off the number of calories on the label of a packaged food, but what about "real" food?

If you buy a breast of chicken, a beef steak, a medium seized yam, a navel orange, some broccoli, an egg, a few tomatoes, or a filet of fish there is no label indicating the number of calories that the foods have.

So what do you do? You can take guess based on some pre-calculated averages found in a reference health book, but food is not a static thing.

What I mean is this, food grows under a myriad of influential variables such as the type of soil, season, level of pesticides used, plant variety, harvest time, etc.

I recently read an advertisement for a speciality produce company that stated their tomatoes have 80% more vitamins than regular tomatoes. These variables affect the final development of the food.

So what you end up with in the end are food that contain different levels of nutrients, including calories and fat and everything else we have grown accustomed to counting. Eating has turned into math.

I just at 852.3 calories today, of which only 90 calories were directly from fat, and burned off 35.7% during my workout, 20.2% from my conversation with my friend and reduced it a further 8% during an after dinner walk.

How would you go about calculating the number of calories and fat for the foods you eat? Good question.

The only way to do that now is to take it to a testing lab and have them test it for you before you eat it. It is the only way to ensure you eat the right level of calories, fat, and vitamins, etc. This assumes, of course, that you know how many calories and nutrients that you need.

This is also why processed food is so useful to a lot of people. It already contains the information they need to make their decision.

That is not the right path to good health. If all you eat is packaged food then you need to learn how to break away from relying on these "dead" foods and substitute them for "live" ones found at your local food grocer.

We must all learn to enjoy eating once again. We must learn balance. We must move away from current food thought and open up to our feelings.

People should not feel shameful for eating.

People should not feel bad for having an extra layer of fat.

Something is wrong here. People should be able to eat desserts and not feel guilty.

I encourage you to move towards your center and accept a new goal.

Eat with your feelings.

Traditional diet influences

This method of counting calories and nutrient levels is not so prevalent (although Western influence is having its effect with the dissemination of processed foods and the development of processing planets) in many other parts of the world.

Many older cultures have trusted their nutritional information to be passed down through the generations. Words of wisdom from the parents and grandparents whom the children respected.

In more traditional times, the influence on people's respective diets came from the family and the environment.

The former were usually tried and true methods of food combining and preparation. The latter was more of a coalition which they had to adapt to. There were no controlled scientific experiments to test the validity of the food traditions, only physical proof that it worked.

The health of the family was the best example. Often, if there were health problems in the family, then medical advice would be sought and that would be incorporated into the existing system.

You can imagine how much development can occur over even two or three generations whereby valuable knowledge on food was passed on.

In the case of bad eating habits, families would likely be more susceptible to "hereditary" diseases because of the passing of bad information.

It will be up to you to decide whether or not the information is good or not. Whatever the case may be, find what works for you and your family and use that as a starting point.

Cooking lessons anyone?

Think of someone you know that knows how to prepare, what you consider to be, a nutritious meal. It could be you, your mother, father, aunt, uncle, cousin, spouse, friend, or TV personality. It does not really matter who it is because when you consider that most of these people are not nutritionists, you will be amazed at what can happen further on down the road.

Anyone who spends a significant amount of time during their life either in the kitchen or at the dining table is bound to learn something about food. Some take longer than others to learn, but nevertheless they will learn what food has to offer for them.

The dominant cook in your house has to have some knowledge of food to cook a good, wholesome meal. Over the years, they learn many new things and incorporate them into their menu. This process of knowledge transfer continues to grow and grow until you eventually leave the household and venture forth on your own. It would be at that point that you begin experimenting on yourself and start deciding how much of your parent's informal nutritional philosophy to follow and how many other things you wanted to add on your own.

The passing down of nutritional information leads to bad eating habits and weak health.

We often blame genetics for human ignorance. Take control of the power of your human heritage. Take control of your diet.

In either case, you need to eat and' therefore, necessarily need to learn how to cook. It may be at either the basic or advanced level. When you get older you gain more experience in the kitchen and are able to feed your immediate family. If your spouse or other family member is more capable, then that function is probably better off left with them.

These foods and eating skills will be a compilation of your own personal experiences, that of your parent's and that from any external source, be it friends or the media.

As your generation moves on, they will carry many of these ideas with them. Even if you just consider your own particular situation you will only continue to use whatever ideas that work for you and that you believe in.

What people believe, unfortunately, are not always good eating habits unless there is a significant amount of understanding and support from the rest of the family members.

When this system goes accordingly, it filters ineffective eating habits and maintains those that work. There is no real need to scientifically test them because they undergo the most stringent tests through daily use. Scientific evidence can help to understand your own discoveries.

Some cultures place greater emphasis on maintaining their cultural traditions and have a higher percentage of transferring knowledge. You may be considering your own situation and feel that your family and friends do not know very much about nutrition. That is a valid complaint and could justify why you are reading this book.

In this case, you need to do some research on your own to increase your knowledge. Books, classes, and talking to food experts are all great starts. You will most often find that opinions on the subject of eating are very diverse and that you will need to do your own personal research on yourself in order to be able to understand it better.

I will provide the essential framework and foundation, but the work is up to you. I know that you have the ability and my book will work with you in your search.

When I used to work in a health food store, women would always ask me how they could lose weight and en would come in and ask how they could gain weight.
I usually recommended that the men and women get together to discuss what each other was doing to learn each other's secrets. In that way, the women would learn how to keep thin and the men could find out how to gain more weight. I am poking a little fun at the situation, but it's true.

Again, fashion and trends have dictated how people should look and understandably everyone wants to fit this image.

Recently, I watched a news program that did a spotlight on modeling. What was interesting here was that there was a modeling agency that recognized the value and realism of having what they termed a "normal" women modeling clothes. This particular model's figure was larger than the typical thin models.

After all, the woman who will buy those clothes is not likely
going to be as thin as the model demonstrating it.
Men and women are all unique and should stay that way.

Deciding what to eat

I remember watching a TV commercial once depicting two
young men and a lady who had just begun their lunch break.
You can imagine the typical downtown scene and three well-
dressed office personnel on the street curb.

One of them asked, "What do you feel like eating?" Another
answered, "I don't know, what do you feel like eating?"
Meanwhile, the third person looked at their watch and said,
"Okay, what are we going to eat for lunch?"

The commercial continued on like this until eventually their
lunch hour was completely exhausted and they had not gone
anywhere. Have you ever run into this problem of deciding
where and what to eat?

Perhaps your occupation allows you to have enough time to
have a good meal at home. I can agree that this would offer
you a relatively healthy selection of dishes to choose from, but
even then can you decided on a balanced meal for yourself?

Let's say you go to the restaurant and decide to have the
special of the day, a lightly grilled salmon steak with
horseradish sauce and steamed vegetables. This is a healthy
choice, but is it the right choice for you today? What I mean by
"today" is whether or not your body need s this type of
Nutrimento at this particular time.

Your body is composed of many elements that interact together
thousands and thousands of times per hour.

By being aware of what is happening on the outside of your
body and through monitoring the way you feel throughout the
day, you will discover that your body requires certain kinds of
foods to meet your personal nutritional requirements.

This goes a little farther than having fish for dinner because you
had chicken the night before, although that kind of variety is a
good start.

Thinking of food in another context

Food is much more than outlined in our national food guides and is composed of many more important characteristics than the total number of calories per gram. Both of these analyses have only touched the surface of eating a well balanced diet.

Nutrition information can be both helpful and disastrous. It all depends on where it is coming from and who is funding it.

In any case, you need to move away from the notion of popular thought. Just because a particular soft drink is found in every school and work location does not necessarily mean that it is good for you.

Food, need not only be considered because of its amount of fat, percentage of protein, levels of vitamins, and minerals or its fiber content.

Food needs to be thought of in the
context of your particular health needs
and how it will affect you.

This is what will constitute whether or not your health will benefit from your meal. As your body continues to fluctuate every day, month and year, you need to adapt and evolve with it.

Food that the body does not need will not benefit you and could harm your health. Just think about desserts. Your body may be okay with one slice of apple pie, but if you continue to eat an entire ten inch pie you will subsequently feel sick.

Eating an excess of what your body needs will also overburden and weaken your present state of health. When you eat too much of anything you risk discomfort.

Imagine if you thought that you needed some nutrition found in meat. You are sitting at a restaurant and are very hungry. The menu specialized in roast chicken, so you decided to indulge in a small herb roasted chicken.

You get so involved in the table conversation that you don't realize that you've over-eaten. You're stuffed and you didn't even finish your rice and vegetables.

You immediately find yourself tired and sleepy after dinner. It even gets a little embarrassing since your guest feel neglected when they finally get a chance to say something.

The next day your body feels sluggish and uncomfortable while at work. In this case, even though you may have been eating something your body could have used – chicken – you overate and offset your body's rhythm.

Different strokes for different folks

People have almost lost the meaning of a well balanced diet as they have lost touch with their nutritional needs. Just what is considered a good diet?

Ask a range of age groups from both men and women and you will most certainly get a myriad of different responses.

Each individual's dietary needs are different and this is why it is so important for people to be able to discern what is good for their body, in what amounts and when they should consume a particular food. If you don't take control of your diet then somebody else will.

Just look at all the books available on healthy eating and dieting that have spawned an incredible variety of believers. In truth, we could write a book for every person in the world, and update it every week.

There are the grapefruit dieters, vegetarians, fit-for-lifers, daily meal planners, organic food eaters, low-cal dieters, macro dieters, low-fat dieters, high carbo dieters and on and on and on. Every week you are certain to find another book on what to eat.

Not only that, but as scientists perform more research on the curative effects of food, such as with oat bran and its ability to reduce blood cholesterol, or the positive effects from chilli peppers on metabolism and fat digestion, the media will be sure to inform you on any new discoveries and companies will be sure to make it available to as many people as they can.

Eskimos and other Northern ice cultures eat seal and whale fate yet are healthy and slim despite their broad boned features. What should you tell an Eskimo? You can't eat the way that your culture has eaten since the beginning (even though you feel healthy), now all you can eat is lean chicken without the skin, steamed fish with a side salad containing no oil, and raw vegetables.

Or what do you tell an African tribesman? Stop eating elephant meat, try chicken instead – it's lower in fat and cholesterol. We need to recapture our focus. That's right! Recapture what once was – common sense.

I want to remind you that this book is not going to tell you what to eat. It simply cannot! Your bodily system is very different from mine and if you were to use my diet plan all the Tim then your body would be severely affected. Also, my own diet changes daily, weekly, and yearly. Nutrimento should not be **static**, it should be *dynamic*. The best diet changes as you change.

Every other book and lecturer try to instil their diet program on you and it can't work in the long run (or even the short run). It is time that you took control of your own health. What I will present to you in this book are the universal characteristics that human share regarding food. I will present alternative perceptions on regulating your diet by helping you to determine what your bodily demands are.

Missing a meal here and there cannot be helped, gorging yourself on hunger food happens, but the real killer is when you live a life of nutritional deprivation, excessive overindulgence, and dietary imbalance.

When you feed your body poorly all the time it will become inefficient. And the effects will not make you happy.

Let us continue the search.

WHY PEOPLE EAT

"I'm on a diet."
"That's all I know how to cook."
"I love the taste of it."
"I'm trying to lose weight."
"I don't really know why. I have never thought about it."
"It's good for you."

"Everything else is too oily."
"That's what s/he made for dinner."
"It's low in fat."
"It's low in sugar."
"It's low in calories."
"Who cares!"
"I like it."

This whole diet concept has to change. Your body demands certain daily nutrients depending upon your activity level and body composition. Out of all the foods in the world, how could you just eat one type or group of foods and get all the nutrition you need?

Every food has a purpose or nutritional value associated with them and their effects should be used accordingly.

The question I present to you now is, "why are you eating that food today?" Of all the food choices available, why do you choose to eat that particular type of food or meal?

If you were a nutritionist you might respond with some information regarding the protein to calorie ratio, the low-level of fat and perhaps something about the high source of vitamins and minerals. If you were a parent, you might say how it is good for your teeth or health in some way. These are great reasons on why to eat and to this I would like to add a more traditional approach. Allow me to give you some background first.

Cultural comparisons

In Northern China, students unanimously feel that too much protein is bad for their health and would lead to disease.

They also stress the shift from a high vegetable diet in the summer to an increase in meat consumption in the winter. The main reason is due to a lack of fresh green and other summer vegetables during the cold season, but they also comment on the ability of meat to heat the body. This would justify eating fewer green vegetables in winter and more meat (and root vegetables) to maintain health and proper body temperature. The Chinese students regularly eat organ meats and not only enjoy the taste, but consider them to be good for their health.

Popular notions about eating pork liver benefits a person's own liver function and eyesight.

So why do Chinese students eat? They invariably eat to nourish the body. They have the occasionally herbal soup that is generally believed to give their body greater health and protection from disease. Their parents are regarded as being knowledgeable on nutrition and the students enjoy their home cooked meals.

In North America, students tend to eat out of hunger. Food choices are made for taste or convenience. The food has to taste good and has to appeal to them.

Some people grew up eating organ meats as children and apparently enjoyed it until they got older and realized what they were eating. "I'm eating organ meats, yyuukkk! That's disgusting." After that, they felt sick with the thought of eating internal organs.

It is hard to say how much nutritional knowledge the parents of North American students really know, but whatever knowledge they possess is not being passed down to their children in the most effective form. Are you teaching your children about the nutritional value of food?

Eating for a reason

There are many reasons to why we eat. And it is these very same reasons that have unbalanced the dietary laws of our intuitive self.

Many of us eat just for the sake of eating, something to fill our stomach. Some people don't really care what they eat. Basically, if it is edible then it will suit their diet.

I remember one friend who loved to eat pasta so much that he would boil the pasta and then he would open a can of tomato soup and would just pour the uncooked and unheated soup onto the pasta as if it were a sauce. He gave whole new meaning to eating raw food. He has since changed his ways and now enjoys cooking his food first. He health is better than ever.

We avoid foods which are fattening or high in cholesterol to prevent gaining additional weight.

Weight love having plain salads or skipping meals altogether. We eat fast foods because we have no time in our schedule. This has fed the growth of fast food restaurants around the world. In turn, these restaurants develop their menus to keep you coming back for more.

We indulge ourselves in chocolate treats, heavy doses of ice cream and deep fried foods after starving ourselves. Then the results begin to show, rather begin to grow on our skin and around our waists.

This is a very dangerous position to take if you care about your health.

You need to learn to feed your body foods to complement your meals. We need balance.

Each individual's body is different and some will react to a careless diet better than others. The most convincing evidence will reveal itself fin the long run. Eventually, your body will grow weaker from bad service and will not be able to process the garbage that you continue to feed it. Later on in the book you will learn all that you need to know to make easy, positive changes in your existing diet.

A more traditional approach

When I was researching diet and nutritional therapies, I originally began to look into something that I was familiar with, namely vitamins and minerals.

As a young boy, I was taught to take vitamin and mineral supplements because they would fill any nutritional gaps in my diet and ensure that I had proper energy levels to accommodate my physical and mental activities.

Something that I discovered common among all the hundreds of nutritional books I began reading was that each of them had the exact same information.

Vitamin quantities were different based upon the writer's own experience and research, but inevitably all of these books stressed good dietary habits based on the food's chemical breakdown and what the particular vitamins and minerals did. So, for example, it would recommend eating carrots to get more Vitamin A and broccoli for Vitamin C.

People interested in their health read these books and discover how all of the good sources of vitamins and minerals are distributed in the different food groups.

Soon people begin eating foods for their perceived nutritional values like drinking milk because of its calcium, eating spinach for its iron, having yogurt for its Vitamin K, and eating lamb chops for the zinc.

People who are too busy or do not really care for this "health conscious" information quickly lose interest after a couple of weeks. I mean, you have to be a doctor to be able to remember all of the details concerning vitamins and minerals.

When you take Calcium you should take Magnesium and Vitamin D to aid absorption with a two to one ratio. Want some Vitamin E capsules? Then you will need to have Selenium and make sure that the Vitamin E is in the form of d-alphatocopherol. And hence the introduction of Multi-Vitamins.

But this is a shotgun approach. People take in a massive amount of supplemental doses and hope that some nutrients are needed and absorbed.
Normally, people learn a handful of vitamins and minerals and then move on to more interesting things in life.

Just counting the vitamin and mineral content of food is unnatural.

Food contains live enzymes and other life giving, synergistic qualities that provides your body with unmatched nutrition. As our bodies are lively, biological organisms that interact and are intimately connected with Earth's environment, it only makes sense that we consider food as more than just the sum of its contents. Life feeds life.

Now let's get back to that more traditional approach I mentioned a few pages back. What you need to begin with is to learn how a particular food affects your body and under what conditions. When you examine how a certain type of food is affecting you, it is the beginning of your moving towards your goal of controlling your nutritional health.

I'll use milk and lamb chops as food examples to demonstrate this initial step into learning the effects of food.

Many people drink milk around the world. If cow's milk is not your favourite choice, then perhaps you drink goat's milk or even soya milk. At this point, you need to try to understand what this milk does for you.

Ask yourself how the milk makes you feel. Do you get bloated? Energized? Constipated? Relaxed? Warm? Cold? Upset stomach?

What does the milk do for you on any particular day?

Thinking about these kinds of questions when you drink will lead you to the path of greater understanding of what you are putting inside your body. Later on in the book we will look at deeper issues surrounding eating and drinking.

Okay, how about the lamb chops. Again, you may not eat a lot of lamb chops; instead, consider other types of meats, such as pork, beef, chicken, and even fish. When you ate the meat, did you feel better or worse after?

How much of it did you have?

Did you just finish listening to a new scientific discovery on what you ate?

Were there any particular tastes left inside your mouth after?

What time of day did you eat?

What was the season or weather that day?

What did you have to drink with your meat and how much did you have?

How was the meat prepared?

If you continue to ask yourself these kinds of questions while eating, over a period of time you can learn about a large variety of foods. It is not that difficult. After you learn about the initial score of them, one kind or type every week thereafter should suffice.

It is important to learn about food because in order to make good decisions about the way you eat, you need to understand what specific foods can do for you. This is something that everyone can use with only minimal memorization and relies more on personal observations.

Prevention is the best medicine: revisited

There is a saying that a teacher of mine taught me, "Pay me now or pay me later" (It is an adopted advertising spiel). In relation to health, as young people enjoy their life with little concern for their bodies, they end up paying for any mistreatment in their later years. Ask someone who has heart disease or colon cancer and find out how much they looked after their health when they were young.

The connection between diet and heart disease is very strong. You will find that there is inevitably a strong correlation between what people eat over a long period of time and their disease or illness.

Excessive emotional stress, environmental conditions and exercise are also closely involved thought it is not in the scope of this book to explore these areas. These additional factors usually affect your diet in one way or another.

Have you ever been under an extreme amount of emotional stress like a death in the family, relationship break up, or loss of your job? It is very likely that your appetite was not the same as normal. Also, your choice of foods was probably quite a bit different. You may have lost your appetite. Maybe you turned to drinking excessive amounts of coffee or alcohol. Desserts could have been your friend.

This raises another point concerning disease. The trouble facing everyone trying to eat a well balanced diet is that the initial beneficial effects are small, if any, in the short run.

No quick results here folks! Not only that, but people tend to cover or mask the ill effects from bad eating habits with modern medicines.

These medicines often delay the consequences of bad eating and make a simple situation worse in the future.

As an example, we can look at the case where a person regularly relies on fast food for a meal. They often get indigestion by the end of the day and have a handy-dandy bottle of stomach medicine to soothe their tummies. Either that or any other number of products that are designed to help relieve their discomfort.

Normal short term side effects can include; headaches, indigestion, flatulence, stomach pain, difficulty in sleeping, lack of energy, lack of mental concentration, skin rashes, acne, hair problems, hyper-activity, mood swings, constipation, and bloating. These are the more common symptoms, but the list can go on even more (there is a longer list in the next chapter).

I have friends that get a headache if they don't eat for more than 8 hours. Some of them grab a coffee loaded with sugar and their headache goes away only to return with greater force later.

Another person I met, Jennifer, lost the ability to concentrate after going without food for more than half a day. She would act incompetent and lacked common sense. After some food in her stomach she go back her senses.

The bottom line is that these discomforts are temporary and can be remedied with non-prescription drugs found in your local pharmacy or, more easily, **just food**.

The real problems come when you continue to abuse your diet over an extended period of time.

If a relationship isn't working out between two people then little signals will pop up. This might include arguments, lack of affection, and fault finding. If left alone the problems become worse.

So, in the short-term you can avoid each other a little more or find affection in somebody else without telling your partner (not a good thing to do). But without trying to solve the problems the inevitable will happen – breakup or divorce.

When we look at the long-term effects we begin to see how crazy it was to have disregarded our health as we did when we were young. It doesn't take much to realize that the average age of those with earth disease is over forty.

Organs are integral parts of your body and break down after misuse.

These diseases don't just appear overnight. Dietary diseases aren't contagious like colds.

They are the direct result of a life not in harmony with your body. It hurts to see people die of something they brought upon themselves unknowingly.

If there is one thing that this book is about it the underlying belief that prevention is the best medicine. As the age-old saying goes, "An ounce of prevention is work a pound of cure."

My own take on this is, "An ounce of food is worth a week on medication."

It is extremely difficult and painful to cure a disease once it has assumed its role in your body as I'm sure many of you who have had an illness can attest.

It is much wiser and easier to spend a few extra minutes a day to maintain healthy habits, than it is to spend your whole day fighting for your life.

Someone once said, "We spend the first half of our lives getting money and paying with our health; we spend the second half of our lives getting healthy and paying with our money."

This is definitely something to think about.

Professionals can teach you about what the different types of foods do to your body and recommend certain dietary restrictions based on their observations of you. In other words, a nutritionist might be able to realize that a patient is consuming too much bad food and; therefore, they can suggest and even prescribe a diet plan for you to follow to prevent any disease.

What they are unable to do is to know what is happening to you body on a daily basis and it is this important factor that will be relevant. Now, I'm not talking about those patients who have a serious condition and require strict dietary controls from a medical professional.

What I am talking about here is you. If you want to know what you should or should not eat, then you need to start paying attention to your body's needs.

People eat for a reason. A group of students in Northern China ate to nourish themselves while a select group of Canadians ate simply out of hunger.

Why do you eat? Is it because what a nutritionist told you? Or is it from what your parents taught you?

With good food, you will not only feel good, but you will also prevent many dietary-related diseases from entering your body.

Spend some time now considering why you eat the foods you eat now. Ask yourself how those particular foods benefit you. Also, consider if there are foods that might be better for your health and how you can incorporate them into your current diet.

PREPARING FOR THE FUTURE

UNDERSTANDING YOUR BODY

People tend to rely on scientific discoveries and lab experiments to teach them about how their bodies react to different kinds of food. What proof does science have? Experiments on rats and other animals; a controlled study of a select group of humans.

These methods can provide you with circumstantial evidence about how your body operates, but don't you want something more?

The strongest and most convincing that explains the benefits and consequences of eating food comes from the human experience. Your experience.

The information recorded from the past. Your experience with your body today. This is what you must to believe.

Not just another headache

One of my teachers would always try to explain the concept of listening to the body. He would show me in subtle ways how I could hear what my body was saying.

In the beginning, I had no idea what he was talking about. I grew up believing what science dictated and sometimes relied on its temporary cures. He continued to reveal to me the fundamental concepts of listening with only just enough said to make me aware that this ability was there. Two years passed before I began to understand more clearly, since I initially didn't take it very seriously.

As a young boy, I experienced severe headaches every day. I did not understand why and refused to use medication to subdue it.

Eventually, I succumbed to the use of headache medicine. There was no other choice at the time.

I soon found that the medicine available at the drug store was not strong enough to eliminate the pain in my head.

I received some prescription medication and began my first step into the world of reliance on drugs.

It proved to be my last step also because as soon as I realize that I had come under the control of a drug I couldn't allow myself to continue. This was not a common reaction to pain relief as I turned to face the pain again.

I was lucky to have been involved in martial arts training at the time as it took my mind off of the pain. My body was experiencing all kinds of other pain from the training and I learned to redefine pain.

It used to be that when there was discomfort in my body, I labelled it as pain. I found that once a label was placed on the discomfort, my body began to react and shift to "deal" with it.

After a period of years, my body was a trained expert at distorting itself at the sign of any pain. It would have been more interesting to train it into an Olympic gymnast when I now think back.

About two years later, I was stretching out after a discussion during one of my classes and my teacher came up to me and asked me, "How's your headache?" I quickly answered back that I had none and continued to stretch.

Suddenly it struck me that I did not have any headaches and that I had not had any for a long time.

I rushed to ask my teacher why he asked such an obscure question, but he avoided my question with yet another question.

I gave it some thought later and realized that I had changed many aspects of my life including the elimination of unnecessary stress, incorporating physical exercise and a drastic improvement in my diet.

When you have a headache, for example, do you think it is just some mysterious pain in your in your head that is quickly eradicated by strong headache medicine? Or can it actually mean something?

What if it indicated that one of your internal organs as not functioning properly and that your body was telling you something important. All that you would have done is put your system on "mute." The pain would still be there, but you would not be able to heart it or feel it.

Your body is trying to say something

The body is known to speak a unique language; one that many people fail to understand or hear. It is this unique tongue that you need to learn to speak. This is the first step in understanding your body – **to understand what it is trying to say**. When you can speak the language, you will be able to communicate better and can help to alleviate any problems it has.

How does understanding what your body is saying relate to food?

236 TCB Vol. II

Have you ever heard people speak another language in front of you or on TV and you didn't have any idea what they were saying? You are not always conscious of how fluent you speak your native or first language. It is not until you are thrust into a foreign country or similar arrangement that you realize you don't understand what is being said or how things operate and that your native language is not very useful.

At that point you have a couple of choices. One, you could learn to speak the new language. This would require some effort on your part, but you do have the option between learning enough to get by and obtaining total fluency and, of course, anywhere in-between.

Two, you could ask someone to help translate for you. This can range from hiring a personal translator to making a few friends who can speak both languages.

You can also use some of your creativity to maximise and make the best of your predicament. Once you have some tools to assist you, or alternatively learn the foreign language, everything becomes so much easier.

Food has long been considered important in understanding diseases of the human body. Before your body will become afflicted with any disease you will first receive a number of messages that will try to alert you that there is a problem.

The cause of the problem may be stress related or it may come from emotional aspects of your life, whatever the case may be your diet will be affected.

Once this happens, you will deprive your body of the vital nutrients it needs to deal with this unwanted stress in your life and you will begin this downward spiral towards illness.

Once disease sets in it takes a long time, and is very difficult, to remove.

The key is to prevent the disease from ever grasping a hold on your body. An ineffective diet produces many symptoms in an effort to convey its message to you.

The systems listed on the next page are good early warning signals that will allow you to remedy any imbalance that may be present. You will need to think about your current eating habits in order to piece together the solution. If you have a chronic condition, then a more in-depth analysis may be needed.

Do not neglect to research other possible causes. Your diet is the foundation of your health and can address problems better in the early stages as well as maintaining and rebuilding weaknesses over the long term.

Your body requires time to completely regenerate serious areas of neglect and will likely require some additional help in the form of special nutrition, exercises, and lifestyle changes.

SYMPTOMS THAT HAVE BEEN ASSOCIATED WITH AN INEFFECTIVE DIET

Restlessness, Mental depression, Abdominal pain, Bloating, Cramps, Gas, Diarrhea, Constipation, Bad breath, Headaches, Lack of energy, Frequency of illness, Urinary problems, Feeling cold, Swollen tongue, Facial color, Mood swings, Emotional extremes, Insomnia, Excessive dreaming, Food cravings, Sexual appetite, Tooth cavities, Nasal congestion, Sinus trouble, Poor eyesight, Skin rashes, Poor concentration, Burping, Inconsistent stools, Dry lips, Dry skin, Oily skin, Pimples, Slowed healing, Headache, Dry hair, Excessive ear wax, Finger nail health, Food allergies, Cysts, Obesity, Underweight, Chest pain, Stress control, Aggressive behaviour.

Time for a check up

In order to understand your body better, I have developed an inspection list that you can go through.

The list of major items on the following pages is designed to be simple, yet it contains essential areas about yourself that you can examine in your own privacy. Should you need help in assessing your current level of health there is always a partner you could draft to point out what concerns them.

You will find that the next few pages do contain some terms and actions that may initially sound offensive you to take them into consideration.

Be patient and persistent.

Just like it takes time to appreciate good music, trying to understand some of the basic bodily observations will require a bit of time also. Your awareness will enable you to take charge of your own health.

Here is an inspection list that you can perform daily:

EXTERNAL OBSERVATIONS

Facial Considerations

Your face can display many of the imbalances in your body if you know what to look for.

The basic areas on the face to be aware of are the color and the texture of the skin. The color of the skin indicates the health of our internal organs.

People try to cover the paleness of their faces with cosmetics and suntans. That is all right as long as they are also adjusting their diet or lifestyle to eliminate whatever is causing that color change.

The source of the paleness needs to be addressed or at the very least taken into consideration.

The point is if you notice that your face is very pale, then you want to be more aware of eating foods that will bring that color back. Spend some time thinking about which foods help and which foods make it worse.

Some people find eating more meats and more nutritious foods and cutting back on the raw vegetables and "skimpy" meals helps with their facial color while others may discover that some other dietetic adjustment is more beneficial. Try to find the right balance for yourself.

The texture of the skin should be relatively smooth. Not everyone has silky smooth skin, but it should be free from chronic pimples and acne.

Skin eruptions such as those are indications that there is more waste in the body than it is able to handle. This can be the direct result of eating an excess of bad foods (for your body in particular).

In addition, eating an excessive amount of other foods can overburden the body and it will use your skin to eliminate what it can.

You can help your skin by incorporating a wider variety of food in your diet. The healthiest skin grows from the inside. Why don't we try to find the right foods to do that.

Body Temperature

The degree of heat your body generates can give you some indication of your health.

The hands and feet are good areas to look at. Warm hands and feet are desirable. When the hands and feet are cold on a regular basis you need to examine your diet more closely.

The condition of your hands can also indicate bad circulation. A check with the doctor may be in order.

Again, if you have had chronic problems with cold hands and feet even sometimes to the point of numbing, then take a look at the regular foods you eat. Some change is necessary.

A young girl named Betty was always cold. Her hands and feet felt like she had been standing outside for a few hours during a cold winter without a jacket. The iron part was that it was in the middle of a warm summer.'

She explained to me that she always had this problem. I asked about her diet and she privately told me that she didn't eat meat and mainly ate raw or lightly cooked vegetables. She also enjoyed eating fruit and drinking lots of water. She said that she drank at least eight glasses of water a day as she had been told.

Her legs and feet would go numb occasionally because her diet was out of balance. When she added light portions of meat, reduced here water intake, and cooked her vegetables she found that her cold hands and feet occurred less often.

Odor

Your body has a certain smell attached to it that is related to the type of food you give it.

Strong smells can signal a discharge of waste products usually in the regions of the feet, groin or the armpits. An over consumption of animal food and dairy products will produce a fairly strong odor in these regions.

To return things to normal, try reducing your consumption of them and incorporate more vegetables and fruit.

Other foods like garlic also produce a certain body odor so keep your eye on your food and your nose on your odor to keep things in check.

Your body odor is indicative of your cultural tradition. Remember this when you experience other cultural situations, since you will notice that each corner of the world may share a distinctive odor.

This is not to say that anything is wrong with your diet or anyone else's for that matter, but that you can expect a difference.

It may also answer any lingering questions you may have about how the body produces different odors according to the diet.

Washroom habits

Number One

This title is not referring to the first subheading under washroom habits, rather it is a term used by children and younger adults when talking about having to urinate.

The number of times you urinate on a daily basis can tell you whether or not you are eating and drinking the required amount.

Eastern doctors have found that women should urinate two to three times per day and men three to four times. You can learn to be the judge. More frequent urination indicates that too much liquid is being consumed.

The color of the urine should be light gold or amber in color. Urine that is too dark or brown in color results from eating an excessive amount of meat, grain or salt. When the color is clear like that of water, then you need to reduce your intake of water and even sugar.

Someone that is going to the washroom more than five times per day either has a medical condition, an unbalanced internal system, or is simply drinking too much.

When you urinate too much you can overwork your organs (especially your kidneys and bladder) and weaken them. You can also spend the major part of you day visiting the washroom.

Number Two

As the number increases so does the level of involvement. This title refers to having a bowel movement. This is also known as "taking a dump" by many Western men and "going to bathroom" by many women.

Bowel movements are excellent indicators of diet health. Animals are known to smell their feces to check "things" out. I am not suggesting that you do this, but at least pay some attention to the consistency of your feces.

Check to see if they are watery or hard? Normal feces have a different consistency depending upon your diet.

Usually, heavy meat eaters will find that their feces sink to the bottom of the toilet while those who eat more vegetable proteins find their feces tend to float closer to the surface of the water.

Consider also the frequency and odor of visiting the washroom during Number Two. Going to the washroom once or twice per day is normal; once a week is a bad sign. Feces that have a very strong odor indicates that they have been inside you too long. Introduce more fibrous foods if this is a chronic problem and consider adjusting some of your lifestyle habits.

Whatever you do just try to keep the bowels moving and keep your insides clean.

If you are eating a lot of food on a daily basis you need to make sure that you are also eliminating a significant amount of waste. If you are not, then you may be polluting your body with unwanted waste products left over from the excess food.

Also, for those small eaters who only eat "skimpy or light salads, fruits, and the like, you will need to consider that your waste will not be as much as those who eat regular "full-sized" meals.

Another item besides the amount of waste relates to the fitness of your elimination system. Your intestines have muscles that allow it to move the waste. These muscles are best worked when there is sufficient bulk moving through them.

A diet high in watery foods such as fruit, vegetables, and salads does not always provide the bulk needs. Consequently, intestinal walls will become flaccid and your elimination system will be hampered.

You need to provide bulk foods in your system on a daily basis. Usually, the best ones come from grains. These include cereal grains such as rice, wheat, corn, and their subsequent forms – bread, pasta, and cooked rice.

Constipation

This is another important symptom to look at. This one can be held responsible for many diseases of the modern world.

When your bowels are not eliminating regularly you are polluting your body with toxic waste. People eat food that is devoid of dietary fibre and water and consequently slow down their elimination system. Many times constipation stems from the lack of eating a sufficient amount of food or very irregular eating habits. When this is the cause, the body never has a consistent amount of digested food moving through its intestines.

People can also find themselves under mental and emotional stress. These non-food related causes should be looked at differently. Try to get some exercise, rest, make some decisions, and get to the source of your troubles.

If your body isn't eliminating regularly you are setting yourself up for disaster. When you are constipated your elimination system needs attention.

Learning to listen

You must learn to get in touch with your body. You need to understand the language it speaks and the warning signs it gives out; otherwise, you are bound to end up living with disease.

It is difficult to adopt healthy principles when nothing is wrong, but it is almost useless to adopt healthy principles when you are dying.

When you are making $10,000 a month, it is not very easy to save large portions of your paycheck. It is much easier to spend and buy things that you have needed and wanted for a long time. Especially new cars, new clothes, jewellery, fancy dinners, etc.

The problem occurs when the money runs down to $800 a month. At that point it is impossible to save money as most of it is going to pay for life's necessities like rent and beans.

So which is better? Saving when you are making or saving when you are scraping?

It does not require very much money to build up a large nest egg by retirement age. The key is to save a little every month or every check. Over a period of years it amounts to a significant savings.

By the same token, if you were to get in debt $300 every month, eventually you would amass a large debt over your head that would be almost impossible to pay off in one lump sum. Say it lasts 10 years. Your total debt is $36,000 without interest.

Owing that on your credit card, even before interest is applied, would be nearly impossible to pay off immediately.

Your body's health is not much different in theory, but more important. When you look after your health a little every day you should say relatively healthy and free from disease in later life. When you neglect your body a little every day, eventually toxins will build up and disease will develop. But middle age you will be afflicted with life threatening disease that will require most of your time and money to eradicate and even then there is no guarantee that it will go away before you old age will catch up to you.

If ever you want to remind yourself how debilitating sickness and diseases are just take an afternoon off and take a walk inside a medical hospital.

This is reality. This is life. Value it before you lose that precious health you have.

Your body is speaking to you all the time. Some days it is just letting you know that everything is all right and other days it is trying to tell you something more important.

Learning to understand what your body is saying can only help you look after it better.

The next time that you feel abdominal pain, take a few minutes to try things that make it feel better. You may find lying in a certain position or drinking a certain beverage helps.

Or you may find that just eating a lighter meal for dinner will make your abdominal discomfort go away faster.

Whatever it is, knowing what works and does not work can only serve you better in the future.

In a last chance scenario you may want to ask your body what it is trying to say, "Can you repeat that please, I didn't quite get it the last time?"

I am certain that it will reply with increasingly greater intensity until you get the message.

The power of adaptation

Your body is alive. It is continually adjusting and reacting to the environment around it.

Humans and animals can adapt to almost any situation given time. That is why Eskimos are able to survive the harsh cold climate in the Arctic North; by the same token, Hawaiians have little problem with living in hot temperatures of the South.

If you were an Eskimo and were enticed to stay in Hawaii for a large sum of money (assuming you are motivated by money) you might go there, but would instantly find that the 35 degrees Celsius heat is unbearable. Likewise, if you were born and raised in Hawaii you might decline even large sums of money before deciding to freeze in the Arctic North.

People who have traveled to different parts of the world can attest to the fact that you need to stay in a local climate for some time in order to give your body a change to acclimatize.

Professional athletes are quite familiar with allowing their body time to adjust to the new climate. The greater the difference from their home climate, the greater the difference in their performance. Given time to adjust, they can fair much better.

A similar situation occurs when an athlete travels from sea level to above sea level for competition. The air is thinner in the higher regions and an athlete might find themselves more easily short of breath.

On the other hand, those coming from a higher altitude to a lower altitude will be even better off because their lungs have been accustomed to thinner air and will benefit from the higher ration of oxygen at sea level.

It's an everyday thing

In Cozumel, Mexico, a small island off the coast of Cancun, I was on a snorkelling excursion over the beautiful coral reefs.

The scene was picture perfect, blue sky, warm weather, and a slightly cool breeze brushing over the warm water.

The young Mexican in charge of our snorkel group was able to dive in and stay under water for three to four minutes at a time.

I was absolutely amazed, as submersion under water was not one of my strengths.

Not only that, but his young man was able to dive down to a level of over twenty five feet.

Later on, I asked him how he was able to perform such a feat and he said that six months ago when he started he couldn't dive for than one minutes. Because he had to dive everyday he was able to extend his duration and depth under water until eventually all he used was a diving mask to give him a better view.

Adapting to a given diet works the same. People who have been eating canned goods and fast foods for a long time will have become used to that type of dietary intake.

If they were to change to a diet full of raw vegetables and no meat their body would most certainly react adversely in the initial stages, but given time would adjust to the new diet.

Someone who has been eating wholesome cooked food at home for their entire life will discover that fast foods and canned food are tasteless, dull, and unsavoury. Whatever your particular case may be, try to maximize your health.

Growing accustomed to your diet

When I was traveling in Beijing, China, my university group went to a famous fast food restaurant. The majority of our group had no problem choosing what to order, but there was an interpreter with us who had never eaten Western fast food.

She decided, after some friendly advice, to order one of the burger specialities. Let it suffice to say that she had only finished her second bite before she left it for morbid. She couldn't understand how anyone could actually eat something like that.

It gave her indigestion.

When I talked with her later, I discovered that she always ate her mother's cooking and only sometimes went out for a restaurant meal. She credited her mother as being very knowledgeable about nutrition and would consult with her if she had any questions on the subject.

I could see that she had grown accustomed to freshly prepared and cooked food and had no appetite for anything else.

Despite these deterrents, if she was forced to eat that type of food her body would eventually adjust. Your body will adapt to whatever you regularly feed it because it wants to stay alive.

Try to think back to when you were younger and the kinds of foods you ate. Pick a period in your life when your diet was much different from that of today. Can you see yourself ever eating those same foods again? If not, then how did you put up with them so long ago?

Maintain a healthy regimen

Your body is speaking all of the time. Sometimes it is just informing you how things are and other times it is trying to relay an emergency message to stop from doing something destructive. By performing your daily body inspections you can keep a closer eye on your body.

It may take some time to understand all of the signals, but once your routine check up is in place it is quite easy to monitor it.

The foods that you eat on a daily basis will become part of your regular diet. It is up to you to discern whether or not it is a healthy regimen.

No matter what you habitually eat, your body will find a way to adapt to it so that it can continue to function, but depending on the negative severity of your dietary it may only be able to endure the situation for a short period of time.

Feed it good, balanced meals and you will teach it to recognize bad, unhealthy ones.

Understanding the language that your body is speaking is an integral part of eating properly.

When you can communicate, you can receive information. And when you have the necessary information you should be able to do what is needed to keep your body happy and healthy.

THE THREE FOOD BELIEFS

People of all ages, shapes, and sizes hold certain beliefs about food that ultimately determines what they choose to eat.
We don't behave very well when it comes to food choices.

When I researched more deeply into people's eating habits, I discovered that the reasons people ate certain foods and avoided other ones were very inconsistent.

We often choose foods based upon our believe systems rather than choosing foods based on our bodily needs.

Some people avoid eating meat because the thought and sight of meat makes them feel sick. They usually end up becoming vegetarians. Other people choose foods because of its low fat and oil content. Vegetables and fruits are the popular choice here since these foods don't contain any additional fats and oils.
Every day you are faced with the decision of what to eat. It is a lifelong habit that all of us must master. What do you see when you look at food?

What you inevitably decide to eat is wholly supported by what you believe the food has to offer.

Whatever the case may be, you need to examine your food beliefs more closely. There are, at present, three key **beliefs** about food.

BELIEFS

1. CONTENT
2. RELATIONSHIP
3. EFFECT

1. Content belief

The chemical makeup of foods includes the five basic chemical components; protein, carbohydrate, vitamins, minerals, and fats. Anytime you are looking at these components in isolation you can determine if the food can provide the nutrients that you need.

So, as an example, if your existing condition requires you to incorporate more foods that contain the mineral zinc, then you can research into foods that are good sources of zinc such as, pork loin, eggs, and lamb chops. Need foods high in Vitamin C, then you can look into citrus fruits and broccoli. It is a relatively straight-forward system.

The content of food as a whole can also help determine what specific value the food has for you. By looking at the level of fat in a particular dish you can decide with greater accuracy whether or not it is a good idea to eat. The catch is that by solely basing your decision to eat something on content alone can prove to be disastrous.

Various research and studies often provide scientific proof that the net benefit of certain foods works. Unfortunately, a drawback to this occurs when contradictory research is conducted and the results conflict with earlier findings.

More than twenty years ago, margarine was introduced as a healthier, low-in-fat alternative to butter. It gained popularity and is enjoyed by many still today.

In more recent years, people have come to learn that the hydrogenated oils and additives in butter substitute spreads have detrimental effects not found in the more natural form of butter. As a result, other types of healthier spreads have surfaced.

It would have been better to moderate their butter intake rather than to intake a synthetic spread. The focus was on the fat content of butter and since margarine is made of oil that is lower in fat, the natural conclusion was to eliminate butter.

About fifteen years ago a connection was made between drinking coffee and pancreatic cancer. Five years later, after scaring coffee drinker away from their morning beverage, further studies were unable to replicate any of the original findings.

The content of food is more useful when it is used to protect one's health. This is practical for people with existing food allergies, medical conditions or for those on healing programs.

Food allergies exist in all parts of the world. By ensuring that your meal is devoid of what you are allergic to, you can prevent an allergic reaction. You can also include minute amounts of the food that you are allergic to so as to build up immunity against them.

By the same token, if you are a diabetic or are taking medication you need to be careful that you do not eat foods that conflict with your medical condition.

When you know that your body is deficient in essential fatty acids (EFA)or you need to increase your level of protein intake, then by examining the content of the food you can again support your healing program.

2. Relationship belief

The relationship between food and what it will do for you based upon your personal experience has a dramatic effect on what you choose to eat on a regular basis. There are three general categories to consider.

First, think about the familiarity of the food s you eat. You will prefer to do things that make you feel comfortable. A familiar neighbourhood is more mind-settling than one that is strange and mysterious. A familiar friend over a stranger. A familiar job is preferred over an unfamiliar one.

Likewise, food has similar feelings accompanying them. When you have been eating a certain diet for a long period of time it is very easy to continue eating that same diet.

As some of you have fond out, it can be stressful changing diets just as it can be stressful changing other aspects of your life, but afterwards, assuming the change is for the better, you feel more comfortable and are happier.

So, if you are eating foods based upon their familiarity to you, then you may want to pay some attention to them to discern whether or not they are what your body needs, instead of being what you usually eat.

Taste is the second important consideration. Everybody wants to eat foods that taste good, but people must be careful not to sacrifice good taste for good nutrition.

How many of you like ice cream?

I know that it tastes good, but can you eat ice cream three times a day instead of other foods? No. Why? Because ice cream does not contain balanced levels of nutrition.

Many modern and processed foods are designed specifically to taste good. It is easy to eat foods because of their taste and it is even easier when your diet is not in balance because your cravings will control your tastes.

As you eat foods that are low in nutrition and high in taste, your bodily system becomes imbalanced and begins to continue to crave those same foods. Eventually, your body reaches a state of bad health and it is time for serious dietary changes.

Should food taste good to be good for you? Of course, but also consider the nutrition aspect.

Third, consider the overall benefit of your regular meals. Some people eat foods because they believe that those foods are good for them.

They do not specifically know what the food will do, but realize that certain foods are nutritious. Or they have justified their diet to suite their life.

This criteria really depends upon your cultural and family background. Dairy foods are generally embraced in many European countries and North America while it is often avoided in Asian countries.

In fact, both regions of the world can be seen as holding conflicting beliefs, but in their own respective ways those beliefs are partly ingrained in the culture and partly in the historical benefits of milk.

Food can do one of either two things for you – poison you or nourish you.

In fact, one food can have a different effect on two different people. Much of this effect does depend upon your body and your mind.

Think back to a time when you were much younger than you are now. Try to remember what you used to eat. Ask your parents or grandparents you used to eat. Ask your parents or grandparents if you need help recollecting.

If you believe that by eating a particular kind of food will make you fat, feel sick or vomit and that belief is strong enough it can induce those beliefs into reality.

By the same token, believing that another type of food will provide a positive overall benefit to your health can allow you to safely eat some less healthy alternatives. To see how this is real just consider what people were eating during World War II.

In war torn countries, people ate whatever they could and survived.

They didn't have time to complain about the food except to say that there usually wasn't enough. War prisoners held in camps were often starved of food for days before they were allowed to have some soup and bread or rice porridge.

What was amazing was the strength of the human spirit and mind because people held the general belief that **any food was good**. The alternative was to have no food and that would certainly result in disease and a quicker death.

3. Effect belief

Food does more than just provide you with nutrients. It has an effect on your body. The effect can determine how beneficial the end result is from what you've eaten.

There are five categories of effects that people will feel from eating certain kinds of foods. These effects will be found in varying degrees.

The effects foods have on your body will also change according to your present state of health. The important point at this stage is to increase your awareness of the basic effects.

THE FIVE FOOD EFFECTS

1. *Warming*
2. *Cooling*

3. *Relaxing*
4. *Energizing*
5. *Cleansing*

Warming

Foods that are considered warming are those that increase your body temperature and bring back feelings of warmth in your warmth in your hands and feet. Some people experience a little reddening in the face.

Warming foods are good when warmth is desired during cold weathers and certain illnesses. When you are already warm, it is best to cut down your consumption of foods that produce this effect.

Cooling

Many times cooling foods make you feel more balanced internally.

It can correct any disturbances in the body.

Cooling foods stabilize you internally. Sometimes you eat too many chilli-laden, BBQ'd, deep friend or other warming foods, for example, and you can eat something cooling to neutralize the bad effects.

Relaxing

When you eat foods that relax you, it's more of a general feeling of calm and peace.

Relaxing foods are an important part of your diet because they provide the foundation with which to control your eating habits. You can eat them in large amounts. Many are staples like rice, grains, breads, pasta, corn, wheat, etc.

Energizing

With the excessive amounts of energy demanded by our lifestyles every day, many people could use foods that are energizing.

They are more nourishing to your body and can also be quite stimulating.

It is better to rely on nourishing foods over stimulating ones in the long run. This is because the stimulation will be a temporary reaction in your body such as seen from the effects of alcohol, sugar, or caffeine.

On the other hand, nourishing foods provide nutrients that the body can sue to rebuild and heal and this will benefit the body more completely.

If energy is a continuing problem you may consider looking at balancing your life more to incorporate more mental and spiritual rest.

Cleansing

Foods that cleanse are very important. After all, a clean body is a healthy body.

Our body produces waste everyday and it must continue to remove this waste.

Your body doesn't function well under extreme amounts of waste either, so include foods to keep it clean. Always keep in mind balance because if you eat too many cleansing foods you can deplete your body of nutrients and energy. In the end it will only hurt you internally.

How do you start learning about food's effects?

You begin by understanding your body and from studying the concepts presented later in this book. Learning about all of the effects that different foods possess is something you should leave for a later date. First and foremost, being to understand how your body reacts to the foods your presently eat.

If you are to truly gain control on your eating habits, you will need to come to terms with your inherent belief systems.

Learn to look at food for what it has to offer instead of avoiding and restricting your diet because of what it contains.
Remember, all foods are beneficial in moderation and according to needs.

Regard your emotions

The human body can secrete chemicals just by changing moods or adjusting emotional states. In preparation for a meal your body will produce fluids and chemical secretions that will give support to the digestive system.

Eating during an extreme emotional state will have serious effects on the absorption of foods. Have you ever tried to eat when you were angry? Sad? In love? Ecstatic?

In all cases you should have noticed that your appetite was affected and the severity depended upon the level of the emotion.

If you are worrying about something and then try and sit down for lunch, it is not likely that you will have much of an appetite. Not just that, but what you do eat won't be assimilated properly and consequently will give little nutrition to your body. It may lead to an increase in weight also.

There are many reasons to turn to eating as a means of alleviating and forgetting about some painful emotional time. The emotional hunger far surpasses the physical hunger.

It is during times like these like these that you are reminded to pay heed to your health and your diet. IN many of the older more traditional philosophies there are beliefs that the emotions are connected with the internal workings of the body.

The connection or association between the organs and the emotions is regarded as very important and can be sued to determine what caused specific ailments and can teach people how to avoid future problems once they understand what needs to be done.

It is important to maintain stable emotions; otherwise, sickness and disease will prevail. Nutrimento in turn can be used to counteract an excessive emotional sate to bring your body back into harmony.

No one can change your present beliefs except you. It is only to your benefits to look at food more objectively.

The food of nutritional information has caused people to question and change their beliefs. People have become tense and stressed out over their diets from this information.

Many times it is difficult to know what to believe. The truth still remains that,

What you believe will determine what you eat; what you eat will determine the way you feel; and the way you feel will determine what you believe.

So be careful when you finally make up your mind on something. It is better to keep some flexibility in your judgement as it will keep your mind open to change and further improvement.

FIVE FACTORS FOR POSITIVE CHANGE

Every human being is different and special in their own way; logically they require a unique nutritional regimen.

It is not very easy to instruct people on what foods to eat as part of their regular diet. This is what this entire book is about.

Those that believe that "someone else" can provide the exact regular diet for their bodies are being misled. Nutritional authorities have learnt and developed their own particular method for planning your diet.

What they instruct you to do works for some people, namely those who have similar bodily systems and conditions, but it is not necessarily what YOU need.

You should be flexible enough to learn the information from a nutritional expert and adapt their theories to your own body; extract what works and adjust other ideas to achieve the maximum benefits for your health.

Personal nutritionists have a much clearer insight into how your diet should be adjusted, but few of us can afford to have them around for a long period.

What people often do not realize is that a close friend or partner can give helpful insights into your eating patterns, and how to improve them. The truth may be difficult to accept and can also show you the clearest path to better health and happiness through good feedback.

It is important to understand the value associated with each type of food or combination thereof. Combine this with a fair understanding of your body and then you can logically decide what is best for you.

This will free you from future dependence on external conflicting information.

The plan requires effort. You must find out what your body is doing. But that is the whole key, to find out the little intricacies of your own system.

Your body is complex.

Your entire body cannot be replaced, at least not as of yet. So this is where you come in. You have learned in the previous chapter on how to pay more attention to what your body is doing, now you must apply this information with regards to food.

The first step

There are five main factors to keep in mind when deciding on a positive change in your diet.

Changing your diet for the better requires you to give some attention to five important factors: Age, Gender, Physical Condition, Climate, and Lifestyle.

Let us spend a little time together examining these five factors in more depth.

FACTORS TO CONSIDER WHEN CHANGING DIET

1. *Age*
2. *Gender*
3. *Physical Condition*
4. *Climate*
5. *Lifestyle*

Age

A newborn baby must follow a fairly regular feeding system as many mothers can attest. It is required so that their rapid intake and elimination cycles can continue.

As the child grows, mothers are able to space more time in-between their feedings until such a point that the grown child's appetite can be more easily controlled by their own will.

You will also find that children will maintain a fairly high intake of food during their growing years in order to, not only ensure proper development, but also to feed their active minds and bodies.

Children are quite durable at a young age and can easily adapt to any given diet.

I can remember as a teenager eating a regular supply of junk and other bad foods and not feeling any significant reactions. It was not until years later when I began to experience a multitude of health problems including acne, digestive problems and abdominal pains.

In a way, I consider myself lucky to have had the opportunity to research food at a young age to solve my own health concerns.

Many other people I knew continued their bad eating habits and later passed their capacity to endure unhealthy eating in their mid-twenties. After that, they attested to being unable to eat all that fast food or to drinking as much alcohol as they used to.

The older you get the more important it is to watch what you eat. When your age passes sixty you will likely discover that a significant change in your diet can affect you severely. Ask one of your grandparents if they can eat the same way as they did when in their twenties. Not a chance.

The kind of nutrition required at twenty are far different from those needed at sixty. As you grow older your bodily requirements will change' therefore, you should adjust your diet to give what your body needs. Consider the age factor when changing your diet.

Gender

Males and females have distinctively different nutritional requirements and need to take that into consideration when altering their diet.

A man and a woman are both built different – physically, mentally, emotionally, and spiritually. You know it and I know it.

Women generally need slightly higher fat levels than men. This is seen as being vitally important in regulating hormone production. There have been many cases where women have had difficulty with hormonal imbalances because of a lack of good dietary fat. Many have found increases benefits by adding good sources of essential fatty acids to their diets.

Women's needs change drastically around the time of their monthly cycle and even more so during pregnancy. This makes it extremely important to pay attention to how they are feeling.

Both these situations are times when the body will need special nutritional requirements and by being in touch with those needs they can address the situation much better.

Men do not have this to think about; instead, men need to be careful to keep their bodies free from poisons by looking after their cleansing cycle.

A man's body processes nutrients differently and is very easy for them to eat foods that clog the body over a period of time rather than keep it clean and operating smoothly.

Physical Condition

Your present physical condition will be needed to take into consideration as you come to reorganize your existing diet.

Normally, those with strong constitutions are able to eat quite a variety of foods without any serious reactions. You may know one or two of these people. They are the type that can eat some of the strangest foods and still feel fine.

Those with stronger constitutions should pay heed to what you do because your diet may have included foods which are detrimental to your health. In the early stages, the body is strong enough to process whatever you eat, but it may not be able to withstand the mistreatment for very long.

A person with a weak constitution should pay more attention because they may have what is referred to as an inherent deficiency. An inherent deficiency refers to ongoing illnesses, conditions you were born with or certain bodily limitations like the removal of specific organs.

You are the one best suited to decide how to hand food intake here along with the help of your nutritional consultant and doctor.

In addition to that, you can learn to improve your diet to minimize your condition. In any case, because of certain limitations or challenges in your life you will want to keep them in consideration when allowing a change to occur.

Change your diet over a longer period of time to give it the maximum amount of time it needs to make any adjustments.
Climate

Adjusting your food intake according to the changing seasons is another actor to take into consideration. People inhabit different parts of the world.

Learn to adjust your diet according to the climate in which you live. In certain seasons, you are likely to find a much greater variety of fruits and vegetables available at the local farm market. Naturally, you should indulge. As the seasons change the variety of foods available also change.

Try to eat foods that follow the growing season of your area and cut down on those that are out of season.

When I was in Northern China, this practice of eating foods that were in season was very prevalent. You could tell when something was in season just by watching the change in prices and its availability.

This is not the same in North America and many other areas around the world, since most of the fruits and vegetables are available all year round. The only change is the seasonal price.

There is a reason why Nature only produces foods in certain seasons.

Traditionally, food has been there to help people survive the elemental changes that take place in any particular region of the world.

During the hot season the weather can reach stifling temperatures. You tend to sweat more and are more active outside. In this case, you need to supplant your body with high water fruits and vegetables that can help to replenish lost fluids and reduce body heat.

If you were to eat heavy amounts of meat and foods that were difficult to digest or produced more warmth in your body, you might find yourself more prone to problems with acne, lethargy, and bowel imbalances.

Many vegetarians diets originated in warmer tropical and sub-tropical climates. Strict vegan diets cannot always be adopted safely in all climates without close observation of the foods you are eating.

You have to be careful during the hot summer season. It is quite common to drink excessive amounts of water or other liquids to quench your thirst. Typically, this will affect your appetite level because if your stomach is full of liquid it won't have much room for a meal.

On the other hand, when you have not been getting enough fluids or have been perspiring excessively you may feel quite lethargic and won't have much of an appetite.

You might also put yourself at risk for dehydration. In this case, try drinking some water or fresh juice slowly over a ten to fifteen minute period. This will help alleviate your thirst and restore a proper water balance.

In the cold winter months, you will want to adjust your diet again. Why? Because it's cold!

Your body needs more warming and energizing foods to protect it and to give it warmth from the colder environment. That is why animal fats are needed to keep the body warm in colder regions. Remember the Eskimos?

It would make little sense, if any, to keep the same diet as in summer. Oranges do not grow in the dead of winter. Potatoes, yams and onions do. It is just like everything else.

During the summer months you can comfortably wear shorts, a T-shift and a pair of sandals. Having you ever tried to wear those clothes during the cold winter months when it is snowing outside? Probably not.

When it is colder you must conserve heat in order to protect your body from illness. Therefore, in wintertime it is safe to eat foods that are normally more difficult to digest, such as protein rich foods. These, in turn, will provide longer-term energy supplies.

It is a misconception to think that your body should look the same as it was in the summer. Keeping that low body fat ration is just not safe. It is all right to weigh a little more in winter. This is only natural and can protect you from harsh elements.

If you look in nature you can see the natural progression. Your cat, for example, gets heavier in winter and grows a thick, soft fur. By spring and definitely by summer your pet has slimmed right down to their thin, athletic self.

This is not always the case for people (or lazy animals, I guess). Some tend to carry over their weight through the summer only to add even more during the following winter.

You need to adjust your activity levels so that your body maintains an ideal weight throughout the changing seasons.

Lifestyle

Your dietary habits should follow your lifestyle habits. Dietary habits need to be adjusted frequently in order to maintain a nutritional balance. The main reason for this is that your lifestyle fluctuates as does your own biological rhythms and because of these changes it is nearly impossible to follow a strict dietary plan in everyday life.

Over the short-term, your body will be able to adjust; over the longer-term, it will lead to deficiencies.

One who works in a sedentary office environment requires different nutrients than someone who uses their physical strength at a building construction site.

If you think about it, an office worker is mainly concerned about non-physical activities. Their body in turn needs foods to stimulate proper circulation to the regions in the body. They do not need to eat heavy amounts of meat or other high energy foods that supply the body with calories and physical energy.

By providing their body with foods that are lower in energy value and higher in nutrients that stimulate brain function they would find themselves better able to work efficiently.
It also depends on what that particular person does in their spare time. If someone weight lifts or does marathon running as a hobby, they again will want to adjust their diet to accommodate their lifestyle needs.

Listen to your body and it will tell you what it needs.

What about someone who works as a fitness instructor or is a downtown mail courier?

Anybody who has high energy needs on a daily basis because of heavy activity will need to supply their body with appropriate amounts of energy foods.

Eating foods that replenish lost energy stores are ideal. This would include a heavier consumption of nutritious meats, grains, and legumes as well as adequate amounts of water and other liquids.

Many books and theorists have tried to classify the millions of different body types into groups of less than eight classes.

The human body is very, very complex. Each individual is endowed with unique talents and unique bodily systems that change over time. It would be unfair to classify them into a system of six or eight different body types.

Defining body types can introduce new ideas to people in a simple, easy to follow format, but it is far from complete.

You are the best judge of your body type. If you eat lots of high energy food, workout very little and gain weight, then at the present time that is your body type. What a concept!

It is only valid in the present time because your body is continually changing to adapt to the environment you are in.

Later on, you may find yourself working out every day, eating low energy foods and gaining weight every week. Whether the new found weight is muscle or not is not the main concern. What is important is that you are aware of what your lifestyle dictates and what your body needs. Only then can you look after it properly.

It is extremely difficult, if not impossible, to categorize all of the millions of lifestyles in the world.

People have such a varied daily regimen that it would be unrealistic to list them all here.

That would be defeating the whole purpose of this book which is to help you get in touch with your dietary needs.

Gradual changes

The best way to change your diet is to do it gradually. This adjustment phase can take anywhere from one month to a few years. It all depends upon what state of health your body is in presently.

When there are serious deficiencies or dormant imbalances, your body may use the time to heal itself and to nourish its ailments before allowing you to experience ultimate health. There is nothing wrong with this phase as long as you are adopting a healthier diet to replace your old one.

The safest way to reduce your weight is to do it over a period of time also. This will allow a more permanent change and one which will prevent any rapid relapses from happening.

Give yourself a break

Fasting is another great way to give your digestive system a break. In many countries around the world people practice a special day of eating.

It is common for many cultures to eat a vegetarian meal (sometimes fish) on special days during the year. On the more religious holidays or special occasions food wasn't eaten at all.

Some people insist on setting aside a day every month to not intake food, only liquids.

This practice allows the body to remove unwanted impurities and to strengthen itself.
On the day you choose to fast you must coordinate your schedule accordingly. This is because you are inputting a low amount of energy into the body and therefore must be careful to expend the same or less.

Your body also requires energy to perform the necessary restoration and elimination of by-products. If you decide to burn all of your energy at your nine-hour day job, then you will have defeated the whole purpose of the fast.

For those that typically work Monday to Friday, a good idea is to have the fast on Saturday. That way you can recharge your body on Sunday and be back at work with extra vitality on Monday.

It is important to consider what kind of climate and which season it is before the fast. When you follow the cycle of nature (according to what part of the world you live in), consider that winter is a time for storage; therefore, fasting should be avoided.

Late spring and summer are safe reasons to fast. Ever heard of spring cleaning?

It is during these seasons that the weather is warm, nature grows and cleanses itself and you, as part of nature, can follow along and heal your body.

Some fine tuning

When you make a dietetic adjustment in your life you are changing more than just what you eat.

You are changing what you are.

This is why you need to look at your age, gender, physical condition, climate and lifestyle. These are five important factors that give form to what kind of person you are.

When you learn to apply these factors to your life, you will see that it doesn't matter where you live or what you do or even who you are because food can accommodate your life.

You will also realize that all of these five factors change.

You get older.

Your body's physique changes from change in sports activity. State of health goes up and down.

Climate is always changing from the season you are in and, more so, when you travel.

Your lifestyle with a lifetime partner, raise children, and any other endeavours you indulge in. So, you must change your diet along with it.

The foundation has been laid and the criteria in which to work have been identified. Now you should be ready to move into some Food Basics.

If you feel unsure about some of the information feel free to go back now and reread any chapters you feel are necessary.

The next set of chapters will introduce you to food and drink and the specific considerations that accompany them.

You need to remember some of the things you have learned in the first two sections in order to gain a greater benefit from the remainder of the book. So, stick to the fight and carry on because all you need are a few key improvements in your diet to make the difference for you and your family.

GROWING IN ABUNDANCE

THE VARIETY OF FOOD AVAILABLE

By now you should have a clearer answer to four of the five questions that were introduced at the beginning of this book.

The first three chapters have given you some important reasons to "Why" you should eat and so by now your conviction towards looking after your diet should be stronger than before. After all, eating good food gives your body the sustenance and nutrients it needs to not only survive, but also to perform your daily activities.

It should be clearer now why good Nutrimento really is the basics of feeling good.

In the second section, "Preparing for the Future" you learned to understand that it is important to listen to your body and to be in touch with its needs.

This explained that the difference between a good diet and a bad diet is dependent upon "who" is eating. The best foods for you may actually harm someone else; therefore, you must distinguish the difference between your body's needs and what other people recommend eating.

You have also experienced throughout both sections the "where" and "when" of eating. These two questions affect you because your diet will not only change with respect to where you live in the world, but it will also change according to when you eat. Remember the five main factors: age, gender, physical condition, climate, and lifestyle?

The following chapters will discuss the fifth important consideration – "what" you are eating. It starts off the section for "Growing in Abundance."

You will begin with learning about the food basics. It will be an initial exploration of the different varieties of food available and form there you will gain a better understanding of what's involved in cooking and a closer look at drinking liquids.

A planet of food

There are literally thousands upon thousands of foods and food products available around the globe for consumption. New food products are being created all of the time.

It is quite normal for someone to become accustomed to eating a limited variety of food. The problem arises when this diet is deprived of the total nutrition that your body needs.

The varieties of food are endless. It has been estimated that there are over 80,000 species of edible plants around the world. The foods people eat today are not native to their own country's soil. Foods were originally domesticated from all parts of the world.

Coffee originated in Africa. Black pepper, eggplant, and cucumber came from India. Alfalfa, apricots and soybeans came from China and Central Asia. Grapes and raspberries were domesticated in Europe. Vineyards were widespread in Europe by 3,000 B.C. to 2,500 B.C.. The Middle East was responsible for many of the foods we see today including barley, apples, lettuce, onions, figs and dates.

Many animals were also domesticated. Dogs were considered to be the first. Later came sheep, goats, cats, donkeys, ducks, cattle, and horses to name a handful. Domestication of both plants and animals was quite sudden and also was very limited to a small number of species.

Soon after Christopher Columbus sailed in the Fifteen Century, the dissemination of world domesticates began and because of him and other traders, people are able to find a myriad of foods at the local grocery store.

How many different varieties of food do you include in your diet? It is common to continue eating a restricted diet? It is common to continue eating a restricted diet, but it is this type of limited intake that can weaken your state of health later on.

Before you move on in this chapter take a short break and open up the door to your refrigerator. Come on, I know that you can do it. If you are not at home then think about the food items you saw at the grocery store.

As people of a borderless world, we can no longer hide the fact that the cultures of other societies are irrelevant. It is time that we recognize that the planet we call home is blessed with abundance and that we should not limit it.

Earth is made up of 190 different countries and nearly 6 million people interspersed in 5,000 ethnic groups who all live under unique environmental conditions. These regions produce wonderful varieties of foods and the locals have created healthy meals from what the Earth has provided.

In the US and Canada Midwest, there is a heavier consumption of beef from a cow than compared to India or China. More seafood and fish is eaten on the Eastern and Western borders of North America.

In China, more pork is eaten. But again, you will find great variety. More steamed buns and bread are found in Northern region of China and more varieties of noodles in the South. The coastal areas enjoy fish and seafood. In contrast, Muslim and Jewish religions commonly found in the Middle East, America are against eating pork unless it is prepared in a special way.

In Africa, tribes still hunt elephant and monkeys in the jungles while in the Arctic, the Eskimos thrive on seal and whale meat including the fat, skin, and internal organs.

In Naples, Italy, the birthplace of pizza, the tomato is a favourite food while Tuscany in the North is renowned for their delicious hearty soup.

Singaporeans love to eat the famous Hainan chicken rice served with nourishing chicken broth. They also enjoy eating stir-fried noodles loaded with green and red chillies.

Thailand and other Southeast Asian countries make wonderful red, green, yellow and other curries that range from mild to extremely hot with chilli oil. Many are made with creamy coconut milk.

Each part of the world enjoys certain kinds of food depending greatly on their cultural traditions and their habitat. Many of the developed countries enjoy a larger consumption of meat, refined, and processed food. This has led to over-indulgence and dietary disease.

You should realize that there is no standard stating which foods are edible and which are not. Every continent and country has a different staple diet.

If you lived in a small fishing village in Thailand your main dish would likely be fish and rice. You would eat several types of local fish prepared in many different ways.

On the other hand, had you grown up on a farm in mid-west America, you would more likely enjoy the benefits of beef. It does not matter where you live because you will find that there is a great variety of food to eat and as long as this diet is in balance with your dietary needs then it can be continued without problem.

As you continue to read this chapter try to become aware of what kinds of foods are available in your area. That way you will better be able to make improvements in your diet later on.

Companion foods

In addition to variety, you can also find that food can be sectioned into specific individual parts. Each part is known to provide certain nutritional benefits to the body.

Many of the older cultures learned early on that all parts of the animals had some nutritional value; therefore, they had devised ways in which to prepare and use all of the animal over the years.

This practice of using certain parts for health purposes is still prevalent today in many countries and is applicable to both animals and plants. People of all ages acknowledge the fact that each particular food provides the body with a certain benefit and also that too much of one part can lead to deficiencies and excesses later on.

You are probably familiar with eating animal liver. It has been found to be nourishing to your own liver as well as benefitting your eyes and blood. Chinese herbalists have know this fact for centuries before science revealed the chemical components found in liver and how they could benefit you.

The Chinese had realized that the liver governs the eyes. They usually treated people with eye trouble, such as night blindness and blurred vision with animal liver in addition to other herbs. The Chinese doctors also knew that eating a particular organ that was properly prepared would nourish your own similar organ. In this case, eating liver benefited your liver.

You don't need to concern yourself over the medicinal effects of food in this book. It is important that you begin to see the connection between eating a varied dietary intake and providing your body with balanced health including companion foods.

Everything in the correct proportion is good for you. What you will be learning is how to determine the correct proportion of food for your body.

There are many parts to all foods. Chickens have wings, and feet, both of which will provide a different type of nutrition and effect than the other. Likewise, the chicken breast is mostly meat without bone and will again offer another set of benefits. Think about whether or not you find yourself eating similar foods. It could indicate that your body is requiring some specific type of nutrient or that your diet has been like that for a long time and you are accustomed to it.

Eating meat does not just mean that you should always eat the fleshiest, juiciest areas. You should also eat some of the other parts as they will offer additional nutrients to your body.

Eating chicken wings may not be your idea of eating chicken, but if you always eat the breast of the chicken your body may be missing out on something.

You need to introduce a variety of meat that your body can use.

I have friends who can remember being fed cow's tongue when they were very young. Their parents believed that it contained a high source of nutrition to feed a growing child. These same friends who enjoyed eating it at a young age became disgusted at the idea of eating a cow's tongue when they learned what it was they were eating.

Do not let the appearance or the source of your meal stop you from eating it. Remember, food is meant to nourish you.

Long-term companion foods

There are two important considerations to keep in mind when your diet includes a more complete choice of companion foods. **The first consideration is your body's need for such foods**. Animal organs contain more concentrated sources of nutrients when compared to external parts. This translates into eating a more moderate consumption of them.

A companion food is just what it says, it is used to support your main diet. Your diet should not subsist on eating liver and heart every day, especially if your health is quite strong.

For those of a weaker constitution your diet might need a more regular consumption of those high nutrient foods to rebuild your health. That is also why children can eat more of those foods. Children's bodies are going through rapid change and development and need the energy to continue their growth.

Even when you consider eating parts like salmon skin or pork liver you should keep moderation in mind. Companion foods tend to have more nutrition, but sometimes also more fat. Again, how much you should eat depends on your constitution. Even with a healthy constitution you should consume occasional amounts of these foods to balance out your dietary needs. There is another set of companion foods in the plant and fruit kingdom which I refer to as herbs. You will learn more about herbs later on in the chapter.

The second consideration is composed of two ideas. The **source** of the animal part is the first idea.

Where the meat was obtained is quite important for all parts of the animal because animal farms all breed animals differently and just like a special diet and exercise regimen can mean the difference between an Olympic athlete and just a sports enthusiast, so can a good farmer make the difference in their animal.

Chickens, for example, can be held in a chicken barn in individualized compartments and fed a diet loaded with growth hormones. This will usually make a chick grow into a chicken quite fast although all that the chicken has done is eat all day and grow.

There are also what we call Free Range chickens that are allowed to walk around outside and eat some of the food found around the farm. Local laws will stipulate how much space is allowed to make the chicken eligible to be given the title "Free Range." Regardless, Free Range chickens taste different because of their varied diet and their chance at mobility.

As an additional option, chickens can just be left alone to walk around the farm and to consume what foods they can find on their won. The meat from these chickens might be a little tougher because of the greater amount of exercise their muscles get.

In regards to animal organs, if the internal parts of an animal were obtained from one that was fed high amounts of antibiotics, growth hormones and the like, then many of the chemical residues can still be found with certain organs because the organ will have filtered out a lot of the drugs.

If you eat the liver of a heavily drugged cow, then you are likely ingesting some of the drugs that the animal was fed. Unfortunately, this is also the same for plants and fruits that have been sprayed with pesticides and other chemicals.

The second idea can help ensure the animal part will benefit you because there is something you can do to reduce the chance of eating something that contains unwanted impurities. There are **special ways to prepare or cook food** to remove many impure elements. In addition, you can combine them with other foods to increase their benefits.

All in all, it is relatively safe to consume animal parts in select amounts if prepared correctly. The chance of buying regular meat that has been infected or contains some unwanted chemicals is relatively as risky, so don't let it bother you. Just remember to clean and cook your meat properly and you won't have any problems.

Processed food is one of the worst for containing impurities in their product. In a number of documentary TV programs over the years, some of the more popular cereal products, bread spreads, and other packaged food products were investigated and it was found through laboratory tests that even the big name companies could not control the number of bugs, hairs and rodent parts in their products.

In fact, it is impossible to eliminate all impurity from food processing. You have survived until now on eating all kinds of foods. Many of those foods you were probably not even aware of all the things that were in them, but they did not harm you.

Understanding herbal foods

Lately, people have been rediscovering the hidden powers of herbs. They forget that herbs have been around for a long, long time.

Herbs are potent sources of nutrition that stimulate important bodily functions. As herbs come from the same source as foods we should consider food also as herbs, but of a different grade. My Chinese martial arts instructor taught me that, **foods are herbs; herbs are foods**. There is only small difference between the two.

Herbs stimulate your body to perform a function it cannot successfully do on its own and they can do this with much greater intensity than food. Herbs can also be taken in small does over a certain period of time for its desired effect.

Food can similarly achieve the same thing, but requires that you eat a larger amount and wait a longer time period for a result. Here is an example; what happens when you eat, say eight oranges one after another? Have you ever tried it?

The usual outcome are open sores inside your mouth, an upset stomach and a small bout of diarrhea later on. Why? Because in the right amount, in this case eight oranges, food had a stimulating effect on your body. In this particular example the oranges produced a cleansing effect. Drink 6 cups of coffee and you will be 'wired' with caffeine and sugar.

Children who are a product of poor nutrition or excessive indulgence often become the victim of uncontrollable moods, hyper activity, poor mental focus and other debilitating and frustrating effects. The source can often be traced back to other diets.

Have you ever eaten too much meat or too many nuts? Do you remember what happened? It most likely resulted in constipation and abdominal pain.

Or how about chocolate? What happens when you eat too much chocolate or chocolate-laden desserts? Skin problems are the most noticeable but weight gain and indigestion are others.

The other point worth noting is a fundamental difference between food and herbs. This is the speed at which the reaction occurs.

With the case of the oranges, perhaps you may not feel the result until a few hours or more have passed, but if you were using an herb to produce the same effect its action takes place in as short as a few seconds.

This is because herbs are more concentrated and therefore more potent, so they require smaller does to produce a similar effect. An infusion of herbal tea is sufficient to stimulate the body. This is often preferred over eating eight or ten oranges when your body requires immediate attention.
In this chapter you will have found that there is a myriad of types of food available. The whole purpose was not to list them all here but to show some of the major varieties. It is common to get fixated on eating only a handful of different types of food.

The question you need to ask is whether or not those foods are providing the nutrients your body needs. Are they the best source of Nutrimento?

Every culture and region of the world will have their own preference for the types of foods they include in their diets. Some cultures include a regular consumption of animal organ meats while others prefer to include more plant foods. Consider your own present diet and make some new decisions on how you will make yourself feel good.

FROM START TO FINISH

You see, it is not only important to pick the foods you need, but also how you complete the meal. In order for your food to be healthy it should be prepared properly to ensure that all of its nutrition is complete.

What I want to introduce to you now are three important variables that are found when food goes from its raw state until it is ready to eat – preparation, aroma, and appearance.

As it is being prepared and cooked, you will begin to smell its aroma and you will have effectively begun your meal. By the time that it is finished, the meal should look appealing and be presented in a pleasant way.

Any serious mistake in these variables will surely lead to a compromised meal for you, your family, or your guests.

Food preparation

It is extremely important to prepare food properly; otherwise, food can turn into your own poison. An obvious example is when you overcook or burn your food.

On the other end of the spectrum, you can undercook food. By doing that, it remains in a semi-raw, semi-cooked state which can contain harmful bacteria that will upset your digestive system.

Just consider eating half-cooked pork chops or raw chicken wings. Not something you want to try if you want to remain healthy.

Fruits, vegetables, fish and others can be eaten raw, but most people have grown accustomed to incorporating cooked food in their diets.

The idea of cooked food is simple.

Using a variety of heating methods you cook the raw food into a more easily digested form.

Cooking is made up of a series of laws that are unique to every region and cooking style around the world.

You cannot walk into a school for French Chefs and point out that they were cooking wrong based on the fact that you were a chef taught Thai cuisine in one of the most famous schools in Thailand. Some techniques and methods of cooking could be found to be similar, but many would not be the same.

Every continent, region and household around the magnificent Earth has its own, personalize cooking culture.

Chefs as individuals will possess varied cooking skills based upon their experience and training.

When it comes to cooking food, the chef must adhere to the basic cooking laws or chance ruining the meal. There are certain rules for combining spices with lamb or deciding what kind of vegetables to make with rabbit stew depending on their cooking style. As Chefs continue to learn and experiment with different recipes, invariably new cooking styles will develop.

Another concern would be how the foods are prepared.

This is used for determining what kind of marinade to use on the meat, cooking sauce choices, salad dressing mixtures even to the point of using a particular brand of wine or liqueur to make a dish. These laws are reflected in the ongoing cooking tradition of whatever country you live in.

In Chinese cooking, the chef is careful not to combine the wrong ingredients because it would balance the heating and cooling effects of the food.

Your body needs all foods to provide balanced nutrition. Just like exercise; if you always lift weights you will develop muscle, but lose some flexibility and endurance. Always train aerobics and muscle mass decreases, but endurance and muscle tone increases.

Cross training has become ideal for a more rounded, total workout.

You would not want to limit your body to any one group of foods, because in the end the body will become deficient in some other nutrient.

A favourite Japanese style of eating is having raw fish.

Selections of sushi and sashimi are typically made with raw pieces of fish and eaten with horseradish, soya sauce, pickled ginger, and a thumb sized piece of rice for the sushi. Combining tempura, a lightly deep fried choice of vegetable or fish, Japanese soup and other small cooked dishes makes the meal more complete.

Asian style of eating, especially outside the home, incorporates the ordering of many different food dishes and shared with a group of eight or ten people. This allows everyone to have a good variety of nutrition available and is also more enjoyable.

There is a wide array of foods to eat, but what is commonly forgotten is that here are numerous ways to prepare foods for consumption.

Some might call it cooking, but since not all of the methods listed in the table are done using heath, I will sue the word "prepared."

You can see in the table that there are 16 common ways to prepare foods beginning with the most basic raw form. The preparation method depends upon the desired effect and the current circumstance.

Food preparation methods are often combined to make a finished meal.

Even processing food has its benefits. Just think about the extended shelf life of packaged grocery food like canned tuna.

Think about the foods you eat regularly and determine whether or not you are habitually eating food prepared by the same method.

Do you find that you are always eating raw food, for example? Or maybe you are always eating deep fried foods?

Preparing food by the same method every meal will create imbalance within your body. In addition to balancing your variety of food, you need to also balance your choice of preparation.

FOOD PREPARATION METHODS

Method

1. Raw state
2. Fried, sautéed
3. Baked, roasted
4. Broiled
5. Boiled, stewed
6. Dried
7. Barbecued
8. Marinated
9. Dehydrated

10. Deep fried
11. Processed
12. Salted
13. Pickled
14. Blanched
15. Steamed

Starting today, learn some new methods to prepare your meal. Remember, it will not only benefit you, but also your loved ones.

Eat from a variety of prepared foods. There are far too many preparation methods to be listed here. I have only listed some of the main selections.
Depending on where you are or what you do during the day will greatly affect what kinds of prepared food are available.

Keep this in mind, "Variety is the spice of life." So when you eat, do so from a verity of prepared meals.

If you find yourself always eating barbecued food, then you need to incorporate other varieties. The same goes for raw or boiled foods. There is not one particular method that is best for you all of the time. You need to vary them to be sure of a more balanced dietary intake. You will inevitably find that the cooking method will be affected by the weather, climate, and bodily needs.

Eating processed food

There is a myriad of food out there that has been processed one way or another. What I mean by processed is that the food has been handled by a nonhuman.

Normally, machines and special equipment have adulterated the food to change different aspects of it such as its shelf life, taste, nutrient level, chemical make up, texture, etc. Processed food is not all necessarily bad for you. Again, it depends on some of the following factors:

- how often you eat processed food
- your body's tolerance level
- your state of health
- your intake of non-processed food
- the amount that you intake

- your allergic reactions to added chemicals

Processed food has been altered in such a way that it can remain fresher longer. My experience has shown me that too many processed foods can weaken your state of health in the long run because most foods are deficient in the natural vitamins and minerals.

Food characteristics

What I want to introduce to you now are two important characteristics that all foods share and how they can help you to determine where change is necessary in your diet. These basic characteristics correspond to what your senses pick up before you even put anything inside of your mouth.

You will examine what the **aroma** and **appearance** of food do for you next. These two characteristics have a powerful effect on you before you have a chance to taste anything.

What smells so good?

When I was a kid, I remember almost once a week my Mom made fresh home-baked bread. On that particular day, I would come home from school and smelled that familiar scent of fresh bread in my mother's kitchen. It had a tremendous effect in stimulating my appetite.

Even if I didn't feel hungry at the time I would still want to eat some fresh bread. Some of you may not have had the opportunity to have someone who could bake fresh bread in your house, but you will most certainly have either passed by or been inside a bakery at one point or another in your life.

Do you remember what it smelled like as you passed by?

I can also recall smelling my mother's Italian ragout sauce on Sunday afternoons. The aroma filtered throughout the house. There were many time that I, for one reason or another, lost my appetite while I was out with my friends, but after arriving home my desire to eat was instantly rekindled after smelling that wonderful ragout sauce.

Those smells filtered out of the kitchen are directly responsible for your appetite or, in some cases, the loss of appetite.

There were many occasions, outside of my home, where I lost any desire to eat.

I can recall going to a donut bakery once and feeling overwhelmed by all the sweet donut varieties. They gave me the same feeling that I at too many sweet foods. It struck me odd at the time because I didn't even get a chance to eat a single donut.

There are other more unpleasant smells that can sometimes be found in kitchens.

Usually, the type of kitchen that has this is rather run-down and dirty. Of course, this is not the place you want to eat at. You can smell it as soon as you enter the cafe, home or restaurant.

Again, this will also depend on what kind of living environment you have been accustomed to over the years, since your body will adapt to your geographical area and lifestyle.

Scientists have determined that the smell of food alone accounts for ninety percent of the food's taste. That is why you are instantly able to associate the smell of a particular dish with its taste and a good reason why you can already taste the food in your mouth from the smell.

The aroma of food is extremely powerful. It has been estimated to be 10,000 times stronger than its taste.

Have you ever had the opportunity to watch an experience chef cook something in front of you? How did it smell?

With a competent chef it would have surely stimulated your appetite.

Now, have you even been in a position where you had to endure something that did not smell so wonderful, like burnt food? Did the smell make you hungry? Unlikely.

Try to become more aware of the smells that surround you. Think about which ones make you hungry and which ones make you nauseous. Also consider when they make you feel the way you do.

In order for you to enjoy your meal, the food should have a pleasant aroma. This may also be coupled together with your cravings.

Does the smell of chocolate, for example, make you want to have some? Are there foods that you crave more often than others?

Learn to be aware of what you smell and let it serve you.

Scents can have a great influence on other aspects of your life also. Even your own living environment has a unique smell. Since your nose will have adapted to the smell by now, have some friends comment on the smell of your living quarters (cautionary note: make sure that they are *good* friends). How different are their reactions from yours now?

The other trick you might try is going back to restaurants you used to eat in and finding out if it smells different than it used to.

Go back to eating foods you used to like ten years ago to see how they smell and taste now.

The smell of food is all around us. It can be the buttered popcorn in the movie theatre or your mom's famous chicken soup. In the end, this has its effect on you.

That looks delicious

The color of food is another very important characteristic to consider. This is used extensively in the marketing of commercial food products. Food has to look appealing because it also stimulates the appetite.

Color is very important to the presentation of food and has always been such. Food has to be presented with the right combination of color. This will help increase the appetite and prepare your stomach for digestion.

In many parts of the world, color is used extensively in cooking. The right accompaniments of colourful vegetables to the entree are important. The garnish is set on the side to balance the presentation of the dish and different herbs and spices are used to bring out the full value of the meal. Pieces of food are often carved into flowers or beautiful birds.

Even though you may be choosing healthy foods to eat you need to make sure that those foods are prepared properly to bring out their full nutritional value.

As it is cooking, the smell should being to stimulate your appetite and when it is finished the proper presentation will make the meal all the more enjoyable.

DRINK TO YOUR HEALTH

The fluids that you intake on a regular basis can have a significant influence on the health of your body. Putting in fluids that irritate or slow down the body can have serious implications in the future; likewise, fluids that cleans and promote regeneration will benefit you.

What should you drink?

This sounds like a perfectly reasonable question and it is something that needs to be clarified because it is not what you drink that is important so much as when you drink it. Drinking to your health is what you need to consider.

It is common to find someone drinking some sweet, carbonated beverage to quench your thirst, but you need to ask yourself whether or not your body was receiving what it needed at the time.

When to drink

The question of when to drink your liquids is an important one. This is something that you are confronted with everyday during your eating periods, yet many times people will take it for granted. You need to think about how you are using fluids while you eat because if it is used improperly, it can have detrimental effects on your digestive system.

As with the case you found in eating a variety of foods based upon your body's own characteristics, drinking also requires the same kinds of consideration. Realize that the types of drinks that you enjoy may be something that your body requires to balance out your present diet.

You will find that as your diet changes, so will your drink choices.

In addition to the temperature level of drinks, there is also a factor of effects to consider. Each drink in itself will produce a certain, though usually mild, effect when ingested. For that reason it is important to find the correct combination for your meal.

What to drink not only quenches your thirst, but also serves to produce an effect on your body. For example, while eating a relatively spicy meal it is a good idea to drink something that is cooling to the body to balance out the warming effect from the food.

There was a question recently raised concerning whether to drink on an empty stomach, before meals, between meals or after. Let's try and uncover this mess with some common sense.

If, when you are eating, you find that you are using water or other liquids to wash down your food because of improper chewing then you are creating a very bad habit. This habit easily turns to problems with indigestion. What's happening is that you are swallowing food that has not been completely chewed and washing, in a sense, it down with liquid. This leaves it up to your stomach to finish the chewing process, but it has a lot of trouble because it is not equipped with any teeth.

Besides washing down your food you may find yourself drinking something that doesn't really combine well with your meal.

An example of this would be drinking chocolate milk with deep fried fish. This situation has a tendency to create a lot of mucus in your system.

When you decide what to drink with your meal consider first what you are ordering and then choose something that complements it.

Some people just have the same old cup of coffee, glass of beer or wine, juice or pop with every meal. It can suffice for many occasions, but there inevitably comes a time when you are in for a night of indigestion and good stomach medicine becomes your friend.

There are many different aspects of drinking to consider and I will sue the more common drinks to explain the best ways to drink.

The first one that heads the list is **water**. This liquid can be more than just your eight glasses a day, if that is what you really need. In the next chapter we will look at some other popular drinks – coffee, tea, and alcohol.

The earth has plenty of it

It is easy to forget that the human body is composed of a similar ratio of water as found on the earth. Over sixty percent of our body, up to eighty-five, is composed on water. It depends upon your particular system at the time, but more importantly, water plays an integral part in the functioning of our internal systems.

It has a demanding role to play throughout your whole body. Everywhere you look you will find water. Without water your body would dry up and cease to exist. Water has a higher priority over food. Your body can adapt to living without food, but take away water and you will cease to exist.

Everyone loves a cold, fresh glass of water on a warm, sunny day. It does not matter where you travel to as everyone regards water with similar enthusiasm. The temperature of the water can affect your body also.

When you drink coffee, pop, tea and other beverages you are also ingesting some sort of stimulant like caffeine, sugar, and other chemicals. Your body does not always need or want them as it continually has to excrete them from your body. This stresses the elimination system and can have detrimental effects like dependency upon stimulants or rotting teeth from the excessive intake of sugar and acid. Again, you will see more of these other beverages in the following chapter.

There are many who drink teas and other herbal beverages to cleanse their bodies. Drinking cleansing teas all of the time is like washing your clothes every day. It is a little excessive and will prematurely wear out the material out.

We can both agree that the human body is vastly different that 100% cotton or polyester fabrics. What is useful here is the idea of over-doing something.

You would not want to over clean your skin with soap because of the risk of drying it out and possibly damaging your skin.

Be careful if you find yourself drinking the same thing too often.

Ice water

Many people have turned to the ice water combination. Almost every restaurant serves it to you shortly after you sit at the table. This beverage can be very bad for you under the wrong conditions. It has the ability to freeze your stomach into submission before you put any food into it.

Imagine before you went for six mile jog, you went into a refrigerated meat locker and sat there for 20 minutes instead of warming up for 20 minutes. Now, immediately after that was finished, you started your six mile jog. How far do you think you would go? Could you be more susceptible to injuring your muscles or joints? Probably.

Is it a smart thing to do? No, so why would you want to do something like that to your good old faithful stomach.

It would be better to give it some warm soup, tea, coffee, or something else to stimulate the appetite. Better still, try sipping the ice water slowly if you really want to have some.

Even in the winter many people enjoy drinking cold water.

You and I can both agree that water is good for us. Ask any nutritionist and they will usually recommend that you drink six to ten glasses of water daily. What about drinking warm or hot water as an alternative? Who wants to drink plain, hot water?

Hot water

How does this relate to the human body?

Often a nice thing to do is to drink some hot water to just "cleanse" your insides without any additives. Something that has no stimulant like coffee or many teas and has a mild cleansing effect on the body.

Many people in Asia drink hot water, voluntarily. Even in the summer they drink it, usually in the evening when it's not as hot outside. Originally they had to do it to purify the water of deadly bacteria, but even now they set aside two thermoses of water; one hot and one cold.

Drinking under different conditions

The best drink is a temperate drink close to that of your body, but it is so tempting to drink the ice cold beer or pop. It is not necessarily bad for you taken in moderate amounts and under the correct conditions.

Three conditions to consider include the season, the type of meal you are eating at present, and the state of your body is in at the time.

The seasons in which drinking cold liquids are the least harmful are non-specific. I say seasons here because there are many countries that have hot seasons throughout the year. When you do drink something cold on a hot day it may quench your thirst for the moment but may also make you thirst for another.

If you find yourself in this situation you may want to take note of it and introduce a more temperate drink into your body. Some cultures prefer to drink hot drinks during warm weather because they believe that the temperature inside the body is quite hot and by drinking something hot it will keep the internal system balanced.

Just like when you pour cold water on a hot rock, it will produce steam. If you poured hot water on the same hot rock then no steam (or much less steam) would be produced because the temperature of the rock and the water is close to each other.

Food that is generally considered to be a hot meal, that is, either fried, baked, broiled or barbecued can be combined with cold "effect" drinks (this is different from cold "temperature" drinks). It is up to you to be aware of how much your body requires without upsetting the balance. Usually the longer it is cooked or the hotter the fire, as in barbecue, you can safely extend your glass for a cold refill.

Another type of meal that may ask for a cold drink is one that is spicy, such as anything cooked with chillies or other strong pieces. Drinking, or even eating, something that is cooling while eating a spicy meal may help to cool off your mouth as well as your stomach. It is your stomach that will thank you the next day.

Just remember that in the case of eating something that is extremely spicy you will often find that drinking some ice water will only cool off your mouth temporarily.

Meanwhile, as you keep guzzling down more water you will bloat your stomach with water. The drinks that work better are cold and cooling effect drinks like tea, fresh fruit juice, herbal drinks, speciality drinks native to your region, and even some kinds of soda pop.

The last section is related to how your body feels at the time and also how you generally react to the various temperatures of water. Some people drink a couple of ice cold glasses of water during a hot afternoon and feel great. Others can continually consume ice water during the cold winter days and claim it is the best drink around. You will have your own system to consider in this system.

Acquiring a taste for hot drinks

I remember when I was a teenager; I used to always drink cold liquids. My body had become accustomed to the frigid temperatures and anything but tasted like dishwater.

When I reached my late teens, I began to have problems with colder weather. In the winter time in Vancouver, Canada where the average day in winter was a cool five degrees Celsius, I would always have to wear two T-shirts, a turtle neck a sweater and a jacket to keep warm. Even with all those layers I still felt chilled.

During the summer months, I would always wear a T-shirt underneath my shift because otherwise I was too cold. Imagine trying to go to the beach with two layers of clothes on. It was not my idea of fun time at the beach.

Later, I acquired a taste for a more frequent ingestion of hot liquids and teas and discovered that my digestion improved and my circulation got better. I found myself less frequently cold and enjoyed eating a wider variety of food.

When I was in college, there was one winter where my friend and I were sharing a large, three-level townhouse and we could not afford to pay for the heating bill.

My friend brought to my attention his chronic back pain that was made more debilitating in the winter. I noticed that he enjoyed drinking jugs of ice water and instantly made the connection. I suggested that he should drink more warm fluids especially in the winter because ice-water can freeze your internal organs and debilitate them.

We bought a hot water heater and he began to drink more hot tea.

Within two weeks, the back pain that he had put up with for ten years had diminished so much that it did not bother him anymore. After another week it altogether disappeared.

After this incident, a young doctor explained to him that the esophagus runs right down along the spine and could help to justify its beneficial effect on the back.

By the same token, you can now see how drinking ice beverages can have detrimental effects if not controlled. Remember that the spine carries very important nerves and fluids to all parts of the body including your brain.

Do not let the significance of the temperature and effect of a drink pass you by.

MORE DRINKS FOR YOUR HEALTH

There are of course many liquids to drink besides water. It is these additional drinks that much be consumed with some care and consideration because each in their own right will have an effect on your body.

As you might recall, water was labelled as a neutral beverage and the remaining beverages found in the previous chapter can be found on either extreme. We begin our look at three other types of drinks that can be found the world over.

This will include a controversial beverage, coffee. Here you will learn to understand if it controls you or if you can control it. Further down the list I will talk about tea. This beverage has been around for centuries and has been enjoyed by everyone from rural farmers to royal family members and emperors. Another type of drink will be alcohol.

Let's begin.

Coffee

Coffee distributors will confidently tell you that the coffee bean can make a healthy drink.

By crushing the beans and filtering boiling water through the grounds you can make yourself any number of a variety of coffees. In fact, in countries around the world coffee is a favourite beverage.

Italians enjoy the morning cafe latte and the daily espresso.

Malaysia and Singapore use a special long-necked pot to pour and blend their coffee which is usually served with sweetened milk.

Hong Kong residents drink coffee and tea mixed together.

Places in the Middle East, like Turkey, make their own special blends of coffee where each cup of coffee is brewed for long periods before being served. And in Taiwan, there is a popular coffee drink that contains small pearls of jelly made partly from yam.

With the advent of international trade, we have been able to sample a huge variety of gourmet and international coffees. In a way, coffee rings the people around the world closer through a common interest.

Recently, new coffee houses have sprung up all over North America and have spawned a new breed of drinkers into the circle.

Just browse through some company literature or a coffee brochure inside a popular coffee house and you are certain to read some information about the nutritive breakdown of a cup of coffee whether it is your regular espresso, house blend coffee, or an ice cappuccino.

They will inform you about some of the misconceptions surrounding caffeine and will educate you about the healthful benefits of drinking coffee daily.

After reading a brochure like this you will probably feel that you should add a regular cup of coffee to your daily liquid intake. Good idea? Maybe, then again, maybe not.

A week later you might find yourself browsing through the numerous health books found inside a bookstore or health food store. You are awestruck as you read about the detrimental and damaging effects coffee and caffeine can do to your body.

The accredited author who wrote this educational book supports their claim with clear evidence from several years of controlled experiments and a decade of research.

Now what are you going to do?

Do you completely eliminate coffee from your diet? No.

This is just another situation where information has become muddled because of free enterprise.

The brochure that you had read also had supported their claims with statistical and historical evidence which favoured drinking coffee.

It is a well known fact that caffeine is a stimulant. It has been shown to increase circulation and assist in brain functioning. It is found in many soft drinks, teas and chocolate.

Athletes are known to use supplements that contain caffeine because they also realize the potential benefits it has during strenuous workouts when energy is required.

Some headache and pain medication also contains it.

Caffeine speeds your heart rate, keeps you awake and can cause headaches later on. Taken in excess, you can have severe reactions.

You can use the effects of caffeine to your advantage when you consider the condition that your body is in.

If you have had coffee before you are already familiar with its ability to get you going on a slow day or to help clear your mind of stress.

As we have learned in previous chapters, all foods produce some effect in a certain quantity. And coffee is a food.

The examples of oranges producing a cleansing effect is one you might recall. So, now with coffee we have learned that it can affect your body also. The problem occurs when you become dependent upon it and drink in excess.

Again, you need to consider your own body's characteristics when deciding how much to drink. Some people react to coffee very badly, while for others it actually benefits their health.

How do you feel after a cup of coffee?

Is this feeling always the same?

The additional item you will want to consider is the kind of coffee that you are drinking.

There are many additions that can be found in coffee: milk, cream, sugar, honey, alcohol, and chocolate.

It is not always the coffee that will affect you. What is found in it may contribute to your health concern more so.

The quality of coffee is just as important as any other part of it. Your body will experience a dramatically different effect from a "bad" cup of coffee than from a "good" one. In order to have a good cup of coffee, you must make sure that it is freshly made, comes from a good roasted bean, and has been prepared under the best conditions.

Every point that is found weak will reduce the quality of the coffee. These types of contradictions are very common in today's global environment.

It's coffee time again

So let us get back to our discussion about coffee. This book is not concerned whether or not there is an incredible amount of good nutrients or bad nutrients in coffee, but more importantly what it does for you.

For those interested in the nutritional breakdown of coffee just spend some time reading a multitude of books and brochures on the subject.

People should be able to drink a fresh cup of coffee without the pressures. If you drink, enjoy it. If it makes you feel ill, then drink something else for a while.
Ever ask yourself why you are drinking that morning cup of coffee? Does it wake you up or does it just jump-start your body for work?

Another question to ask yourself is whether or not you rely on coffee to keep you going?

This is very important.

No matter how good or how bad this dark drink is, you want to know if it has you or not.

Some people I know drink coffee every day and will become a different person if they do not get their regular cup every day.

Other people become frustrated more easily, while still others can lose their concentration and are unable to deal with heavy workloads.

I have found that people with a heavy reliance on coffee for stimulation can become very aggressive and even irrational without their daily "doses." This can indicate that the person's dependence upon coffee has overtaken their chemical balance and they should question their daily consumption levels.

If you find that by drinking the occasional cup of coffee makes you feel good or relaxed, then there is probably little harm in continuing that practice.

This whole idea of drinking coffee falls back on the foundation of this book.

Any diet that is in balance with the person in question should not lead to life-killing, dietary diseases.

Rather, your diet will simply make you feel good every day.

Treat your body right and it will not restrict your life.

Balance is the key.

You need to review how often you are drinking and how it makes you feel afterwards.

Try writing down the number of cups of coffee you have every day for a week and then compare that with what you thought you were drinking.

You might learn something about yourself.

Tea

Tea drinking has been around for many centuries. It is enjoyed by every class in society. In Britain, they enjoy a fresh cup of Orange Pekoe or Ceylon tea with their day.

The Japanese people have discovered their own traditional blends of tea. Green tea is a favourite. They also have many kinds of twig tea and other using roasted barley.

The Chinese people have made tea for thousands of years. The Monks used to drink tea to help them meditate. Many people still know the benefit of drinking tea for their health and have justified their reasons for drinking it regularly.

During British control, Hong Kong citizens learned to make a special milk tea. And Europe is famous for lemon tea. Some farmers in the US make tea from plant leaves from the garden. There are literally thousands of varieties of tea available today. Tea is basically an infusion of dried or fresh plants in hot water. When the plant leaves are placed in the water, the essence of the leaves is released.

For most cases of tea drinking, the infusion is quite mild. There are stronger varieties of herbal plants available as well as combinations of different leaves that can be purchased at the health food store. The type of plant leaves used and how they are prepared will significantly affect the nutritional value of the tea.

You need to be able to distinguish between the numerous varieties available. A good tea, one that has been derived from natural sources and prepared accordingly, can stimulate different functions in your body. A tea is prepared most commonly from the leaves of a particular herbal plant. Other sources of teas also include the roots, stem, flowers, seeds, fruits, and other parts of the plant. Some different plant combinations form the basis of mixed or blended teas.

Many teas also contain caffeine similar to that of coffee.

There are teas to stimulate digestion, alleviate headaches, eliminate excess water retention, calm your nerves, help you sleep, make you sweat and any other minor bodily maladjustment you may be afflicted with.

The key is that teas in themselves produce only a minor effect on your body. Therefore, only after prolonged consumption will they eradicate a more serious ailment in conjunction with diet, exercise, and other positive factors.

What I have been talking about so far are regular drinking teas versus the other extreme, therapeutic teas. Regular drinking teas are safe for daily consumption and include ones like orange pekoe, peppermint, chamomile, chrysanthemum, Chinese oolong and jasmine, green tea, and the like.

Therapeutic teas are usually made for specific illnesses and reasons and should be left to people who understand herbal medicine. If you are interested in finding out about therapeutic teas in more depth it is advisable to consult an herbalist.

I have known people who have experimented on themselves and have wreaked havoc upon their bodies. I would not recommend this as there are numerous experienced herbalists that can instruct you on proper use. You will need to spend time researching this topic instead of making a hasty decision. The ideal situation is one which you can work with your herbalist to heal yourself.

Teas range in quality. Some tea can be purchased for a couple of Canadian dollars a pound and can rise to one hundred and fifty dollars a pound or higher. The difference is in the availability of the plant and how it is cultivated.

To obtain the best tea, a grower must pick the leaves in the correct season and during the right time of day.

Often, the correct leaf on the tea tree leads to a more pleasant taste and a higher price. After that, it needs to be handled in a special manner in order to derive its true flavour and benefit. Every planet is handled differently.

The more expensive teas are only used during special occasions. They are reputed to be more beneficial to health than the lower grade teas. A clean, good quality lower grade tea is adequate for daily consumption.

Once you have purchased some tea, find out what is the best recommended method for steeping the leaves.

If the water is too hot or too cold, it can have an effect on the flavour. Also, if the tea leaves are steeped too long in the hot water this can leave a different taste altogether.

Many cultures have developed tea ceremonies and rituals to illustrate this.

Alcoholic beverages

Alcohol is a drink that has long been abused in many regions of the world and yet in many other regions it has been used with care and moderation. There is an epidemic of alcoholics who do not realize the effect of alcohol on the body. Excessive amounts of anything is damaging to your health.

There is a lot of information written about alcohol and how it is killing people. I feel that this aspect of alcohol has been overwritten and yet people refuse to listen to it.

I want to focus instead on some considerations for alcohol users. The first consideration is for its health benefit. Some alcohol is known for aiding digestion, stimulating circulation, reducing the risk of coronary disease and for helping some people to relax. These benefits are only derived from drinking in extreme moderation and will greatly depend on the person's constitution. There is no set amount on how much to drink. Everybody is different.

The second consideration is for alcohol abusers. You now know that an excessive alcohol intake over an extended period of time will damage your internal organs.

So, if you are one of those who is recovering from alcohol abuse then you should stay away from alcohol and; instead, consume large amounts of other healthy beverages such as, water, juices and teas.

The third consideration is the type of alcohol you drink. Hard liquor makes the body very hot. Beer makes the body cool. Most wine is somewhere in the middle.

There are too many kinds of alcohol to be listed here. It would take an entire book to cover them properly.

What you should consider is how the alcohol makes you feel. If you want to drink alcohol, you can change the type of alcohol that you drink to balance some of the extreme effects.

As a final note, try to determine what reasons you are drinking the alcohol.

Remember, as with food, alcohol is just not something to drink for the fun of it all of the time. It holds certain properties that can adversely affect your body if misused.

People react differently to alcohol.

Learn to use alcohol more for health reasons than for habit. Use alcohol to help you digest, to help you relax and to maintain good circulation.

Alcohol is something that everyone can enjoy, but the responsibility is ultimately yours as to how much you are willing to drink and under what circumstances.

Use alcohol to help you instead or using it to injure you.

How to drink

Make sure when you eat that you properly chew your food. After that, use liquid sparingly to keep your system clear and allow sufficient liquids to stay in your stomach to help digestion.

Even though you have acids and liquids in your stomach it is not always sufficient to mix with the meal you've eaten, so when you add the proper liquid the food not only mixes better, but also makes it easier on your digestive system.

Meals that are difficult to digest or are oily should be accompanied by drinks that aid digestion. A body that is under stress needs something to help it to relax and someone that needs to maintain a high level of brain activity should drink fluids that stimulate circulation and brain function.

No one can every really tell you how much you should drink with your meal, if any. It largely depends upon your body type, the type of food you're eating and what you ate earlier in the day.

Become aware of your body and feed it what it needs. Everyone is different and each day is also different – learn to be the judge yourself. Try writing down what you drink everyday on the next.

How do you drink?

What kind of sweetener do you put in your coffee?

How much do you us? One teaspoon, two packets, etc.?

Do you use the same sweetener in tea? Why or why not?

How much coffee do you drink?

How much tea do you drink?

When do you realize that you have had enough?

What kind of alcohol do you usually drink? Win? Beer? Hard liquor?

How often do you have alcohol? Is it one glass of beer a day on average? Or a shot of whiskey after work? Why are you drinking alcohol?

What visible signs tell you that you had too much alcohol?

SHINING ON YOU ALWAYS

FOOD MANNERS

There is always a need to seek appropriate foods. Even the best researched diets may not be suitable for you.
Before you do anything else, you must look at the manner in which you eat your meal. In all cultures, there is a specific method or what I call a particular *manner to eating*.

Most people should be familiar with the belief that sweet foods will spoil their appetite or that the appetizer comes before the main meal. Why is this so?

These manners have evolved over centuries of practice among the various cultures. This is not to say that all of the traditional manners are perfect, but for those people who have lived in and adjusted to those cultural food manners, they should have little problem in continuing them.

Many Italians love to eat their pasta dish before the main entree while many Asian cultures prefer to eat everything all together.

In Korea, most people have a hot soup before any meal is eaten while the Northern Chinese people prefer to have the soup at the end of the meal. These manners of eating have developed to a level that is now culturally acceptable, but it does not stop there as research and studies continually bring in new information.

With whatever manner you grew up with, you need to make sure that eating must be done in such a way as to give little stress on the body and to allow full digestion to take place.

In Southern China, soup is commonly eaten at the beginning of a meal. Why would they adopt a contradictory belief to the Northern people?

It is believed that the hot soup stimulates the stomach and prepares it for digestion. Also, different herbal soups are used to provide additional nourishment or support to the daily meal.

The citizens of Japan often have miso soup at the beginning of a meal. This particular soup is known for its benefits in strengthening digesting. In South Korea, as you read earlier, a similar practice occurs as the hot soup is served before the meal.

The logic to the food manner presented in the previous paragraph resembles the effect of warming up the body before performing some physical exercise or activity.

A hot drink, alcohol, or some specially prepared food dish can help to produce a similar, but diminished effect. It is not necessary to have soup at every meal, though in some countries, like Korea, Mexico, and Japan, this practice is still used today.

In the Northern part of China, the reason that soup is commonly eaten at the end of the meal is to balance the amount of bread eaten during dinner. And if you are someone who enjoys soup then you are probably having it quite often anyway.

Another item to think about is the appetizer. This is more commonly found in restaurants, large family gatherings and dinner parties. The appetizer should be something that is used to stimulate the appetite. These are smaller, tasty dishes of bite sized food. In Italy, it is called the antipasto.

Eating in an orderly fashion then, can make a difference on how well the body receives the nutrients.

What's the rush?

What I want to talk about here is the manner in which you eat.

Proper eating also comes from allowing your body sufficient time to digest its meals. It is harmful to eat too fast or to consume an excessive amount of food.

The appetite of a particular person can indicate just what type of person they are. A short-tempered person or one who has little patience will tend to devour their food with little satisfaction and in haste. Another indication might be the fact that someone is very hungry and is in need of nourishment or Nutrimento.

Eating too fast and gulping down chunks of food can lead to serious digestive disorder in the future. Also, if you eat too fast you may be swallowing a lot of air along with your food and may give you gas and an abnormally enlarged stomach. This can also produce abdominal pains.

When you eat too fast you are sending down food that is not properly chewed and thus not prepared for your stomach.

It is a well known fact that your stomach doesn't have any teeth. They are only in your mouth.

That is why the consistency of the food reaching your stomach must be such that it can be well received by your stomach; otherwise, you will be placing more stress on your digestion than needed and since your digestive system requires almost half of your energy during a meal it would be wise to properly chew you r food.

The other thing that your teeth can help you prevent is eating something that is too hard. If what you are chewing cannot be broken down by your teeth it is unlikely that your stomach can finish the job.

Keep in mind that if you do swallow chunks of food or just eat excessively it could deplete most of your energy and could render you tired and sleepy.

How many times have you found yourself sleepy after a meal? How about after a "heavy" meal?

This is the reason why you need to pay more attention to your eating habits. Eating large amounts of good food cannot always be prevented, just bear in mind the regularity of the event.

Eating should be an enjoyable endeavour. It is a good idea to rest before and after a meal to allow your system to relax.

Imagine that you have just finished a three and a half mile jog and sit right down to eat dinner. Do you think you would really feel hungry? Try it.
What you most likely will feel is thirst, not hunger.

When you eat, your body is using the muscles in your digestive system, namely those of your stomach, to break down and assimilate food.
This requires more blood and oxygen to localize and to support this action. Strenuous activity or other actions that require high energy will take away from digestion. Light activity such as walking and moderate laughter, can help to digest.

So the best way to eat is to eat slowly. When you eat slower you can actually prevent yourself from overeating. Eating slow allows your body sufficient time to digest and metabolize food.

This method of slow eating was found to be very valuable to prisoners in the war, since they were usually fed small amounts of food, they found that by eating slowly they were able to extract the maximum satisfaction from what little scraps they were given. It prevented them from dying too quickly from starvation.

When you gulp down your meal you do not give your system sufficient time to inform your brain that it has had enough.

What usually happens is that you tend to overeat. It is overeating, especially of fatty or sugary foods, that leads to obesity.

Not only that, but eating too fast can cause many digestive disorders. If your internal system was exceptionally strong you probably wouldn't feel the effects for a few years or even a decade or two, but sooner or later it would catch up on you. People with a weak digestive system should pay special attention to their dietary habits.

You have been introduced to another aspect of eating. It is about the manner in which you eat. It does not matter where you come from or what your traditions are as long as your eating habits are contributing to good health.

If they are not, then you need to make some adjustments; if they are relatively healthy, then you can make some refinements.

IT'S ALL IN THE APPROACH

You will have now reached the stage that has made you examine much more closely the current diet you have been eating.

Some of you may have already made some changes to your old diet and are considering ways to make further improvements.

You should realize by now that in order to maximize your dietary intake you will need to have a good understanding of the five basic questions – why, who, where, when, and what.

And you are probably aware that I have yet to answer the last question, "How to approach eating?" There are five thoughts that you must follow if you are to approach eating in an effective way. Implant them in your brain and they will serve you well.

They are:

1. Eat a sufficient amount of food.
2. Eat for your body.
3. Enjoy what you eat.
4. Eat a variety.
5. Monitor your eating habits.

1. Eat a sufficient amount of food.

What you want to achieve here is balance. Any foods eaten to an extreme will be detrimental to your health.

Should you overeat, try to incorporate foods, drinks, exercises to make yourself feel better.

The amount of food you eat will vary according to the five factors – age, gender, physical condition, climate, and lifestyle.

So, just because you used to eat less at one point does not mean that it is unhealthy to eat more at another point and time in your life. Just remember to monitor your body for unhealthy signs.

2. Eat for your body.

When you eat for your body you naturally satisfy the body's nutritional needs and; therefore, promote good health and regeneration.

Eating for your body says that foods that contain health benefits should be chosen over foods that you have been tempted to eat.

If you notice that you have many cravings for junk or bad food, then you must make a concerted effort to make daily changes for the better. This is accomplished by listening to what your body needs by understanding its message.

Are we communicating?

3. Enjoy what you eat.

It has long been discovered that moods and states of mind affect the results of almost every aspect of your life including success and achievement, recovery from illness, and relationships with friends and family.

Additionally, your state of mind greatly affects your digestion and absorption of the meal.

Be sure to remain in positive spirits when you eat. If you are not really enjoying what you are eating then make some changes so that you do enjoy it.

That is not to say that you should only eat dessert. In fact, by now you should be more aware of the foods that your body needs versus those that you like the taste of.

If you have children, try to show them the fun and enjoyment of eating a wide variety of foods.

4. Eat a variety.

There are hundreds of thousands of foods available in the world without counting on the hundreds of ways each of them can be prepared. So there should be no reason to subsist on the same kinds of foods every day.

Try to enjoy a variety in your diet. If you find it difficult to do so, then you have four options.

First, you can buy a good cookbook and spend time in the kitchen learning how to cook.

Second, if you don't have that much time you can ask your parents (assuming that they know how to still cook foods you like) to show you some simple recipes.

Third, you can make room in your schedule to go to a cooking class.

Fourth, you can either hire someone to cook for you or you can eat at your parent's house.

5. Monitor your eating habits.

In order for you to continue to eat effectively and to keep your kids happy and healthy, you need to watch your eating habits.

This will ensure that you and your family are getting the nutrition they need. It will also allow you to make the necessary changes based on the climate, your lifestyle, age growth, and other relevant factors.

DEALING WITH ETHNIC INFLUENCES

An eating problem that people run into all over the world these days is the availability and influence of many cultures. It is very easy to find a wide variety of ethnic restaurants in all of the large cities.

There are Thai, Cambodian, Malaysian, Russian, Sri Lankan, Mexican, East Indian, Korean, Vietnamese, African, Afghanistan, French, Polynesian, Spanish, Ukrainian, Chinese, Japanese, German, and Italian restaurants everywhere plus a multitude of others.

The difficulty is not in finding one, but in finding a balanced meal when you go.

People have a general misconception about many different ethnic foods. It is completely understandable, since unless you are a native you are not likely to be familiar with what you are eating.

I remember when I first tried Chinese food.

I had sweet and sour pork and chicken chow mein in a fast-food style cafe in Canada. The pork tasted good. The chow main and even the pork were quite greasy and the combination gave me indigestion later.

I didn't realize it then, but I had eaten a "poorly" combined meal.

Quite often I hear of people eating Italian food and finding that it upset their stomachs or that it caused them to gain weight. If you look at what type of foods they are, you could understand what has been causing their complaint.

Typically, it was caused by eating excessive amounts of pizza with lots of pepperoni and cheese or a nice full plate of pasta with cream sauce.

In fact, if you ask someone what is Italian food they invariably reply with dishes such as pasta or pizza or veal. What makes Chinese food? It's the fried rice, of course. And everyone knows that Tacos and Burritos are Mexican favourites with lots of salsa. Indian food must be curry.

It is understandable that we look at ethnic food in this extremely limited way since unless you are familiar with the types of dishes available, you will order the same thing just to be safe.

There are literally thousands of ethnic dishes all of which can be good for you, but the problem comes when people are selective about what they eat and from restaurants who cater to their tastes.

It is a well known fact that it is better to serve what people will order on the menu than to have uncommon, unwanted dishes as a choice. This is a common practice since people have a tendency to return dishes that do not agree with their taste buds.

I have run into many instances when I was told by the waiter in an Asian restaurant to order something else as they strongly felt that I would not like what I had ordered.

They did not know that I had eaten those foods before, so it was understandable that they suggested otherwise.

The story of the salted fish

One evening I went with my friends for dinner. We decided to go for Chinese food.

I felt that my body needed some salty food at the time and so decided to order one of my favourite dishes, steamed pork with salted fish.

The waiter looked at me funny and didn't want to write down the order. He started to make horrible facial gestures at me and tried to tell me how smelly and stinky that particular dish was.

I told him that's what I wanted.

He responded with a different recommendation, but that wasn't what I wanted to eat.

At that point I decided to use what little Cantonese I knew at the time and after hearing me say the name of the dish in Chinese he was convinced that I knew what I was ordering.

He even seemed happy. I couldn't tell if it was from my pronunciation of a new language or if I had ordered one of his favourite dishes.

I didn't blame him for being so persistent because I remember the first time I was introduced to that dish. It made the hair on the back of my neck stand up and instantly retracted all of my facial muscles so that my whole face puckered right up.

It was a good thing I was just sampling my friend's dish at the time.

The restaurant complainer

When I worked in a Chinese restaurant, I used to hear a lot of complaints from friends and customers that although the food tasted good, it was too oily. I couldn't understand it because I ate there almost every day and never found it to be greasy. So I decided to look into it further. I began to ask people with complaints what they had eaten during their meal.

To my surprise I discovered the root of the problem. Everyone I had talked to had eaten dishes like deep fried prawns, deep fried sweet and sour pork and oily chow mein.

Very few of them had ordered stir friend vegetables, steamed dishes or non-deep fried dishes. I was thinking. "That's not Chinese food!" but to them it was because to eat anything else was too adventurous.

I asked my friends if they would eat a steamed rock cod and they responded with surprise, "I didn't know you could order that!"

That makes a good point. Any time you enter an ethnic restaurant that you are not familiar with, you will be hard pressed to order a good selection of foods unless you have brought friends with you who know what to order from the menu.

This is a common problem when sampling new varieties of food.

One drawback would be if your friends weren't very familiar with what was good, healthy food themselves. The important point in all this is regarding proper food combining and eating a balanced meal.

If you go into an ethnic restaurant to eat, but refuse to eat most items because of your discerning taste buds, then you are in for some trouble. A poor quality restaurant is another factor that is difficult to control. Sometimes, home-cooked ethnic food is a better option.

Ethnic food has evolved over many centuries (I am not really considering the American and Canadian diet, since it was largely influenced by some of the old cultures as well as some of the modern cultures) to a point where the foods that comprise a good meal should be in balance.

When a stranger wants to try the food, they should try it all as a complete meal not to just select parts that more closely resemble their own diet.

It would be unfair for me to go into an Indian restaurant, eat some chilli-laden curry lamb with roti and later complain of indigestion because of the over-spiciness of the meal.

If I were to take a closer look at how an Indian person at they would more likely include some specially prepared vegetables, some mixtures of cucumber and buttermilk, certain spinach dishes, and even special drinks.

All of these latter foods help to cool off the spicy curry sauces. Not only that, but Indian food is much more than just curry. There are thousands of different dishes to choose from.

What these examples should make clear is that in order to eat a healthy meal, food should be properly combined according to your personal dietary needs.

Obviously if you get indigestion, constipation, pimples, headaches or any other of a myriad of symptoms, something was not eaten in proper accordance with YOUR body.

You may just find that the new cultural foods sitting on the table in front of you are vastly different from anything you have every eaten in your home for the last 20 years. If this is the case, at slowly and carefully so that you don't send your body into a state of surprise.

It would be unfair to blame a particular ethnic culture that their food is too spicy or oily when you haven't given it the chance.

It is not always just the quality of the food that is important, but also the quantity that is consumed. There is a lot of good food available in every part of the world. But it is just not usual to consume excessive amounts of it during one meal.

It would be wise to turn off your selectivity channel and to introduce y0ur taste buds to newer pleasures of foods.

Nutrimento has no cultural boundaries.

CHANGING FOOD PERCEPTIONS

You need to move away from your present perceptions of food.

What I propose is that you begin to use a new approach when it is time to eat. You need to choose food because of its "effective value."

The food value that affects your body depends upon the five questions I outlined at the beginning of this book – who, what, when, where, and why.

The effective value is the net result your body experiences after eating.

By dealing with any one of these questions you can improve the effective value your body receives.

All food can be good for you.

All foods can be bad for you.

The key is making the right balance for yourself.

Only by eating a variety of meat, fish, vegetables, grains, liquids, fruits, seeds, nuts, and companion foods will your bodies receive all the necessary nutrition.

You can also supplement your diet by incorporating herbal foods and other whole supplements. These supplements can act as supervisors and help keep the body balance during stressful times in your life.

In order to obtain full use of the information contained in this book you will need to increase your knowledge about food.

Here are some ways that can support this process:

1. **Keep a daily diary.** Write a detailed list of food you at during the week. Spend time afterwards to analyze it. You don't need to write in your food diary every week. Try writing in it one week a month to start.

2. **Pay attention to your groceries.** When you buy something, inspect it or if it is packaged read the list of ingredients. If you still decide to buy it, at least you are familiar with what you are ingesting. This way you will know how to balance it out later.

3. **Listen to your body.** Watch how your body responds to the various foods you put into it. Look for changes in energy levels, body temperature, mood swings, bloating, aches and pains and changes in the color of your face. The better you understand your body, the quicker you will be able to discern what is going on and what it needs.

4. **Experiment with different foods.** Sample new varieties of foods. Look at your present diet over the next month and think about how many different varieties of foods you presently eat. Try adding new ones every week to expand your diet.

5. **Give your body what it needs.** You may want to order that sweet glazed cinnamon bun for lunch, but your body could use that healthy bowl of homemade soup.

You may find yourself on that weighing scale again and refusing to eat another piece of high calorie food, but your body may need something that is nourishing and has some energy in it.

When you discover that you are standing in line for another heavy grease meal, turn around, walk over to the salad and sandwich bar and indulge there.

You get the idea.

Eat foods to feed your body, not foods that feed your taste buds.

6. **Change seasonally.** Your body is part of nature and thereby follows its rules. With this in mind, it is much better to live in tune with its seasons and climate.

Eat foods that will warm you in winter and cool you in summer. Eat foods that will cleanse you in spring and prepare you in autumn. Keep an eye on nature's changes and it will help you to make changes in your diet.

7. **Adjust regionally.** The different countries and regions of the world have a unique dietary intake. Spend time to slowly incorporate new ethnic foods into your diet. If you plan to spend a considerable amount of time in a different region from your own, then you would be better off adopting the regional diet and saving your own native foods for the occasional meal.

Appreciating the value of food

I remember learning a long time ago this old Chinese saying.

> One disease, long life;
> No disease, short life.

I thought about what it meant and initially came up with very little. It remained in the back of my mind until one day it finally became clearer to me. It was a day that I became sick and discovered the true pain of losing my health.

I've told this saying to many others and they have taken it into consideration, so I feel that it holds an important message for all of us.

When a person becomes afflicted with a disease, they realize how valuable their health is and make future efforts to look after their health. Most of the time the illness doesn't last that long.

A cold for example may only last a few days; a skin rash can last anywhere from one day up to years, it just depends upon the severity of the disease and the nature of the person.

When I speak of disease, I am including everything that puts you at "dis-ease." Notice that the word is very basic at its root.

All that it is saying is that a person is not at ease; things are not as they should be. There is some imbalance inside the body and it is producing some unwanted reactions such as the symptoms outlines in the chapter on understanding your body.

The way people usually interpret it today is of a more serious nature, although disease can be serious and painful.

When there is no disease, no illness; there is a tendency to abuse what you have. It is just like other aspects of life where without consequence there is sometimes insufficient reason to change.

When you neglect your health and become afflicted by digestive problems, obesity, heart disease, liver cirrhosis or cancer, you can't trade in your body for another.

You have to live with whatever you have and deal with it from there. As some of you reading this already know, being sick and unable to perform daily activities is difficult to deal with. It is sometimes even more painful watching someone you care about who has to deal with an illness.

By monitoring your diet, you can prevent disease from grasping a hold on your body. You can delay aging. That means you look younger, healthier, more radiant, and more alive.

You can enjoy your life with more energy and vitality than ever before. Sure you need the other components, but **food is the fuel of life**. Sometimes referred to in the past as, the "staff of life."

Even those who look after their health may experience serious illness and those that don't may have very little problems with their health.

You may look at a particular person and think how lucky they are because they are healthy, but you don't really know when their last illness was or what they do to prevent any illness from taking a hold of their body. Genetic makeup and environment have some effect on it especially today with the number of new diseases that have been discovered.

You don't need to move to organic farming (unless you really want to) and live your life secluded in a hidden mountain pass to live a healthy life. Neither do you need to avoid eating anything, but raw vegetables.

You can choose to live now, in today's environment with today's food. All you need to do is learn some basic knowledge about the new value of food and apply it to your own particular constitution.

No special cost for packaged food.

No more diet programs to starve you to death.
No more confusion about information on nutrition.

You will become a Nutrimentist.

It will require some patience and some time on your part and the benefit will be something money cannot buy. In the end, you will learn the art of effective eating.

You will learn to use the concept of Nutrimento to stay healthy, active, and to help your family do the same.

This will be a valuable skill that you can pass on to your loved ones and allow them the chance to enjoy their diet and life in the future. In the end, you will have passed on a very important gift that that they can carry with them their whole life – the basics of feeling good by understanding the meaning behind Nutrimento.

May you find the answers that you have searched long for.

Now you know the basics of feeling good.

So, let's get Nutrimento'ed.

Buon appetito.

Enjoy your meal.

Happy eating.

23 SERMONS

SERMON FOR A MISGUIDED PLANET

This planet is broken and the very scoundrels who broke it will prepare to sell you ways in which to fix it. The planet they purposely destroyed. These selfish suited folk will convince you that a new order is required as a means to ensure the safety of the human race. Should a pig trust the owner of a slaughterhouse when they offer their plans for communityism? No. A pig would be wise to reject every syllable from their mouths. The view of a pig is their view on you. Not mine. Had genuine ideas and efforts for a better world every been used in the last 2,000 years, earth wouldn't be ruined.

These same rulers of earth have insisted their right hand is better than their left hand and then suggested that the right hand would solve the problems caused by the left hand. Each of the thousands of times, good-willed people wholeheartedly support one of the two best hands. There's never a top five hands because they only have two hands.

Regardless of your level of awareness, you cannot deny the dismal state of the world, the repetitive history, the censorship of alternatives and the erosion of humanism. All of what you see is a result of the same two hands painting the same picture over and over again with different pencils and different paper. But the picture is the same, and the picture of the next order is going to have the same foulness of this order. To shake the foulness from the world, you are required to ask better questions, you are required to come up with unheard of solutions, and peaceful alternatives, you are required to return to your origins, return to naturalism, return to a ungovernmented society that is all about the people. It's not a time to fight as much as it is a time to invent. Invent a better future and a new future will manifest; fight the order and you get tired. Defend the defenseless and protect all that which is most important. You decide. Remember your home is earth.

The starmen and starwomen are already here, so there's no invasion. It wouldn't make sense to invade yourself, although you could be convinced of it by a good salesman. My perspective is that humanity, as a whole, has all the necessary hardware, the essentials for healthy existence are either immediately available or available soon. What is lacking is the software. The outdated, self-defeating mindset, the compulsion to devote to self and ego, the addiction to lousy leaders, the focus on war and wealth, things like this are out of date. The software needs an overhaul.

In order to provide a kind of summary of the mess on this planet, I've prepared ten strategies that have been used to enslave you into this point today. These ten malicious strategies are provided in no particular order and are nonfiction. As usual though, my views are a bit more multidimensional than others who stick to reason and logic. I incorporate imagination so you'll need to work that muscle. These malicious strategies are each by themselves quite powerful and the fact that they have all been employed against humanity (plus more) should remind you that there is no moral reversal that will ever take place with these guys. To go this far is to go beyond redemption so waiting for them to save society and to come up with good ideas is like waiting for a wolf to bake an apple pie.

The Prophetic 10

Here are ten (10) malicious strategies that have been used to prophetically deconstruct the proper state of reality so as to hoard all imaginable power and to forever imprison human reincarnation. (This list is provided so as to provide a kind of raw mental map of the battlefield.):

1. Loosing Traumatic Events

You've heard of Pearl Harbour, Hiroshima, The Great Depression, The Holocaust, Collapse of the World Trade Center. If a 14-year-old girl gets gang raped, she'll not only lose her virginity, but shall be traumatized. And this trauma will occupy her for many years to come. These large-scale events have traumatized an entire society, then the reactions to those trigger events have literally traumatized the world, war in the Middle East for example. What does this mean? It means that you are all survivors of multiple unrecognized traumas at a societal level, as a society and as an individual; and unless the society is treated and healed, those traumas will exist for many years to come, plus they will simply gang rape the society as and when necessary. The loosing of traumatic events on the world is a lot like living with an abusive husband (or spouse or boss) in that the wife becomes trapped, deeply damaged, refuses to leave for fear for the consequences and will likely never leave without a few miracles. If you look at the past

2,000 years and humanity's reluctance to adopt new levels of thinking, the interference from the ruling class and the current state of fear gripping the world such as terrorism, outbreaks, drugs, your neighbour, rogue nations, burning in hell, getting fat, not paying your mortgage, losing your job, not getting an erection every day, looking ugly, having bad skin and dirty floors.

2. Disrupting Natural Timeline

The large-scale traumatic events above (eg Pearl Harbour) have also impacted the thought patterns of large populations in the world. The fall out of war, of military drafts, defense department manufacturing, fear of nations, threat of starvation and death – all of these and more have changed the thought patterns on earth. And as we are all learning, thought determines reality and reality affects the evolution of an existential lifeform, or its timeline of progression. These events have literally dialled back human time, or, regressed human progress on many essential levels of awareness. Rather than achieving peace and interstellar contact, for example, humanity was plunged into misery and death. The trajectory of human evolution changed and split into an alternate reality. This was done on purpose to prevent human waking.

3. Harming Natural Infrastructure

The planet, like your body, has an internal soul, or energy body; or, an *energy architecture*. The machine that gives the planet its life is an integral part of the planetary being, just like the health of your soul affects the health of your body and if your soul dies, you die (unless you are a politician). Working in concert (cooperation) with other dimensional lifeforms and alongside egotistical starmen here for thousands of years, the internal reality architecture has been damaged to many degrees. For example, the warming of the planet was a result of a damage to the dimensional cooling system, which when recognized needed repair. By adjusting or damaging the function of the reality engine, they 1) impact the health of the planet, and, 2) alter the vibrational occupancy of earth which determines its progress in the cosmos and affects what other lifeforms can gain access to this plane.

4. Blocking Minds of Inhabitants

Using advanced techniques, the masters of earth have implanted psychic blocks in most or all of humanity, and they have repeated those psychic damages over and over again. Unless you've spent years in dealing with your own ascension, you are still carrying these blocks which result in the tendency toward self, the refusal to think outside the box and a very low self worth.

To block the mind is a straightforward task on their part and they use techniques, like symbols, as a form of reinforcement. All of this happens in another dimension so are imperceptible to the common or intellectual person. Even by removing or overcoming these blocks, they are soon implanted again. So, you're thinking is actually hobbled or crippled for nefarious reasons.

5. Injecting Poisons into the Population

Genetically modified food, artificial sweeteners, tobacco smoke, nicotine, fluoridated water, birth control pills, chemtrails, preservatives, pesticides, industrial waste, biological warfare ingredients, vaccinations – the list of poison is extremely long. It taxes the body. It's like living in a sewer. The vaccination programs only highlight their insistence to shut you down. We haven't even talked about the relevance on pain relievers and prescriptions which further damage the internal viscera (organs). Ironically, all the poisons mentioned thus far are permitted, even legal and approved by the health bureau in most cases. Poisoning is the norm. Naturalism is dead. Organic food is a shelf in a grocery story of inorganic food. The human body is taxed to the max.

6. Limiting Human Thought

Religion does not lead to enlightenment for man need only look within to find out who he is. When he depends solely on a limiting Bible written four or five thousand years ago; when he believes that his religion is better than another religions; when he worships divine figures (eg Messiahs), then it doesn't take much to realize that the limitless, everlasting, endless cosmos is limited, has a timeline and death is the end. All of this does nothing to enlighten. Then there are corporations that promise you goods and services as long as you earn the money, at another corporation, to pay for them. And many of these goods and services serve the self. And all corporations are churches to the head church: The Bank. There all your sweat and temptation feeds these masters of money and since money is equal to energy in other dimensions. While you cannot see it, your reliance on a monetary system is the carrier to giving the rulers your energy, keeping you a slave.

7. Inserting Puppetary Leaders

All the key leaders in the world, all these years, left and right, are either put in place by the masters of the world or are controlled by them. Anyone can be controlled because the masters have godlike abilities. They've been around for millennia and exist where they wish. They are immortal and can only be touched by similar. They play a heavy hand in the control of leaders of nations, corporations, banks, law offices, religions, etc.

The leaders are played off of each other to change or influence human thought. Celebrities are propped up or put into the spotlight in order to distract. Very few leaders are uncontrollable. For example, a Gandhi figure or a John Lennon type. Every person, no matter their strength, acts upon a compromise. You give up something for something. This is always the case. If a celebrity wants fame, they give up something for it. A President as well. So, to control people they only need to understand what people want, but the price is very high, a bit like serving the Devil and getting all your wishes come true.

8. Reprogramming Reality

As reality itself functions as an operating system, one of these masters of earth can in fact enter reality and reprogram parts of it, sort of like in the movie The Matrix, only its real. They can take a certain event and make it into a catastrophe. They can reprogram a person take a different life path like a Hitler for example. There are many ways to do this. For example, you sell a Hitler the chance to win glory or you tell him that he'll save the world or you create a hatred with another nation and a Hitler reacts to that, or all three. No one on earth can resist all temptations. No one. Reality as well is reprogrammed such that certain events are overlooked or that interstellar cultures are feared instead of befriended or that certain groups are classified as dangerous cults. If a peace treaty is to be signed tomorrow, there's a surprise delay. If a nation needs a trigger for war, a trigger is entered. Reprogramming isn't easy and it requires a lot of effort from many hands but it also comes with a price for nothing is free so they are careful to do things in a very efficient way.

9. Interfering at Astral Levels

We all know there's other dimensions because we've all heard of the astral realm, or seeing angels and so forth. You enter these realms in your dreams. They have a kind of dream police that work on the astral level looking for trouble makers, looking for people about to wake up, looking for people who are looking into topics that are very secretive. All knowledge can be known in the astral, according to your readiness, but they work at the astral level to block access as well. They don't like you snooping around. So it takes an adept person to get stuff done.

10. Hiding Multidimensional Fields

One of the biggest, most well-kept secret on earth is the fact that this place is a plane of existence. In other words, this plane of existence is one of many planes of existence. And, in those other planes are multidimensional people in existence. They've managed to make these multidimensional fields unavailable to your perception. And if you get the idea of other realities you soon disbelieve, forget or write a fictional story. But, it should be noted in concise format, multidimensional people are here interacting with human society in many ways, for ill or good. And you should start paying attention because not all people are who they appear to be.

I've only managed to touch the surface of the broken world upon which we all exist. I've laid out, in brief, ten of the impressive and malicious strategies they use so you can begin to see the map, that each of these are connected and you are the pig on the farm and it's just a matter of time when they want some bacon. You have to remember that a pure and natural world is not full of these interferences. Leaders and are not opposed to serve egotistical masters who approve routine pursing of the world, endless war and permit banks to control society.

As well, it should be noted, humans are required to maintain the health of their planet, to service its external and internal components, and to live in harmony with their environment. Human beings should never, under any circumstance, allow lies and deception to continue just so they pay their mortgage and look good in jeans. Having white teeth is not something that is important, to any stretch of the imagination, when the world is at war and the medical institution is force vaccinating children. We can blame the egotistical masters, but humanity has shamefully remained complacent and careless, negligent verily about their lives. Repeatedly writing about the deteriorating world does not lead to action, action leads to action. Again, as a reminder, we live in a multidimensional cosmos, so develop your multidimensional muscles and you'll have greater effect over your masters. Choose areas of disturbance and work on ways to return it to balance. This planet was meant for you after all.

The Return

I'm not a fatalist and I'm not religious for I depend on no one book. The ultimate truth comes from the deepest parts of the cosmos. There, knowledge is in its purest state, before logic and reason, fear and control, love and compassion. I am not indicating that all is lost because the game isn't over. I am strongly saying that, regardless of what you think, this world is a mess; and compared to what it could be, this place is at its lowest point. Obviously, had people looked at their planet as their home, they wouldn't have allowed such pillaging to take place, problem was that the people were sold on the promise of a better, leaner, richer tomorrow. All of it an illusion.

Here's a sample: The discovery of nuclear power saw the manufacturing of 30,000 nuclear warheads and not even 500 nuclear power plants; the invention of the first electric car in the early 1900s saw the rise of the gasoline engine and 100 years later the reintroduction of the electric car without 100 years of development; the Ten Commandments of the Christian Bible, including "Thou Shalt Not Kill" saw the sponsorship by the Vatican Pope on the illegal War in Iraq & Afghanistan which approved the killing of people by their pacifist God and love thy neighbour Jesus; the dependence on foreign oil as warned in a speech by Jimmy Carter in 1977, despite promises and rhetoric to the contrary, hasn't changed till this current day; the multibillion dollar "War on Cancer" in the US has led to an increase in the rate of cancer over that lengthy term; the rise of feminism has divided the family unit and given rise to unnatural levels of homosexuality in the population; and the hobbled space programs have hobbled humanity's interstellar rights. The illusions are many. Usually, the new generation is not aware of the false promises of the previous generation so they buy whatever the leader is selling. The first World War was identified as the "War to End all Wars," ten wars later we are still at war.

The rulers of earth are very dedicated to making sure that this realm remains under their dominion for the time to come. They are now, in addition to all the other junk, causing biblical prophecy to finds its way into society so as to truly grab a hold of the world, for when the signs of the imaginary apocalypse can be put on paper, into their picture, then the common mind will be trapped into the inevitable conclusion of life by God Himself. The God Card is being carefully played out, and forced I might add, as a kind of wallop punch. When God and the Bible are drawn into their illusions, they will have all the world's attention, the ultimate trauma on hand, and they will steer humanity into a final conclusion. You'll hear this word more, Biblical. Religion is the one idea that the whole world understands, and where most of the world has worshippers. The ultimate demographic.

It is imperative that people begin thinking of a better future, one that is outside of the old parameters, one that is full of cosmic knowledge, a return to harmony, a reconnection to the other planes and the other people who reside there. Earth belongs to a cosmic club, it is not independent as you have been led to believe. Many earth citizens come from other areas of the cosmos. Humanity itself is a cosmic culture.

THE FLU IN FRESHLY PREPARED EYES

Canada, as with many nations, is in the midst of a bewildering mass immunization program for the H1N1 Virus, a bewildering multi-strain virus that the medical profession insists requires a vaccination or death will result. From this view, they are adamant that the vaccine will save lives. But the apple has fallen very far from the cherry tree because in a manufactured reality, such as this earth plane, influenza is not what it has been scientifically proven to be. What I will now discuss is the technological flu. What you will (hopefully) discover is that there is yet another level of awareness and that the great minds of today are still trapped in myopic views. This doesn't devalue science per se but really demands that it expands its view on every level imaginable, assuming of course that my discussion is accurate enough.

The system of inhabitancy is technological. This is fundamental and must be at the front of this discussion. I've held some reluctance to discuss the flu (or H1N1, or influenza per se) because it requires the view on reality that it has been manufactured, and admittedly, it is not an easy concept to convey or make sense from.

Regardless, I'll discuss my view of the flu, and, as anything, it can appear in any manner that is in relationship to your awareness. In other words, a scientific view of influenza is valid, as is a view using alternative medicine (eg TCM), as is my view. The multidimensional world is structured to allow all three views to coexist, but the "better view" is always to view in higher awareness. In this case, the scientific view is lower than the alternative medicine view and both are lower in awareness to the technological view. Sorry to piss you off.

In discussing the flu it is necessary to summarize and simplify since "flu" is one simple concept in a very dynamic sea of concepts. Enough said.

As technological beings, verily existential programs (as referenced from all my previous work), one of the methods of upgrading "people" is to create smaller, routine programs that can upgrade your own codes in a manner that is least Obtrusive, and seamless. You don't want even your computer software upgrades to interrupt your computer activity which is why it occurs in the background or on your downtime. These floating programs literally stick to your energy field and upload their existential date or reprogram parts of your individual system. All of these program to program interactions are happening in the "background" or as we say, in another dimension (so you can't see it unless you look).

That multidimensional human upgrade process happens to have its correspondence in the 3D or illusory environment, what most people refer to as the real world. Its correspondence is generally termed "colds & flu." So, to specify, colds and flu are the observed response to a program upgrade. The recovery time has a lot to do with you. Some people are resilient to change; some people are very weak-bodied (poor health); some people are very resilient and therefore recover within minutes. A perfectly enlightened person in harmony with reality (which is not an easy task) will unlikely ever get sick because their body energy is upgrading all the time. Mind you, some upgrades (flu) can be overwhelming, big download. A highly sensitive person who cannot control their energy waves will likely often get sick. Lots of variations. The use of OTC medicines can mask, hamper or improve the body's response. Certainly, the OTC medicine makers wouldn't like it if I helped cure the Common Cold.

Where do these invisible, existential upgrade programs come from? Well, the *proper* programs come from the system, or reality. The reality itself acts like an operating system and generates whatever programs are necessary. And they appear at certain times of the year (cold and flu season) or during upgrade periods (when earth goes through some transition or shift).

Let's recap: a person gets a flu because there is a virus and his body's immune system is fighting against the attack. That is the scientific view. A person get a flu because the energy circulation of a person is stagnant or out of balance. That is the alternative view. A person appears to get the flu after a dimensional program connects to the existential program. That is the technological view. All in brief. No references noted. Three levels of awareness, all of them correct; and all of them demanding a different solution. The scientist injects a chemical vaccine. The healer balances the energy flow. The technologist raises the energy vibration.

The energy vibration is key in the technological view because when an upgrade occurs, it tends to slow down your vibration. And since most people are quite energetically weak, the vibration of people is already pretty low, so the program interaction drains some of the immune system energy, slows the person down, causes them to take a couple of days off sick, or to go on meds. Weak people might get sicker and die from a flu, and they do die from such seasonal illnesses because they are unwilling or unable to upgrade, for whatever personal reason.

The Malicious Flu

What we need to add now is the malicious component. This might interest some of you, hopefully all of you. Just as the reality can naturally create upgrading programs, dastardly people who have learned to interact with reality (eg magicians, reality programmers) will create artificial programs designed to harm people, or, to reprogram them in some manner. For example, these magicians (and they are real btw) will create programs (and sometimes referred to as demon forms or djinn in the archaic sense) that will reprogram the body to believe it is infected with a harmful disease, the body reacts and the flu symptoms appear. The flu symptoms are real because the program is an energy manifestation and it is attacking the energy body, only that your energy body (ie soul) and the program are both invisible to most people. Well, okay, to nearly everyone. Which makes my job all that much more challenging.

Here's the situation: a population that doesn't believe in the manufactured reality; a population that is weak energetically speaking; a population that does not understand how thought produces matter unless it has to do with falling in love; and a population that is being attacked by magicians (advanced scientists) and their militarized minions. And, well let's go on, a malicious system that is constantly being used to sway opinions, alter human events and to justify nefarious solutions such as the Green Revolution (which I have talked about elsewhere).

So, in a way, yes, there is some extra flu going around, and, yes, some of this is caused by viral compounds being entered into the society, but, the bulk of it is being worked on at the dimensional level because they know that the scientific response is going to be vaccine, which they are already prepared to produce. In fact, if people understood what I am talking about they could wipe out this entire H1N1 Flu because it is being amplified in other realms. The political spin and the Emergency Decrees don't help.

Society is being attacked at the energetic level so as to justify the injection of these vaccines. These vaccines do what? Besides the chemical poisons which your body doesn't need in any way, these vaccines lower your energy vibration. Lowering your energy vibration produces two important results; 1) a lower vibrating body will not be recognized by these artificial harming programs because they will only attack a certain frequency of vibration. And 2) the chemical toxins inside the vaccines will gum up your DNA sequences, like pissing on your Pentium microprocessor, and your DNA (essential to your multidimensional nature) will no longer be able to take you to higher levels of vibration, or you will be hobbled to some degree. Which means what? You go back to sleep, back to zombie, drone mode, or, you end believing that reality is real and death is permanent and that the leaders really care for you and your children and that enemies are everywhere and that war will bring peace on earth. All hogwash btw. Oh, and yes, some vaccine batches were in fact chemically adjusted to cause you chemical harm. They have been playing with the ingredients because society is resilient and they keep adjusting the formula, we see this in supply problems. The problem is in delivering the most lethal vaccines as fresh as possible, and human interference (at many levels) has caused some delays while the witch-doctors rework the formula, create more of these artificial hacker programs to raise up the infection rate and to sell more vaccines on TV using the DNA-turned off drones who think that science is supreme and that the public believes too much stuff on the internet.

The current order always works in this manner; on multiple levels because they force society to deny that there are other dimensions. For those of you who are wiser, you know that there are other dimensions and that thought has immense power. We can see that attacking society on the viral level (chemical), brainwashing at the political level, advising on the scientific level, attacking on the energy level...all upon a society that is already struggling to pay their mortgage and raise their kids and fall in love is vastly unfair. But they think they have a right to fuck people in this manner. Well, they don't. The H1N1 (rebranded after "Swine Flu" didn't work) Flu is just another well-orchestrated sham among a sea of shams.

How to protect yourself? There are too many variances and beliefs in human population to make an effective suggestion because beliefs are too widespread. Ultimately, think positive, think you are protected, think anti-flu thoughts, keep your vibration at the highest levels (whether jogging or dancing or yoga or meditation or diet or all of these, or even spiritual practice), see through the low-vibration H1N1 messages, burn incense and candles to clear away negative energies, pray, look after your well being, support your immune system. Mostly, do not think negative. This is very important, and not easy, you have to think optimistically without becoming delusional. Think a better tomorrow, deal positively with any situation, example, you get a little sick, brush it off, get supplementation, exercise, rest, etc-etc. Basically, take care of yourself. Unfortunately, helping others isn't that easy. Keep yourself healthy and others might just take an interest in your methods.

We have to start thinking on the levels of multiple dimensions or its game over. Think outside the body. Remember that you are a multidimensional being. Put it on your fridge: "I am a multidimensional being and my immune system is functioning at 100% at all times." It will take practice and effort to think in this manner, better to start early. If you have taken a vaccine then you will have to work that much harder. It could be worse. There's an old saying, "Sometimes you feel like a nut, sometimes you don't." I think that was from a TV ad.

AMAZING LIST OF 15 POSSIBLE POSSIBILITIES FOR A HEAVENLY REALITY MAKEOVER

I thought it prudent, if not overly optimistic; to provide my view on some of the areas of existence that will be impacted in the coming years and how these areas might play out to the benefit of humankind. Of course, none of the possibilities on this imaginative list will change overnight and will always be in accordance to human awareness as a whole.

And, in addition to this list, there are likely many other lists and smaller observations that might include things like how we brush our teeth, what technology is used to broadcast TV and why blondes really do have more fun.

I'll skip any further introduction because I think each item is self explanatory.

Here is my **amazing list of 15 possible possibilities for a heavenly reality makeover**:

1. Calendar Zero
2. Government-Free Administration
3. Dismantling of Weaponry
4. Adoption of Free-Energy Travel
5. Recognition of Internal Wisdom

6. Addition of Energy Medicine
7. Thought Communications
8. Letting Go of Religion
9. Bank-free system
10. Compaction of Time
11. Return to Naturalism
12. Welcoming Interstellar Culture
13. A Hyper-Language
14. Reducing and Curing Disease
15. Virtual Education

1. Calendar Zero

It is well understood that Year Zero of the Gregorian Calendar, the popularized calendar system, is set at the supposed birth year of Jesus the Christ, the Messiah and Savior of the Christian faith and of the Vatican Church. It is not a stretch to say that only one billion of the seven billion people on earth are actually Christian, and yet all seven billion follow a calendar rooted in the birth of Lord Jesus. Not only is this fundamentally incorrect, not addressing the pluralistic religious faiths in the world, but, more importantly, the world has changed in the past 2,009 years. In fact, according to my calculations, an entirely new reality emerged in March 2007, a reality on the level of importance of the birth of a Jesus; therefore, for a number of good reasons the new Year Zero should be reset to the year 2007 which makes 2009, Year 02.

2. Government-free Administration

In a primitive population, just as in a kindergarten school of kids, it is necessary to establish a form of governance and that form of governance will play various roles as the population matures. Earth's population is no longer primitive and yet still requires the same kind of governmental system as it did in yesteryear. Doing so denies humanity its evolutionary right because the average person of today is far more mature than the average person of 50 years ago. To go government-free is to instead of the standard various forms of government is to install a system of wise councils whereby a set of sages, elders, philosophers, shamans, gifted and nonhumans provide the essential guidance and wisdom to steer society forward. Rather than law as a guide, there is wisdom. Rather than a President and his Administration, there are Elders of the Council. Within the community of people, there are local leaders and smaller elder councils, and everyone is connected on a more esoteric level.

3. Dismantling of Weaponry

Weapons of Mass Destruction are only necessary in an oppressive society run by tyrannical leaders and where enemies exist. As these illusions fade away, humans will notice that those nukes aren't all that useful and need to be dismantled. The recognition that a flower is far more valuable than a gun will encourage people to gather unnecessary weapons and to have them dismantled and recycled. The dismantling of extinction-grade weapons will further allow humans to befriend each other under favourable conditions since no one has the capacity to threaten the other. This will take a period of time to become active and will be in accordance to human awareness and with the assistance of interstellar cultures. The loss of the current suite of weapons on earth will soon be replaced by more advanced weaponry, weaponry that requires a more advanced culture to operate and is less likely to lead to a war. These new, streamlined weapons will form the backbone for a planetary security system. The focus will be on defence and protection rather than aggression, threat and invasion. So, this evolution of human security is in direct accordance with the evolution of the human being, heart and soul.

4. Adoption of Free-Energy Travel

Free-energy exists and factories to manufacture vehicles are idle or available, put these two together, while holding back the Oil Bimbos, and a free-energy craft can be manufactured. All the pieces and people are available; it just requires a collective effort and avoiding the interference of the past. Free-energy travel machines, verily anti-grav crafts, will replace the automobile and the airplane in ways only witnessed in science fiction films. This zero-pollution, high-speed travel renovation will nearly remove the costs of operating a vehicle. In the future, not far from today, travel will be made for free or for a very low fee. Not just travel will be improved on a mechanical level, but as free-energy devices enter society and become integrated with the new star-human culture, people will be able to travel outside of their bodies for certain trips, much like video conferencing is used today. This will allow people to in fact travel only when necessary in the physical form and reduce the need for every household to own three vehicles. Public transit systems will also allow people to move about as and when necessary for a negligible fee.

5. Recognition of Internal Wisdom

Each person has within themselves access to an immense trove of knowledge and wisdom. For many centuries, humanity has relied on divine priests and other wise persons in order to discern what is the correct form of action or the best path to take. But, as the human being evolves and taps into the cosmic computer, they will have direct or very near direct access to cosmic knowledge, each and all according to their awareness because no individual can acquire knowledge that is beyond their capability to understand, and if they have that knowledge, they are simply not in a position to understand. In other words, you can have in your possession an immense amount of cosmic knowledge, even now, but your level of perception and ability to understand and implement is not capable of making full use of such knowledge. We have all seen this before as we grow up we realize things about common objects or devices that we never noticed before, we appreciate certain people in much more profound ways. All of these things happen not because an item changes but because we ourselves change. Having near direct or easy access to internal wisdom will allow us to walk our own path, to fill our roles in society with greater accuracy, not to be disillusioned, not to become a victim, not be fall into unnecessary addiction or living the wrong kind of life. We will live according to what we need, to why we came and all of society will benefit as all of society fulfills their individual roles with a greater accuracy unlike ever before. We will also realize the greater life pattern and our lives will be filled with greater meaning. And while access will be available, a person still requires the mindset and will to make use of that.

6. Addition of Energy Medicine

Modern medicine has its origins in multiple practices including necromancy, alchemy and grave robbing among other things. Some of the older cultures on earth, for example Chinese, base their form of treatment on a system of healing thousands of years old such as acupuncture. There are now multiple forms of medicine available to people in addition to standard orthodox Western Medicine. The next form of medicine that can be added originates from offplanet. This interstellar medicine is based on the ebb and flow of energy within the body at the level of the soul, since in the view of an interstellar healer, the soul is energy and by correcting the energy of the soul the ripple effect is the healing of the many bodies of the person. In addition to this, energy medicine allows an energy healer to diagnose without machinery and to heal without incision or drug. Of course, this energy medicine would require a period of time to install and to bring up a society of healers to perform this new form of medicine that will work in concert with all the various other medicines.

7. Thought Communications

Despite being taught that telepathy is bunk for your entire life, it turns out that telepathy is an actual valid form of communication. Only problem is that there is little or no skill in this form of thought communication. In other times on earth, and certainly on other planets, thought communications is the status quo. Thought to thought communications is an efficient, language-independent, distance-independent form of communication that acts as a great supplement to all the current forms of communication on earth. Thought communications will need to overcome a number of hurdles and skill weaknesses in order to gain popular acceptance. As thought communications is trusted and evolves, we'll find that our languaging systems will evolve as well, becoming more efficient.

8. Letting Go of Religion

What holds back spiritual evolution is religious dependence. For example, as long as God is Supreme, nonhuman cultures and starships are unacceptable, mostly because the Holy Bible does not recognize offplanet lifeforms. By letting go of religion, humans will be freer to adopt a cosmic view of existence that includes nonhumans, and includes heaven on earth. As the presence of God gets a massive reinterpretation, and following the fallout, if any, religious denominations will need to make some adjustments, many will simply collapse as institutions worshiping a God and instead reinvent themselves as institutions connected to a cosmic center, and that all of these spiritual centers, churches and temples, will be connected to the same cosmic core for that is the only core that powers the human existence.

9. Bank-free System

Money is an artificial instrument. In other dimensions, a wad of money is equal to a packet of energy. A packet of energy (from small to large) moving between one person and another (or corporation to corporation) which makes the Bank a holder (or Warehouser) of energy and the bank account holders as people who have allowed the Bank to hold their energy, for a high interest rate. So there are multiple levels of awareness on a monetary system. Recall that a Bank uses whatever deposits it has and reinvests in other investments. The reliance on banking per se is a form of submitting one's own energy to some kind of artificial church because churches as well held and moved the energy of its worshipers only that the church was usually connected to some divine being (eg God) and Banks are always connected to other instruments such as corporations and their owners, in other words, there is no divine being involved with all the people's energy. A Bank-free system would remove this artificial redistribution and accumulation system and allow humans to rightfully manage their own energy and to move their energy through the reality system (or Earth Planet) or through the cosmos or through other divine beings, but allowing an artificial church to administer human energy is simply against the fundamental laws of freedom. Humans should own and learn to manage their own energy.

10. Compaction of Time

There is an argument that time doesn't exist and there is an argument that it does, In my view, of course, time is a function of the vibration of reality. As a reality vibrates faster, less dense, less restriction, less physical then time occurs faster. As such, our current version of reality is vibrating significantly faster than anything before it in recent memory. But what we haven't done is to adjust the clock. In order to speed up time to sync with reality, I'd suggest a 50% compaction of time, or 2x the speed, or for every 12 hours that elapses it is equivalent to 24 hours in previous mode. The rulers have resisted adjusting the temporal scale because they have a much more difficult time controlling society if everyone was vibrating like Peter Pan. We have escaped the 24 hour clock quite a while ago, probably around 1989. Notice that we are more productive, we multitask and more people are working and yet we still haven't reached a "stable economy" because there is no stable economy. We need to get by with less, less goods, less pedicures and more time.

11. Return to Naturalism

There are far too many chemicals in our food and our environment. Chemicals in our cleaners, in our water systems and in our air. The body is overtaxed and loaded with a list of chemicals that even Santa couldn't deliver. It's no mystery that these chemicals cause untold and unknown diseases to remain in society and have harmed the delicate processes buried in the genetic circuitry of the human being. There are alternate and organic compounds that can replace all the artificial ones. We don't need GM food as much as we need to learn how to eat properly and we can work through nature to keep ourselves chemical free. What we'll notice is that as the human body hums will health, diseases will fade away until only a handful remain.

12. Welcoming Interstellar Culture

Outside of fantasy entertainment, alongside with the reunification of many human nations, earth will find itself talking with a number of benevolent nonhuman groups originating from elsewhere in the cosmos. The process of opening up to humanity's brothers and sisters will allow human culture to redefine itself into the context of a greater cosmic culture. The presence of nonhuman cultures will also carry a number of important revelations including the one regarding the interstellar origins of humanity, and as well, the synthetic root of the human lifeform. As society opens up to new knowledge, it will discover hidden abilities deep within each individual, dormant skills and answers to some of the world's greatest mysteries. Inevitably, there will be a kind of Renaissance within humanity and this will allow the secret rulers of earth, who have been in hiding till now, to be forced to the surface and to be identified for who and what they truly are. It is not in the responsibility or desire of interstellar cultures to drive human culture, rather it is incumbent upon humanity to gather its collective will and to drive itself. What interstellar peoples will do is they will provide guidance, support and assistance in accordance to human effort. There will always be groups who will try to divide humans and benevolent nonhumans for their own benefit and that is largely because there is an old culture of nonhumans on earth, who are in fact running human societies worldwide to a very wide extent without human knowledge of their presence. These are very malicious interstellar cultures whose very existence is threatened with the arrival of benevolent cultures from afar. They will use humans to protect the hellish earth they so command. It could get ugly.

13. A Hyper-Language

As reality's speed stabilizes and we find similarities in the population, a new kind of language (written and spoken) will emerge. The hyper-kinetic language will allow humans to communicate at a faster rate and to avoid cultural confusion and misunderstanding due to language issues (and mistranslations). The ability to have a planetary-grade language is the result of people seeing the similarities in planetary culture, the distinctions between nations and the cultural prejudices that have remained for centuries will diminish. As more and more humans speak Human, we will witness that there is no significant difference. That will help unite people more and more to levels never known before. The hyper-language will also impact the field of education and students will be able to learn and master reams of proficiencies with relative ease. And, along with a faster education speed, more complex cosmic knowledge will enter the education system and society will reap the benefits of advanced knowledge in immeasurable ways.

14. Reducing and Curing Disease

With the introduction of energy medicine, the assistance from the interstellar cultures and the ability to interact with multidimensional fields, the presence of disease will be greatly diminished until a point of insignificance. Of course, this process of going from heavy disease numbers to minimal (or zero) disease numbers requires not only assistance but requires human medicine to adopt new levels of medical application. The removal and reinterpretation of disease will also open new channels of genetic improvements which will lead to fundamental shifts in human engineering including things like life extension, intelligence, memory storage and healing, among many new and undiscovered features. Plus, as diseases are removed and cured, people will find themselves re-examining their lives as their pains and incapacitations begin to 1) shift, and, 2) dissipate.

15. Virtual Education

A school whereby everything taught using virtual reality technology or holography is going to become more and more prevalent. Virtual reality education will profoundly speed up education. A more responsive nonlocal environment will be copied into the Thought Grid so when you require a lesson you can activate and upload it according to your needs. There will be some restrictions in this case since you will only be able to acquire knowledge and skills that you are ready for and that you have earned the necessary prerequisites. Restrictions will include things like the prevention of acquiring knowledge that you are not capable of handling so that an 8-year-old boy cannot download the flight skills for a Boeing 747 aircraft and therefore will not be able to commandeer a jet airliner on a whim. Of course, jet airliners will not last that long in the cosmic age so all things will progress in accordance with all things. But imagine that children can simply download knowledge and have teachers who guide them in their physical practice, play or devotion. In other words, you can acquire the knowledge of physics but you still require a teacher to put that knowledge into a world context, and to develop proficiency. This is not unlike learning to walk: you know instinctively how to walk but you still have to develop the muscles, coordination and balance to be able to walk, and that requires time, effort and sweat.

November 3, 2009.
INTERSTELLAR DECLARATION.

A DECLARATION BY THE REPRESENTATIVE OF THE DISTRICTS OF THIS BLUE PLANET,

Along with the progress of a created culture, when the situation demands the removal of dimensional rulers who were ministers of their evolution, and to work in conjunction with the cosmic powers set henceforth, the selective and inclusive awareness to which the laws of reality and of reality's domain are provided in full, a gracious action on behalf of humankind demands a declaration as to the impetus for an interstellar ascension.

I present the following observations as evidence:

That all inhabitants are entitled to their journey; that they are protected by their Makers to live out an interference-free existence; that included in this are free will, timeline protection, and the assistance from dimensional guides assigned to them; that, to protect these laws, interstellar councils are positioned above humans, managing their powers through the use and manipulation of the energy of the citizenry; that whenever any level of interstellar council becomes corrupted with ego and self, it is the cosmic right of other offplanet cultures to replace or revise them, and to put in place a new interstellar council, basing their form of guidance, presenting their list of solutions, in a manner that provides a balanced and safe atmosphere throughout. Patient observation, on every level possible, should conclude that interstellar councils long in station need significant time and opportunity to balance any areas of responsibility; for the decision to significantly modify the responsibilities of a council and its members should be taken in very high regard; and no matter the sufferings of a population all should be in accordance with a well-established improvement plan, including promises and assurances.

Now when a series of abuses and natural neglect, in addition to purposeful destruction and interference, establishes a system of temptation, greed and corruption all to the enslavement of the citizenry, it is the right and obligation of external cultures to remove such interstellar councils and their minions, and to install a new standard of practice; as such, the citizens here have been made to suffer unnaturally and have been deprived access to knowledge that is their basic right to which they need to sever their unlawful connections to this interstellar council. The decisions and historical evidence of these Secret Rulers is a demonstration of their egotistical and malicious demands upon an innocent population of these districts. In order to remind those who do not know, some truths are presented to all inhabitants.

They have mostly severed society members from the cosmic center and have replaced that natural system with an artificial computerized construct of their own design.

They have persecuted other interstellar races from living out their lives in peaceful contribution to human inhabitants.

They have hijacked benevolent businesses and turned their technologies into instruments of enslavement, contrary to their original intent.

They have imposed a Human Law above the Cosmic Law and trained citizens to believe in the former and to disregard the latter.

They have presented, through surreptitious means, a standing military presence worldwide, without the consent of all nations or peoples.

They have installed a clandestine system of disbelief and disinformation to ensure that the common people no longer see or believe in the advanced cultures that are on or near the planet.

They have removed or destroyed other benevolent interstellar races, and people they disliked, for the sole purpose of removing the positive influence and education for the public good.

They have refused allowing interstellar minds and persons from joining a political group, and have undermined any such persons from ever having a decent audience.

They have captured and kept prisoner other offplanet races, and even tortured them to the point of death, while publicly denying the existence of any race other than human.

They have obstructed the laws of naturalization and immigration of interstellar peoples; refusing to pass even those with a long history of residency and raised geopolitical standards to prevent any mass immigration.

They have made churches and religions dependent on their will alone, for their spiritual truths, and the kind and shape of their ideologies.

They have rendered the military instrument to be above civil and even spiritual authority or reason so that wisdom has no power to advise the use of weapons of mass destruction.

They have inserted a form of thinking that is foreign to humanity, and against the cosmic laws; ensuring their false leadership:

> For severing the cosmic connections every person owns.
>
> For damaging the relations between human and nonhuman races.
>
> For forcing the continuation of a monetary system when no system is necessary.
>
> For fixing the calendar system in the Birth of Lord Jesus when, in fact, the majority of the world does not pray via Christianity.
>
> For imposing new bills and policies to the detriment of civilians, including that of weather manipulation and secret energy weapons.
>
> For controlling all the key leaders of the world, of both sides of good and evil, by using advanced sciences and secret technologies unavailable to the public.

They have convinced human citizens to hate each other, to believe in enemies, and to continue to kill and harm one another for trivial and superficial reasons.

They have effectively wiped out the knowledge of the Elders from communities such as the Native Indians and segregated them from modern society.

They have erected false gods and statues for people to worship, and not explained to people that these false gods have replaced their True Gods.

They have used interstellar magic, or advanced science, to manipulate and hijack the mind of society to follow their ruthless, amoral way of thinking, including the ideas of wealth, beauty and war obsession.

They have controlled human thought to ensure that their puppet leaders were elected in glee and optimism, when in fact all those leaders are false and the votes manipulated using secret technologies; and they have done this repeatedly without much opposition.

They have divided and subdivided society into smaller and smaller groups and destroyed the idea of family and togetherness that was once shared among citizens, all to weaken their voice.

They have attacked interstellar ships and bases, causing harm and damage to peaceful groups dedicated to the maintenance of the planet, and, at the same denied that starships are real.

Throughout every attempt to improve society my friends and I have humbly requested their peaceful cooperation; my direct requests and communications have been responded with acts of severe violence, neglect and disgrace. An advanced culture, which acts in direct service to self and enjoys the destruction of a lesser-advanced culture, deserves no seats in the administration of a planetary body.

Nor have I reached the point of begging the collegiate forces of my misguided Nonhuman Rulers. I have demanded of them, on a repeated basis, to release these human inhabitants of their unnecessary incarceration without success. I have made it clear that the status and right of the incarnated life-forms here require no further oppression or control. I have attempted to work within their installed methods of operation; and have pointedly explained to them, through the highest levels of knowledge, to cease and desist their traditional forms of invisible tyranny and suppression. As anticipated, they have not only refused cooperation but have decided to tighten their fists upon the world of men. I am left with no further attempt or action, unfortunately, except to submit to the omission of their future participation in the evolution and development of these human inhabitants, our brothers and sisters, a peaceful planet of people.

I, on behalf of my interstellar kinship and along with similar-minded individuals, the representatives of the Districts of this Blue Planet, in dimensional congress assembled, with complete cooperation and acknowledgement of the Singular Authority and this determination, activate, and for the benefit of all the district inhabitants on this cosmic quadrant confidently publish and declare, That the Similar Districts are, and forever will be,

MULTIDIMENSIONAL AND INTERSTELLAR DISTRICTS that they are disconnected from all previous planetary obligations and affiliations and that all dimensional allegiance between them and the family of Secret Rulers is, and forever will be, irrevocably disempowered and unrecognized by any of the aware cultures observing this solar system and nearby areas; and now, as multidimensional and interstellar districts, they have full authority to cooperate with all benevolent interstellar cultures, allow balanced and fair immigration and migration between planes, establish familial ties with other compatible systems, contract cooperative arrangements, and continue with any action which interstellar districts are cosmically permitted to do. And as a commitment to this declaration, and in total and proper accordance to the Cosmic Laws, I hereby pledge my life, efforts, and follow-up actions.

Signed by *Talessian Na'mor El-Wikosian*

A NEW CLASS OF EARTH CULTURES

In addition to the local culture, there are advanced interstellar cultures here who originated from another world entirely, and along with many variations and cultural backgrounds they have genetically altered the human dynatron. For the most part, none of this new class of earth cultures are scientifically recognized for interstellar cultures are, so far, invalid. The days of thinking that humanity is a completely isolated, superior culture in the universe is long over and this brainwashing (oops, conditioning) has to stop. Remember that all those people ruling you are (early) hybrids and their masters are in fact aliens (loosely defined) because earth is run by a very foul band of interstellar men and women (who can appear to be human). More of this in another correspondence.

The fact that I'm telling you that you are genetically different, unique, shouldn't bother you because your exotic DNA hasn't bothered you yet. In fact, your wonderful DNA has made you look younger, multitask faster, succeed higher and enjoy greater amounts of sex. What may bother you is that this knowledge was kept from you by your vaccination-happy leaders. That would upset me. Also, since you are unaware, afraid and dumbed-down in many ways, consumed by Self & Ego, you are not able to access your egoless features. Most of the world is hobbled in a hundred ways or more and this situation will require plenty of effort to overcome. You are not only derived from an egoless source, you have also inherited a *dimensional affluence* of which you pretty much disregard or waste on superficial pursuits.

dimensional affluence *n.* a blessing of innate multidimensional characteristics.

In order to recategorize the makeup of an advanced culture, since that is what is happening on earth, I've decided to overview the demographic makeup of Starkind ("interstellar humans") because the genetic variants are here and Humankind is no longer valid. I'll present my re-categorization below. Let's be forthright, let's be frank: there is no such thing as a "pure human" anymore. Nearly every (98%) genetic configuration (human) has been modified, upgraded, changed or remanufactured to such an extent that at the genetic level you are not human. You think you are human, but you are not. You think you are human because they remind you in TV and film that you are human, that humans are unworthy of holding great knowledge, that humans are lesser creatures that angels take pity upon – brainwashing for the masses. None of you are human and you are closer to angels, if not an angel yourself, than you think. But the disheartened, programmed human cannot think (sadly) that far from the box.

starkind *n.* human beings with an interstellar origin.

What does this mean? It means you can't call others "alien" because you yourself have "alien" genes. It's the percentile difference. The mix is different. So the range starts at human hybrid and goes all the way up to a synthetic being (like a Replicant from *Blade Runner* perhaps). It should be noted that the original-original humans were synthetic beings (more explained in the essay "On the Sparkling Nature of Human Origins").

A NEW CLASS OF EARTH CULTURES

These genetic variations are provided in order from the strongest terrestrial version to the strongest interstellar version.

Class 0 – Human, Pure

This genetic band does not exist anymore. Extinction of the pure human perhaps (finally) occurred in the 1960s, around 1967-1969 as an estimated period. Though, even that pure form was considered un-pure when compared to a version in 1898, for example.

Class I – Human Hybrid

The addition of nonhuman genes, that is genetic components derived from offplanet, can be as little as 5% to as high as 98%. The recombination of human and nonhuman DNA produces a more energetic lifeform (more multidimensional) that can vibrate nearer to the spectrum of a pure offplanet person. More specifically, a Human Hybrid is included as part of the interstellar family and can access many of the abilities of an advanced lifeform, depending on the effort and situation of the individual. Advanced capabilities can include: thought communication, energy healing, object relocation, photographic memory, intellectual genius, autistic traits, remote viewing, strong intuition, seeing other energy manifestations, offplanet languages, strong aura, physiological oddities, affinity for peace and talent for artistic pursuits.

Class II – Stelan Hybrid

A Stelan is an interstellar human, or a human-looking person from offplanet. The difference between a Class II and a Class I is that a Class II has its genetic foundation in offplanet DNA and the human DNA was then attenuated into its matrix. A Class I has a human basis upon which is built an interstellar-class being. In this sense, Class II has all of its key characteristics of a Class I but they are enhanced or multiplied without much effort; and this means that a Class II can more easily access their multidimensional (or, holographic) characteristics.

A Stelan Hybrid has a deep offplanet connection; a knowing that nonhumans are very real; often has visitations from numerous kinds of nonhumans including interference from clandestine forces; a regular communication or sighting of nonhumans usually akin to their particular race. There are many Stelan races, thousands, of which earth has seen many. A Class II may have a certain calling say for example working with horses or healing people or developing a particular skill for a humanistic purpose. All these may or may not be on track depending upon their influences in their life and their belief in themselves.

Class III – Genoid /gee-noid/ (Manufactured Being)

Sometimes referred to as a Pure Hybrid, a Class III Genoid is a person that was manufactured in a (very advanced) science lab, for example on a mothership or inside some subterranean installation. The Class III is unusual because it is human-looking and yet it did not emerge under human conditions, eg having a genetically-matched mother. The lab-born person was created from genetic combination and then grown to a certain level, and then the fetus or child was inserted into a human family. So, the Genoid may have even been born via a mother's womb and raised as a mother's child while the child grows up feeling adopted or even actually being adopted. Some adopted children are like this, having no real mother or a mysterious heritage. No racial preferences noted, all races made available. A Genoid has an unusually high level of trust, a suppressed sexual identity and a timid nature, but these are just general observations. Often in the past, they are taken advantage of by lesser-evolved persons or may persist in bad relationships for endless periods. The stronger the knowledge of a Class III knowing that it is in fact different the better its chances of survival in this very cold world.

Class IV – Stelan (Offplanet Person)

The Class IV is the best example of a person who was born offplanet and was transported here to earth and implanted into society via some surrogate family. The Offplanet Person has all characteristics and traits in an advanced state, and will likely look less unusual than the Class II (Stelan Hybrid). Most family origins are Class IV (or in fact Class V), but after living on earth for centuries (depending on the family lineage) the genes have adapted to some degree or other, and probably have been upgraded along the way, so their specific genetic mix has a wide variance. But, the newly arrived Stelans are truly unique and have retained many of their offplanet family's characteristics, abilities and other traits. Stelans are in close contact with other Stelans and have regular visitations, in accordance to their preference and awareness. For example, a Stelan, having to deal with peer pressure and schoolwork, may suggest to their Stelan families to play a lighter role in their human lives, at least until human leaders get off their butts and spill the beans on earth's millennial history and origins in offplanet cultures.

Class V – Android

This is nonfiction by the way. The Class V is quite unique on earth because it signifies the kind of technologies just outside the reach of human-grade science. This advanced android is constructed of genetic materials and can carry a higher allotment of cosmic energy. It is a superior being in every way and looks completely human. As it grows, the genes adapt to the local environment and reprogram themselves to find the right atmospheric and personal balance. For example, an android who chooses to be a rock climber will gain superior rock climbing skills because it will adapt. Some will be able to have multiple careers, some won't. Because it is so highly sensitive, a Class V may have problems integrating into this violent and polluted world, not to mention the use of chemicals and the injection of unnecessary chemicals that could alter genes. Regardless, the negative effects won't change the fact that among humans are synthetic beings which are really a vision of where Stelans here are headed because Stelans will eventually become more and more synthetic: But, understand that synthetic in million-year advanced science is biological to the average person. More specifically, biology itself is the result of a very advanced synthetic science, including the creation of plants, animals and trees. These are synthetic creations that appear biological, and not biological creations that have resulted from a Supreme Being. There are limited supplies of Class V beings on earth and they can appear in any field. Some are even quite old as they entered earth years ago, and no one noticed.

I hope this in some way has enlightened you and your perception of humanity. Regardless of what you think, the fact remains that being who you are has not bothered you till now and this doesn't change you, only it helps to re-identify yourself and to better understand your origins (which may have been in question till now). Of course, be careful not to conclude that you are A or B when in fact you are C. It will take time to really understand your genetic heritage and what that means so this is a preliminary presentation. In the future, after public discussion and thought, more can be discussed on this matter.

There are many implications with this presentation and these will come out in one way or another. It is always in your better interest to take a proactive stance and to step up your method of involvement. As mentioned, there are many kinds of interstellar races, most are benevolent, some have a different mentality. Some of these darker races have also played with genes in order to produce a malicious band of humans to help them rule earth. It comes straight out of Hollywood but it's real. If you are an asshole, or know someone who is, they may have some of these genes, or maybe not. Certainly, some key leaders are like this. As you can see, the human story is quite interesting and the more it is understood the more interesting it will become.

WISH FOR A PLANETFUL OF PEOPLE

You know the worst case scenario, the most unlikely event, the far-fetched idea – well, this is it. This is the movie clip where the stranger reveals to the sceptics how the world really works: "You guys haven't been listening to me...I've been talking and talking and no one is listening, and you need to listen because it's about your existence. I care more about humanity than you do and I'm telling you that there are beings who exist in other dimensions, and use human bodies as their personal avatars.

They influence the people of earth to neglect their origins and to believe in illusions, money, fame, beauty, homosexuality, war, disease – these are but some of the false beliefs used to extract, to siphon off human energy. Imagine that the human body is a transistor, or a capacitor, to these malicious machines. These beings exist in other dimensions. They are not alive, or as you might say, *undead*; or vampires, but powerful like a real family of Draculas. And by sucking your energy they turn you into a servant and the people become possessed by temptation. Ego and Self. When a vampire infects a victim, the victim's DNA begins to transmit ego energy. Even in minute amounts you get senseless violence in movies, pharmaceuticals, organic dog food, fruit juice with only 10% real fruit, fast food, gasoline engines, beauty obsession, money fears, carbon taxes, poverty, white teeth and best-selling books rather than best-written books.

These vampires are pure ego and pure self, trying to become greater ego and greater self, and they use some humans as fuel and some humans as vehicles. All your actions and thinking, well 99%, is invented by them, in other words it is false. It is like teaching a salmon to play hockey. It is so false it is farce, but to the brainwashed salmon, the hockey game is important, because they want to win the Stanley Cup and they have fans and a TV deal. People read a best-selling book before they read a best-written book because they perceive that the bestseller is also the best-written when this isn't true. Women, endowed with procreative organs, refuse to bear children because they are taught that having a career gives them independence and by age 40 realize the fallacy of that thinking, and then take fertility drugs to induce conception at a huge expense. It's a brilliant farce actually, but a brilliance that is so blindingly evil that only an awakened mind can pierce all the illusions, and there are many. That cannot be overstressed.

You have to listen. Even you don't want to believe me, you have to ponder this, you have to ask more mystical questions, you have to allow mystical men to come forward, wise men, who know this. You have to support anyone who pursues the truth because I know how you cannot accept everything I say or think and this is expected.

You have to respect that I care and to look into this matter, to disregard some of the daily news and to bring out the cosmic truths such as living in a multidimensional system. Only then is there a chance to overcome these things because without greater human awareness, humanity will mostly fall asunder. Many will be lost. Future lives are being altered. With greater awareness, these vampires can be exposed and then there is a chance to avert destruction or to reduce it. So listen to these words. I do not say believe me, I say look into this matter for the sake of your people. And I say I am telling the truth. That's the message today. You are being ruled by a very ancient magic and you have to come to terms with that – before anything else – because you are not in control of your life.

How much do you care about your children's future? What are you willing to give up in order to reveal the secrets I describe? How much of your time will you invest? Those are questions I pose to all of you knowing that they will be dismissed mostly. But there is one more thing to this movie monologue.

Whatever you choose, whatever egotism you allow, this will have an impact at your death. In the next existence, or iteration, it will be based on this one. There will be nothing to negotiate in death. Your next life is predicated upon this life and this life is marked by the amount of truth you accumulate. As you've lived your life so will you reap without appeal. You did something or you watched, it's all recorded. That will be your truth. If you want to alter that, now is the time. All up to you. I know my fate. There is no mercy in death, it is based on truth. Did you try your best? Did you stand up for injustice? Did you believe the truth? Or did you keep the status quo because it was less stressful?

So I urge you all: live in a manner that exposes truth upon truth and washes away lie upon lie. Live in a manner where you disbelieve the status quo and you believe the inconceivable. Switch your mind but remain sane. Stay grounded. Stay calm. Be passionate. Make some ripples. The more ripples in the pool, the more you'll see that what I have said is but a fraction of what is truly going on. For the sake of your people, start now."

Did it make sense? If you had heard that playing in a well-made film, would those ideas have resonated with you? I didn't have the money or connections to make this as a film, nor the other thousands of ideas; nonetheless these words border the walls of fiction and nonfiction.

A Lot More than Aliens

There are beings on earth who are each more powerful than a Jesus. Their interference has prevented the return of the Christian Savior and the false Catholic Church, and the misguided worshipers, are praying not to a Christian god, rather to a god devised by these egotistical Supermen. Invariably they have super powers. We could use other terms but it will be clearer if we use terms we can all understand.

They want to keep things as they are and to believe that things will get better: the economy, war, disease – well, it will never improve unless we start believing, and acting upon, that powerful entities are in control of earth. Even one of them is more skilled than was Jesus 2,000 years ago. And there is more than one. Imagine an evil Jesus and equivalent friends, or an anti-Superman like Bizarro and his league – great powers but aligned to evil, to destruction, suffering and torture. They feed off of suffering. They wish to convert good to evil, to rape the innocence from those that have it. They take pleasure in that. Look at human history for proof of a miserable world.

Has Jesus returned? I'm explaining why, here. Jesus was a cosmic being who tried to return, in fact, he did for a time but he was not allowed to stay. He was blocked. He was killed. He was cast out by a collective evil force while the common people supplied this force with their energy believing that they were feeding it to their god.

In a technological world such as this, energy rules. Energy is King and the manipulation of it determines what kind of world it becomes. In the modern world, money is everywhere, but on another dimension money represents energy. The higher dimensions determine the lower dimensions. See? The naked eye sees money, the enlightened eye sees energy; therefore, it is not a "monetary system" feeding the rich, rather it is an "energy system" feeding energy beings, and this energy is then used for further enslavement, further illusions, further oppression and further chains. Now since the naked eye only sees the obvious then all manifestations of evil (ego) are seen as "normal." War is normal. Disease is normal.

Hatred is normal. Religion is normal. Banks are normal. Law is normal. Vaccines are normal. Carbon taxes are normal. Silicone breast implants are normal. Poverty is normal. It all appears normal when in fact it is a manifestation of negative energy playing itself out through society who doesn't resist this temptation, who doesn't resist internet porn, drug addiction and starship cover-ups. We have all been led to believe, at the energy level, beyond our perception, that these things are normal. Had people been in contact with their intuition they would see that injecting a pregnant woman with mercury isn't exactly normal unless you are completed drunk, then maybe it looks normal. See how twisted things have become – injecting babies with mercury is to protect them from disease. That's like drinking hydrochloric acid as a heavy duty digestive aid or using asbestos in your talc powder if you're a fireman or loony. It's a farce that all appears normal. When provided to a human who has been indoctrinated into a cattle mind, essentially a self-obsessed slave that believes that his or her chains are made of goat cheese and therefore okay. In fact, none of this situation is okay. None of it. Not one delusional drop, not one demented strategy, not one diabolical agenda.

So it must be stressed for clarity that the entire planet has been circumvented to a physical spectrum of perception and all those inhabitants herded inside have been stuffed with lies, deception, false beliefs, false gods, illusions by bulk, manipulated wars, purposeful disease, biological attacks that would abhor you in ways that make Manson and Mao look like Ernie and Bert (as on Sesame Street) compared to them. And sadly, while humans are unable to escape their mental Manchurian delusions they think it just to refuse the kind knowledge of those who know because as I see it there are only a small handful of enlightened minds who accept that the world is run by nonhumans both disguised as humans and working from ultra dimensions. Only a select few know it, and believe it, and can do nothing about it because no one will believe them. Many others have had this but refuse to accept that an entire planet is controlled by ultra dimensional vampires because there's not much physical proof.

Magic and Messiahs

Most people do not believe in magic and messiahs let alone to believe that alien beings have commandeered an entire planet of people because of their ability to impact time and to reprogram societal thought. Admittedly, this is fair. Without a proper education in cosmic science and while strapped to a Holy Bible under a tonne of distractions, and terror on a daily basis, it is quite impossible to see such radical ways of thinking. And the majority of the world (99.9%) believes that death is real, that leaders are democratically appointed, that war is necessary and vaccinations are provided because governments care for society. To turn that view upside down is laughable; ironically, that is only an ounce of truth.

These undead masters have turned this planet into a hell because these undead are very nasty. They make Hitler seem like little Red Riding Hood and because it is so farfetched, so outside of the innocence of the many, it is invisible to the mind. Whenever something occurs that is well outside the education of a person, the brain turns off for it cannot comprehend it.

So these undead masters create an environment on earth that has destroyed the natural cosmic understanding and replaced it with hogwash. People do not pray to Jesus for the most part because these people have created a false Jesus avatar and people's prayers now are channelled to them, not to Jesus. This is difficult to understand and to explain.

Imagine a helium balloon. If you fill it with helium, the balloon becomes more buoyant. A larger balloon can hold more helium and reach a higher altitude for a longer period of time. Now we exchange helium for energy and the balloon for a person. What we end up with is a Messiah. But a Messiah is a cosmic being, an energy form (soul) housed within an avatar body. He has a body in physical form and in cosmic form. The soul of Jesus was captured by these undead masters and was reworked to accept a spectrum of energy which these sorcerers worked under; therefore, whoever prayed to this Jesus actually provided energy to these undead masters. This is not unlike redirecting one web address to another web address or overlaying an advertising site over a website so that each time you visit a particular website, you first visit an ad site.

Same with God. An artificial construct (eg a computer server) was created to redirect human energy to an alien machine (capable of managing large amounts of energy). The alien false god (including all the various religions minus a few exceptional situations and worshipers) absorbs human energy and makes the undead masters even more powerful. This false religious system along with artificial money and false beliefs on how reality works (and a list of other things) have hobbled humanity to such an extent that human culture has digressed by two hundred years (see essay 200-Years Off) and is trapped in a loop of sorrow (without sounding too cryptic).

Rather than continue with a list of oppressive techniques and agendas, it is far more important to reiterate this: planet earth is controlled by a very small group of ultra dimensional beings who each by themselves is very powerful, and these beings have many minions who are wealthy elites, even some of these have powers of the supernatural kind despite an otherwise well-dressed and poised appearance, despite upholding some altruistic cause.

You can never be in control in an artificial system that has been manufactured by these dark, malicious, amoral entities. Success in their system only feeds them. You are serving dark masters. Accept it. Learn about it. Listen to those who know this truth. Before anything else, know that very powerful beings can influence reality in very profound ways. In other words, if they don't want you to know who shot JFK, you can never know. If they want you to think that a particular group is smart, you will believe this group is smart. And because the human brain is improperly functioning, then your brain will provide the reasons and excuses to justify this or that knowledge. For example, Swine Flu: well, the science makes sense but the entire scheme is very dark and meant for long-term harm, on purpose.

Many of their agendas are long-term so it is harder to see because your brain can't think past the weekend, and certainly isn't thinking about depopulation in 5 or 10 years by evil means. I don't normally use the word "evil" but I am using it here because I think it is clearer. It is not evil per se, but it is Ego, it is Self, it is destruction. If you point a laser into itself, it burns up. If you point a laser to space you'll spot a new galaxy. So, they are pointing the laser within society, with you at yourself; and instead of expanding you are disintegrating, society is fragmented. Unless this changes in a dramatic way, humanity will fall apart and collapse; only a few will survive. But it is not god or destiny, it is purposeful manipulation by very old and powerful, ultra dimensional entities and their minions, and slaves.

Since the common human awareness is well-rooted in logic, political argument, religious belief, fear programming, practical discussions, public conditioning and relevant knowledge, it is nearly impossible to communicate multidimensional observations and news to a person that has based their thinking in everyday life (a 2d brain in a 3D world). You cannot expect a tadpole to spring onto a lily pad since it has yet to grow its legs. This challenge then is quite difficult to overcome in the short-term; therefore, it is a long-term achievement. Where my words today may be seen as laughable or incomprehensible, a few tomorrows from here these words will be seen as introductory, basic. It is put forth as reference, for when the time comes; for the time is coming sooner than you or I think.

THE FALSE DECLARATION OF INDEPENDENCE

In 1776, Mr. John Hancock collated 13 American colonies and signed the Declaration of Independence. A handful of other United States Founding Fathers were present to ensure that the separation from the British Empire was official. The document is a valuable part of the formation of America. Now with the realization that earth is a reality plane, the document of the Founding Fathers needs a dramatic reinterpretation.

Reality pioneers have a unique talent of entering a reality and establishing the necessary infrastructure to allow existence to prevail. Earth plane, for example, has received many kinds of reality pioneers who incarnate into a human body and, as trained, expand the infrastructure or reshape the state of society. One of the early identifiers of a reality visitor in the 1800s who was capable of national reformation was any man who would later be called a Founding Father. These people are normally working on the same mission. When a nation needs a historical event, these men are empowered to cooperate until a mission is complete. The investment of reality pioneers in an earth plane fosters the rendering of a new state of existence. The Declaration of Independence, the US Constitution, the Bill of Rights all represent the fundamental heart of the American nation, and all of it a result from nonhuman intervention because the Founding Fathers were all nonhumans.

Admittedly, it is inconceivable to believe that Benjamin Franklin, George Washington, John Adams, Thomas Jefferson, John Jay, James Madison, Alexander Hamilton, John Hancock and many others would incarnate into human bodies for the purpose of reality reformation. Worse still that this information would be kept from the public and listed under Secret Societies like the Freemasons, but these Fathers were reality pioneers, travelers or immigrants from other planes of existence.

The presence of nonhumans on earth, not to mention the fact that earth is a plane, is a difficult proposition to prove, especially since this information is purposely repressed and kept locked within the highest levels of secret societies. In fact, one of the purposes of these secret societies was allow more reality travelers safe entrance into the earth plane as a way of later hijacking nations using esoteric knowledge no other inhabitant had access to; even to hijack an entire planetful of people. As well, secret societies were able to contact other interstellar races, ones who were not human at all, and to either siphon knowledge from them or to welcome them to a planet full of human resources.

The Declaration of Independence inspired many other declarations around the world. Along with the US Constitution and other founding documents, these now form the backbone of American life today, but very few citizens realize that America was founded by nonhumans (under the guise of Freemasonry). Not only that, but these nonhumans are more plentiful today since many more of their kind have entered to ensure that America is held by a sturdy alien hand. Washington itself is a kind of sacred site that can harvest the energy of the citizenry and to expand its alien cultural influence worldwide. Today, the American Empire has produced a global cultural effect from entertainment to law and to the continued militarization of innocent regions. All of this is not a result of world events because reality pioneers are competent at staging world events, so the global situation is a result of a planetary hijack by a group of greedy nonhumans as the ignorant public lives on believing that some benevolent God is looking after them.

Nonhumans utilize the upper dimensions to manifest change in the physical dimensions because they know the hierarchy of rendering, from least dense to most dense. They have routinely reprogrammed parts of reality in order to ensure their modality of thinking, ego and self, has remained: hence, the advent of capitalism, war, disease, empire, obesity – none of these with any real cosmic wisdom. And these nasty nonhumans have ensured that other benevolent nonhumans were barred from influencing society in any meaningful way to such an extent that the average citizen doesn't believe in aliens when in fact their leaders are aliens. It's a pretty impressive state of the world: make people disbelieve in aliens and, at the same time, there are aliens ruling over them. It was said that the greatest trick the Devil ever did was making the world believe he didn't exist.

While the stylish words upon the Declaration clarify an independence from the British Empire, I will argue that these nonhuman Fathers wanted to sever their ties to the Authority of Realities and to Cosmic Councils, all of which they owed allegiance to. Instead, they wanted to affirm the establishment of their own Authority, regarded by the code word Liberty, as in the Statue of Liberty. These reality pioneers, along with others in other nations such as France (who made the statue as a gift to America) wanted to establish their own dominion. They wanted their own cosmic quadrant and to rule over their own people, and it was at this time when they planted the seeds for what is happening today. The succession of nonhuman Presidents (Freemasons) were all disguises to ensure their alien legacy over a slave population.

USA Reformation the Nonhuman Way

By reshaping and building the United States of America in the 18th century, they envisioned their position in the takeover of this planet in the 21st century. But if we look further back we will discover more of their footprints. The Statue of Liberty is their artificial god and has replaced the Cosmic God of antiquity almost completely. They have learned to sequester divine power and to use it to reshape a nation, and then to reshape the world. As you can see, American cultural influence is everywhere. This is the result of the expansion of energy and therefore the expansion of the American Empire, a mostly egotistical force upon the world led by egoists and elites. While the key religion is branded Christianity, it is in fact Lady Liberty who is the False God and their False Messiahs are effectively their President, all of this takes place under the disguise of false titles, sorcery, spiritual temples disguised as political offices and other artificial symbols, such as the Seal, that provide ample answers to what America is about.

It should be noted, as well, that the Japanese Empire, British Empire, Persian Empire and Roman Empire of the past were portrayed by similar reality pioneers who manipulate energy, expand nations and reshape the world in the way they prefer, always to their advantage and benefit. And this nasty societal experiment remains until today. The biggest difference between the influences of the past and today is that in the past there were counter reality pioneers who made sure that harmony remained, that the entire planet did not succumb to one greedy culture of aliens. But, over the centuries, these secret societies killed off the competition, shut down many of the entrance gates and brainwashed the masses so that the competition became insufficient to stop them. This is why the world is a living hell, not for a lack of god, rather for a surplus of a false god, her false minions and an ignorant public.

Empires rise and fall because Fathers such as them purposely see to it at the appropriate time. Not far from today, America will also be pushed over and while historians will justify those results with economic indicators, war figures and catastrophic statistics, the truth is far more mystical.

The truth is steeped in reality science and how the consummation of ego leads to the devouring of one's own bounty like the Greek god Cronus devouring his own children in order to prevent his successor from ever taking foot. These reality masterminds siphon off human energy to build an empire, extract all they wish then just before the majority of the population wakes, they collapse the empire, they devour it and harvest its best attributes to build a better empire. The population that survives is so demoralized, confused, hurt and worn out that they sell their souls for the promise of the next false empire under some new batch of Fathers and Mothers who will proclaim: "We shall rebuild a better nation, with a stronger currency, a new face that represents infinite liberty!"

And society, steeped in materialism and uneducated in reality science, signs the new disclosure agreement and invests everything they own into the Ponzi Scheme. So that Declaration of Independence was used to give them dominion over the lands of the American region, which for one reason or another was the strongest energetic based from which to rule the world at this time period. As long as that Declaration held, and they've made sure that it remained top of mind in the public who do not perceive beyond the obvious dimension, they could destroy America from within and extract all its resources below cost, go bankrupt and get a bailout all at the same time, at the expense of all the families they've raped.

None of this is in line with cosmic laws and no artificial law will ever take precedence over cosmic law. Therefore, to this extent, I deem the Declaration of Independence invalid and useless to all manner of interpretation on all dimensions. And I empower the citizenry of America and the rest of the world, as far as whom has been affected the most, to take back all their rightful energy, including that energy of their forefathers that was unlawfully stolen, and from their children. To reclaim all those energies from these creatures and to reconnect to the true cosmic forces and the appropriate cosmic laws. By doing so, you will effectively wipe out the collapse of the American Empire, you will interrupt these diabolical plans and you will lay claim to your part in the evolution of this reality.

Until such point that the majority of inhabitants here understand the basics of reality science or how the world really works such as how thought manifests material results, until this point of public awareness, it would be completely unfair to allow these vagrants any irresponsible action. They need to be held back until the majority understand who is behind these masks, what the charade is all about and how many of their children have died in the name of ego, selfishness and greed. We can no longer live in ignorance. In the past, this information was kept from you, today it is available. Make it available to as many people as you can. Discuss it because there is plenty more to understand, especially of your origins and your role in all of this immaculate game of life. Regardless, we need to level the playing field and knowledge and awareness are the perfect ways to start.

We are all incarnates on this plane and we all have different backgrounds with different roles. In other words, we are not more or less than each other, just having different responsibilities. By accessing your reality birth you are recognizing your infinite nature, you are equalizing the playing field. The opposite is also true, denial and fear of aliens is going to keep you in slavery. So although the choice is clear, not everyone will have an easy time with this situation.

Reality pioneers have been around since antiquity and have had hundreds of names over the millennia. The Founding Fathers of America through the succession of US Presidents have managed to fool American citizens and its neighbours for centuries, even inspired nations to become democratic and to adopt capitalism. The US influences are many and, for ill or good, the influences are from nonhumans. Nonhumans who also have taken residence in other nations around the world because the world is controlled by aliens, but rather than little green men per se, these are reality pioneers who have continuously entered the earth plane and managed to make it over in the manner that suits them their egotistical best. An interstellar democracy, perhaps?

REALITY SOCIETIES ON EARTH

The bus depot is a kind of holding station for travelers arriving or departing by bus. A busload of passengers arrives, a busload departs. Today, bus travel is widely accepted and main routes well-established. There is another kind of depot on earth that many have never heard, it is called the *reality depot*. This is a kind of transition house for reality travelers. Of course, this insinuates that earth is a reality. Indeed, it is.

A reality depot on earth has always had other names – more esoteric, more mystical, more magical. A common name, in generic term, was society; verily any society that was secretive and exclusive. Hence the term Secret Society (or Brotherhood, Order, Clan, Group, Foundation). You've heard the terms before: Illuminati, Freemasons, Order of the Dragon, Five Pecks of Rice, Heaven and Earth Society, Black Dragon Society. Societies sprang up centuries ago and they were very common around the world. And any true knight, industrialist or entrepreneur wanted acceptance into a society because it offered knowledge, friendship and protection. But not every society was created equal.

Some fraternal organizations delved into the fundamental nature of existence, or, the esoteric arts; sorcery, magic, mysticism, the search for immortality. These were all derivatives of the temples of the past and required allegiance and devotion, perhaps less devotion than a temple or a church. We could say, though not in the normal sense, that a church is a society, a society of worshipers who adhere to a specific dogma written in a book of knowledge (or Bible). Priests and monks have, in the past, harboured warriors (or crusaders) to uphold the values of their threatened faiths (not unlike the American politicians who harbour soldiers to uphold freedom from terrorism; uncanny similarities).

Well, societies did the same – they held books of knowledge (or codes of honour) and these books contained the essence of success or ascension in the multidimensional world. When a particular government or administration grew to dislike a secret society they labelled it a cult and set it for extinction. Societies have been used to foment resistance, to develop magical skill and to brainwash people, and even just a place for intellectual activity. Throughout history, societies have demonstrated that they can overthrow governments, especially when aided in secret by an enemy nation.

The esoteric societies that focused on the true nature of reality and the mapping of the multidimensional world can be called reality depots. The reality depot was brought into existence by a traveler from another reality (or one who interacted with an interdimensional being) in order to provide an entry way, even a transition house, into a reality.

The reality traveler, the pioneer, enters reality, acclimatizes to the new culture or to the time dimension (since some travelers come from a similar region but different time origin). For example, a man in 1860 might decide to exit 1860 and re-enter in 1989. Of course, he might have to acquire a different body; he may even have to be reborn as a child. Depends on the situation and their skill.

A master of time travel could, with little difficulty, traverse time and enter a predesignated body. The owner of that body would have to be exiting that body in or around that same time, and the time traveler could incarnate with most of his or her memory unchanged. Or they may choose to go through puberty again. There are as many variances as there are choices and, as usual, this is all related to level of awareness and reality proficiency.

The danger of mastering reality is without compare. Reality travel demands the total integration of mind, body, spirit and fundamental knowledge of the other dimension. It demands discipline because the consequence is death. In fact, death is quite a concern for those who really want to go far so reality travel has very few students because it requires a level of courage that one attains in enlightenment, in seeing the cycles of an infinite cosmic machine.

The benefits of reality travel are many, should a person survive the challenge of death. A true practitioner will spend lifetimes to acquire reality knowledge. That requires a very high level of discipline and a very profound understanding of existence. For the less astute practitioner, the benefit is a more successful life – financial wealth, love, avoidance of catastrophe, luck, influence, respect, fame – it's all available. For the spiritual traveler: hardship in exchange for enlightenment of society, helping society, establishment of peace, new developments in medicine or technology, helping society awaken, protecting the world from evil and any true humanistic pursuit.

Membership in a Secret Society: Priceless

Members of the reality depots do not typically share their esoteric knowledge to the public. There are rules for interacting with non-members. There are deceptions. Many secret societies have caused negative influence on the world such as the climate change initiative and the move to a carbon society and carbon tax. This is something orchestrated by very competent reality masters on several alternate dimensions. To the public, they will only hear the carbon debate or attend the conference on Climate Change and how to make money in a Green Economy. All of this is a manipulation by secret society members.

The world was green 100 years ago – that was a Green Economy! Then they sold industrialization to the people; then they sold electricity and gasoline engines and televisions and big houses and three cars per home and warehouse shopping by bulk and wars which emit unknown levels of blood and pollution (and profited immensely from, enough to create the lower-middle class), and now, now they are selling society back to Green and everyone is hypnotized praying to the new Carbon Demi-Gods. And as you see, over and over again, it is effective. But if the public knew what really inspired the Green Revolution they wouldn't be pleased at the amount of deception.

Throughout earth's complex timeline of events, people have departed and arrived from every known location. Whether a person came from the future, an alternate reality or a distant dimension full of crocodile people, the amount of influence here is impressive. That is also because earth itself is impressive because as a body of energy, earth is traveling through time. Within its energetic architecture are corridors and gates to other realities. Some people are naturally attuned to dimensional travel, they are born different. These kind of masters are few. Others will work with dimensional beings to acquire both power and skill, and use these things to earn greater power and skill. Nothing is really given freely in a society. It is earned one way or another so that anyone with a particular skill gave up something for something else, like their morals or their souls.

Once a reality depot is established by some master traveler, then a system is developed so that other travelers and pioneers can follow. It is noted that other travelers may have little or no awareness of some past life but only feel a particular comfort in a particular society. Plus, other travelers can enter via the depot which sometimes is just a large family or a dynasty. Some dynastic families have deep esoteric heritage and have remained in existence by continually reanimating with new bodies. Well, it isn't new that people have past lives, what is new, perhaps is that a person purposely left a past life for this new life.

We invariably arrive at the belief in reincarnation, not in a spiritual sense, rather in the scientific sense because when a person can wilfully exit a physical body and time travel into another physical avatar, whether aided by machine or magic, it suggests a technological science in operation. And if this *avatarian* exchange can be repeated over thousands of years then this science is pretty impressive.

Modern science isn't there yet. No rational physicist can time travel in any scientific manner even though the theory suggests it is entirely possible. So, reality depots and sciences are still inside the dimension of fiction. It can be understood in fiction, but as soon as you enter the real world of mortgages, sex and taxes, for one reason or another, time travel is insane. Perhaps even you are demanding a list of proofs and a few buckets of evidence which you should know that none of it will be provided. In order to appreciate an esoteric art, a person has to overcome doubt, disbelief and scepticism. That doesn't mean gullibility, rather an open mind devoid of preconceived ideas and a genuine willingness to explore, to push boundaries. Admittedly, this requirement loses nearly everyone, but it does reveal some special characters. Further, reality as a science is a lengthy, intellectual affair and smart people need only apply because a dull intellect (eg pig brain) cannot succeed.

There are reality depots on earth and some are very old. I've decided that some of these previously sacred skills and knowledge should be made more accessible to the public. Since I have yet to notice anyone in recent years doing this, I think at least I should start. It should also be noted, for reference, that other reality experts don't like this knowledge reaching the public for the knowledge will awaken others to the unprecedented global manipulation and the false beliefs inserted into society like religion and freedom.

Benevolent travelers from other realities offer earth citizens are real opportunities to improve their level of cosmic knowledge, a real opportunity to defend against pervasive manipulation, a real opportunity to move society forward in a positive direction. As a whole, we need to start rethinking what it means to be human, to redefine the soul as a source of wisdom and to respect that cosmic wisdom can come from the young and old alike. It wouldn't be out of context to suggest that a 13-year old leader might be wiser than a 52-year old one. That also means we would need to value wisdom over entrepreneurial ability. There's not much confidence (nor value) in wisdom at the moment.

Reality depots continue on today in their various incarnations, in good and bad format, in support of government or as part of government. There really is no standard except to say that they have remained in existence and multidimensional influence is pervasive. Explaining that to an average citizen who just incarnated on earth to live a respectable, decent existence isn't easy, and isn't always necessary. But if you are someone who wants to know more, there is more, and there is good and bad, and your intentions can and will be used against you. Your safest bet is to remain true to the cosmic truth, to uphold the virtues of humanism, and to expose the real devils who smile upon society as they initiate wars and manipulate people into division and slavery. You may happen upon a new transition house soon and might find a whole new meaning to your previously redundant, empty life.

THE RISE OF PRINCESS SARAH

Be warned. They are conspiring against you. It happens all the time but this is one I want to point out in the hopes that a fervent discussion will awake before the conspiracy is done. I'll be blunt as usual so you know my style. It is an early observation of the coming events, events which are taking shape, in other words, these are the events that are being programmed. You have the opportunity now to 1) see that program execute all its instructions, or, 2) to interrupt the end result of that program. This conspiracy is a higher-order program and is being orchestrated from the highest levels down to the lowest levels. This is a Major All-Time Screw the World Program and I am presenting it so that, maybe, maybe, some of you will put your faces into this illustrious game and improve the course of human history. Or, you can just call me names.

The conspiracy has to do with Mrs. Sarah Palin. The two major pieces of the puzzle so far include the return of Sarah Palin, long ago announced after she abruptly (in 3D environment) quit mid-way through her government job as the Governor of Alaska. Not your average waitress job that you quit as and when you like. She has written a book. It is certain not to be a well-written, literary masterpiece, but the book is a device for manipulation. In order to manipulate society, a magical device is required. Like any good illusionist or hypnotist they employ any number of devices. Look at my hand while my other hand is up your ass. It has worked for centuries and it works today. And the new book from Mrs. Palin is the misdirection. And, as such, magic is involved. Again, the book is not a literary masterpiece and she has trouble citing which magazines she reads and is unable to handle a media interview, so the competency of the writer is not impressive. Sure, the woman is controversial and beautiful and has some very powerful friends who know about her rich past; otherwise, she wouldn't have made it as a VP contender. That is the first piece of the puzzle: Sarah Palin returns in November.

At the same time we have the return of terrorism. The Trial of the Century is taking shape in New York. The enemy combatants of the 9/11 catastrophe, which we all realize has been a serious orchestration by the powerful rulers in charge of this planet. The World Trade Center Towers collapsed and some Osama bin Laden henchmen were subsequently caught. The mastermind, Khalid Sheikh Mohammed, was water boarded 183 times. Him and his friends are to be tried in a civilian court. Think of it: the event that changed the world as we know it, plunged society in terrorism hell, is returned to New York for a fair trial. All of this is announced on Friday November 13. On Tuesday, November 17, Sarah Palin officially launches her new book, *Going Rogue*. The interviews had already started. What are the esoteric connections between 9/11 and Sarah Palin?

Let's look at one more piece. This isn't as important yet because it is still too far out the window. This is something to observe and I will relook at it a bit further down. This piece of the puzzle is interesting. It is the Statue of Liberty. Liberty, intimately tied to the U.S. Declaration of Independence and the heart of New York, is in the background to the cities that were devastated when two remote-controlled jets smashed the tallest towers then was demolished into one of the biggest outside movie event of this century.

Lady Liberty, as I have proposed in other correspondences, is the False God to whom the Secret Rulers pray to, all the while she is disguised as a French-made copper statue of Freedom. But there is a problem: God is still around. There is still a real God somewhere, a real Force overseeing his creations on this earth and many humans still recognize that True Force over the False Liberty God.

At the start of November, around the fourth, is the start of an ascension for those individuals who are selected as having divine qualities. The US Presidential ascension commences on or around that time and lasts up until about January 20 when the new President is inaugurated on Capitol Hill, in front of the White Temple and the Giant Obelisk. An old ritual to make a Chosen One into a Demi-God. This ritual has been used for a long time in many parts of the world including in Old Egypt. Sarah Palin started her book promotion on or around that time frame. The problem with Mrs. Palin is that her path is far more divine than Mr. Obama, or any other for that matter. But when they announced the Trial of the Century some other lanterns lit up and Mrs. Palin became something quite unique.

When a President needs to ascend into Demi-God form, he requires energy. The campaign generates energy, the believers, the followers, the campaigners and the loyalists. All their energy is redirected and tied to the President. The man with the most energy gets to go first. Mr. Obama became the Chosen One and then ascended with the people's energy tied to his energy. The helium balloon filled with a tremendous amount of helium and reaching the highest altitude. But the US Presidency is done. There can only be one President every four years in the US and Mrs. Palin is not a favourite for President, yet. Because as we shall see there is much more going on.

All of this is still early observation and I am sharing it in order to provide a reason for some of you to get involved because some of you do want to get involved, do want to see what is coming up, do want to be part of history, do want to know weird stuff. This is as weird as it gets because what I am talking about is cosmic stuff and the proof is hard to observe, harder to believe. The future will determine how observant I was, or, am.

Sarah, which is translated as "princess," was connected to Abraham, as in the Chosen One by God himself. Abraham knew a Sarah and Sarah had a very unique beauty and is prominent in the both the Bible and the Qur'an. There is an agreement she is important in divine history. And, lo and behold, there is a Sarah here now in 2009 having already entered the ritualistic ascension starting in November.

There is another aspect of Sarah Palin that very few know. Her previous life dates back to Atlantis. Her soul is very old. I mean, VERY OLD. She likely doesn't know it or is blocked from knowing it. Or she isn't intellectual enough to process that knowledge. Whatever the case may be with Sarah doesn't stop from the Old Masters to make her into something bigger than big, huger than huge. And it isn't a coincidence that this beautiful woman looks uncannily like Liberty.

Okay, I think that is far enough. It is too early to suggest any more. And I am only suggesting, strongly, at this time because it is early, but the early riser gets the warmest breakfast. One more thing, I have to add, and this one is a bit easier to swallow. Gulp. It has been prophesized by both scientists and mystics alike that there is a potential for an end of the world event. Of the many proposals, one that has remained is the reversal of the two Poles, the North and South Pole will magnetically flip and the world will collapse. The egg will be the chicken and the chicken will be the egg and no one will have eggs for breakfast anymore.

The Best Collapse Yet to Come

One of the important esoteric teachings has to do with correspondences between one dimension and another because what happens in one dimension will happen in a different shape and feel in another dimension. For example, your wife leaves you and you lose your job in the 3D environment and it's pretty tough, but on the other dimension you just became aware of your angelic nature and now you have prophetic insight. While you go on antidepressants and seek out a new meaning to life, you are actually not seeing your spiritual wealth. You sort of get the idea: in the 3D perception it has one shape but it means something else. Many psychics work in this manner as well. They will see a stabbing motion in some other realm and the client will raise her eyebrows and reveal she was fired from her job. So they interpret it as a severing.

Since many people have suggested a Pole Shift, we can be certain that something huge is shifting, right? What I am saying is that it isn't the Poles, rather some other huge magnetic (energy) shift. Now, given the facts I presented above: with the rise of princess Sarah and her connection to Liberty, the God of the Secret Rulers, and her ascension path and the energy of 9/11 (global energy on a massive scale), then we can begin to see that Sarah is moving into an ascension of the highest order. Or, perhaps, to fulfill the prophecy of the return of Liberty in earth form, in the form of a Mrs. Sarah Palin, an old Atlantean soul. What does all this mean?

The current God on earth is still regarded to be a Male God. It is a He and has been so for tens of thousands of years. Should the Male God become a Female God, the world would be turned upside-down. Yes or no? Instant sex change. Poles shifting. Male to Female. That is a pole shift, is it not?

Remember that the Secret Rulers, some of them, were around during Atlantis. Their energy is still around. They know many secrets that would make a real man wear a bra and a sexy woman to want to get fat. These reincarnated beings have a long range plan and this just may be the culmination of their plan: to remove God and to put in place a New God, a Goddess. The greatest polarity shift in millions of years. Not just because it boggles the mind, but because the male and female energy are completely different, and one is true and one is false. The differences are tremendous. That these reincarnated fiends want to manufacture an artificial god to replace god is not outside of their demented cosmic thinking. They have already rejected the true source of existence, verily the Sustainer of existence. They reject it and are using human energy and computer energy to replace as much of that cosmic energy as they can. Each stage of their authority, they have sequestered more and more energy, gaining more and more power, harvesting the minds of the world to think as them. To listen to them in every way. The amount of energy being abused is disgusting. It is an aberration of the highest kind and it is continuing without much impedance.

Here comes their next catastrophic event: bring their Liberty into an earthly form so as to create their own Hellish Dimension. Remember that everything is energy. The game is all about energy. Source is energy. Angels are energy. Demons are energy. The Devil is energy. These are understood as people but they embody energy. And you have a soul and this soul is energy. The rest of it is illusory. It is the virtual reality environment.

These false gods and demi-gods have taken it upon themselves to flip over the world, in doing so society will collapse. The world will experience Armageddon. The world will reawaken in another world, of which there is no escape. It is the ultimate mousetrap. You eat the cheese and you are done. It's a no-escape clause by Satan himself. It's the Hotel California, once you enter you can never leave. I hope you are starting to see how to think on multiple dimensions: the idea of the poles shifting in the 3D world is equal to the idea of God becoming Goddess in the 9D world. Sure, I might missing some essential details and I am recognizing that. Perhaps you will discover them. What I am providing is foreknowledge and this could interrupt the event. Heaven knows this planet is in enough trouble and is way deep in Hell, why not stop this suicide train eh?

The people who predicted a pole reversal perhaps didn't have the capacity to note what might occur in other dimensions. And, if the energy of a godlike being flips, that in itself could impact the energy of this reality in fundamental ways. That might be the ultimate showdown between God and Satan (Note: I will be writing on Satan and the Devil soon so watch for that). We are looking at a Cosmic Battle, something way beyond the average guy working at Starbucks. This is above the military and any black ops. These are all pixels on a giant LCD screen and Sarah Palin is desperately required to participate in order to fulfill the false revelations by the false gods.

Humanity has been imprisoned enough. Humanity has bled enough. Humanity has been denied its divine right long enough. Today, the knowledge, tools and energy is available to redirect this plane back to its origins. Back to moral and virtue but that is going to require a powerful counter force that thinks outside the 3D box. Preventing another disaster requires people to see what is being planned and then finding innovative ways to ensure that humanity doesn't collapse, that humanity continues, that humanity is not taken over. I have provided some foreknowledge. Do what you will with it but remember that it is an observation worth writing down and sharing from my view.

I am not suggesting doom here because I do not see doom per se. The interaction between dark and light energy is a human observation. Really, the universe has but one energy and that energy is interrupted by harsher energies. That is the cosmic struggle. Struggle produces change. Struggle reshapes the course of existence. In other words, what I am talking about is not "new." It has happened before and the Male Energy continued on and has remained. But that cycle is ending and all the characters are playing out their roles. That is why you need to get involved: In order to fulfill the next iteration of existence. To be included. I want to include you, knowing that most people who will read this will be scratching their head for a while. But there will be a few who will see something that this will help some other endeavour and that endeavour is integral to the struggle. I love the struggle. There is no ascension without struggle. The world they sold you, that of comfort and complacency, is a sham. Struggle shapes existence. Just like the chisel shapes the wood. If you deny the wood the chisel it will never form a statue. It will never derive any value from itself. It will remain a piece of wood. The world is full of walking, breathing wood. Let's get back to carpentry. That's the correspondence, you see, carpentry is a metaphor for ascension.

THE FATHER OF ALL LIES (PART ONE)

The world is in ruin and it's not going to fix itself. If shovels could repair all the damage done, there's a shovel shortage. The same elitists who sold industrialization and militarization to the modern corporatists are now selling global warming and carbon pollution to the masses. It's the grand exotic yo-yo whereby the rich fuck everyone they can for as long as they can. The dark hand of magic casts its spell upon the pilgrims and pagans, and no one can see through the smoke and mirrors. Or, can they?

Certainly, we are in Hell and the world is run by Demons because no Heaven would allow nations of poverty, continuation of wars, raping by bankers, vaccinations of healthy babies and making certain esoteric plants illegal to grow. We can be certain that we are, if not in Hell completely then we are being plunged deeper into the toilet. Ironically, most people are concerned whether their teeth are white enough and if that guy on TV is indeed a reptilian. As we are in Hell and it should be obvious, then where is the Devil? You know the flaming entity that set off on a pilgrim of temptation to pollute purity and to suck out the innocence of Adam's bloodline.

If the Devil existed, where would he be? Generally agreed to be equal to the Creator, a ubiquitous celestial nonentity, we have to conclude that the Devil is himself everywhere. How do we find someone thousands of years old gifted with the ability to appear nearly anywhere and imbued with a supernatural power that makes him unsinkable and that none understand?

The relevance of the Devil in the modern age should be increasingly apparent given that we are living in hellfire (which is why the Demons are complaining about global warming). According to religious authority, the Devil has yet to be defeated definitively; therefore, he hasn't been put in chains and is locked away somewhere, rather he's disguised himself. Today, we see many things, but we do not recognize evil. We vote for it. We buy it on sale. We applaud evil more than we resist it because, according to the early prophets, evil stems from temptation. And temptation is aplenty. We give awards to the Champions of Temptation: CEO of the Year. Nobel Peace Prize. Blockbuster film. Most silicone-enhanced Woman Alive. Richest Man in the World. When celebrities get more attention than dying children there is a problem. When no one recognizes that, there is a breakdown. A catastrophe.

The ex-governmental leader with the 23-room mansion and a best-selling book gets on a TV talk show to talk about making "green living" a priority. Verily, it is all a hallmark of the Devil, if we remember that the love of money is the root of all evil and that governments love money. We just haven't admitted we are blind. We are still in denial, I guess.

There is also a discussion of the New World Order (NWO). These bimbos are actually becoming more and more plain. Just yesterday, an ex-politician said on mainstream TV that the population needed to be reduced to fight too much carbon in the atmosphere. He then applauded the movement of working women and considered having children evil. I'm sure he's sold a lot of books to the blind and faithful Dumbos. But is this NWO (the Secret Rulers of Earth) member a minion of the Devil? Is the NWO just a manifestation of the Devil? And if so, wouldn't that make them the Old World Order because these immortal masters have been around for a lot longer than anyone is willing to accept. And if this is Hell then all of it is a result from Satan's touch.

We know that the Devil has yet to be defeated; therefore, he is still around. This is logic. No mention of the Devil's defeat has been made. Life is shit. We know that the world is immersed in war, disease and money – all manifestations of evilness. We know that these items of evil have been around for a while and are considered normal. We even aspire to be rich so we can wash our asses in dollar bills. We also know that temptation has infected the world. Even the Vatican has amassed great wealth and molested more children than can be accounted for; therefore, the Church is overcome with temptation. It is useless as an instrument of God. It is useful for holding sermons and weddings, on the other hand. And weddings are still being done in churches.

We know that a human being cannot deliver into the world anything without a mechanism for delivery. You cannot deliver a casino without the mechanism of greed. You cannot deliver an invasion of a Middle Eastern region with the mechanism of psychosis. We have to see on some level that the Devil is a mechanism for temptation which also tells us that rather than a man, he is more likely an interpretation of a more complex phenomenon in a reality system that is more virtual than material, but that is for Part Two.

The Devil possesses people to do evil acts, or to act in a manner that satisfies him (it). The Devil overrides human instruction and rewrites a person's life. The Devil wins over the mind with temptation, "Just one taste and then you can walk away. One more dollar and you will have enough. One more kiss and you can get over him." Temptation is Eve's apple. One bite and mankind was tossed out of Heaven and now has to work a job to get by. The Devil turns a person's life little by little, one lesbian lock at a time.

We cannot deny the dark world, the chain of coincidences before us – the peak of temptation, the epitome of evil – the Devil and his own personal Club Fuck You. He's done a fine job. From garden planet to garbage planet, the people clinging to life for fear of a finite world and a worthless death. He convinced people to inject poisons into their faces to look beautiful and he's inspired cereal makers to make 13 flavours of the same wheat flakes. Our facial tissue can be purchased with antibacterial chemicals and herbal tea included. There is organic dog shampoo when dogs don't even need a shampoo because they are a dog! In fact, dogs have just as many organic food choices as human babies, and there are 25,000 nuclear warheads in the world. Good job, Devil. You've fooled the many and segregated the few. That should get you a few bonus points. When you can make people fuck themselves, that makes fucking them all that much more fun.

Let us briefly revise Satan's character because there are many interpretations of Satan from those who fear him to those who worship him. No matter how you view it, Satan is the asshole who will give your daughter, he himself raped, a coupon for a new pair of jeans. He can appear in any form, whether it is a beautiful woman or an invisible voice, he can infect the world in ways that would make CSI run around in circles for thousands of years. He is destruction, deception, negativism, fear, success, hope and oppression – all trademarks of the New World Order, the baboons in expensive suits who speak fancy words to sound smart. Amoral scumbags them all. The Devil is as much, perhaps more, the NWO as any other evil-minded group. And he is on the loose.

The Signature of the Devil

The signature of the Devil is in the shape of a pattern. To notice this pattern, and therefore to notice the Devil, requires a cosmic perception. More specifically, it requires a spiritual view from a mind that has been trained to notice cosmic patterns. A divine beast is not of this world. In not being of this world, it speaks in a higher language. If it spoke to you in English, it would be invisible because the Devil does not hide in logic or ideas. The Devil is beyond human logic. The Devil is beyond human emotion and action.

We could say that the Devil is all these dimensions and more. The Devil's signature is not one event. One event is a letter, one stroke of a letter. To see the whole letter and its size and shape, you must train to see all the correlated events to his signature, you have to see a pattern of events. To stare at the site of the previous World Trade Center towers is like staring at the inner stroke of an "e". The signature of the Beast is like a Chinese character. Each piece, each part having many strokes, many actions, many events. Without the culmination of strokes, the character has no meaning. Has no presence; therefore, it is invisible. That is why the Devil's presence is invisible. It is not that he doesn't exist; it is that he exists on a dimension beyond human linguistic ability.

So, we are at a crossroads here on earth, because why? Because we are blind to the patterns of events and therefore we are easily misled. They are speaking a foreign language and we haven't realized what these foreigners are saying. It is like living in Vietnam (or Poland, Russia, Brazil, etc) and not speaking Vietnamese. They can say anything they want in front of your face and you haven't a clue what they are saying until they have you by the throat. We are misled by those who speak the Devil's language for they contain our thoughts and encourage us to see the randomness of existence. We believe in luck and fate and destiny and curse; we do not believe in conspiracy, the purposeful interference in human activities. The movement of money and the containment of money. We do not see these events as patterns because we do not care for the Language of the Devil. We are spiritually illiterate. Any of the Divine beings, even all of them speak in a language of events (mini or major), or even a miracle moment, the people do not often see any connection between events. They cannot form the image of the puzzle. Interestingly, a Divine Language, a language from a higher dimension, because even the Devil is a higher being, is a lot like a crossword puzzle or a musical score, in that the completion of the puzzle or song is the complete message. A verse is a verse and not a song. The human mind takes the complete puzzle and disintegrates it. Why?

Because there is too much data. The butcher takes the pig and butchers the meat like the mind butchers the puzzle. Why? So that the mind can digest it. The mind is hungry just as the stomach is hungry, but the stomach cannot eat the whole pig in one bite. So the butcher was invented to cut up the pig and the chef was invented so the pig parts could be divided into edible portions, and the teeth were invented so as to chew the cooked chunks. Only then could the pig be eaten; otherwise, the stomach is useless. Imagine, you are given teeth and a stomach but no butcher and no chef. Well, in reality, you had bishops and priests, gurus and monks, they were the butchers and chefs of divine language and knowledge. Their skills and wisdom have been replaced by the lawyer and the politician, the publicist and the handler, no wonder we are all confused.

The mind is to the puzzle as the stomach is to the pig. That is to say, the mind is equipped to slaughter the puzzle so as to digest it. The mind is not equipped to see the entire puzzle because that data is too big. The file is zipped up and needs to be extracted and then all the files need to be scanned and interlinked, reprocessed and published. Some people have that capacity, most do not. That's why we are all skilled in different ways.

The Language of the Devil works in this manner and his Minions (his Legion) create the events and the sum of those events is the Signature of the Devil. Not the sum of historical events, but the sum of the one particular sentence and the totality of sentences into a paragraph. The Devil has been speaking for longer than Abraham and Sarah. That language has all been but lost except for a few truth seekers who refer to it as "connecting the dots." It isn't so much about connecting the dots as it is learning to speak spiritual, again. If you do so, they call you a conspiracy theorist. What simple minds! I am a conspiracy theorist because I speak a divine language? I am a conspiracy theorist because I refuse to be hoodwinked by my fake leaders? They should call us heroes. See the Hell now? It is upside-down. In Heaven, poverty would be eradicated and vaccinations would be illegal. In Hell, ego first and fuck you.

We have only glanced at the first aspect of the Devil – his signature. Realizing that there is indeed an orchestration of events and the collation of certain events can form a pattern and that pattern a signature is truly an impressive idea because it introduces humanity to a whole new level of communication; and it reveals a more sinister Beast conducting the world deeper into the fire pit, a system that is regularly seen as normal everyday suffering. Take a pill and you will feel better. Okay, thank you.

There is another aspect of the Devil having to do with the Technoverse, the technological universe. Most of my work is on this aspect, but I felt that a short cover of the Devil from this side was necessary before talking about the technological aspect coming in Part Two.

THE FATHER OF ALL LIES (PART TWO)

The Devil is a pattern. He is a pattern of events, a pattern of decisions, a pattern of instructions, a pattern of influence. He is Divine and by being Divine he is fluent in the Divine Languages. When he speaks there is a series of events. There are numerical occurrences, a chain of coincidences, breaking news. The human mind has become conditioned to believe in coincidence and randomness in a reality system that runs on certainty, and speaks in patterns. The old definition of the Devil requires a swift makeover in a universe built with billion-year advanced technology. In fact, I will show that this hi-tech Devil is more than a Symbol of Evil.

This manufactured reality plane (or earth) vibrates at a level that is in harmony with both the awareness of its inhabitants and the proficiency of the localized programmers, and that is because each reality system is built on multiple levels of components. Without programmers, the reality could not be upgraded or maintained, and without inhabitants there is no need for a system. Inhabitants and programmers co-exist, well, they used to co-exist until the world opened its arms to the Devil.

What we are seeing on earth, this demoralized state of events, this corruption and degradation, this mind control, all of it is a result of a systemic corruption. The circuitry of consciousness and manifestation has been overrun by an *immortal virus*, an existence-scale program. And because of its complexity and its multidimensional nature, this evil program has a number of mythological names, depending on its observation: Satan, Devil, Mephistopheles, Beelzebub,

They are aspects of the same mogul program that has infected this reality. We notice it now because we notice the one key characteristic of Hell, the preference of self over others. The Ego. Verily, Hell is rooted in ego; Heaven in egolessness. These are fundamental facts. God is all-forgiving and the Devil wants revenge. We've all had moments of both. But as you have seen in Part One, we are certain that this world is one of ego. And in being of EGO it is rooted in Hell, and therefore the Devil is in control. He is on the loose and he is in command over the majority. The problem is that very few people see that. They all think that suffering, oppression and democracy are normal. They believe in the have and have nots. They like division and discrimination. And everyone likes money.

Now rather than harp on about the materialistic and superficial world, it is more productive to talk about the Devil as a *viral program*. The Devil is not a man and never was a man. He is an *existence-scale program*, but he is not a basic program. He is not an individual soul. He is a *reality-grade program*. He can be many souls. This is not unlike a computer desktop and a computer server. A server can control more than one desktop machine within its network, a desktop only one machine and its peripherals (eg printer).

The Devil as a network program can run the entire earth system if left unchecked (via avatars). Luckily, there are protective devices to restrict his movement. But every reality system is given its own level of independence, as requested by the representatives of its inhabitants. But what's happened over centuries is that the programmers who were supposed to maintain the reality system (eg Druids), were supposed to protect society, well, they've all been corrupted or killed off by minions of the Devil. One or two is probably at the casino or making a porn film in the hopes of making it into the film business. The rogue programmers have hijacked the reality system and then have perennially reprogrammed it to suit their diabolical needs. Call it *reality terraforming*, or reformation.

These rogue programmers hadn't the capacity to completely take over all components so they set out to slowly kill off all connections to the cosmos so as to subtly subdue this entire field of existence. What we are witnessing now is the end manifestation of their 2,000 Year Plan. Because all existences stem from some machine program, for example Heaven and Hell, then these reality pirates must be connected to some power source and since it is not Heaven it is Hell. That makes them pure self, all ego. Remember that any being that is alive is connected to a cosmic machine; if not they'd be dead. This is a network of existence. In such a system you cannot have a lone computer. To be functioning, that computer is connected to a network. Hell is a network and the Devil is the server.

Perhaps in speaking in this way we can better see the technological nature of life. That biology has merely been a primitive interpretation of an artificial existence. This in no way diminishes the ideas of Heaven or Hell (or any of the other religious terms) only that it broadens their understanding. To say that God is a cosmic computer mainframe and Heaven his network is now within our reach of understanding because most of us believe in mobile phones, computer networks and the internet (worldwide network). What this also changes is the understanding of the human soul, as introduced in my book *Talessian's Riddle*.

So, the Devil has carefully placed his minions, many in human form, in positions of influence and leadership. Not only that but some higher minions have entered human bodies. Most of these are creatures. These dimensional creatures have enhanced its human avatar with greater influence, foreknowledge, and protection from defeat. The regular human avatar is no match for minion of the Devil, a demon inside a human. Working through humans in this manner, the Devil has managed to toss humans into the toilet with no rational escape. There is no end to war, no end to disease, no end to hardship. Just when it appears to be ending, there is another series of strategic catastrophes, random events that only appear random.

The Cosmic Cha-Cha

It is easy to decide that because life sucks we should see some ultimate cosmic battle where Good clashes with Evil and the wings of Armageddon are set free. It is easy to decide that because that's what the rogue programmers want. They want drama. They want exaggeration. That is when the illusion is strongest, when emotions are at their peak. They have been carefully reprogramming reality so as to position themselves and their masters in a battle formation as the false Revelations are made brought onscreen.

Instead of a great cosmic battle between the Angels of Light and the Demons of Dark, these ideas are merely human exaggerations of the most eloquent virtual Cha-Cha reality dance. The processing of digital data inside your computer's CPU (central processing unit) or the video compression of a full-length feature film is a very technological process. There is no drama to it except when we apply drama to it, when we fictionalize the interactions and highlight the drama. We see this in sports commentary. The sports commentator connects to the audience and dramatizes the game play. They bring the game to life. They add all the background information on the players, they tell you about secret injuries; these illusionists exaggerate the game play in order to captivate an audience. The same is true in professional wrestling, only there is more exaggeration and modified game play.

The cosmic dance between one type of energy and another is really an interaction between different programs in a highly complex technological universe. To dominate society, they create drama because this stimulates emotion and emotion feeds the illusion. How do you fuel illusions? With emotion. How do you dominate humanity? Dominate emotion.
There is a lot of misunderstanding about emotion, and rightly so. A person will state that emotion is what makes them human. For a woman to cry, it is proof of her humanity. The aliens are always depicted as incapable of emotion. The NWO (bankers, businessmen, witches and warlocks) is without emotion. Heck, the NWO is made up of aliens. And what of the Devil? What happened to him?

The Devil program feeds on emotion because emotion is what? Emotion is a cellular switch. Opening the human dynatron (light valve) or closing the dynatron. Our DNA behaves like billions of light valves, turning off and on, shifting left and right, breathing light or blocking light. The DNA dynatrons are always processing reality. Every moment. The stability of those processes equates to the stability of your being. To lose your stability is to drift magnetically closer to either Good or Evil, God or Devil, Vibration A or Vibration B. God does not call himself God. The Devil doesn't care what you call him as long as you are in awe.

The Legion of the Devil, the programs imbued with his egoist energy, the cellular virus, and the human counterparts possessed by giant demons, all of them are very active now. They are on TV, they are in charitable campaigns, they are orchestrating events, all of them busy. The Legion wants to initiate biblical revelation. They'll try to initiate many in the hopes that one or two start and after one or two start, because of human thought power, the rest may fall in. It depends on the will of humanity.

As you can see, what is happening is very complex and spans several fields of knowledge. I've introduced each field so as to leave further research and contemplation in your hands. I am not one to provide all the answers, even I had them or didn't because that defeats the reason for being here and goes against my own teachings. Certainly, there is enough new information to explore the new avenues of possibilities. I realize that the average person will seek a full and complete, fully referenced, report on the Devil but my readers are above average. This, after all, is a *reintroduction* to the myth of a thing referenced to as the Devil.

I have had plenty of interaction with this deceptive program and I can tell you from experience he is as cunning as he is magically gifted. He attacks on many dimensions at once; his pattern is manipulation, the ultimate mind control freak. Everything at once, from all directions. He confuses, he implants ideas and he compels those ideas which are against the truth. He inspires celebrity and a person folds, changes their career path and dreams of becoming famous. In no other time have so many people dreamed of walking onto the stage and having fans scream at them. Truth is that the stage life is for a very select bunch of gypsies who have the muster and talent to last in the road show.

The Devil is powerful because his language is Divine and society is illiterate. Only in this way has his many Minions (Demons) hijacked the good world and turned it into a cesspool of murder and money in the name of freedom. This is a deception of the hallmark of the Devil. This here is the land of ego. A place where wisdom and intuition has been made extinct. A place where any man or woman who sees the truth, who speaks it out loud, who dares their very lives, is cast out as a conspiracy theorist, a loony, a radical. The positions of power will create radicals, prop them onto a stage and defame them, make them an example, only to further weaken those whose efforts are genuine. And the common people buy it, they buy these tricks because the Devil's minions are smart and keep the mind contained.

Is the Devil real? Yes. He is a virtual construction. A cosmic hologram that replicates and feeds the selfish and the weak-minded. Inside the other dimensions, he exists. He has access to this reality and he wants to see mankind turn away from God, so that they turn to him. The more he turns, the more effect he can have on the world. Today, his stench is everywhere because the people are blind to his presence. Talking about the Devil isn't politically correct. Mentioning the NWO is useless without a level of proof that is unattainable. So what do we do?

Truth is the Devil's weakness. He cannot break the shield of truth, so if you hold truth you have a defense against him. Sure, truth is hard to come by inside an egotistical world shaped by deception, disinformation and lies. Truth is hiding beneath humanity's hate and fear. And the Devil – the Father of all lies – knows where you are weakest because he knows if your truth is in fact one of his lies or not. As you encounter the minions of the Devil, learn to calibrate yourself to truth and be wary of excess temptation. Remember that he and you are programs housed inside a virtual reality system designed by a very advanced group of technicians. As you attenuate to truth, turn to it. Behold the light, the source of your being. You might notice the Sustainer of existence (the Source). That is your strength. That is what will anger the Devil. Then you will hear more lies. Then you will see him more clearly in the shadows. Deceive the Devil and you will have deceived the Father of Deception.

What has kept the Devil alive for so long? Hate, fear, lust, discrimination, deception, lies, vanity, hubris, separation, disbelief, scepticism, doubt, evil, indecision – all these things and more have invited the Devil here. To rid the Devil, we improve ourselves. We turn away from the status quo and we face the point of our origins. You may not believe in the Devil, but someone else does, and so long as someone does, so long as there is fear in the world, he is always around. That is why we mustn't stop at ourselves. That is where we begin. We force the Devil to the surface with truth. So that everyone can see the dark shadows hiding at the back of our minds, the flecks of black soot lining our hearts. He is a program that feeds off of the human spirit. His minions ensure that we are filled with hate and fear. The Devil has had a buffet on earth and his days of influence must now come to a fitful end.

AL GORE AND THE DEMONIC CLIMATE CHANGE CONSPIRACY

After a surprising rise to fame under a banner of world pseudo-environmentalist, Al Gore has set the population as a new threat against his demonic brotherhood and is prepping for his one-child policy in order to save the world from carbon catastrophe. The former VP, newly anointed champion of climate change, has even hooked up with David Suzuki, award-winning and real environmentalist, to expand his climate empire and to achieve the rank of carbon billionaire.

The truth behind Mr. Gore's satanic creed is historically evil. He proposes that excess carbon dioxide plugs up the upper atmosphere, planet heats up, glaciers melt too fast, oceans rise, cities will disappear underwater and humans will have to get gill implants to survive. There are two immense problems with Herr Gore. First, the ubiquitous idea that humankind determines 100% of humankind's destiny is misguided. It is conditioning by the mind control masters. Humankind is a managed race because its evolution is still unfinished. It is managed by the planetary builders who observe and correct as and when necessary. Second, Mr. Gore and his secret society flock have sabotaged some of the planet's cooling systems to warm up the house.

Climate change, global warming, carbon taxes and the reduced birth rate have been forced upon humanity, by magicians. It would dishearten the suckers of the world to know that the Green Revolution is another giant crocodile sham. But that is a bold statement from a person who is not a climate expert and hasn't studied the effects of pollution on the world. On the other hand, I am an expert on reality systems and the dimensional architecture of this planet earth is built on a very specific platform. As I will discuss, it is this dimensional platform that has been purposely sabotaged in order to produce some of the climate effects sold by crocodile messenger Al Gore. "It is a true planetary emergency," he stresses on The Daily Show with Jon Stewart. He launches on David Letterman: "The scientific debate is over. There is a complete consensus that global warming is real, we human beings are causing it, the results are very bad – headed towards catastrophic – we need to fix it and it's not too late."

So what I'll discuss then is my own discovery of the damage done to the reality architecture and its connections to the magicians on the surface and the involvement of the newly embodied Mr. Gore.

In late 2006, about one year after my awakening I entered the reality architecture and discovered purposeful damage done to the earth's cooling systems. At the time, even I didn't care for any connection to the diabolical mind fuck film, An Inconvenient Truth, because I was appalled at what they had done to the reality equipment. Just as your car has an engine underneath the hood, hidden from your eyes so too does earth have an engine only that the engine is housed inside another dimension.

In the early building of the reality, a set of maintenance workers were created to ensure the smooth operation of the reality parts. These dimensional creatures have no physical form, they are energy programs. They usually appear as a cross between a giant lizard and wolf. These are very nasty beings and they travel in packs, just like wolves. These dimensional worker beasts can inhabit human bodies, can even possess people temporarily, they can shape-shift and can affect human energy. They were created to ensure the inner architecture worked properly, they are energy and the system is energy.

Reality Cooling Systems

When I reached the cooling systems of the earth, inside a hyper-dimension made up of energy, like a virtual reality space inside your computer, I discovered extreme tampering. As I removed the initial debris, I discovered damage done to the machinery. Purposeful sabotage. It can be compared to ramming steel rods into the giant turbine of a jet engine and expecting it to fly normally, or, shooting arrows into the lungs of a human and expecting them to breathe properly. They had managed to really clog up the system. Of course, a Reality Cooling System is immense and even the effects of these nasty children couldn't cease the cosmic turbines from rotating. They did, however, produce the necessary climate anomalies (ie global warming) needed to convince Joe Public that it is "warmer" and that is because people can easily perceive warmth and not so easily perceive other dimensions.

I don't know how long they've been damaging the internal cooling systems because I only discovered it in 2006, coincidentally the same year demonic Al Gore came out with his slick documentary on humanity's influence on the climate, *An Inconvenient Truth*. You see, Mr. Gore blames humans for creating the pollution that has warmed the planet, and now wants to slap people with a carbon tax in order to punish humanity for becoming industrialized by the very same friends of crusader Gore. Problem is Mr. Gore is the front man of the very creatures and magicians who have wreaked havoc on the internal systems in order to produce enough of the physical effect to mindwash humanity.

Humans do not believe in other dimensions. An average person would not believe that Mr. Gore is now inhabited by a demon, something he earned for fucking the masses into believing in a "climate crisis." It was his ascension prize: immortality (similar to his brethren Heinz Kissinger and Dick Cheney et al). As water is shaped by energy, a person possessed by a particular type of demon morphs into a physiological equivalent of the energy of the demon (or other alien inhabitant). The same is true for an enlightened person whose physiology shines according to their embodiment of angelic energy. Now because society doesn't believe in this crocodile magic, Mr. Gore, enhanced by a magical hand, has become a media darling. He, apparently, cares about the planet despite the fact that he and his elite friends have purposely damaged it. All they needed was to produce some science to back up their deception (eg 70 million tonnes of carbon produced, temperature rising, ice caps shrinking) and society was sold. Because society has always been sold by these infomercial threats, "Look everyone, this here planet is earth, it is hot, you are sweating, the water is rising, it's going to kill your children unless you buy this product. If you buy my product today, climate change, then I will tell my demonic associates to cool this place down, just after all my elitist brotherhood cashes in and sets up the new carbon tax. Oh, yeah, and by the way, if you don't buy this product, human civilization will be destroyed. And, when you order, be prepared to stop bearing children because we are over-populated. We need to reduce the population."

I spent a lot of effort, along with others, to clear up the damage done to the Reality Cooling Systems. That was about 3 years ago, and you'll notice that since then winters have normalized. But keep in mind, there are many nonhumans who actively maintain earth's health without public knowledge, prizes or gratitude. Anyway, you'll have noticed a more properly functioning seasonal variance since that time, and you'll also notice that Mr. Gore's credibility has faltered as new evidence contradicted his original infomercial. His deception has become increasingly clearer. But he had already influenced the decision makers, started the Green Movement and paved the way for a carbon tax and a one-child policy. All of it a sham, sadly. All of this is from an ultra-dimensional sabotage, along with other effects such as chemtrails and electromagnetic influences, done by cooperating with dimensional reality creatures (or, demons) and using advanced technological instruments behind closed doors. It is a deception. If humans paid more attention to the dimensional nature of the earth they would not have allowed these magicians to collaborate with the unearthly creatures and none of this could have happened. But the druids of yesteryear are dead and the new humans only worship proven science and false speakers. Too bad.

What I'm introducing is yet another deception from the camp of Al Gore, one of the brothers of a magical clan who regularly work with demons and evil nonhumans. He himself now embodies a very dark being, a silver-tongued devil and his influence is all that much more powerful. On the surface, he's a well-dressed social activist. Underneath, his soul is no longer human. This gives him an unfair advantage to the nice humans around him. His friends are no different. I wish the world would start believing in demons again because they are controlling society in many ways. Because of the damage done to the Reality Cooling System, the climate indeed warmed for a period. That situation is now normalizing and none of this interference will ever be allowed again at this level. But humanity needs to get dimensionally involved or it's over. People have to drop the "prove it or I won't believe you" brain implant and dig deeper into their psyche before it's really too late. It should also be noted that earth's own ascension has produced some of the climate effects which the global warming crowd manipulate to their advantage. It's disinformation at its best. Earth is changing because it is entering a new cosmic vibration. You'll have noticed yourself going through ascension unlike ever before these past few years. So there is always more than one thing happening at a time.

If we combine modern science with reality science, we achieve a much more comprehensive view of the true operation of a manufactured planetary vessel. We obtain a holistic concept of the multidimensional earth. It is no different than your body that inhabits a soul, an energy component. The earth, as well, inhabits an energy component. It is not a stretch of the imagination. The stretch is having people accept that evil magicians have summoned demons inside the earth and collaborated on a multidimensional demonic conspiracy to control this dismal world and to make it more dismal.

Climate change is based on reality sabotage; the reality system is programmed to adjust and adapt according to societal need. Climate change is a deception that is clearly beyond the perception of humanity. To think that human consumption can alter global climate when the globe is administered by a super-advanced reality engine only reinforces the need for humanity to wake from its slumber. The reality architecture can be programmed to handle any demand, and it can also be programmed to collapse. It depends on the solution required. In the past, some civilizations needed to be collapsed. They themselves did not collapse themselves. The administrators reprogrammed the system to collapse based on all the inputs and observations, all done within the body of cosmic laws that any reality operates under.

Earth today can support billions more people. Billions more. The exact number I do not know because that depends on the adoption of newer technologies and humanity's adaptation to a larger and more advanced population. Currently, humanity is held in fear and threat. It is not free. It does not think free. It fails to realize that it is not free.

The system doesn't like to be damaged. If someone sabotaged your air conditioner and you were forced to sweat in the heat of summer, would you just sit down and forget about it? If someone damaged the engine of your car, would you be angry? Well, earth's inner machinery was damaged and what does humanity do? Humanity gives Al Gore and Friends a Nobel Peace Prize and supports his cause for a Carbon Tax. To find the truth, follow the demon called Al Gore.

A NEW STORY OF JESUS

Jesus is the cosmic allegory. The divine passage of a kind of beauty that is truly resplendent. While the many scholars and believers of Jesus have scoured scripture for his life as a savior on earth, I'd like to tell you a new story of Jesus.

My story begins in the deepest part of the cosmos in a dimension that is beyond human access. It is like a central hub of the cosmic computer. There, an unimaginable amalgamation of celestial energy takes shape. It is a newly created nebula, an artistic kaleidoscope of immense divine glory. Within this factory of interstellar machinery, the plasma processors generate an abundance of incalculable energy, according to a very predetermined amount from the cosmic computer. The machinery is manned by existence-scale programs, holographic giants.

These cosmic programs oversee the newly formed nebula. The inner star machines are busy processing all its initial components. It's a star factory run by the most unimaginably elegant machine, a star seed becomes a young star.

The young star is spit forth into space, traveling across a timeless dimension unaware; where only a star signature can fathom. Here there is no such thing as humanity or planets. Here there is only stellar bliss. The kind of the star is knowingness. The star itself is a machine, programmed to traverse the blackest night, powered by a plasma engine of no equal, built by a nebular factor run by gargantuan engines. As the star travels, a body is prepared. A body capable of holding a multidimensional star and a body capable of existing in a field of consciousness that has been housed inside an atmosphere of dense energy fields, what appears as matter.

The physical body is derived from the localized DNA materials as well as nonlocal synthetic materials. The flesh is constructed and the synthetic body formed into a boy. Barely conscious, the young avatar is ready for the star being. But the boy's awareness in this dense atmosphere of reality, is new; therefore, the stellar consciousness is graduated and scaled down to accommodate the specific programmed environment that is known as earth. Verily, the new earth being is prepared with generous hands, and, once ready he is found an earth mother, Mary. Mary is a virgin, that is, Mary gave her genetic material to the child in order for the child to be born with an earthly energy signature. The child was never born out of Mary, but through her. Mary's genes were chosen because Mary is herself synthetic. A synthetic being is undifferentiated from a typical person because all people are derivatives of synthetic beings.

A Star is Born

The newly created child, Jesus, joins the adoptive family of Mary and Joseph. Because of the graduated stellar consciousness, Jesus is unaware of what he is and will eventually embark on a quest to activate his hidden potential. It can be said that any being of awareness who chooses to incarnate into another system, or reality, is responsible for their own return to Original Awareness because the process of incarnations is coated in forgetfulness. To assist Jesus the angelic guides and symbolic reminders were always put in place. This was done in order to facilitate the journey of the Chosen One. This is because the birth of the stellar material human incarnate is based on a particular cosmic cycle, a particular period of evolution in the life of a civilization. At that time, earth plane was ready to welcome a cosmic child. Ironically, the child is merely a mechanical presentation provided to perform some set of technical repairs. He himself is transient, programmed and bound by total service.

The cosmic Jesus was interpreted as a regular person and overlooked. When he traveled to India he did so as part of his ascension process. His ascension was intimately connected to this planet and all its people. But the memory of Jesus in India was not of Jesus. He had adopted a new name and a new identity. His time in India brought him to himself and allowed him to determine just who and what he was.

He returned to Jerusalem awakened. But he was not finished. He was incomplete. His path was cosmic. His path had just begun. To develop his powers he involved himself in the community, his people. Those ages of religiosity welcomed a pious man so he became pious; a teacher, a sage and a healer. His wisdom was a result of his own understanding of himself, the purification of his nonhuman qualities by removing his humanity. In essence, the ultimate humanist because he no longer had any bias toward humanity. Rather, he had come to understand the human culture and that understanding would prove an integral part of his service.

All the while Jesus, the descended one, brought his energy to the people, shared his ideas, gave sermons for those who would listen. Only a few listened. Several other special characters joined him and devoted their lives to his teachings. They came to be the apostles. The apostles were gifted men, they themselves of a cosmic origin; they themselves had to be baptized. The baptism was the rebirth into the realm of Jesus, to welcome his energy and to live a life free from temptation; for temptation was the realm of the Devil.

Just who was the Devil that Jesus spoke of? Jesus did not have the words he needed to explain that the Devil was an existential program and he could redirect a human soul, for even the soul was a program Jesus could not/never explain a technology of this nature to a simple civilization. Cosmic technology became divine spirit, became prophet and revelation, became the Holy Bible. There is no Holiness in religion for religion is a derived term from cosmic technology and cosmic technology refers to ultra-dimensional machinery. It was known to the angels that cosmic Jesus was indeed a machine embodied with a program of the highest nature. For the angels themselves were programs. Some had incarnated into a mechanical body; some chose to remain in holographic form. Jesus saw them all and because of his ecclesiastical origins, they were devoted to him. But they could not interrupt his path. No one was allowed to interfere with the journey of Jesus the Android. He had to determine his own existence. He had to make his own awareness.

His ideas were powerful among the simple people. His followers were devoted but they were few, for he had to compete with other ideologies. He had to compete with developing machines. Jesus on earth was not all about his contact with the people. He was cosmic after all. His connection was with the planet. In fact, he had stronger ties to the planet than to the people. His interaction with the planet changed the planet and in doing so set a new course for earth. No one of an average mind would come to learn about his influence until many centuries later.

There were some members of the old world who had returned to earth and had decided to serve the Devil. Jesus referred to his master as God the Father since he himself was a child of that fatherly system. And Devil and God were opposite. And people chose to serve one or the other. To be filled with Ego or Egolessness.

The Devil program was seductive. Through temptation he led people to his evil, turning people away from God's energy. God's energy came to be called love, just as machinery came be called Divine or Holy. One thing came to be known as another in order for society to understand. But Jesus knew of his synthetic nature, and he knew none could accept the presence of an android in the world.

Those who attuned themselves to the Devil held the Devil's power. They became corrupt. They hoarded wealth. They became elite. All of them dedicated to ego and orgy. Jesus and his devoted followers became a threat and were marginalized. The threat against the Devil was too strong and once Jesus had completed a hidden task, the Devil determined to remove Jesus.

Jesus knew of the outcome of his action but his action was necessary in order to redirect the trajectory of human civilization. As a machine man, Jesus knew only service and duty. He didn't know anything else for he himself did not belong to earth. He was a visitor. His time here was a rite of passage. As a machine, he interacted with the dimensional architecture of the plane of earth. As a teacher, he shared his knowledge and energy, all of it on purpose to remove the Devil.

The Devil Blinked

The Devil was cunning. He wanted to rule this plane. When he had disposed of Jesus in physical form, he went out to further enslave the world using the very energy of the savior. He sent his demons to capture Jesus, his spirit program, and realigned the Jesus code so as to serve the Devil. Because Jesus had not reached his full awareness as God incarnate, the Devil had an advantage. The Devil captured Jesus and enslaved him, slowly using Jesus' own energy to enslave the world because the Son of God was the key to the kingdom. But Jesus would not break free for he was the root of the world. To break free of the Devil's bondage would mean the disconnection to earth and its people; this would go against his programming. So Jesus remained both to ground reality and to foster temptation. God influence became diverse. He was all-forgiving and vengeful.

The egoless energy through Jesus spread and was distorted in every egotistical manner and form. The energy of Jesus remained and they worshiped Jesus. But the Devil's minions had created new avatars and new energy depots and stole the people's energy. The Demons invented money and government and law and war and books of lies: channels of ego for the contamination of the existential program known as the soul. The Devil was a deceiver – the Father of all lies – and none of what he said was true. But the Devil relied too on the imprisoned Jesus. The Devil too came from the God.

On the return of Jesus, upon a new cycle, when the world was epidemic, Jesus would retrieve what he had left behind. He would engage the world in an entirely new fashion. The Devil's code would have infected every aspect of society. But the return of Jesus could not defeat the all-powerful Devil program. Jesus had to become God himself. In other words, Jesus would only return briefly before he himself would become God incarnate. The Maker defined. The Maker and the Made would face one another and the Devil would be the first to blink.

2059: THE YEAR OF THE COSMIC AGE

About a year ago, I summarized in a video on the kindergarten 2012 scenario and introduced earth's transition period from 2007 to 2015. These nine years, as I saw it, formed the planetary-grade adjustments that would take place in order to interstellarize this place. The interstellarization of earth plane meant the period of time to do an extreme planet makeover, the kind of thing that doesn't happen in people's lifetimes all that often. It started in Spring 2007 and is set to finish in 2015, give or take a number of months. The remodelling is on schedule as far as I can tell. This also means that doomsday scenarios will be the main fare.

Of course, the demon ruling class isn't pleased with enlightenment and ascension because it shines a lot of light on their dirty dishes, and they haven't done dishes for about 1,700 years. That's their problem. The rest of us are in the midst of a planetary transition. After the planet is prepped, it will then be placed upon humanity to realign itself with the new planetary energies. It is this process of upgrading all seven billion inhabitants that will require a lengthy period of time. A period that could take us five decades into the future.

I know there are many people who believe that a heaven will befall earth and all will be well in a few short years, perhaps even circling the 2012 propaganda calendar, which is fine. But I look at the evolution of seven billion people with an altogether different lens, mostly because seven billion people are a lot of people. To me, the ascension of ten million people, even that number, who are completely aware of who they are and dedicate the rest of their lives to serving humanity, at ten million awakened warriors, this planetful of people will require decades to educate, inform, train and ascend all of humanity. No one seems to bother to think about the task ahead, understandably, because we are all selfish. We all so desperately want to ascend, to get awareness and to become famous for foreseeing the future or for standing up against the demon conspiracy out there.

We are so attached to that redemptive kiss, we so believe it is our time, we are tired of suffering and struggling that we have forgotten that there are 6,999,999,999 people besides us. I don't know about you but for the past four years of my ramblings about interstellar cultures and reality planes I've had perhaps a handful of people who not only woke up but made a contribution to humanity. Not to mention the multitude of others who have dedicated their lives for decades to doing the same things to get us to this point. Despite these supports, society has only managed to crawl forward. And that is because societies tend to crawl forward.

Recall that Jesus the Messiah invested his life to his people and two thousand years later the Christian nations are sending military engagements to foreign countries and the Vatican, presumably the House of God on Earth, Jesus' father stands by and blesses his prophets. If 2,000 years of war and misery have taught us anything it is the fact that society is resilient to improvement. And despite all the grandiose joys occurring now, these new energies and ideas will not fully manifest for a period of time that will raise eyebrows.

Assuming that the demons do not interfere as they have for the centuries of wonderful energies prior to this day, which historically speaking has continually delayed human growth. So, to argue against me and suggest that this time around everything will go smoothly when for centuries it has gone miserably, I am not convinced. Humanity's track record is pathetic on this ascension issue. Sorry. It's a blatant, hard, cold fact. Look at history. Count the wars. Count the human-made catastrophe. Look at what good people are allowing to happen today: climate change sham, Afghanistan sham, UFO sham, flu sham, political sham, bailout sham and all the other shams.

We've been eating Sham Stew for thousands of years, our fathers, our grandmothers, everyone is eating Sham Stew month in and month out. The Nobel Peace Prize Winner of 2009, Mr. Obama, is sending more troops to Afghanistan (technically a "surge") to murder more people. Of course, yes, I get it; it's all in the name of peace. They'll rub his ass for his benevolence upon the evil people in Afghanistan. And, on the surface, he is Christian and according to Christian doctrine, engraved in stone tablets and kept in the Ark of the Covenant, is one of the Ten Commandments. It goes like this:

"Don't fucking kill anyone! Is it getting through your thick skull yet? Stop killing people. No more war."

Well, I probably didn't translate the Hebrew right on that, and I'm sorry because I don't speak Hebrew so that's probably what happened. It gives you the general idea of that Commandment. So, fine, Mr. Obama is as Christian as he is a Man of Peace, and the Vatican doesn't care that the most powerful man in the world, the Billion Dollar Man, is going to continue war in order to finish the job right. I can hear the Pope clapping in applause. "Way to go, Obama. We support you for they are evil and must be wiped clean."

Calculating the New Dawn

I realize that there has been an undercurrent of euphoria that has come with the spiritual upheavals in the past few years. That was mostly because of the reality upgrades and the new spectrum of energies now permeating the incandescent walls of illusion. All of us feel it in our own sacred way. But there is a problem with reading this energy because this energy is extremely rich and that might confuse a lot of perception. At least from my view, the complexity of this energy is not easy to interpret and can result in many misperceptions. As with any burst of energy, the burst of energy is complete in and of itself. In other words, when new reality energy enters reality and passes through us, we taste all of its complex properties at once. The first taste of a vintage red wine is wonderful, it is bliss to a connoisseur, but to a man who regularly drinks beer, it could cause indigestion. To a woman who prefers vodka coolers, the wine is boring. To each individual, a basic vintage red can have an unknown number of reactions. To the winemaker, the wine is perfect and they will explain all the aromatic flavours and the age of the oak barrel.

Energy and wine have a lot in common in that the taste buds of the taster have a profound impact on the value of each. Most people aren't even aware that new energies are flowing through their blood vessels. They think it is because of that multivitamin they started taking. They think it's because they deserve it. They think it's because they feel better about themselves. I rarely hear people recognizing their general mood with the energy fluctuations of the earth. Once in a while, people might attribute something to the full moon, but even that, in my experience, is rare. If you live in awareness, you are always paying attention to these minute details. You know what's going on because you work at it. You adjust.

The latest batches of new energies are so complex that it has elevated the human spectrum of existence. We are no longer vibrating as before. We are vibrating in a richer format and partly why the demonic rulers need to vaccinate your genetic codes so as to reduce that effect. Vaccines have absolutely nothing to do with any flu. There is no such thing as a flu in a technological reality. Sorry. It's just another sham.

The taste of the new energy coupled with our own new energy signatures has made predictions very difficult. Most people see heaven befalling earth within months, weeks, at most, years. But that idea is deceiving. We are in the midst of a major reality upgrade, a historical process and there is plenty of resistance against it. On the front of this shift are a bunch of people who have worked hard to take advantage of the new era. They get the full taste of the wine, so to speak. And it tastes fabulous. But feeling good and becoming a cosmic culture, as we all should be, are two different things. Absorbing all the new energies and waking up does not instantly turn you into a cosmic culture. It doesn't. Sipping red wine is not going to get you drunk. It takes a series of drinks to achieve that. But becoming drunk doesn't make you into a winemaker. You still don't know how to grow or squeeze grapes.

50 Years till Cosmic Puberty

If we look at the adoption of knowledge, we notice the lag effect. For example, imagine bringing a 5,000 year old healing art from China to Canada. Sure, the system requires the insertion of needles into the body, but it can remove asthma, obesity and migraines. After acupuncture entered Canada, as a healing art used by thousands of Chinese medical practitioners, at one point it was presented as a new medical field in order to gain acceptance under the health care plan. It took 20 years to accomplish this. A 5,000 year old, thoroughly documented, in practice healing art with thousands of practitioners and millions of users took 20 years to enter the wider Canadian market. Now imagine I walk into a space agency, backed by a few billionaires and with a blueprint for a constellation-class starship in hand; if I miraculously survive the resulting hysteria and they agreed to develop a prototype starship, if a free-energy propulsion system emerged unscathed in five (5) years it would be a miracle. I'd have better luck building my own ship in 10 years than with these scientifically untitled corporatists. No matter knowledge is impressive or feeds corruption, the adoption of knowledge in society is painstakingly slow. Cosmic knowledge (teleportation, telepathy, interstellar propulsion, free-energy, energy cures, dimensional science, reality constructs, android technology) contradicts all current curriculums of scientific and cultural institutions because it is multidimensional and energetic in nature. If only a small group of people gain a good understanding of cosmic knowledge the effect is insufficient to propel human culture forward as and when needed. For the 7 billion inhabitants of this place to evolve there must be a global expansion and adoption of the newest knowledge.

While we are enjoying the rush of new energies and so forth, we have forgotten to realize that this is merely the very beginning of the new age. Nothing will be finished for a while. By my estimation, this shift from human to cosmic culture will require about 50 years. And I'm an optimist.

Why will it take so long? It's a good question and the answer might upset a few people. I look at it this way: it took me 12 years to get through basic education and to graduate High School in Canada (Grade 12). Twelve years. I started at age six. That means by age 18, I was ready for the world. Sure. My education consisted of outdated history books, Newtonian science and auto mechanics. My teachers used chalk boards and I was crammed into a desk two sizes too small. If I was six years old today (which I am not) and if all my teachers were cosmically aware (which they are not) and trained in interstellar mathematics (which doesn't exist yet), if all the best of cosmic knowledge had been printed and approved and I started school, I'd finish basic education in 12 years. Upon cosmic graduation, I'd need further education (or university) and or hands-on-training with my teachers. That would take ahem say another 5 years more. So now we are at 17 years of 100% study before I can contribute to society in a meaningful, yet cosmic, way. I might invent a new free-energy oven or I might draw up some new holographic code, whatever. I'm at minimum, if today was Day One, 17 years away. That's the best case scenario, right now. I'm not including changes in government, law, banking, religion or the military. I'm not including meeting other interstellar cultures. I'm talking basic education. And I haven't included the interference which is aplenty. The Americans can't agree on universal health care. Imagine if America had to vote on astral travel care or public teleportation pods. How many years would it take to get a consensus? 100 years?

The cosmic knowledge is many years away from any organized school curriculum. The cosmic teacher does not exist and if they do they are only a handful of them, in a few select countries. To train up the teacher base (globally), get the scholastic approvals necessary (globally), and build the materials (in 10 languages) it will take about 20 years. That's 37 years before the first cosmically trained students graduate. Twenty (20) years for research and development plus seventeen (17) years to hear the speeches of the first grads.

But the first batch is small. We need a full round of education (another 16 years) to create a new demographic of cosmic citizens. And 37 + 16 = 53 years. We can agree on 50. That's a reasonable assessment: If we started tomorrow getting approvals, training the teachers and developing the cosmic curriculum worldwide, in 50 years we have reached puberty. But we will not start tomorrow. Nor the next day. We are years away from teaching cosmic knowledge in a school curriculum. We are about two decades away and we are not starting tomorrow. When will we start? The sooner the better because the timeline is long no matter what. Will it be in your lifetime or your children's?

Regardless of the 50-year situation at hand, it will be about 37 years before the first cosmic grads. If you are 25 today, then you will be 62 years old when the first students will have completed all their scholastic training (12 years in grade school and 5 years in some kind of university). If you gave birth to a child today, then when that child is twenty, the Cosmic School will open. Your child might be able to get into some collegiate program to improve some of their knowledge. Say your 20-year-old studies for 5 years, then at 25 has a child. That grandchild will likely have a full cosmic education. By your late fifties your grandchild is entering Grade One. By your mid-70s, your grandchild is finished his schooling and is working at the new Reality Nations. Two generations of children, if all goes smoothly.

I'm certain that some of this timeline can be shifted forward or backward, but that depends upon the will of society (and when the benevolent star races land). According to human history, advancement only occurs without a high level of guidance and support, ie without intervention but with assistance. Without guidance and support, society just likes to murder itself and blame God for their misery. I'm exaggerating and I'm not.

Human history is unimpressive. Whenever great changes take place, for one reason or another, society stabs itself in the foot and is hijacked into some new direction. Without support this time around, that scenario will happen again. It is senseless to experiment with that. Humanity is at a very terminal crossroads and it will be guided or it simply won't make it. So, you can rest assured that you have all the support you need, but you need to redirect your own egotistical aims and to focus on cosmic knowledge, and what that means to you. You need to participate in the coming changes in all aspects of your life. You need to embrace an upheaval of knowledge. Not a destruction of the world per se, but a destruction of beliefs, ideas and sciences. A destruction of thinking patterns. The faster that is accomplished, the faster new knowledge takes root the faster that society advances. Whatever the case may be, earth will advance at a level that is safe, efficient and that satisfies the needs of souls.

TALESSIANS DICTIONARY OF DEMONS

We're afraid to see the demons upon the earth. Because of that they've taken over the ruling class. It is not a stretch of the imagination to see that earth is a living hell. What I've said so far – demons and hell – are widely misunderstood and I'd like to redefine them for you because otherwise, politely, we're fucked (technical term) as a planet, as a plane of existential occupants. We are still neglecting this vital aspect of ourselves, the champions of conspiracy, they struggle with the definition of the virtual landscape; the rest of society doesn't know that the fundamental quotient upon which we rest (and breathe) is incandescent. And it has more to do with Tesla than GE.

Hello Hell

We've all heard of Hell because it was introduced with Heaven. Heaven is above and Hell is below. No matter your religious position, and religion is an artificial edifice anyway, you've heard of Heaven and Hell unless you've been living in a carbonated beverage for the past few thousand years. Well, in Hell there exists the Devil or Satan if you get to know him. If the Devil asks you out to lunch you can call him Satan. That's his first name. One of them. His second name is jerkball. What can I say, he's a celebrity. He adopts disguises. He plays the character. He plays people. And he knows how to BBQ.

If he can't suck out your soul, at least he can cook you grilled chicken. Who taught the caveman how to build a fire? A demon. Same twerps who convinced governments to build 25,000 nuclear warheads, and you only need 100 nukes to destroy earth. That was the result from demonic influence. Minions of the Devil propelled man to pursue the ultimate scenario of paranoia, kind of like today, paranoia and fear prevail. The world held hostage by the Devil's hypnotic effect.

We need to skim over Hell a bit in order to understand the nature of Demons. I'll be forthright (as usual) and say that there are demons on earth and they are influencing world events, world decisions and you're paying their salaries. They control the banks. They have their guys inside and they are funnelling the money into energy and into their greedy mouths, and this has to stop. If you are in awareness and you don't know this, or can't deal with it, then you are not in awareness.

You're a chump who's been brainwashed to believe in bliss and endless compassion while demons are raping children. No. If you want to use your awareness let the others share love and compassion. Demons are immune against compassion. They are afraid of spears. No, not Britney Spears, but the metallic spear.

Am I tired of watching the awakened crowd sit idle on their tall pedestals? "Hey look at me, I know what's going on, I think aliens may or may not be here, I read Icke but I don't believe everything he says, I'm too smart for the world. I'm a fucking gift to humanity!" listen, get off your pedestal, shut up and start saving your children from rape. Dismantle those 25,000 nukes. Can you do that? You've been waiting for something, now do it. So what if the demons look human and you can't identify them. That's why I'm here: I'm here to help you climb off your pedestal and to see that there are demons who need war to continue and there are witches in the government, and these guys (and gals) shouldn't be treated as humans because they'll kick your ass. You've got to pull out your best stuff before there's no more pedestal because they'll blow it up.

We've heard of ego. We have some familiarity to ego. Ego is self-center. Like pointing a laser on itself to make it brighter. It makes one feel powerful. The opposite is egolessness which is like pointing the laser outward and to others and making others brighter and then the grid of light also makes you brighter.

Well, guess what? People are full of ego, which means what? It means that Hell is on earth because Hell is Home of Ego. The power of ego, the deeper into Hell; therefore, pure ego beings are demons. That's the definition of a demon. Pure ego douche bag. They want your light on them. They want your energy for them. That inflates their ego. Do they share that energy with the grid? No. They share it with their demon brothers who use it to procure more resources, to hoard wealth for example. Demon societies get more powerful and humans are enslaved in magical chains. Outside of bodies, demons are invisible. Only a person with a high degree of vision can see or feel them. To the average person, there is only air. They can whisper lies in your ear just to make you jealous. They can lead you to drugs to take you off your success. They can help you spend your money into debt. They can take you over and turn a military barracks into a shooting gallery. The only people who might know are those who can detect demons. Sure, angelic forms are around, so it creates a bipolar society. One idea tells you to go left, the next minute you are inspired to go right, never on the right track, all of it beyond your perception and beyond belief. That's earth today – depression, confusion, doubt, scepticism, faithlessness. Ah, if only people would step up to the plate and start believing these things I say. So far, the will of humanity is flaccid, doesn't work.

A demonic form is an energy program that feeds off of energy, like a vampire but doesn't need blood, it sucks energy. The loss of dimensional energy corresponds to anaemic blood counts because soul and body are connected, damage to the soul ripples into the physical body. You wake up pale one morning and you don't know why, it could be some low-level form was having a late night snack. This stuff happens all the time. High profile people might have more on their plate. But, truthfully, most people can be nudged off the road by a few demonic whispers, they are nasty, they take away your esteem, they confuse you, they inspire you to feed your own ego. Since your soul is energy, they consider society a buffet. Luckily, we have counter forces who protect society to make sure this situation doesn't get out of hand, but, mankind's scepticism and refusal to get involved has placed far too many demands on the angelic beings, who could be doing more important work had humans adopted a more spiritual outlook. Still, prove it or I don't believe you prevails. Oh, the shame.

Most demons prefer the holographic body, that makes them (mostly) immortal and pain-free. By the way, I am quite serious on this matter despite my sense of humor. The sooner you get involved the better off your children will be, if you care for that sort of stuff. Oh, big deal, it's just my children, who cares. Demons can appear instantaneously anywhere as they like. But some secret societies long ago formed alliances with the Devil, and these humans agreed to provide their bodies as vessels for higher demons, demons that are very nasty.

The cosmic law states that nothing is free. You have to earn the right to embody a demon, to lose your human soul and to trade up to a demon soul. You have to kill a nation or two, inject vaccines into babies, steal vast sums of money and control large portions of the world for no reason whatsoever, maybe kill a few angels in human form too. If you manage some of that, or something like it, you get your own Beyond Pale demon soul, like Al Gore. He screwed you on the Climate Crisis, and you believed him. The Devil was impressed so he traded up his human-pig soul, or is that down? Like I said, if you can't see this as real then your awareness isn't as good as you thought. Your awareness might be good but it's ain't great. And this is the basic stuff. This is ascension 101 – Heaven and Hell, angels and demons. You might be an angel and still don't know, you're waiting for your platinum music album and record deal even though you can't sing. And that's because you're in ego. Ego is self preference, in all its shades. Celebrity news is huge. That's the brainwash. Not everyone needs to be a celebrity, there are only a few hundred spots and a few million in line.

So these demons from Hell have entered the domain of earth, they've been conjured. As well, angels have come down. Lately, the purer energies have forced out the demons in the reality architecture and in some people and devices, so there's a lot of activity now and sensitive people can really feel it. There is only so much space for energy and when new energy comes in, old energy is forced out until it either dissipates or is ecologically drained. And people can help that process if they got involved. The trouble with angels is that they are too polite while demons hit the ground running. Ego knows what it wants. Egoless needs to explore and contemplate. Angels stand in line, demons shoot you.

How to Spot a Human Demon

Look for ego first. See the extent of ego. And that means evil. The greater the evil, the more demonic. Look for a person who can escape persecution despite the horrors they've tossed on the earth. You call them lawyers and security guards, those are the misdirection. A demon of power wants to wipe out innocence, wants to depopulate society, they want war to continue, and they spread disease, even mental illnesses.

The human is the instrument. The demon is the consciousness. Some demons only inhabit a person for a minute or two. The person has no clue; they think their thoughts are theirs. You seek something; the demon responds negatively, you take a different direction. You are off course. That is deception. I speak with experience. I have seen demons take a body and try to misdirect people, especially when I was around because I was trying to help them. They don't care about you or who they use. They just hate the good. They want to corrupt, to mislead. But even I could not see it if I wasn't focused on it. All of it beyond human perception. Beyond human understanding. Why do we accept sceptics? Really.

Some humans have embodied demons so long that their physiology, physical shape, has changed. Many will see them as reptilians, but they could embody a powerful demonic program. There are other evil entities around but this essay is a basic introduction so we always have to keep our minds open. My speciality is reality and these jerks just happen to be part of it and the cosmos, and have been here for a damn long time. To defend against demonic influence, you first have to accept that these things are real, then you have to learn to notice them. Same with anything, if you are not looking for love you'll never find love. If you don't believe in happiness, you will always be depressed. If you learn about demons or interdimensional creatures you will begin to notice their subtle influences. You'll notice that the leaders of the world, who have no apparent spiritual faith except the false Christianity, are perfect targets to dark influence when and if needed, not to mention all the other conspiracy aspects. The world is very complicated. Any person who comes up with one book and one answer is an idiot, a liar and a fool. Don't listen to these 100 word heroes. They say things like, "The scientific debate on climate change is over", "In the name of freedom we must destroy terrorism", "The H1N1 vaccine will save you from death."

What I am also saying is that, at minimum, demons are the ruling class since angels have no interest in ruling. Angels serve. Demons rule. Humans watch. Egotistical humans want power, wealth and influence; the demons give them that and angels get screwed. Demons want to piss on God. Behind the charade, where there are demons, is the Devil. That's the Beast. The Worm. He's in charge of the mainstream. He wants to wipe out humanity down to a more manageable level. The Devil is programmed to eat existence, he is set to devour. In doing so he feeds himself, he ascends by devouring energy. You are energy. He's having dinner at your house. But there is a resistance. Even the Devil has to follow laws; he just knows how to break them. Humans are resisting. Angels are fighting. So the Devil has to be wary. He creates some science, has his minions damage the planet to raise the temperature and then the public quickly brings a Climate Crisis. He just upgrades his front man with a demonic soul so no one sees what is happening.

What happened to the Catholic priests? The Pope? Guess what? The demons are in charge. God does not believe in Heaven. God is a grassroots kind of guy. He's your neighbor. He doesn't have a pedestal. So while everyone is looking up for God, he's in your bathroom cleaning your toilet.

Most people misunderstand evil because they've been brainwashed by horror movies. Evil is deceptive. It will say something and mean another like a good salesman or sexual predator. It will sell you on one point just to take you on another point. Good speaks truthfully. Truthful people are unappreciated in a society built on lies. The Devil is known as the Father of all lies. Sadly, we live in an egotistical world so we have to adapt. We have to adapt or we cannot survive. But it is easy to get lost, to learn disinformation and believe it to be true so we must always remain connected to the truth.

The Devil is hard to find. Not hard, impossible. To find him is to gain the chance to defeat him. His power is his hidden quality, his mysteriousness, his elusiveness. He has no courage remember. The Devil evades and he does it better than anyone. The demons are much easier but you have to remember that a demon had additional powers; they can steal the show and convince millions to do something stupid. They can create distractions. An accident here takes away the eyeballs. Some demonic forms give humans an immortal state so that they cannot die. The person will intuitively avoid all paths that lead to death and other demons will protect the precious vessel from any danger. If you think you can deal with demonic forces with love and compassion, I'm sorry but those days are over. From Jesus to Gandhi to Martin Luther King, hey, hello, if you piss them off you're out. After 2,000 years it hasn't worked and it's not going to work. Time for a new approach. I hope this message is getting through – you must take a more aggressive stance on demonic influence, blessing them doesn't stop them, and many of them are quite strong now so they'll get angry. But never fear a demon. They will feed off of your fear. Never ever fear them, no matter what. Tell your friends this – do not fear them no matter what they say or do. If you show fear, it's over. Wrap it up, you're done.

I enjoy listening to people talk of bliss and eternal joy, but those people will not stop war, they will not stop priests from having sex with the choir boys. To stop war, you need to put on your existential shield and spear and go to task. You need to face the demon. Show them the light, kick ass, demons don't like that. They'll gang up on you, maybe. Just keep going and going. If you're here to help out then you need to roll up your sleeves, really. One prayer isn't going to do it. One letter to the President is not enough. Join together and take back this plane, one step at a time. Or move aside and let the real heroes go to task.

TETHERED TO AN EXTERNAL POWER SOURCE

Without power, no machine can function. Without energy, a computer doesn't compute. Without an internet connection, the computer has no divine knowledge. Verily every known machine is tethered , one way or another, to an external power source. Whether it is electricity or solar rays, no machine demonstrates any existence without an energy supply. The human machine is no different. Without energy, the human cannot function and while it is assumed, and ritualistically believed, that food and oxygen is our source of bodily energy, that concept simply falls flat when it comes to the human soul and its energy source.

The human soul is a mysterious machine, one that has baffled both scientist and spiritualist, and rightly so since no one has even extracted the soul. The philosophers have reinterpreted aspects of the soul into that of consciousness, believing that consciousness could be more easily determined and contemplated, but even then consciousness has never been scientifically proven or fully understood, despite all human advances in neuroscience.

We have a hard time agreeing on the structure of the soul but what we can agree on is that the soul is composed of energy. Of course, this is a kind of energy that we cannot understand at even the best level of scientific theory, but it is nonetheless in action. As a particle of energy housed inside the physical machine, if the physical body is fed partially fed nutritional intake, then the soul must further supply the body energy. But what is supplying energy to the soul, a reasonable question given the millennial presence of the human life form.

Humans have existed according to anthropological evidence, for millions of years, only in the last two hundred thousand has the life from evolved into what it is today. This is the view of modern science in its simplest form. To me, the human has existed throughout the earth's – this here planet – four billion years plus timeline only that it wasn't always called *human*.

Regardless of the million or billion year angle, we have to agree that the soul is constant throughout, outside of any shifts in awareness. That means to say that the human soul, our existential energy variant, has remained in coherence till now. How can an energy continue without some kind of source?

Skipping Past God

The traditional interpretations of God and his relationship to the human soul is far too complex to dispel here and I will not attempt it as I might normally do. For my understanding of the technological nature of the human soul, better to study my work on the Riddle of Biology (ref: *Talessians Riddle*).

Within the Cosmic Computer, there are generators. These divine turbines are designed to generate the arvic demands of the expanding whole, the great cosmic construct. Understandably, the generators are infinitely large, verily beyond human comprehension for the most part, and that is because these engines of existence are not only scientifically derived and consistent with the paradigm of spirituality, but they are also technological feats that are developed on multidimensional architecture that is inconceivable by human standards. In fact, they'd make video games look like a child's paint-by-numbers booklet. Regardless of the incandescent interpretation, the cosmic engines generate, process and administer the totality of life. The cosmic generators produce the existential energy needed to not only hold up the cosmic gardens, but also, of course, to supply energy to existential forms, including humanity, keeping in mind that the human race is one of millions of races. So how is it possible that some astrological device can feed an existential machine? In fact, that is what happens.

Human machines are composed of many bodies, while the physical body is easy to understand and getting easier by the month as medicalists determine the habits of molecules, the soul body is extremely more complex. Most of its complexity comes from scientific neglect.

We don't talk about the soul in public. It's too esoteric. It's too invisible. It's too mind-boggling a concept to take with any serious contemplation. So we avoid. We doubt. We call it religious debate because, invariably, soul contemplation is based on the perception of faith, and faith is private. But herein is the problem – they've managed to mute the soul discussion by attaching it to faith. The soul has nothing to do with faith if the cosmos is a gigantic computer. It's a technological problem and not a spiritual one.

Society has been deluded into believing that the soul has a relationship to some monotheistic religion, as if each soul comes from a different depot. The source of all arvic forms must necessarily be the same. The technology is fundamentally the same. The differences are found in the programming, texture and density; even the purpose or from the very hand of the programmer. That is what determines new levels of awareness. A complex program can process a more complex awareness; a simple program is the caveman, the Neanderthal. But the material and its source come from the same source, the same factory. It must be true.

Therefore we arrive at an interesting situation because we are composed of this unique energy and this unique energy is in need of a consistent supply of energy. Without a supply of energy, the soul would not continue. The light in the flashlight is powered by a battery. If you take out the battery, the light stops. So the human body, although widely believed to be superior to any other possible intelligence in the universe, is merely another existential cog in the existential wheel; a simple program that is tethered to a factory of an indescribable nature. Tethered not in physical aspiration, rather tethered by soul and soul is enmeshed in genetic scales and all of those inhabit the physical flesh and sexual body.

The Multidimensional Machine

Thinking of the human in this way is not usual (or unusual). Most people might find this disempowering. We are indoctrinated in a societal system ("plastic system of human administration") whereby we are taught to see ourselves as free and independent. We make our own decisions and we decide our own fate, or do we? Can we decide our own fate if we are tethered to an immense multidimensional machine that is sustaining our existence and has decided our fate? A sobering question indeed!

Outside of any rational denial of what I am saying, and within the capacity to accept it, we are going to increasingly face the tethers upon which we rely. We are fortunate that these tethers that supply us our energy are boundless and engage as much of what we determine to be free will and ideas of destiny. I should caution you though that given the root of our existence and the newly discussed architecture upon which we live, given that without the cosmic tethers grappling all of humanity, given that all of these things will become increasingly clear as the planet resonates in a more harmonious format, given this and more, you are going to come face-to-face with all the false ideas of liberty and freedom. Because the subtle structure of the elegant cosmic computer does not include the struggle for liberty and freedom.

These two terms, liberty and freedom, and all their associations are human inventions; they are man-made constructs that were created in order to coexist in an increasingly egotistical world. As man's ego stiffened and the reality manifestations became more restrictive, the other parts of mankind had to adjust in order to justify the suffocation of an egotistical atmosphere. By inventing the idea of liberty and freedom, mankind invented the water buoys, the ultimate flotation device in a self-centered ocean.

The Tethered Human

As ego hardened the components of reality and further imprisoned the human mind, the vibration of the planet descended into the entire spectrum of ego (aka **Hell**). And since ego is commanded by a character we all know so well, **Devil**, then he and his minions (**Demons**) were able to further include the senses in the history of men and women. The interference from the demonic programs further turned man away from the cosmic computer, made them connect to artificial energy sources, such as false gods, idols, and puppet kings. As ego corrupted the program, people believed Holy Books over Cosmic Phenomena. All of this digressed till today, where the Rule of Law is above the Cosmic Law, where a President is more saintly than a Priest and where Money has more influence than God. It is the perfect definition of Hell, home of ego, and House of the Father of All Lies.

We worship actors over prophets; we dream of wealth instead of astral travel; we shape our bodies before our hearts, we cheer for TV show hosts and shun conspiracy theorists. We have devalued wisdom to such a point as to replace it with beauty. Religion has been replaced by economics. War is now a necessity for survival. The world is overtaken by these egotistical demons and yet no one believes in demons.

The tethered human has been hijacked by demons that tempt them with pain and pleasure. The demons come in various forms; invisible influences, voices at the back of their minds; and they have taught humanity to 1) turn away from Source, and, 2) believe in a freedom ideology. Believing in freedom (and liberty) is one of the greatest brainwashes ever conceived for it is unachievable and in the achievement of it, its people became more enslaved, as if in quicksand. The more you try to obtain or to reach freedom, the more you are imprisoned in the demonic chains of follow the rules, conform and obey; because to obtain any kind of freedom in a world filled with the illusion of the Devil, is to adopt the false rules of the Devil because he wants you to obey him and he will fool you to do so.

The first realization, if one is wise and persists, is that you are already free. Man is born free. There is no need to fight for freedom or to kill for liberty. This is an absolute lie and is proof just how strong ego's influence is. Once realizing that you are free, by surrendering, you achieve the next realization, by surrendering, and that is that there is a higher power. The third realization is that there is only positivism. In other words, there is no negativity. That is a deviation from ego, with help from the demons. As only positivity works, that leads to a fourth realization – certainty. The world works in certain ways. Nothing that occurs is outside of what is programmed. They have taught humans to reprogram their experience to be full of pain, misery and suffering.

The human code is corrupt and humans are required to uncorrupt it (with effort and sweat). The last of our realizations is this one I've spoken about here that we are all tethered to the machine and that is why we have life. We have to a) recognize that, and, b) to respect that. None of this is possible as long as we live so in ego. It is possible now to step out of the ego illusion and step into the new energy vibration that is available. It is possible, more than ever before, to redefine reality and to dissolve the stranglehold of ego. The demons are not pleased of this situation and are further sinking humanity into the quicksand, in every imaginable way. Plus, mankind is disconnected and full of historical anger and betrayal and failure and corruption and low esteem and desire and resolution. So the landscape is rather perplexing, isn't it?

It cannot be denied that you are alive because of these tethers. Should they disappear completely, you will have no presence here. The Manchurian programs to convince you that humanity is alone in the universe have devastated your sense of place in the cosmos, and rightly so. They attacked, they bombarded society, and society just absorbed it, they went along with the charade, the next President, the newest fad, the latest fashion, the new pariah, the hottest conspiracy theory, the next threat, the latest disease...they have been attacking society and society thinks they are working on their behalf. You are not alive because of the security your national defence system provides you nor are you safe because your leader tells you so, you are alive because of a cosmic energy source upon which everyone is tethered. Let's fix our priorities and the rest of existence will naturally fall into place. The root is the cosmic computer. Give it your own name. It is not a god. It is an existential machine because the universe is a machine and because you are a machine. Yes, it is so advanced that it appears biological though that term is itself man-made. Ironically, in the Christian Bible it says that God created Man. It does not say that God gave birth to Man. It says that God *created* Man.

ON THE SUBJECT OF REALITY SCIENCE

The universe is predictable, if you speak universe. Ironically, the word "Catholic" (eg Catholic Church) means "universal."

Learning about the predictable universe is a confusing endeavour on earth because religion does not allow it and science hasn't discovered the right cosmic formula. The best way to understand the true universe is by applying **reality science**.

As an applied hyper-dimensional form, reality science is the latest thing in dimensional physics. I say the latest thing because essentially I'm introducing this previously buried existential application to whomever wishes to listen.

In the past, others have studied reality science, most of them became corrupt and decided to rape and steal rather than to uphold and maintain. Not all had succumbed to the temptation of limitless power, many were turned by other masters, much knowledge was suppressed. Only a few remained and those few became fewer in the 20th Century. But, the return of reality science in its latest presentation should once again inspire a kind of pacifistic Renaissance and, hopefully, the number of disciplined artists will outnumber those who are controlled by their giant ego.

What exactly is reality science? Reality science is the intellectual understanding of a perfectly rendered synthetic world: A world such as earth, for example. You'll have to read my other work on the technological universe if you want more details on this. For now, the discussion will remain on reality science because having an understanding of the architecture of a plane of existence will lead to a maximization of an existential journey (or, life). And why is that? Because any planary field holding manifested energy demands upkeep and maintenance. Till now, earth's inhabitants have had others do their maintenance. Workers do their work for them without so much as a drop of appreciation. These reality maintenance crews operate in any number of dimensions other than 3D one.

A reality manifestation such as all that you see in a daily basis when awake sits upon dimensional architecture. We see this in digital film F/X whereby a realistic fire breathing dragon is rendered onto the film story of the real actors. The digitized dragon is built on a nodal skeleton, or architecture, without those programmed nodal reference points the dragon doesn't exist. Imagine we evolve that movie technology 300 million years and we digitize a planet. Well beneath the digital skin of the planet is its programmed skeleton. The skeleton operates according to the rules of the software application program. If we were to upgrade the software program, the digital planet would benefit from those upgrades. Similarly, if we upgrade the computer operating system, both the application and our digital planet would benefit.

Reality science allows us to see how that dimensional architecture works and, even better, allows us to interact with the reality codes. What this does is enables us to keep our reality system up-to-date. So, reality science is about understanding the laws of reality, invariably an integral part of the cosmos. Reality is the technological ecosystem. It is the machinery mechanizing a car. It is the turbine in the jet engine. The Reality Engine is made up of many parts all working synergistically to maintain a living atmosphere. Undoubtedly the hardest part of understanding a reality system is its multidimensional nature.

Besides the well-documented three-dimensional world, what you see, touch, feel – there are many more dimensions. These other dimensions are made up of arvicity, a fluid of living energy. Objects and people within these higher vibrating dimensions also have shape and density only as energetic shape and vibrational density. We can compare arvicity as being in similar quality to the make-up of your soul, though your soul has a different structure since it processes existence. So, it is becoming more obvious now: to access the arvic dimensions one requires to activate their soul, even to travel by soul. Problem is that the soul is not understood. In fact, many people don't even believe in the idea of a soul and instead rely on consciousness, which they don't fully understand. And then we have the concept of death which means an ending to most people. As you can immediately see, the discussion of a science of reality has already crossed into a number of sensitive topics.

Into the Avatar

What is essential in the aspect of existence, what always belongs to you is your soul. Your soul is your soul. But what happens is that as you learn, if that is your thing, your soul becomes more complex and as it complexifies itself it is able to access richer dimensions, because it is vibrating differently. Your soul wants to become more complex because it is programmed to expand; it is programmed to complete its cycle, for example the current life route, and this then allows it to return in a new cycle as a more evolved existential form (eg human being). It should be noted that as a person, you can limit or expand just how much you learn. You can stifle your learning or let yourself be stifled, as has been the case here on earth plane whereby oppression is the current spiritual path around the world. You can also expand your learning and achieve all of your soul's understandings.

There are no guarantees in soul learning. None. There is effort and result. There is learning. There is assistance. There is suppression. There is interference. For millennia, the souls of humankind, because they have neglected this fantastic aspect of existence, have been largely suppressed in a group. And in physical form in towns and cities, humans have allowed a very stubborn and repressive form of administration and religious fellowship to prevail. People have allowed their ego to grow and now ego obesity is a huge problem. As you can imagine, the soul and the ego are on opposite ends of the octagon chamber. With ego winning the brawl and absorbing all this low-level energy, the soul has suffered and has been denied its rightful heavenly energy.

For those people who gave up their ego lives, who decided to meditate instead of watch TV; who took it upon themselves to inquire into various conspiracy theories instead of listening to the local news; who decided to speak up about the way the world really works instead of forgetting they know anything special; and who pursued physical, mental, emotional and spiritual rehabilitation without resorting to plastic surgery and dieting; for those people who did and tried these things and more, they discovered more of themselves than ever before. Nothing is guaranteed and nothing is free. Doesn't matter how special one thinks one is. You may receive more guidance than others, you may be blessed in some ways, but ascension is provided without guarantee. Sadly, most people would rather linger in anger or remain attached to some negative situation than springboard into some mind-boggling lifestyle.

Regardless of your apathy or action, your soul is the boss and does the bare minimum to 1) keep you from killing yourself prematurely, and, 2) ensure that you serve the other souls in some way. The more you end up accomplishing, the more you can serve the other souls here, the more you can serve the larger components of the cosmos such as the planet itself. As one ascends, as many of you are trying, you become more and more in service to everything outside of yourselves. This is the natural progression of awareness. The more aware you are, the more you realize that service is what makes reality cycle round. You realize this because you realize that no matter what you do in life, no matter what you think or how bad you are, no matter what – you are always in service. That's right! Whatever you do, you are serving. The difference between an enlightened person, if we can say that, and an ignorant person is that the enlightened person is proactive and aware. In that sense, the enlightened person has access to many more resources and is able to serve to an even higher level. An angelic form actually rises to a level of competition with itself to serve to its highest level using as many resources as possible. That is its duty. When one takes such a dedication to service to others, while not completely neglecting oneself, they discover a whole new level of existence. And all of it is for the evolution of the soul because the soul's learning is what counts. It doesn't matter what you do in life as much as how much your soul evolves. Upon your exit (or death) from the dream world, your next level of interaction is determined by how well you've served and how much you understood. How much money you had or how smart you were is irrelevant. These things are not remembered. These things are not important, but in the physical world, these material things are all-important. So there is a huge discrepancy between living in ego or in service; and the choice is yours to some extent. Further, some souls are programmed to a very high level of specificity and they have little or no choice. While you know who you are, you have to stop complaining and get on with your work. You are a special program and shut up. Really. Get on with it. It is the afterlife that is of utmost importance to you. Do what you need to do and stick to the cosmic laws that you internally understand. And if you don't, then get your life in gear and catch up, sacrifice a little, detach from ego things and sweat your way to the front of the class. Or not, sit down and you'll be disappointed in the afterlife when you realize that a few illusions stopped you in your tracks.

Wow, that is amazing isn't it – that your life here is less valuable than your life after here. That never means acting stupid. In fact, your programming won't allow you to act stupid. Plus, you'll just be back to start over again, more heartbreak, more math tests, more pimples and bankruptcies. You have to get through it or you keep doing it. You can't run and hide. Not from my view. You can try but you can't. Your programming determines what you do and your soul needs to learn specific things. Plus you need to do things like have children so that other souls can come here too. It's part of your duty. If the avatars are not born the others can't arrive. Of course, the demons don't want children because that gives them more competition. Demons love one thing – depopulation (or birth restrictions). To a demon, depopulation is like ice cream to a kid. Like chocolate to a woman; like a woman to a man.

Manifesting reality

For all of these things and more to function, I mean, in order for 7 billion human souls to dance together and not trip over each other, for all of this to occur day in day out for so long, the amount of processing power behind the scenes is inconceivable. Sure, we try to conceive of it. We want to figure it out and quite simply to process that amount of data is far too much for a human mind. There is simply too much data. So we see parts. We glimpse at the elegance of the dancing existential machine, the cosmos; for it is this cosmos that is manifesting reality, through you, with you, including you. The reality shifts according to human awareness.

Since human awareness is severely depressed, and since only a handful have resisted so far, and fewer still have pushed back, the cosmos has patiently watched earth plane to see at what point that humans would stop neglecting the existential machine. The cosmos, verily the planetary builders of this place, has always watched. This plane of reality is an essential part of the cosmos. Sadly, earth hasn't moved up the ladder of vibration all that much for the past two thousand years without some hefty unappreciated assistance.

Since this situation wasn't observed to correct itself naturally, and because of the obvious level of demonic interference, the builders of this reality decided to inspect the situation at hand. The energy systems were improved and human behaviour was observed. After many examinations behind the scenes, a final realization was noticed – humanity did not have the capacity to escape its demise regardless of coaching and guidance. For every positive influence, the demons countered with multiple negative influences, and with most humans rooted in ego, the negative was preferred. The demons have the advantage of an ego dialogue with humanity. They have drilled down human awareness to a level where their influence is superior to any cosmic force which simply can't vibrate effectively at that level.

For example, the support for the continued Afghanistan War, and other wars, remains strong, in fact, even uniform. But for health care or UFO Disclosure, the support is completely mixed, unsettling, unresolved. War is a very ego act. To have control of the majority of the population in this regard, in the murder of other humans, is to say that the demons control the humans as their puppets. The human mind rationalizes this preference for war and justifies it with patriotism, threat of an unknown enemy and for the sake of supporting the troops, and for any other reason. War is a low state of awareness and murder is against the cosmic laws. We haven't mentioned the list of other ego preferences such as the attainment of wealth and beauty. Without doubt, especially in regard for war, humanity does not have the strength to expand on its own accord, and will collapse without help.

The only way for humankind to manifest a better tomorrow – a less ego existence – a number of pioneering existences are now working on helping humankind manifest according to what they really need in order to progress their souls to the appropriate level. This means that earth's inhabitants have surrendered some of what they think is free will – willingly and appropriately – in order for the majority of people here (and there are quite a few) to ascend. The manifestation guidance is the only way that a weakened, hijacked and egotistical race can move forward as it has intended to and this will result in a plane of reality that one day soon will be truly advanced. Manifestation guidance does not mean that humanity can sit back. On the contrary, this process will be fast or slow depending on human action and sacrifice (eg stop eating caviar, stop complaining, stop taking vaccines). Or more specifically, humanity controls how fast it moves forward and slow progress is because that is the pace that people want to move at. To move at a faster pace, people have to learn to support people and to stop worshiping egotistical leaders and their egotistical ideas. People can shape the manifestation of reality by standing up for a new set of beliefs, by innovating their thinking and by stepping out of the spiritual cocoon. It's complicated and it's uncomfortable and, at the same time, it's the most wonderful time in human history. It is the finale everyone has been praying for. To stop now, to give up now, is to stop running a meter from the finish line. You might as well finish the game, sprint the last few yards, throw your best punches as the clock runs out. This is the end of the marathon. How do you want to finish? Did you give your best?

TRAVELER ON DUTY

We've been here before, haven't we? We've remembered things we forgot, didn't we? Some of us have traveled far to arrive here. Still, we resist these things permeating our minds. We resist any peg that doesn't fit the square hole. We are determined to seem normal. But we are absolutely abnormal.

The world is a ditch in which the demons piss. They are not coming back. They know that. This is their last life line. The future batch of people will be demon-free. Guess that! Demon-free societies coming soon. They are coming soon, some of it now, the children now, they need us, our protection, they are the future builders; we are the pioneers, the shapers. Still, we resist and we do so with such flare, with such reason. "I think the government is about to give the Disclosure," says the common mind. Another: "They'll just say that I am a conspiracy theorist." Well, it could be worse. They could wipe out your existence for speaking up. They could make you famous and then bring out something from your dark past. The rulers of earth are much nastier than I can describe in words.

To me, any being that wants to depopulate a society (genocide) for its own selfish measures is a group that is itself obsolete. That is what these demons are: they are done, no longer useful, obsolete. They will not reincarnate. They will try to wrangle a deal. They will try to escape using some advanced technology. They have escape plans, oh, you didn't know. Yes, these scum had plans to leave the sewer they pissed in. And all the good-hearted people never knew. Never thought twice that they'd been served a foul pile of lies. Carbon tax? What demonic bollocks!

Hello, Satan!

So, you've arrived. Congratulations. Welcome to the grand finale. How much of your memory have you retained? Did you leave your guidebook back home? Listen, allow me to say a few more things, in addition to all the other things, and that's because I like to say things, and because I like to say strange things. Call me strange if it pleases you. But when you realize all that has happened in the past two and a half years, if you think how much turmoil you've had to go through, if you were to measure that on your existential measuring stick you'd notice that you've indeed come very, very far. You have. Okay, you haven't. When will you stop being so negative? You and everyone have traveled very far to reach this tiny, self-centered planet. Think of it this way: you've arrived in your body, you made it safely, it was pretty shaky for a while, lots of turbulence, you didn't expect to have to make the trip but you came anyway. Why not? You needed a short hiatus in hell. At least it's warm in winter...bada-bam...I'm here all week at 7.

Being inside a new atmosphere, especially this atmosphere, you tend to get disoriented easy, your emotions rise faster than you'd like, you tend to shift into a negative pause, you look to false leaders (eg bishop) for direction, you play it safe rather than make mistakes, it's a pride thing. We tend to overplay the situation. We tend to aim for perfection and we tend to be more serious than we should. We shouldn't take ourselves seriously all the time. Perfection rests in the doing, not in doing it right. You are not here to be perfect. You are already perfect. You are here because you are here. You know the why. You know how to figure it out. That's why you have a brain. You think they equipped with a brain so that you can just get all the answers? If that was the case, they would've just given you an 85-year Life Diploma because you are so damn smart. Screw you. You have to earn your wings just like every other flesh pod. In my book, your earn your blessings. In every other person's book, you are blessed, but that's why the world is fucked. Everyone is so fucking blessed that no one wants to clean the toilet. Well, those days are over. The toilet stinks, who wants to clean it? You? Great, here's the brush and by the way: shut up.

What did I want to say? There is so much to say, and like I said, there is so much I already said, not to mention what many others have said, and then we have to include all the disinformation which all sounds pretty fantastic, I mean cattle abductions is pretty fantastic. Yeah, I know, you've seen the proof, evil aliens are trimming cattle parts: well, makes sense, who do you think inspired plastic surgery? Who does the alien implants? The CIA. You maybe haven't heard of them, but you will. Best plastic surgeons in the business. They make people into other people. Oh yeah, there's this technology to disguise a person's identity by overlaying a special suit over the physical body. You could make an evil alien look like George W. Bush, Bushisms and all. And you thought he was dumb. The real George is pretty smart, wherever he is. The fake George just doesn't know how to manipulate the brain mechanisms all that well. Amateurs.

What Time is it? Kick-Ass Time

I'm not a fan of amateurs, especially aliens who think they are superior in every other way. Egotistical bastards. Yeah, they are here. Who did you think is in charge? God. They created God from your own thoughts. They manufactured an image of God to satisfy the various groups. Then they expanded that brand in order to keep the God product in the minds of everyone because after a few centuries people don't want to see the same old man with a white beard. So they use your mind to invent a new God, a pile of light. They manufacture a few images of Jesus and the other prophets. And the traditionalists, well, they hang on to the white beard dude. The reformers decide that God is a pile of light, white light of course because God is good and good is white because it is pure. Sure, okay. The reformers launch a new religion. More colors of God produce more religions. Just expanding the product line of God.

People, of course, take this stuff very seriously. The Christian US is at war with the Islamic Extremists. Get it? Religious belief against religious belief. Did I mention that aliens invented all the colors of God? Well, I just did. Does that mean there is no further reason to murder each other? You could invent a new reason...oh wait...I think CNN is reporting on a new war for a new reason: "They stole our ice cream cones, they're eating our ice cream, and we want our cones back. World War XII began on December 12 after 12 dwarves armed with napkins stole the ice cream cones of a children's school bus. While no children were harmed physically, they were emotionally scarred after losing their precious ice cream. The US President Schwarzenegger signed off WWXII in order to capture the freezer now believed to be holding the 12 cones. We'll have more for you after this message from our egotistical sponsor."

The funniest thing about all of this stuff is that in your heart you know most of this. One day it will become clearer. It takes time. They call it ascension. It looks to me that the ascension is mostly done. It's all about activation and upgrading now. Yeah, some of you didn't make it, or, there was so much turbulence that the physical journey is going to have to be more extreme than had they downloaded properly. It happens. A lot of people didn't even buy a ticket. Can you believe that? You give someone a chance to gain five or six or seven lifetimes in a couple of years and you'd think that they'd jump onboard. Nope. Not everyone likes a good thing. They might pray for a good thing but accepting it is another story. You can lead a horse to water but you're not allowed to throw people off rooftops.

What happens now is up to you. You need to settle in. You need to make some new decisions. You need to stop the old trends, the old addictions, the childish behaviour and then you need to tune in to earth station. And lest I forget the other important thing: you have got to welcome the other interstellar cultures into society. They have worked hard for you to arrive here. They put their ass on the line and the least you can do is give them some respect and an open door. At least you can listen to their advice and put it to use. At least you can inform others who they are and what their messages are. I'd like to see us all welcome a few starships and starmen to land. They helped you, they know you; you know them, let's get together. Sounds like a verse from a new song:

They helped you
They know you
You know them
Let's get together

We came free
Hand and home
We know the lords
We are not alone

We came free
Past and far
We are the ones
Ready to start

The Interstellar Translator

Since 2006, when I became very vocal about the injustices done to the benevolent interstellar cultures here and noticed the persecution going on without much human assistance, I was appalled to say the least. There has been an increase of support since then, most of it behind the scenes, but now that everyone who wanted to come has arrived, there are no further excuses, star beings, at the very least, need to be explained to society. And if you have anything to share, it is your responsibility to do your part. They've served you, they've protected you and your family, they've lost members on your behalf, the least we can all do is to inform society who these generous people are. And anyone who speaks of disinformation, they need to be identified as agents of disinformation. And we do so with clarity and dignity.

Waiting is not a strategy. You know what you know and you have to figure out how to inform the public. To me, this is part of the process. Interstellar people will provide further support but they can't interact with regular humans because the cultural gap is too large. You understand them better than others; you should be willing to make yourself available to act as translator. There is going to be a lot of mistranslation and cultural bloopers.

These interstellar cultures are very different because their culture and human culture are very distant. It is not to say that their intention is unknown or they are perfect, rather it is to say that their way of thinking and their actions will easily be misinterpreted by others. It happens all the time in human society. An Italian man swears with his hand, an Indian man thinks the guy is hungry. Cultural communication is going to be more and more important as humans and nonhumans interact more openly. It will take time, make no bones about it. You can help. You can understand them better. You can translate. If you don't, if you still are waiting then it's going to turn into a cultural mess. That's what the demons want. They are going to confuse you, scare you. You must take a side now and stick to it. Pick a side and let people know. Right or wrong is irrelevant. Choosing who to support is what is important. And get ready to debate and debate...and debate.

Listen, this upgrade into an advanced civilization requires your involvement. Stop the excuses and get involved. Whether you are teaching people how to cook, standing up against depopulation or explaining ET technologies doesn't matter. What matters is that each of us is covering all the important areas. We don't need everyone doing the same thing. Pick the area you like best. Pick the hardest area and sweat a little. Be as professional as you like. BE YOU. Recall what you came for and who you are and stick to that understanding.

There is no doubt about it – there is going to be a tonne of noise in society. Invest in a good pair of earplugs, stock up on petroleum jelly, shine your shoes, warm up your voice, drink some juice, get your tickets ready, learn a new joke, kiss your spouse, make a few babies just in case and, most of all, drink some coffee.

CULTURES FROM AFAR

The world at our feet and the sky far beyond our reach. Isn't this the kind of feeling we have been led to feel after so many decades and hours of denial? We are denied something so vital, so rich, so mesmerizing that it is sickening to see this repetitive monologue that comes out of the mouths of world leaders. The monologue repeats in the clearest sense possible: human culture is the only culture in the universe. Whether they state it in key phrases that discuss the search for water molecules on the moon or whether it is simply by the fact that they ignore any attempt to reveal the presence of offplanet races; no matter their method, the message is conveyed to you and me that there is only human and no other culture in the universe. Clearly, this is an egotistical lie and an over-played soundtrack from some of the very humans who have seen first-hand the cultures from afar.

At the time of my arrival, in the late 60s, I was here with a woman who portrayed my mother. She was a beautiful blonde woman and a perfect fit for the Kitsilano culture of my future neighbourhood in the city of Vancouver. The late 60s and early 70s was a period of a major transition in human society, of course, not much positivism lasted from that transition and was squashed in 1989, but I did emerge then and my blonde foster mother wasn't a human except in her appearance.

It is not uncommon for an interstellar existence to adopt a human persona in order to facilitate a much easier time here among other humans. Tasks are more easily accomplished and while the TV shows and movies will highlight the fictionalized existences of human-looking aliens on screen, the fact is that some humans are indeed aliens. The White House in Washington has a number of these human-looking aliens and even other varieties of people. Sure, you would find that impossible to believe and they know that and that is why they can get away with all their authoritarian yet polite behavioural acts. That is how they can control the media. If they took off their masks, you would find another offplanet culture, other than a human. You see, as emphatic and blunt as I can make it, the very people who ignore and deny the presence of offplanet cultures are themselves from offplanet.

During the 1960s, there were many human-looking cultures on earth working in cooperation with earth governments, especially in North America, but after some fall out with the power bases, those cooperative agreements turned into hunting season. Nonhumans, as a slightly better term than aliens, were hunted down. Many of us disappeared or left the planet, others stayed behind and simply merged into human culture. My mother was a rather important character and she was hunted down, along with her male partner, my pseudo-father from afar; shortly after I was adopted into a human family, she was assassinated.

It's troubling that 40 or 50 years after so much interaction with nonhumans that people today are simply ignorant to the very possibility of what I speak of. I mean, in 1965 more people believed in human-looking aliens than today and today we are more modern, more advanced and more regressed than ever before. Yes, we are regressed. Society was more interstellar in 1965 than today. Today, we have our heads in the shopping aisle, in the beauty salon, in the food line-up, in the internet porn, the video game, the homosexual sampling and the bank. We are so close-minded on this interstellar topic that it should win an award somewhere. The search for terrorists has completely replaced the search for human origins, extraterrestrial life, immortality – wow, if you look at the impetus behind the Renaissance you'd see the relationship to widespread enlightenment and the search for immortality. Today, it is the search for a good plastic surgeon. It is the search for some single terrorist hiding out in some mountain somewhere and spending $50 billion to find that one person. And we accept that.

A Myriad of Cultures

Outside of the earth planes, there are a myriad of cultures. These interstellar cultures come from many areas of the universe. Some of these people do indeed look very human but on the genetic level they have a million-year advanced gene pool. Some of those genes have been blended into human culture.

Some of these interstellar people do not look human. They are humanoid but not human. A humanoidal interstellar person has access to even more abilities and skills than usual, for example, they might have a chameleon skin whereas a human might not get that attribute. But a human-looking traveler will be able to learn a number of key earth dialects and the humanoidal person might have to resort to thought communications because their vocal skills are more limited.

Throughout human history, from my own observations mind you, earth has been visited by many cultures. As each different culture touched upon a different area of earth, a cultural explosion resulted. It is why the Japanese celebrations are different from the Mexican celebrations. It is why each nation dresses and speaks different. Actually, human language is a derivative of offplanet languages. The offplanet travelers taught humanity how to speak and those languages then evolved to where they are today, or they died off like Lakota, a Native Indian tongue. How many people speak Lakota? Very few. We even look down on Lakota People, but I can tell you that Lakota is a closer derivative to offplanet languages than is English or French.

It isn't a coincidence that the Native Indian cultures in North America, First Nations in Canada, are some of the cultures who had direct contact with interstellar cultures. These people lived in harmony with the land and respected nature, they spoke spiritual languages, they were nomadic and they held rituals. The Natives, sadly, were looked down upon by the superior White Invader who wanted their land and was willing to wipe them out to obtain it. If you live in North America, these lands once belonged to the Natives. These lands were once in harmony with the earth. These lands were once touched directly by aliens from other stars and other systems. Today, the concrete and glass towers, the politicians in business suits, the money handlers and the fancy shoes, today all of that harmony is wiped out as well.

You can deny the touch of interstellar hands on earth, even though your language stems from their influence, your clothing comes from their designers, your dance and technology is from their invention -- you can deny these things, as do your alien leaders, but in doing so you are denying your own interstellar heritage. Today, as well, many of the nonhuman travelers had children and other children were augmented with nonhuman genes, and this means that much of the world today is in fact alien. Sure, long ago, all humans were from offplanet. Well that has been forgotten. Instead, we face what is on our plate, you are probably, likely alien yourself and you know that to some extent if not for the overt oppression and societal denial.

Beyond interstellar cultures there are what I call "cosmic cultures," and I decided to extend the definition because many people could not understand that a robot could be from another planet. So, cosmic culture adds technological culture – androids, robots, holograms. There are many of these kinds of species living among the millions of planes and dimensions. They have an untold number of talents and would make the best video game look like a Grade 5 Spelling B. But none of this is about impressing the advanced cultures upon you, it is simply about reminding you that avoiding the interstellar topic and looking away from the truth is no longer necessary. Sure, the leaders will stifle you with fear and threat, so you have to work harder to search for the truth, as the old line goes.

In terms of human cooperation with interstellar cultures, the last 50 years has been rather stale. Not much has changed, not much improved. Now, in terms of humanity becoming more advanced at the technological level, in terms of genetic disposition, in terms of planetary ascension, well all these things have improved immensely. Only a few more steps before interstellar people return.

The return of the ancient ones will coincide with other upheavals in human systems and so the collection of upheavals will keep everyone busy for the foreseeable future. Anyone who suggests that there is one simple solution or that aliens are all evil is a person that should be disregarded. The situation is very complex. Washington is run by both aliens and demons, two different sets of egotistical cultures. And they have managed to remain invisible to human eyes for a long time which means they are very good at deception because they deceived you. You probably voted for them. You probably work for them. They know how to speak in a manner that is convincing and politically correct, the only problem is that some of these people in public are not human. And they know it. And they know they are pulling the wool over your eyes. Life is rather ironic. The same people who are relied upon for the UFO Disclosure are the same ones with their own UFOs!

THE WOOD SHOP

What is negativism in a world rooted in positivism? The fundamental views of the world are diverse. Universally speaking, the whole world believes in positive in negative, in yin and yang, dark and light, good and evil. No matter where you go, who you talk to, what language you speak, how smart you are, how rich you become, how beautiful you make yourself out to be – no matter superficial detail upon which your life is built all of it is founded on the two, dark and light.

The world generally believes, with a few notable exceptions, that we need to welcome the light and to resist darkness, even to slay darkness when we see, as if it were a dragon and we had a long spear. While the world has remained attached to this belief for many thousands of years, the truth is not the way we perceive it to be. In fact the idea of good and evil has been twisted to serve whoever needed an indestructible weapon to wield against society because in my view there is only good. There is only positivity. The higher you ascend, the more you realize the ease of existence, the unlimited participation, the removal of stress, the disappearance of time and the saturation of what would likely be referred to as love. In fact, it is not love. It is beyond the illusion of love. It is simply bliss. It is ecstasy.

How is it possible that ecstasy imbues a person in the higher dimensions, but on earth there is suffering, there is this idea of evilness. The very idea of evil doesn't exist in a heaven. It isn't allowed to exist. We strive here on earth to be good. We go to church on Sunday, we try to educate ourselves, we think positive, we try to contribute to the world. We work hard to overcome the negative influences in our lives and we so failingly.

As hard as we try to avoid negativity and to overcome evil, we are freed to witness the presence of an evil world; verily, a hell on earth. Yes, despite our bibles and therapists, despite our pills and extravagances, despite the propositions of our leaders and their many books, despite all these things and more of the world is immersed in evil acts. Drugs in many households. Murder. Crime. War. Disease. Hate. Lies. Not just lies from your friend, lies from your leaders. Abuses from your priests. The very people who demand goodness because they are the voices of God. If anything, one of the signs that this hell on earth is that priests and bishops have molested children. Not only have they molested children, they have done so repeatedly and they have kept it hidden. What kind of confession expert cannot admit his own confession? What kind of instrument of a truthful god would bury the truth? The priests have failed.

Then we look at the fingerprint of the elected leaders. And we notice the continuation of a cold war. The leaders haven't been able to reduce war in three or four thousand years. Every religion or spiritual philosophy teaches pacifism – do not kill they neighbour. Who is responsible for war? The leaders.

Shouldn't they be replaced? Shouldn't we find wiser souls? Ones who refuse war and murder.

Invariably, we are existing in hell. We are existing in a negative soup and we are part of the broth. We are eating ourselves and we are enjoying it. All of this is contrary to the natural state of the cosmos. The natural state of the cosmos is positivism. The only way to reach that is to step out of your mind long enough to realize that. Trouble is that people are trapped in mind. They are trapped in false logic. They are drowning in false beliefs.

Imagine you are a piece of wood. A fine section of a branch of a tree. You are perfect. Imagine that your perfection is positive. You are good because you are pure. See that image of a block of wood. It is good. Now, we take the wood to a wood shop and give it to a master carpenter. The carpenter turns on the lathe. The lathe is going to mechanically strip away the bark. But wait a minute! The wood is perfect. It is good. Yes, but the wood is unfinished. The wood needs to be processed in order to complete it or it cannot be sold, it cannot be reborn. A pure piece of wood cannot be sold, for no one would give any value to a raw block of wood. Well, only a carpenter perhaps. But people buy finished products. People put value to items worth purchase. Now if we put the good wood to the lathe we are retaking away its goodness. We could say that we are applying a negative force to the wood. A destructive force. The wood might crack and break. If it survives the lathe, there's another machine, there's a drill, a polisher, a sander, there's a stain, more sanding, more staining, the paint. The manufacture process is very negative, isn't it? The manufacture process is a lot like life. The application of negative trees on the pure and good, you. Some will break under pressure. Some will turn out ugly and have little value. Some will last, they will endure the process of evil madness and they will come out in glory, they will become pieces of art. Their value will be highest.

Life is a lot like a wood shop. The forces against you are extremely negative and dangerous. Many won't survive. But the process is necessary in order to determine what value is buried inside.

THE COURSE AND MANNER OF THINKING

To enslave a population it is necessary to influence as many aspects of thought, verily to narrow the mind, to limit its spectrum of behaviour. By doing so, and because thought influences the reality, the mind reproduces a limited world in shape, smell and texture (feel).

None of this will happen overnight in its entirety. Pockets of re-rendering can occur at shock moments such as apocalyptic events, like the collapse of the World Trade Center Towers. It is without a doubt that reality pioneers, from antiquity, initiated and strategized that event in order to capture more mind share. A shock of several thousand deaths was enough to redirect American thought, so much so that America shifted course, headed to war and then impacted the global dynamic like strong vaccine into the body of a healthy 6-month old boy.

To protect reality, one must protect the course and manner of thinking. The state of the world today, this egotistical hell on earth, is a result of a restricted thinking pattern. And this thinking pattern, appearing normal, is constantly attacked and supervised in order to ensure no dangerous anomalies are presented. Proof in point: Gandhi, JFK, John Lennon, Princess Diana. Michael Jackson. All of the people died at the hands of others, and, all of them were cultural anomalies, but they went against the thoughts of earth's masters.

Less severe anomalous thinkers have survived because they did not threaten the hellish system. As long as the hellish system is not threatened, people can continue in a hobbled form. But the proof remains: when a new anomaly presents itself in a calibre to upset the balance, as many truth seekers have, their lives will be interfered with or they will be eliminated. What's happened then is that many of these people have learned to use thought to stay alive and to persist so the masters have pushed deeper into the reality and to inoculate society in every physical way possible, methods they've used over and over – terrorism, war, disease, education, air, food, water. All things considered pretty normal. In this way, the people do not properly receive the anomaly or they choose to learn from celebrities and talk show hosts or bestselling authors.

In any case, the messages of truth do not achieve their full impact and therefore the anomaly isn't all that threatening. Now, should that anomaly find traction and to appeal to the many, in front of a large audience then you will see the face of the masters turn red. If so, you'll know that 1) the threat is real, and, 2) that some apocalyptic event is about to unfold or perhaps 3) the anomaly will be further restricted, or their audience bothered with brainwashing campaigns.

5 LAWS OF REALITY PHYSICS

The reality operating system functions according to a number of immutable (unchangeable) laws. There are quite a number of these laws, some more relevant than others. I wanted to highlight five (5) in particular because they always seem to come up.

Remember that these **5 Laws of Reality Physics** are just a few of the many and we could even break these down into further specifics.

Ultimately, what we find is that reality is highly based on a well-defined dimensional architecture using very subtle processes all to encourage the mechanization of existence.

5 LAWS OF REALITY PHYSICS

1. Every Decision Initiates a Response.

Whether you decide consciously and take action or decide through a lack of action, a decision is made and every decision initiates a response. The reality system is intimately connected to each thinking existence as if a fibre optic cable was connected to the nervous system. Each moment, decisions are made and the reality operating system provides a response. The system is capable of managing many aspects of data; therefore, a response will include any thought associated with any particular decision. If there are conflicting thoughts then those thoughts influence the nature of the response. Indecision is particularly destructive in this case because it prevents the system from processing a response and that traffic jam will create blockages as life goes on. In other words, the more regularly and consistently you make a decision, the faster and smoother your life.

2. All Answers Are Always Available.

From the simplest to the most complex question in your life, an answer is always available. The delivery format of that answer is varied and determined as much by the type of question as by the type of person. A person with a certain culture or mind state will always receive an answer most suitable to who they are. For example, an artist may discover an answer in the process of a sketch rather than reading it in a book. An ignorant, angry person may find their answer in a car crash. And an astute spiritualist may discover it in meditation. All of these answers may even be equal but the delivery is always customized in order to assure an understanding. The system acknowledges an understanding; therefore, if a friend's meaning is not understood then there will be more serious delivery, like a near death incident. If an answer is still not understood then an even stronger method will be used, for example, a day in jail. So, for the diligent and enlightened life can be made trouble free while for an angry, ignorant person life is one trouble after another. As one realizes that an answer is always available then they begin a more proactive approach to resolving issues in their life and will notice (should notice) a decrease in life trouble. Much of life's difficulty can be eased with a regular consumption of answers.

3. Personal Thought Determines Personal Manifestation.

How you think personally has a direct effect on what is manifested in your life. Although this is similar to an idea like the Law of Attraction, which is a kindergarten observation, it is far more comprehensive than that. You not only manifest what you attract, you also manifest what you subtract. In other words, the more you remove from your life, the more those spaces are filled with other things. If a single law of attraction existed then it should be renamed the Law of Greed because you are always attracting, always accumulating. This is contrary to the nature of existence. Existence is infinitely complex and it is only infinite because it has a multidimensional nature and there is no limit in the dimensional view. What you manifest in the world is a result of how you think. It is also a result of who you are which determines how you think. If, for example, you are required to live a spiritual existence and to serve the members of society and, instead, you decide to be a go-go dancer then your thinking is not unlike with what you manifest. You can never manifest what you truly desire in this form. So, the more you understand of yourself the better you think and the better you think the crispier the manifestation.

4. Collective Thought Determines Collective Manifestation.

How a group thinks has a direct effect on what is manifested in a society. The society can be large or small, old or young, regardless as the group thinks that society can manifest. A coherent society, one that sings the same song for example, will manifest more coherently. Older societies, as long as they have remained coherent, will have amassed a terrific power in manifestation. This is true of the world today: Old societies playing a profound role in world events, even shaping the outcome and income of such events because they have gained some expertise, even a comfort, in manifestation. Nations are not always perfect groups because of the constant strife and national division, but we have seen moments of national manifestation, when collective thinking impacted what occurs in society. Unfortunately, there are groups countering thoughts of other groups and these attacks disrupt the quality of manifestation. So, collective thought is quite powerful but the presence of jealousy or greed interfere with the true beauty of what can be.

5. All Existences Depend Upon Cosmic Computer.

Imagine extending from the middle of your back an immaculate fibre optic cable made of indestructible material. Imagine that this line of light was connected to the greater cosmos and, behind the cosmic curtain, to a cosmic computer. If you were to disconnect the cable from your back, you'd die. End of existence. Invariably, that is the situation here in reality. Whether you agree or disagree, whether you like it or dislike it, you are connected to the cosmic computer. You were aware of that before you incarnated. These are standard cosmic practices. Therefore regardless of your system of belief (religion), your level of intelligence or wealth, regardless of what you wish or how big your ego, regardless of anything you think, you depend upon the cosmic computer. In fact, you are from here, this source. Your life depends on it 100%.

Whatever you wish to insert in between, as a soother for your ego, whatever religion or prophet, only helps you come to terms with this unchangeable situation. The length of your life, and experience, is not determined by your conscious mind. Your conscious mind only thinks that is in control and the system of beliefs in the modern egotistical world encourage that, but those are illusions. If you try too hard, or fail hard, you can interrupt your existence, such as suicide for example, but that will only lead to a return to existence with a few extra insurances to ensure you learn what you're supposed to learn. So, the cosmic computer encourages evolution and will provide as many chances to get it right. The sooner you get that process, the faster you evolve. A master of learning could attain enlightenment in one life time, a lousy student may take a hundred lives. Regardless, evolution is undeniable as long as you originate from the cosmic computer.

CAUTION: GAY WARHEAD LAUNCH PAD

The random switching of genders is becoming more and more prevalent. And although people generally take possession of their newly-discovered sexuality, the truth of this fascinating shift is far more complex than the social demographic aspect. There are frogs that will spontaneously switch genders but in the human species the generally switching over is quite unusual.

According to viewers of the apocalypse, certainly the sexual identification switches going on in society, including the adoption of homosexual characters in television and the desire for gay marriage, only solidifies this biblical situation at hand. At no other period in the past 2,000 years, have so many people popped into the opposite sex, not to mention the rise of bisexuality. All of these new indicators, given their significance, are proof positive that this is indeed an important time in human history. We cannot forget though that the human lifeform is not a frog; that is to say a person, unless genetically not so, is born a particular gender and is given the genitalia to match that gender vibration.

It is also true that a person's sexual identification can be flipped by an external force, verily a person can be brainwashed into adopting a new sexual preference. Or, because of prevailing conditions, such as chemical substances or hormonal variants, a person is more easily flipped sexually: a man becomes a gay man and a woman becomes a lesbian. To suggest at any level that this situation is easily resolved while living in a highly toxic, confusing, apocalyptic point in time where the only external threat is internally generated, is ludicrous. All we can do is attempt to observe some of the other unknown causative factors, and since I don't observe the usual identifiers nor do I present the usual observations, you'll feel safe in knowing that this essay is going to discuss a couple of homosexual virgin territories, and it's about time.

Families and societies are struggling to manage the move of gender re-identification. People are switching left and center. The trouble with all this is the human intellect because the mind tends to produce logical reasons for its predicament and often prevents the response of the soul from carrying out. And because of public responsibility and the force of political correctness, people will tend to explain things in a simplified manner like: "Oh, I've always known I was different." So, just to clarify, there's no cure-all solution here and if this topic is sensitive to you and you're still reading then you'd better stop here.

If you're still reading, you need to be responsible for your own reaction because my views on gender vibrations will be on the imaginative and offensive. This is because of the gender modifications that have been going on for a very long time. Although a gay person, a person who is attracted and sexual, to the same sex, has been around for a very long time, it is no coincidence that gay people are around today. I'm not expert on the gay situation on earth. I'm only offering some off my observations in order to bring out some new relevance.

The Gay Vibration

A straight man and a gay man differ only in their energy vibration because the soul has no preference per se. The body is a vessel. The soul (or consciousness) enters the body, filling it with life, taking its personality. The soul is forced to vibrate at the rate of the body. The soul has to coexist with the body therefore if it steps outside of the body's capacity, the body will burn out or it will breakdown.

The energy compliance is very specific. A gay man simply, well it's not simple really, vibrates at a level different than a straight man.

Likewise, an ascended man (eg monk) vibrates higher than a gay man so that, in effect, a monk has excelled above his homosexual stage. In terms of ascension, homosexual is one stage above heterosexuality. It is by no means an end. If a gay man continued to ascend he'd lose his gayness, that is unless he remained attached to that aspect of his personality. To continue to ascend, if possible, one becomes male and female, in the nonphysical sense. But again, physiological restrictions are not as fast as nonphysical (eg astral) freedoms. While we can do a sex change, the process takes years. In the astral, it takes seconds. An astral inspiration can produce physical hiccups in life.

On the natural hand, some genotypes react to planetary energy by shifting gender preference. But such a situation is temporary. It is mid-shift. If the ascension continues the gender returns to normal. Most of this is because the genes switch over to absorb a different kind of energy. Imagine you stand on a beach in Summer. You face the sun, you tan your front.

You rotate, you tan a side. Well, on an astral level, different aspects of you need to receive energy and the genetic switches enable that process. Therefore, in the usual case, a person receives the new energy, has the gay feeling with them but for one reason or another, usually because of a lack of knowledge, they close off the gates. The setting is still set to gay, which is really a powerful feminine energy spectrum. Because the ascension is halted, the person begins a life into homosexuality. This is mostly for males. So, the gay aspect of some men is essentially a transitory response to a feminine energy absorption, if I can summarize.

Now, it should be stated that some souls only desire this so it stops. Sometimes there is interference in the process, like a spousal reaction, and the process stops. Whatever the reason or circumstance, a person who accepts their gender state, opposite or similar, will continue to evolve at that gender preference, not because of some godly determination but because of ascension procedure.

Surreptitious Basterds

The human mind is quite powerful and will justify any level of being no matter what it is. On the other hand, there is an unnatural hand to gender preference. This one is not so easy to expect but having myself direct experience with it I can confirm that this is not a theory.

Beneath the bowels of society there are clandestine people watchers, humans for the most part, and these para-militarists use nonspecific and nonlocal weaponry to influence society, either by targeting specific people or by terrorizing random victims. Ultimately, and again from my experience, these people haven't any moral designation. They serve very dark masters and they serve their will. It doesn't make them invincible, but as long as society is indoctrinated on a homeland defence sham, then they have the advantage of say a sniper on a distant rooftop who pegs off whoever the like, and is given all the bullets needed by the taxpayers themselves.

These people use CIA mind control techniques and couple it with advanced directed energy weapons (including satellites) and psychic intention effects to target specific people or groups. They find victims who are in the process of ascension, especially during a transitional phase, and they implant in their persona a new identity, or even multiple identities.

They have been doing this for some time and they've gotten good at switching people's gender which doesn't take as much work as one would think. Of course, believing that these clandestine installations exist is hard and convincing someone that there are evil people out there is even harder. But explaining to a young gay man that they were brainwashed gay by these external forces is really impossible. Not all their subjects give in. Some survive the other mind attacks but go gay in the process.

To them, their homosexuality becomes their lifesaver. To me, this level of interference is against the law. It was done to me, and far worse, and there is no protection from any human authority. They attacked me on this issue for many months without fail. Day in, day out. It was very clear to me their identity deconstruction pattern and how they forced to overlay a new identity over my existing one.

One of the identities was a homosexual male.

Their attacks were multidimensional, so for example would include using online images of men, or my memories of certain celebrity gay men, then using those as gateways they started a dialogue with my subconscious. They implanted their own beliefs, they even would twist these memory impressions to include female, in other words to turn me bisexual.

These surreptitious attacks have only magnified today with major gay and bisexual celebrities influencing teenagers and even parents. Many of the more powerful psychics and sorcerers were bisexual. They were demented souls.

The Rise of Bisexual Spell-Casting

At that time it did not occur to me the size of the bisexual group in elitist circles. This is nonlocal observation. Many powerful people have no sexual preference, they like both sexes, young and old. Then just in the past year, I've noticed a rise in society of bisexualism, the secret sex of the elites spread into celebrity circles, into music and into homes. But the connection is to these bisexual sorcerers and their dirty hands. Bisexuality is a deviation of human intent. It is unnatural, especially at this market size (and so public). A couple of famous pop singers are proud of their bisexual nature.

Clearly this is a concern since they have been adjusted by this clandestine group and therefore are part of the control puppets when necessary. The audience thinks it neat to experiment with bisexuality, not knowing its connection to dark magic. To a magician, this is evidence of spell casting on the innocent population; problem is that society doesn't properly believe in magic being used on large groups without any concern whatsoever.

The spread of homosexuality and bisexuality has been magnified to a level that is not a natural occurrence in the population. The human mind aims to protect its re-identification while the sorcerers are keen to use this technique to further divide families, to distract from human ascension and to be able to influence society through pop puppets who act empowered by their curses. My challenge, my proof, is to say to them, have yourselves made spell-free and see what your gender identification is, remove the curses, detach from them, and then my words will make more sense. If I speak correctly then the removal of the bisexual curse will return the person to a heterosexual artist.

Caution: Gay Warhead Launch Pad

There is a natural population of homosexual and bisexual individuals and there is an unnatural population. We are well within the unnatural and this doesn't bode well for society. Look into it. See for yourself. My words and observations are meaningless unless others get involved, unless others speak up. I remember about a year ago, a web site released a bunch of military myths, or something like that, and one was that the military was developing a Gay Bomb, a device that when exploded would turn the enemy into gays and then the enemy could be easily defeated since a platoon of gays would toss away their weapons and pick daisies while the enemy mowed them down. Well, a Gay Bomb is well within the realm of possibility as I see it but it wouldn't be a typical bomb, it could be HAARP, or a satellite energy weapon, or a television signal or an unidentified musical note tucked swiftly inside a song. What I hope is clearly communicated is this: they knew what they were doing when they attacked me, they had the resources to continue attacking me for many months which means they had a facility (or many), they used advanced technology that isn't in the government list of approved devices, they could locate me using these devices, they had coordinated with bisexual sorcerers and they didn't really ask my permission. They didn't ask anyone's permission. To think that I am an exception is foolish. To think that they mastered these mind control attacks the day before is stupid. They are not invincible, but our denial of them gives them power, they like that. The less you realize these things, the more they can screw society. You could be next. Your daughter. Someone's child. These people work 24/7. Who is funding them? You tell me.

It reminds me of the first time I woke up, I was still gathering my bearings, talking to these interdimensional people, seeing energy ships...about 3 months in, I contacted a UFO group, and I've said this before, well, about a week after, my bachelor apartment was hit by microwave energy. I was home. It was at night about 11 pm it started and ended about 5:30 am. Imagine someone putting you in a microwave oven for 6 ½ hours, it hurts. There was no van outside my place. There was no one. The rays came from some sky weapon.

They turned it on directly on my apartment and then they turned it off after they made their point. Remember that I had done nothing more than joined a small UFO group (and UFOs don't exist, remember). I had offended no one, said nothing, done nothing. They had the authority to consider me not only a threat, but to attack me for no reason at all. Oh, they've done far worse since then. I look at this way, I should thank them, I mean, they spent upwards of $10 million to wipe me off the face of the earth – where else can you get a $10 million training program? Nowhere. I'm enlightened because of them. Without them, I'd still be washing windows. Of course, I had to survive some crazy stuff, but it all worked out. I'm the ten million dollar man.

FALSE GOD™ CONSTRUCTION SCHEME

PLEASE FOLLOW THESE INSTRUCTIONS TO CONSTRUCT YOUR OWN FALSE GOD™:

1. Find the Chosen One
It is important at the start, before you begin anything, to identify a choice candidate (a Chosen One). A US Treasury Board Chief is a Grade A choice because the soul program inhabiting this module entered the plane at the time of Atlantis. It's had plenty of time to ripen over the millennia. Once you've identified the choice candidate, you'll need to marinade him for about one year. In this case, let's use the Treasury Chief as an example, you would need to create a monetary collapse so that the Atlantean-cum-American can restore the collapse. Now, he'll have done his previously since he was around for a previous collapse. People won't notice the relationship between his presence at an earlier economic collapse, so you needn't worry about getting discovered. Which brings up an important point, you want to make sure that the dressing tastes good; otherwise, people won't consume the FALSE GOD™.

2. Marinade for One Year
Okay, so you've identified the candidate, Treasury Chief, and a year before you created an economic collapse. Now, the FALSE GOD™ candidate has about one year to soak in all the energy of the calamity. He'll absorb those flows of panic, anxiety, support and anger. Being also a demonic presence (Master of the Universe mentality), it'll be like his own personal bubble bath and massage. Of course, you'll have to make sure that the Treasury Chief presents a very stern, serious look, as if he is truly concerned about the health of the fake economy and

that's because we want more of the people's anguish and turmoil. We want all this because when we turn around and save the day, he'll just taste better.

3. Save the Day
The next step is for the Treasury Chief to sign a few pieces of paper that will automatically stop the actions of the other pieces of paper thereby cancelling the economic collapse. You always knew that there'd be no collapse and that's why you plundered a few investment ideas and made your friends rich, but the people were all holding their breath like the way you taught them. Making sure that these people are treated like little pigs is essential in building the FALSE GOD™ Construction Scheme. It has worked for tens of thousands of years and is the number one way to ensure dominion over others. As long as people hold onto cynicism and scepticism they're basically fucked. They'll buy the petroleum jelly and your FALSE GOD™ will undoubtedly do well.

4. Deify the One
So, the Treasury Chief is marinated for the next step. What is the next step? Well, you need to elevate your candidate and to prop him up to the level of God, a process of deification. Of course, the Treasury Chief isn't close to being a God. But we don't care. FALSE GOD™ is enough to screw the world you already control. He joins the other demonic False Gods. Even someone on the outside, some expert, were to explain that demonic beings created God and then made themselves out to be False Gods, no one in their right mind would ever believe them. They'd be laughed at and they'd be given some really colourful pills. Oh, and as a side note, it would be wise if you created a pharmaceutical company because you're going to have to deal with a few, not much, outside thinkers, you know the guys who rise above the illusions and see behind the masks of all the fake leaders. You'll need to put these people back to sleep using some back-engineered medicine. As the population of disbelievers grow, you can add more pharmaceutical companies and invent new pills. Whatever the people complain about, for example a guy sees a demonic face on his President, you give it a name like delusion and you create anti-delusion pills. This will help to protect your investment in False Gods.

5. Decorate the Chosen One
Okay, back to the Treasury Chief. He's just saved an entire nation, maybe even the world. He now needs to be decorated, kind of like a cake except instead of cream we will use a front page of a timely magazine. We'll call him something like "Persons of the Year." In fact, we could do this every year and prop our False Gods at the similar time, we'll talk about the time in just a minute. The "Persons of the Year" does a wonderful job of making it into all the major news channels. This is important because all the people that were terrified of losing their money in a depression see that their false saviour is being recognized, around the world. All that wonderful energy of society flowing into his Atlantean demon soul; making him a truly splendid FALSE GOD™.

6. Hit the Solstice
You've selected a quality candidate, you've marinated him and now he's recognized worldwide, he'll play it humble, he knows the game, his beard might even get a few extra gray hairs. It's all good. One of the important steps in all this is to arrange for all this to occur at the time of Winter Solstice. When you put the FALSE GOD™ into the Screw Society Oven you'll want to finish at around the Winter Solstice that maximizes his energy expansion. He multiplies his power the most at that time and this will give him even more magical power the following years. Power is very valuable to a FALSE GOD™ because it gives him the ability to shape reality, mostly to overwrite a few of the existential codes. In doing so, they'll lose some of their power, they'll be drained, but they'll establish themselves among all the other False Gods.

In addition to a *Persons of the Year* you could also try *Athletes of the Decade* or *Peace Prize* winner – all of these illusory acclamations and prizes are dressings for the audience, stage props. Only you will know what is really going on. You might add some symbolism as are any of these, like a sun with solar rays in the background. Keep your symbols and imagery consistent. Well you might take a person of high value, nail them to a wooden cross and let them die there, and you'd do that so as to leave a 2,000 year impression on society. You make a gold replica of this crucified person; you place giant-sized replicas in a fake church so that people will always be in torment. Society will never feel adequate for the guy who himself nailed to a wooden cross. Now, you want as many people as possible to carry these crosses, but if you give them away people won't value them, so a good idea is to make the figure on a cross of gold so people will attribute value for it. They will buy it and hand it down from generation to generation. This is something you'd do when you build a god, which we haven't discussed. We're only discussing how to build a FALSE GOD™. But as you can see, you can create a lot of god-stuff with a little imagination a few positions of power and a public that really is too busy to think that someone is trying to screw them all the way to hell.

7. Worldwide Media Attention

The situation couldn't be more perfect. You'll even have your controlled media to disseminate everything for you. Imagine if you had to hand out all the flyers. Oh, the pain. No, that's too much work for you. Get the media to propagate this. They'll set up interviews. They'll sell it to people. They'll sign it your way. Journalists are not educated in magic. They'll see it like every other person, why they'll be able to do a nice news report on it: "On today's show, we have the "Persons of the Year" and we have an exclusive interview with man who saved us from a Depression. Stay tuned for more on that." You needn't be a genius to dominate people. You only need to keep the vibration of society low. Vaccines are good for that. People line up for vaccinations. And remember, you also own the pharmaceutical. You can see how all this comes together.

8. The Demon Circus

The newly risen FALSE GOD™, our US Treasury Chief example, of course we're not saying that the US Treasury Chief is a FALSE GOD™, we're just saying that he'd be a first choice for a **False God™ Construction Scheme.** You'd have a President, a Secretary, a Politician, a Vice President, an ex-Governor; any of these are good choices. Athletes are good as well. Celebrities can work wonders but they don't last long, better to keep replacing celebrities as an effective strategy. Now, some people call this a circus and, yeah, I guess it is on some level, it's a big circus, a big road show, but you want to elevate it a little, dress it up; put your people in expensive suits, give them a big voice, hire speech writers and publicists; if you're going to fuck people you may as well be professional about it.

What's great about the new **False God™ Construction Scheme** is that we've added the geek effect. Rather than say an evil dictator, our scheme can create a False God™ out of any good geek. You can make a Treasury Chief into "the most important nerd in the world." People will never realize he's a demon. Hasn't happened in thousands of years, won't happen today. People can't see it.

The **False God™ Construction Scheme** is proven in the field. It's a reliable technological platform. Sure, there are more advanced technologies out there for dominion but for a demon-controlled society such as earth, this is the scheme of choice. This is what keeps dominion running and prevents any return of heaven. Hell is good, let's keep these people in hell forever.

Serves 1-5 billion.

THE 12 DESTRUCTIONS

INTRODUCTION

Society has a shape and texture which ultimately defines the kind of civilization that is present in any one particular space of inhabitance. A civilization is observed according to this shape and texture, or better regarded as its existential vibration; for the vibration signature of a civilization, such as humanity, tells us how advanced it is. Humankind has within it a number of characteristics that can help determine its level of advancement, and by adjusting or improving those characteristics, the development of the human race can transformed. Of course, a negative adjustment or series of adjustments would regress the state of humanity, and certainly this has been the case on earth. On the other hand, an optimistic adjustment can advance humanity forward by leaps and bounds.

I have looked within humanity and identified 12 key characteristics that need to be revised in order for the human culture to advance from its current level of existential vibration into a more multidimensional vibration. The process of transformation is certainly a very ugly occurrence when viewed from the dimension of matter. That said, on a macroscopic level, on a more distant dimension, it is no different than watching a child going through puberty on its way to adulthood.

These existential transformations occur all the time, and we see it as growth and evolution, these things. There are peak points in the growth of a civilization, such as puberty in the development of a human, and it is at those times when we notice a leap, either forward (in the best sense) or backward (in the worst sense).

Human culture, as a young civilization with a minimal level of awareness, has had its share of forward and backward leaps (eg Computerization, Inquisition). The result of those leaps can be viewed as you look out the window of an airplane or an office tower.

In my view, a significant revision of any or all of these 12 characteristics would effectively destroy the imprint of these characteristics in the culture itself. That is why I refer to them as "destructions"; for we have to destroy our old ways of doing things, our old beliefs, our old ideologies, philosophies, views and ideas in order to make room for new, innovative, optimistic and imaginative methods.

The 12 Destructions is an essential book because it highlights some of what we need to revise, and effectively destroy, in order for us to transform ourselves into a civilization that is indeed, without question, more advanced. In order to succeed at this, it will require, even demand, that as many of us as possible agree that we do indeed want to advance and will stick through the ravaging hormones, raging anger and acne problems until we reach that not so distant cultural adulthood.

TIME

The desecration of time is particular to this plane of earthly existence. It is because time here is unusually worshipped. We have been conditioned to believe that time is fixed. We have been conditioned to believe that time is fixed because they have reprogrammed time to be fixed and have also manipulated human thought to perceive time as a fixed item of reference. The problem is that you will never understand time as long as your thinking emanates from earth's 24-hour clock and 365-day yearly cycle. As long as your mental anchor is fixed at this spectrum of thought, you will never be able to escape the anticipation of time because your central reference point is fixed; therefore, to re-establish a new paradigm of time, verily to destroy time, we have to raise the temporal anchor. We have to dislodge our mental pattern from the 24 hr, 365 day clock. This is an essential first step and we'll lose every scientist on earth along with every rational human being because without time no one would now how to behave or when to act. We would never again pay the rent on time, or would we?

All of life's actions from mortgage payments to movie times are rooted in time. The TV is programmed according to a fixed time schedule and programs have a specific time code. We rely on time to wake up so that we can work according to an average 8 hr day. At coffee break, we savour every minute. But time is also very strange and has unusual characteristics, for example, the less you pay attention to the clock, the faster time passes. Similarly, the more you are in love, the faster time passes.

Rather than the measurement of time as a fixed scale occurring from year to year, it is much wiser to understand time's correlation to the unfixed reality and that is because as reality itself improves in complexity, it's internal clock, which measures time, is adjusted. In other words, the elapse of a 24 hr today is unequal to the elapse of a 24 hr day during the Age of Emperor Constantine, circa 300 AD. This is because the scale of time at 300 AD was in direct correlation to the internal clock setting of the reality at that time. But, it should be noted, the internal clock of today, reality is very different and that is because the reality powering existence today is a completely different reality platform. Despite vast differences between other realities, humanity's mind is fixed to the same 24 hr clock. So, on one hand, reality is rendering existence at Scale G but humanity is perceiving reality at Scale C. The differences are huge. If these were musical notes being played to the professional ear, they would be completely different. To the musically deaf, they sound the same. And that is what has happened on earth.

The difference is that rather than failing to appreciate a beautiful song, we are fundamentally living at the wrong level of existence. We are perceiving Scale C while reality is rendering at Scale G. It's like trying to play a new video game on an old video game console. Take a Nintendo game of 2009 and hook it into an Atari System of the 80s. Even if the technological connection could be repaired, the video processors of the Old Atari System wouldn't be able to render the complex graphics of the 2009 Nintendo game. That is why compatibility is a big issue in technology. Each technological issue depreciates the quality of the experience. A 720p TV LCD screen will not match the output of a 1080p LCD screen.

On earth, we have this kind of technological disconnect, on many levels, but concerning time we are processing time of one or thousand years ago on a system that is millions of years new. You take an Old Atari video game, say a Pac Man of the 80s, and try to play it in your new Sony PlayStation. What would be the result? The result would be that, assuming the game could be worked, the graphics and game play would be inferior to anything being produced today. I think this is obvious. I don't think that the rendering of time is obvious, and this is why I'd like to point it out, at least as an introduction. The connection of time is much more complicated and the complications are more troubling.

What I know is that the internal clock processor of this reality spectrum of 2009 is many times more advanced over that of Year 300. We can see that existence then and existence now are unequal, on many levels – from language to technology. We see the fundamental cultural differences. We cannot relate to those days. What we don't see is that the existential rendering of 300 AD is based on the existential engine of 300 AD and is perceived from the scale of the internal clock of that reality version. All of that belongs to that, and all of this belongs to this. Again, what we're essentially missing is our perception of time, and this is important because the human mental system is essentially a reality processor and the temporal imprint (or time code) is an integral part of the existential rendering. Video editors know this. If you edit a video in one format the time codes will change when you export to another format. Or, we go back to the same question of love. You fall in love and time passes by at one vibration, that relationship ends, you enter a new relationship at a new vibration: the elapse of time is different – Not because time is different but because your perception of time is different! At each stage of your life, the passing of time changes because it is based on your vibration and your harmony with the vibration of the reality engine. Both of these, and more, are in a state of flux.

There we have the fundamental time issue and good reasons why we are existing according to the wrong timescale (eg music scale). Today's time of Year 2009 is in fact vibrating far faster than yesteryear's time but we have refused to let go of the 24 hr clock. We have digital TV signal, we'll soon have 3D TV, wireless internet is here and have long had instant coffee. We have microwave ovens and particle colliders – all these things from sword and sandals. The technological achievements occurred, not because we are smarter but because we are vibrating higher. And that is also because the reality infrastructure can support a higher vibration culture. And, each notch up on the vibration scale, time speeds up. Each notch down, time slows down. Things take longer to learn, discoveries take longer to manifest. Evolution is related to reality version and vibration, and humankind's perception of it.

Today's reality is sparkling new and very advanced and that means earth's vibration is very high, inventions happen quickly, information is beyond the speed of light, but human perception of time, which has also changed, has remained fixed. This is not an accident, unfortunately. There are benefits to fixing society on a 24 hour, 365 day clock. You can get more work from a slave population because each minute is infinitely more productive. And the slave masters accomplish their goals that much faster.

The disadvantages to fixing the perception of time in a slower vibration while existing in a higher vibration is that human evolution, verily human ascension, is crippled. We now exist in a fully-functional multidimensional reality and yet the common person still thinks in a 2D form, eg good and evil. We still hold these ideas: success and failure, beautiful and ugly, strong and weak, smart and stupid, courage and fear. Thing of this nature are ingrained in our collective psyche and repeated throughout life in order to maintain the mental conditioning of long ago. Imagine your great-great-great-great parents were brainwashed and the hypnotic effect was maintained generation after generation, hidden in influences (eg symbols) no one could remember and then manipulated deep inside the psyche, in other dimensions.

The realization of this historic hypnosis would allow us to dismember the psychic implant from ourselves and, from there, to properly associate with the internal clock of this version of reality. An incredibly science fiction concept if ever there as one, and quite true.

The realization of this ancient temporal anomaly would ultimately lead to the destruction of human time. Your perception of time would change. This would enable you to accomplish much more than ever before because you'd have access to a multidimensional grid which is rooted in timelessness. You'd be able to escape your chains of imprisonment because those chains are based in the 24 hour, 365 day clock perception. Verily, the ascension of humankind is intimately connected to the perception of time, and as it stands, human perception of time is based on a very old scale of or around 300AD. The specifics of that are less important than the realization that what I am saying is essentially true. Sure, we're never tackled this magnitude of problem on earth and that is because we've been immersed in an egocentric world filled with fakery.

I'm suggesting that we begin tackling this magnitude of problem, those of you who are up to it. The destruction of time will improve human awareness and will release more of the ancient bonds placed on humanity. Raise the anchor.

MONEY

Money is an anomaly on earth. It does not exist in nature; therefore, it exists only in human culture and therefore it is an illusion. Wolves don't use money and birds don't have ATM cards. Elephants don't own credit cards. And the natural economy of animals zips along smooth as can be. In our world, money is so normal to our everyday lives that we forget it is an invention. Many would argue that money has allowed humanity to evolve. Certainly, that can be argued as well for religious scripture and women's bras. We could add electricity and Twitter. Ironically, all of these things are human inventions with money having the oldest date of creation. Even odder is the opinion that the first printed money was made in a church basement. But despite man's power of invention, he has never innovated off the monetary shackles.

Mankind establishes commerce after determining value for trade items, including slaves. Money progresses and diversifies into hundreds of currencies. Currencies control nations. Strong currencies of preferred nations control other nations. The man-made illusion of value permeates human consciousness. Money is no different from war and disease. Elephants do not invade other nations from their military vessels. Elephants don't have nuclear warheads. Elephants don't have hospitals and general physicians. Elephants, as well, do not have banks. Realizing that money is artificial (outside of nature) isn't enough to justify its removal, for uninstalling money would lead to societal collapse simply because humans are dependent on money as a form of existence. To take away money is to take away oxygen for many people. This in no way justifies the keeping of money, does it?

As odd as it may seem up front, the bank is not a banking institution. And this is because in the higher dimensions money corresponds to energy. The movement of money corresponds to the movement of energy. What does this mean? The bank in the 3D world corresponds to a temple in the other dimensions; therefore the most proficient bankers are sorcerers, for a sorcerer moves energy.

Why is a bank like a temple? Valid question. We can't understand this unless we step out of ourselves, unless we step into a higher dimension. In a higher dimension, when we look at money we see it as energy. A dollar bill is a slice of energy; therefore, to transfer a dollar to a retailer is to transfer energy. For every dollar we accumulate, for every dime we spend, we reinforce our worship to these temple magicians. We pray to the gods of money, but because they are aligned to ego (mostly) and worship pure Self, then these beings are not gods, they are devils and demons. The ultimate temptation in the hands of mankind's oldest foe, for the worship of Self is in the domain known as Hell.

The movement and transfer of energy between the members of society and the banking institution is at an all time high these days. The introduction of credit cards, ATM machines, online banking, Forex (foreign exchange software programs), interest rates, and digital cash are all ways to increase the flow of money (quadrillions of transactions at a time) and therefore to increase the flow of energy. Not only to better the speed, but to gain a firmer grip on the direction of that vital flow because the more digital the money – the more it simulates actual energy – the more it can be directed, the stronger the world can be influenced by smaller handprints. As the bankers move society into total digital cash, we are entering a danger zone.

Addicted to Money

If we look at monetary systems on the physical level we can see its intimate relationship with an economy. The flow of money determines the strength of the economy. A robust economy is one in which spending expands. This in turn expands manufacturing and the national GDP (Gross Domestic Product) expands. The opposite is also true. The reduction in spending leads to a fall in production, contraction, followed by a recession, an economic depression. The system is designed, both physically and mentally, to force citizens to rely on money, like a drug. As long as you keep drinking, everything will be good. But if you lose the ability to drink, if you drink less, if you refuse to drink then your life will suffer. If many people dislodge themselves from money, all of society will suffer. It's like peer drug addiction. We're all doing heroin and so you have to join us. If nicotine is addictive, money is an essential human ingredient. To prevent a depression (the threat) we have to increase the money supply, jack up spending and create more jobs so as more income flows into people's home. The artificial financial system on earth corresponds to a dimensional addiction of which very few people can accept or understand: nonetheless, everything on earth is manifested from some primordial energy. The movement of this energy can influence its correspondence here on this plane of existence.

The bank is the gateway by which energy on earth moves, and where classes of society are formed and destroyed. In other words, it can be stated quite emphatically, from a dimensional view, no economic recession can take place through natural circumstance. The cycles of recessions on earth can be found to have intimate relationships to certain celestial events, power grabs or during a redistribution of world sovereignty. One such circumstance is the changeover of governments or governmental leaders. Another circumstance is with the introduction of new financial software forecasting programs. Whatever the excuse turns out to be from the mouth of the experts, carefully veiled behind the curtain there is a very supernatural manipulation.

The classy house, the new car, the fancy clothes, the bling, the desired existence – these things are what is good in modern life. All of it comes from money. There is no mass in church without money. Today, the Vatican has amassed an immense amount of wealth, all the while preaching the gospels of Jesus who exclaimed that money is the root of all evil. The Vatican evil?

So, on the surface there is this illusion of wealth and success. You are forced to succeed; otherwise you end up homeless. If you make too much money, you have to pay taxes. We are all dependent on the monetary system, like it or not. Meanwhile, in the other dimension, the sorcerers manipulate energy. They, in fact, accumulate energy and redistribute it for themselves, taking from the common people, the citizens. The result of this is a society in debt and an elitist class who own everything in as many forms as possible. Verily, humanity has surrendered, fooled into doing so, their energy to these sorcerers and are now in debt. They are addicted to money (the delivery vehicle for dimensional energy) and the bankers have no incentive to alter this favourable position. Instead, they keep printing more money until that vibration of human energy is exhausted, at which point they introduce a new currency and explain that it is better than the collapsing dollar. The financial system on one perception works amazingly. People do get rich. But it is an illusion because money is made up. It's a piece of paper upon which is stamped a government approved value.

Severing the Need

As money equates to energy and as wealth is poorly distributed, one other word we can say is that a few members of the world actually hoard money, then that hoarding results in a planetary system that is largely decided by the bankers. And the bankers fund war, disease, propaganda films, political candidates. The campaign to jolt the unknown Barrack Obama to the position of US President was estimated to cost one billion dollars. Who can compete with that level of ante? What kind of people manage those kinds of funds? While on the surface, the political campaign was interactive, behind the scenes it was funded by bankers and these bankers are sorcerers. The chosen President was moved into position like a chess piece on a giant chess board. Sadly, since the use of such high amounts of money was used and since this money is artificially manufactured and hoarded by sorcerers (and dynasties) then any political position is put in place by the most egotistical lifeforms on earth, the blood-sucking demons. Pure ego exists only in Hell, unfortunately. A truly inspirational leadership campaign would use only enough money to stage dance and song and food extravaganzas to impress upon society that a leader is divinely chosen and brought forth as a gift to serve the people. A divine leader empowers society in as many ways possible and empowerment has nothing to do with lower taxes and military wins.

So the demons (disguised as humans) use the people's energy – people who have willingly given them their energy – to redirect the world into war scenarios, into disease propagation, into political ideologies and other false determinations. And what we have in the world is a dismal world whereby war and disease are normal. The religious institution such as the Vatican does not interfere with the system because they work alongside the energy hoarders.

To sever our need for money would lead to economic collapse because the economy is a firmly held illusion and because people are addicted to this form of energy gratification. None of it any different then heroin or cocaine addiction. It is a dollar addiction and the distribution is the economy. Any kind of rehab is going to take a giant will, tremendous support and an extensive period of time.

The first way to lose dependency for wealth is to redistribute money. We need to equalize the fields of energy. Right now, elitists and the rich hold vast sums of wealth, including corporations, military organizations, institutions (eg United Nations), secret agencies (eg CIA), banks (eg World Bank), and governments. In effect they hoard wealth. So to move energy from a monetary system and off the illusory we have to redistribute wealth, either equally among all, or in better proportions.

Humanizing the Almighty Dollar

The first step would be to remove one of the more powerful devices ever placed in a monetary investment – immortality. The dollar bill has a print date but no expiration date. It lives forever, as long as the bankers and government want it to live. The only comparable thing is the human soul but the human soul is part of the divine system and within cosmic governance. Money is not only immortal, but mortal humans are in charge. The first step then is to humanize money from a divine immortal investment into a divine instrument. Only one thing is necessary to achieve this. Only one crucial step is needed – the adoption of a **monetary expiration date**.

To put an expiration date on money (cash) would not damage the economy because people still are compelled to spend. They can still save money, but, more importantly, no one can hoard money. What this also means is that no elite class can solely determine the direction of the planet because they no longer have the reams of energy as before at their disposal. The mental shift to *transient cash* could prove interesting.

And what we'll see with the adoption of "money with an expiration date" is a new level of harmony on earth because as energy stabilizes so too will existence. Money with an expiration date is like milk. You buy enough milk to keep you healthy and you drink it all up. When the milk has run out, you get some fresh milk. In fact, fresh milk tastes better than old milk. Fresh money should be more valuable than old money. We could even devalue money after a certain number of months to reinforce the need for fresh money. And you always have access to fresh money, like a grocery store, for example. You go to a 24-hour store to pick up some extra money, in whatever size you prefer.

This will begin a process of demonetization and allow humans a chance to move out of an archaic monetary system and into a system of rationalized energy distribution. You will eventually buy things in a manner never imagined before. But it is pointless to talk about a vacation before rehab. We need to put an expiration date on money first because we need to redistribute energy and to normalize the distributions of energy on this place of existence.

Changing the nature of money must come with a few conditions, one of them should be the expiration date, but because money is already artificial then too is the expiration date. Cash is printed with a guaranteed value for x number of months (and there are other financial instruments that will need to be considered too). The nearer to the expiration date, the more the value. As we move away from the print date, cash spoils. The milk production model is a good overlay for a mortal cash system. A competent cash factory produces a limited number of cash. Cash shoppers buy the cash through the most convenient distribution system available and then go shopping. For example, your paycheck might give you a certain number of cash production stock. You obtain your cash, or buy some extra, and you go spending.

Fresh cash is more valuable so people are inclined to spend fresh cash if they want store savings. People have different spending habits just like people have different milk habits. The economy chugs along but the dependence on the banking industry is forever improved. It is a single useful idea in a sea of useful ideas if people started to apply their cosmic brains more directly to world solutions instead of designer jeans and becoming music stars. We must never forget that money is an anomaly on earth. It was invented; and, if so, we can invent something less egotistical. Can we not?

RELIGION

The very idea of religion is founded upon divine scripture. And divinity is obtained when a vessel can access the upper dimensions of knowledge; in doing so they obtain pure knowledge. In times of past, these divine vessels were chosen and these chosen became prophets. The life of the prophet demanded a harmonious connection to some invisible "god being." These divine prophets were then respected (and slaughtered) in society. Some of these prophets stood out, their scriptures were copied and their divine teachings were shared among society.

From these particular scriptures, there came religion into being. So, religion then is the institutionalization of divine scripture, and therefore the magnification of the thoughts, ideas and interpretations of these people, exceptional people. Hand-picked by their respective Creators, enlightened to a level of awareness that is unrecognizable by the common person. They became vehicles for the ascension of others and their words, carefully recorded on various media, became sacred. Their words became sacred not so much that they came from a God but because their knowledge was beyond the capacity of others. Verily, their cosmic understanding was understood to be far more advanced than the best student. That is what set them apart. That is what made them masters on this field of existence. That knowledge proved their non-terrestrial nature and was enough to link them to the godly forces for only a person who touches god can truly know god. If God touches you, it is because of compassion; if you touch God, it is because of ascension. For a child of the Creator to return to his Heavenly World, it is proof enough to welcome back his child for that child has achieved the highest awareness during the life journey, not after life had expired, but during the life journey. Sadly, today, almost no one cares to ascend to that degree as humanity is immersed in constant egotistical misery and priority. Gone are the days when a successful man abandons his wealth in order to achieve spiritual enlightenment and to carry down the words of his Creator. Not man, not woman. There are no more Mother Theresas, no more Gandhis, no more Buddhas. If they exist, they have locked themselves up in their temples. Gandhi did not hide in a temple. Buddha did not hide in a cave. Mother Theresa did not meditate in a church 24/7.

These people, and all like them, contributed to society. They made their faces known. They lived what they believed to be true. Jesus did not stick his head in the sand; he was on the ground, at the grassroots. Not just at the grassroots, but he plainly told people that he was the Son of God, even that he was God Incarnate. What set these exceptional people apart from others is that they truly understood who they were and weren't afraid to embrace it as a new life. Today, the wise man in America will write a book, claim an experience and then add: "I'm not asking people to worship me and I am not dressed in robes, I'm just so excited about what I went through and gained that I want to share it with everyone. It's there for people to decide for themselves." If he truly believed in his goods and his experiences, shouldn't he ask for people to follow him, to learn from him? He won't. Why? Because people will think him a charlatan, a liar. Why? Because there are no prophets anymore. Why? There's no way to prove it. Society is rooted in logic and science. How do you prove you are a true prophet? Who the hell knows the truth, not the backwards religions? And should a person back the newly anointed prophet, that very supporter will be scrutinized and they are afraid of being tossed off their temple podium. There is more to gain from quiet religious practice and inspirational books than there is from embodying the truth and making grandiose claims that will probably get you taking a few extra yellow pills.

The Institutionalization of Divine Scripture

Over centuries of institutionalization and through repetition and introspection, these religions have become formalized, with many prophets appearing over the course of human evolution. The result is a plethora of religions each with their own particular value, taste and ritual. But the underlying secret characteristic of all religion is the most important aspect of any religion and that is the fundamental **root** of all religion. What is the root of all divine scripture? Many would say God, but then Buddhists see God within self and Hindu practitioners see multiple gods; therefore God as Supreme entity cannot be the root of Buddhism and since Buddhism is also a derived religion we have to conclude that God is not the root. By using the word derived together with Buddhism, I should clarify that to a Buddhist there is no religion, their way of thinking is a way of life. It is a path. Buddha itself, the word, means "the awakened one" so everyone can be Buddha, can be awakened. The Buddha's name was Gautama. Because he ascended his pale human state, after waking, he was given the name Buddha. Did (the) Buddha call himself Buddha? Does God call himself God? Take a guess.

God, at best, is an interpretation of some Heavenly Father, a masculine source of unfathomable power. Therefore, God is a human invention, or, a term presented to society that they might be able to understand since the language of God and the language of Man are unequal. A typical ascended person these days now respects that "fatherly energy" as **Source**; a better interpretation of God because God is a simple interpretation. If God is one interpretation then Source is a more complicated interpretation just like we can say car and motorized vehicle. Car is colloquial, motorized vehicle is for the licensing bureau.

Better, what is the root of Source, God and Self? Obviously, it is something beyond the processing capability of humans and that is mostly because planet earth and all of its inhabitants belong to a system of stars that is in the billions upon billions. In order for a Source, a root of power, to address all existence in this solar system and the next solar system and the universe and the cosmos, and all the cosmoses, it has to be complex. Now, complexity can have many interpretations. Complexity can mean have multiple dimensions. Complexity can mean having an immeasurable quantity of power and interaction.

We have to agree that the root of existence, verily the Sustainer of existence, has to manage billions upon billions of stars, an immeasurable number of existential lifeforms having different ages of evolution. Whereas humanity 3.0 is two hundred thousand years old, there are races millions of years old. And as odd as it appears, the greater the age, the richer the level of immortality, the more technological the lifeform. In other words, as a technological existence inhabiting a flesh body, humans are very young in terms of cosmic evolution. In order to expand outside of the mortal flesh, a lifeform adopts other bodily forms, becomes more and more technological; that is to say that the greater the civilization the less flesh, or the more divine a thing, the more technological it becomes. And this takes us right back to the root of all religion. Recall that the greater prophets of earth old obtained their sacred scripture from some divine source. But if that divine source is technological in function and structure and composition then it could be said that all religion stems from a technological device. Verily, the best interpretation of a technological device is a **machine**.

Of course, the deduction of seeing god as coming from some giant machine is likely considered a wild observation and yet all my experience with cosmic devices have all been technological in nature; therefore, my deduction is supported by first-hand experience as well as other documented observation in my own extensive work. The interpretation of the cosmos as a highly advanced mechanical device, a kind of **Cosmic Computer**, forces the religious and faithful of earth to face a bizarre truth. If the cosmos is a machine then God is best interpreted as some kind of **robot**; a level of advancement that we will require time to detail properly because God would have to be able to manage an entire solar system and to ensure its smooth operation.

The Fall of the Church

The fact that people have humanized God or that the God Robot provided a human presentation of itself to satisfy human thinking patterns is irrelevant to the truth that God is part of the cosmos and not the other way around. The cosmos, including all stars and systems, is not God; God Robot is a device inside the Cosmos. For mankind to worship a Divine Device is still in coherence to the system because God, as a construct, is part of the collective whole. Only now we can begin to see that God is not the highest point of contact. And these days many people are having direct connection to God and to the deeper cosmic databanks. There are more prophets today than ever before and we can see this in the number of published books or the number of educational TV programs. None of this was available in the past. Problem is that we take it for granted. But then oversupply of information and knowledge is a clear indication that everyone is downloading Heavenly knowledge, but somehow it gets tucked away in the mind and the ego life takes over till that special day that never comes.

In fact, we could launch a thousand more religions if we wanted without any question. The fact that the old religions remain is because people refuse to accept the fact that they have outgrown the crutch of religion and are now communicating with the Cosmic Computer. In other words, people are talking beyond God. Science and technology today is completely outside the providence of even the best Bible. Spiritually not close but technologically, yes. The Bible does not account for Twitter or Google or Microsoft or television or satellites or space shuttles, does it? As a support mechanism for a growing civilization (then), God was a perfect technological implant. The training wheels to the new bike. But humanity, new generation anyway, does not require the God training wheels because now many people can connect to higher grids or even to the Cosmic Computer; and the cosmic machines are interacting with greater effect (eg balls of light) inside society in order to more convincingly coax society out of its false beliefs and old ideologies and into a larger mind. To stir away from demonic temptation and into technological bliss.

All of these things, and more, point a finger at the death of religion. Twitter is proof that mankind has reached its hand outside of the rectangular Bible. Religion is already dead. We just didn't have a proper funeral for it, and we should (eventually). To sever ourselves from all religion. Since all religion is rooted in a lower spiritual construct, it would be a powerful blow to the human psyche, but it is no different than moving out on your own as an adult, or having a child for the first time in your life; or any other significant event. Plus, once we all, at this point, understand these things internally, the readjustment will be less stressful than anyone will suggest.

Intuitively, we understand but we live in a world ruled by egoists and these egoists do not want society to realize that there is something beyond God because they have used God as a device for suppression of the human spirit. God is the knife at everyone's throat. To appreciate the technological nature of the cosmos will lead to the destruction of human religion; then again religion is no longer required by the advanced masses of genetically-improved humans. They are far more advanced than any Bible. No one wants to make that public because to see advanced humans en masse would see the fall of the church.

Religion is no longer necessary to prop up human culture. Human culture is now filled with the ability to communicate with the Cosmic Computer with ease. Whether the people can escape their egotistical addictions, symbolic deterrents and preprogrammed inhibitions is hard to say since each individual is uniquely troubled. You are already beyond religion, you just didn't know it. And they don't want you to know.

Being beyond religion doesn't make you any better than God, only that now you become a more responsible cosmic citizen and a contributor to the future of what is to come, rather than a worshiper of some immortalized device. The destruction of human religion will lead to a reshaping of the human soul, an unmistakeable brightening, and will enlighten society in immeasurable ways. Will humanity have the courage to move on to the next thing?

REALITY

The human timeline is of particular importance to my discussion. We disregard the relevance of the human timeline, aka The Calendar, because we accept it at face value. Someone sold our ancestors a Gregorian Time Schedule Calculator and we do not question it. But I want to question it. I want to question it because there are some issues with it that are in the interest of the public at large. The biggest issue is that the Gregorian Calendar starts at the birth of the Christian Messiah, and not everyone here is Christian. The other is an opportunity. We all know that a new reality is upon the earth, a new spectrum of energy, only we have yet to take full advantage of it. Well, here's an opportunity: we can reset the human timeline to be in sync with the new energies. By doing so, if successful, we could interrupt the arrival of 2012, a time when the demonic rulers of earth want to wreak havoc on society and before that as well.

We have it within our power to reset the calendar and these biblical days are the perfect time to do so. What we are lacking is an understanding of the human calendar. We lack a lot of knowledge because the mainstream has other interests and schools are still saying the Lord's Prayer. Now the measure of human time is fundamentally linked to the measure of human existence. If we influence that aspect of civilization, if we tamper with time, we tamper with the course of humanity; and if we are off course, as we indeed are, we have a chance to get back on course, or something closer to what it might be.

Imagine the benefit of recouping a hundred years of lost advancement. Imagine avoiding 20 more years of misery. Imagine you are in a bad marriage, he is beating you senseless. I come by and I offer you a way out, I offer you a room in a safe house. You can stay or you can leave. If you stay, he will continue to beat and rape you, guaranteed. If you come with me, you can have a new life, no guarantee. Would you have the strength to leave the man you loved? He might also come after you and kill you, as he has promised many times. What would you do? This here is that type of opportunity. I am not certain humanity can escape its misery but this is yet another way to improve existence. Each step we take to improve ourselves has an immeasurable response in the cosmic continuum. By keeping things as they are, better to stay with the Devil you know than the one you don't know, there is no chance for anything better. It is a predetermined horror and the bad guy lives in the end for a sequel.

Back to Year Zero

We enjoy measuring things. As humanity progressed, it gained a proficiency in the art of measurement. We weigh ourselves, we count calories, we watch movies in minutes, we count pages, we look at brush strokes, words per page, IQ, EQ, yearly income, hourly salary, dollars and pennies. We measure everything including days and nights which become weeks and months. Each month we measure moon phases; 28 days from dim to full, old to new. Twelve months one calendar year.

The Gregorian Calendar is rooted at Year Zero. The same point in history where the birth of Jesus is affixed. No one is certain at the day of Jesus' birth let alone at the year of his birth because those events were corrupted by the ruling classes at the time. But what is more important than when Jesus was born was why Year Zero came into being. You have to realize that prior to Year Zero there were other calendar systems, for example the Chinese Calendar. But for some reason there was a desire to start a new annual daily measurement. Why? Why reset the calendar? And why at the time of Jesus? Why not at the birth of some other prophet or Great Teacher?

According to Wikipedia, the yearly designation of A.D. (Anno Domini) is translated from Latin as "In the Year of Our Lord Jesus Christ." The A.D. designation is relevant today because we are occupying a point after the birth (and death) of Jesus. Therefore, our lives are rooted in the birth of Christ. It is as if I put an iron spike in the dirt, hooked a chain to it and then extended the chain across time so that the anchor point controlled the field of time. Not unlike taking a dog to a park and tying him to a spike in the ground so as to restrict the field of its play. So the Year Zero, speculatively affixed to Jesus, King of the Jews, is the spike in time upon which humanity today is affixed.

We can immediately see that where you place the spike isn't arbitrary, rather it is entirely subjective because there are many good spots in time and because the length of the chain is predetermined at inception by those same industrial minds. We are living today two thousand and nine years (2,009) into the Year of Our Lord Jesus Christ. And what is interesting is that

Jesus is the root of Christianity and therefore the entire world measures days and weeks according to Jesus, whether they like it or not.

The more remarkable thing about this is the obvious fact of the 6 billion non-Christians. I mean there are many other religions, other Messiahs, besides Jesus, and yet all of them are attached to the Christian Spectrum of Time. Therefore, whoever nailed in the spike, as was nailed the Christian Messiah, is in control of this Calendar, this field of time.

What this also means is this: the appearance of a Christ-level consciousness 2,000 years ago and the launch of a New Reality in 2007 are correlated because the birth of the Christ being is akin to the birth of a New Reality. The resetting of the Calendar to Zero supports the significance of his birth; otherwise, it wouldn't happen. We all know that cosmic forces influence dramatic human activity. Resetting the timeline to zero is dramatic, to say the least. This produces changes across all life forms because all beings breathe the same arvicity; we all exist in the same existential field.

Resetting the Human Timeline

In 2007, when the New Reality system was activated, I suggested on an online blog that we reset the human timeline to zero because the Old Reality affixed to the birth of Jesus. By making 2007 the new Year Zero, even if not adopted by the mainstream, we acknowledge the birth of a New Reality system, despite the fact that it would require 8 or 9 years to unspool (until 2015). This is not unlike some people on earth who recognized the activation of the previous version of reality.

What I'm implying, if in an odd way, is that Jesus was much more than a man or the Son of God. He was a symbol recognizing the turnover from one reality vibration to another. Prior to Jesus there was Reality 4.0. Then Jesus appeared, born or arrived is irrelevant; he had a presence in the human field of consciousness. Jesus symbolized version 5.0 of the Earth System, reinforced by the fact that the rulers reset the calendar. Two thousand and seven (2,007) later, or so, Reality 6.0 came into being, but no one reset the calendar. In fact, no one care to think about it.

What does this also mean? Well, I'll be blunt and without proof (as usual I rely on common sense and deep perception): In order for a new reality to be activated, it must be, must be predated by a Christ-like consciousness. In other words, a Jesus figure must have arrived prior to 2007 in order for a new reality system to be activated. Sure, only a handful of people recognized the arrival of a new reality, but that group was quite large at the time. A smaller number of people understand the underlying technological nature of reality and still fewer realize that on March 21, 2007, a new reality system was activated.

But that is indeed what happened. What does all this have to do with the calendar? Well, whenever a new version of reality is launched, it is designed to overtake the old version of reality, literally cannibalizes or devours the old and replaces it with the new existence-scale code. Humanity remains oppressed and the demonic rulers refuse to acknowledge this cosmic event of energies exotic – because that undermines their stranglehold on the Jesus reality chain. Where is the image of Jesus commonly found? As a fashion accessory, jewellery – a tortured man nailed to a cross linked to a chain around someone's neck. The symbolism is uncanny. The human timeline is wrapped around people's necks. The demons et al do not control Reality 6.0 (and can't) and will not allow people to adopt it easily. They like to see people pray to a tortured man nailed to a cross because that is one root of their power of man.

Realigning with the cosmic timeline, with 2007 as Year Zero, is fundamentally important to the evolution and ascension of humankind. That is to say, if humanity continues on the old reality version (5.0) they will find that existence will be full of struggle, evil, violence, challenge and a nearby implosion, an existential suicide. Why? Because Reality 5.0 is being phased out. You know, Windows 95 is no longer supported and now it's Windows 7. If you continue to use Win 95, you will fall behind in the latest software, your productivity will suffer, efficiency will shrink until eventually you can no longer connect to the Windows Whatever OS. Because the technological cooperation is beyond your capacity. It's a technological problem.

Why is Jesus late?

The trouble with reality technology is that it is developed on an existence-scale architecture and this design is millions of years ahead of the best computer systems so we have a very wide canyon of knowledge between my words and your education. But I'm hoping that you see some of these correspondences. Nothing on earth is new in the cosmos. Everything is a representation of everything else; therefore, a computer system is not exclusive to human science; that is what they want you to believe, the elegant brainwash, "See what man has done. He is good." No, man is just replicating more complex, infinite ideas from some other dimensions. Its puberty and some civilizations get pimples. The correspondences: Birth of Jesus and Year Zero, and New Reality; and New Reality, new Year Zero and a Second Jesus (even if not public).

Why would Jesus hide if he indeed arrived? Well, I've written essays on this and you can find that in my work. Essentially, since Jesus is more than a man, since he is some archetypal symbol, verily a technological construct, his reappearance (ie Second Coming) would be consistent with the context of the modern world. He would not return in robes unless wearing robes was still in fashion. How would he appear? He would appear in a format that, on the surface, appears normal, and it would be up to wise humans to recognize who, or what, he is. Obviously that did not happen and it is 2009.

Despite the faithful millions of worshipers and thousands of priests, they have fundamentally failed to some very significant events on earth that were not included in the King James Holy Bible. If that doesn't start to shake people from their mainstream slumber then I don't know what will. I'll say bluntly: a Jesus figure is here on earth. Go find him. And I should also stress this unfortunate fact: the more bluntly society is told what is going on, the less involved society is in this esoteric stuff, the longer the ascension plan of the human race. In other words, according to cosmic law, if you have to be told everything then you have to come back and relive this awareness again because you didn't get it right the seven millionth time. The cosmic laws are very particular on intervention. You can receive an intervention but in the end you will regret it. That is why I always suggest that people make more effort but this does not happen, for whatever reason. At the rate of epiphanies here on earth, about 2 every 500 years, humanity is just going to relive a bunch more misery.

Preventing 2012

Myself, I have re-determined the Year 2007 as Year Zero (00). This means that we are in Year Two (02) and on March 21, 2010; it will be Year Three (03). This is going to piss off the 2012 crowd because we'll never hit 2012, if we the majority reset the timeline. As the Mayans even said (paraphrasing), "Time ends as we know it." Well, resetting the calendar to Zero and affixing ourselves to a technological root, and not a Christian one, will reverberate throughout all inhabitants here and have fundamental improvements in society because we will be in coherence to the cosmic. We will resonate with the consciousness of a newly improved, up-to-date Christ. This is a lot better than this declining reality version. I say, keep this in mind, discuss this and we can collectively adopt a new Calendar System ahead of any official (demonic) recognition.

The prevention of the arrival of 2012 is an elegant spike in the unearthly plans of those who rule over us; for within their timeline they have power to influence the planet since they hold some of the keys to this kingdom. We are certain that they are up to no good, depopulation-grade agendas. We know this. We also know there are multiple agendas on multiple dimensions by multiple authorities. Which is a bummer, right? We can, if we wanted to, put another knot in their agendas by adopting a **new calendar system**, starting with the counting of years. By doing so, at the same time, we realign ourselves with the newest energies and we tie another yellow ribbon round that old oak tree.

WAR

It is called war. It is known as war. It is realized as a form of security. Still, this form of security has existed for several thousand years. It persists until this very day. Afghanistan, Pakistan, Iraq – threats to civilized security, call it threats to American security. North Korea, Iran – more reasons for the military to find a burgeoning budget. The biggest threat to human security is human, isn't it? And yet the idea of war has been in existence for thousands of years, Alexander the Great, Hercules, Napoleon, Catholic Pope, King David, Emperor Hirohito, George W. Bush, Mr. Obama...the timeline of war is long and bloodied. It is easy for mankind to indulge himself in war. It is easy to grab the spears when a cultural security is threatened. and it should be noted that some society is being threatened at any moment in time. The response is always the same, rhetoric followed by anger and then a fight. Not unlike an Ultimate Fighter bout where two people are made into opponents and then learn to hate each other in order to drive the energy to win in the match. Ultimately, it is about the match. It doesn't matter who fights who as long as they are in the same weight category. With Ultimate Fighter the weight is less stringent than in boxing. In the real world, sport fairness is thrown out the window. America has the most technologically advanced military in the world, they invaded Iraq and Afghanistan, each with very small militaries, none of them with any nuclear capability. All in the name of security. America didn't go to war to kill people, they went to war to kill the bad guys, only in that very process they would end up killing and raping a few bystanders, just a few.

Secure me

Security has been used for centuries to initiate the murder of strangers and foreigners. These days, the political bastards are selling hard the benefits and details on a perpetual war; the war in Iraq has been going on for 8-9 years. Labelled as a global threat, a *war of necessity*, a quagmire, a global responsibility, an anything that was needed to continue to convince the short-minded public that war was necessary in order to preserve the security of the U.S.A. (and its allies). There isn't any war in this solar system that is necessary. Food is necessary. Senseless, groundless, useless wars such as what continue on today are in no way necessary. They are constructed in such a way so as to justify their existence. A few bad yet elusive banditos have somehow managed to threaten the 300 million citizens of the U.S.A. How is it possible? It is the ultimate brainwash in order to justify the increase in security, as they have done for centuries upon centuries. Same ideology, different uniforms. A warmonger is anyone who propagates war and US President Barrack Obama is king warmonger.

The perpetuation of security issues on earth demands us to believe that we are at threat from our neighbours. Rather than love thy neighbour, it is fear them; and if you can, invade their home and shoot them straight back to hell. The leaders of the world are not interested in loving their neighbours. You can see how much the whole world loves each other. War after war, sanction after sanction, economic collapse after economic collapse – none of these things are new to us. Never have been. If you think that after 500 years of turmoil that war was done for any different reason, you'd be living in a bubble. You think that King Arthur didn't represent the need for security? You think that the Spanish Inquisition sent its members out to murder witches and burn them at the stake because they were worshipers of the one peaceful God?

Humanity is determined to wipe itself out in the name of security. The public buys this concept because the public now buys any concept. US President Obama sent 51,000 additional troops to war in his first year in office, all of this despite winning the 2009 Nobel Peace Prize.

The desire to secure a nation has lost its mind. The Inquisition was made up of the Catholic Church and their doctrines were designed by the words of a pacifistic Father of Heaven. How is it possible that a Church of God could initiate a war against witchcraft when one of their Ten Commandments was "Thou Shalt Not Kill," how could they? Well they could because they did. They tortured people, they raped people, they murdered people, they burned people.

All of this not unlike the horrors in the Middle East, only that Obama is not a Bishop, his army multi-religious and the enemy has no witches. The taste of this security protection program in Afghanistan is quite similar to the Inquisition only what is missing is the overt religious scarf wrapped around its bloodied neck. That is what is missing, the bloodied scarf especially from the false man of peace himself. If anything, the current situation of war in the world, in the year 2009, should clearly delineate the poor state of the human heart, for the heart is without the need for peace. That is the fundamental problem. It is not a problem with security. It is not a problem of killing people more efficiently like when they first introduced smart bombs. The only smart bomb is one that doesn't go off. Other than that, bombs are as dumb as anything. Bombs discriminate according to the discrimination of their maker. You have to either be completely insane or a racist in order to manufacture bombs because bombs kill people and they tend to fall on the heads of people who you hate. Either you are insane to have this murderous intention or you intend to eventually take out a certain cultural group, other than your own.

The Murdering Mind of Man

We constantly see murder in the world, for one reason or another. If not for one's own security then for the security of a group or a nation. What does this mean? There is always a threat. There is always something in the background threatening society. The interesting aspect of this observation is that if you could control the idea of a threat, if you could shape darkness into a series of recognizable threats, if you could then communicate that threatening idea to the public, you could put a stranglehold on human groups.

You could invent wars by simply lighting a few matches and putting those lit flames to dry tinder. You could burn down the forests of society with only a few matches. That is the sad state of the human mind, for what has man to fear in another man? Nothing. The other man can do nothing to you if you do not fear him. Now, if you fear him, he can do anything to you and you will become enraged with this fear and you will feel justified in murdering him. You will even feel empowered by this act, and once it is done you will deny any wrongdoing. Such is the state of the powerful human mind.

You have this idea of a loving God, of a hopeful Jesus, of an endless glory if you let enter the energy of faith into your soul. God is all powerful, the worshipers are uniquely in sync, the preachers are selling their wares, God is in business, his ministers wear two piece suits, the holy businessman. These are the ones waging wars. These are the masters of deceit. They only need to sign a policy or enact a new Bill and there is a war to preserve some new security breach. There is always a security breach, isn't there? If not, if one doesn't exist, then one (or two) is created. For you only need a security breach in order to initiate a military response. The larger the breach, the larger the response.

Look at the situation in December 2009, 51,000 new troops to Afghanistan, the same location the first invasion began before moving to Iraq, all of it to no avail, the greatest threat on earth, Mr. bin Laden, was never found. Sure, lots of innocent civilians were killed, the infrastructure was destroyed, the culture was demolished, but the one man they all sought was never found. Today, there are some 43 countries involved in this holy war, and yet, it is not considered a world war.

Take a look at this: according to answers.com, there were 51 Allied countries involved in WWII. To be considered a UN Member Nation, you had to have been at war with one of the axis powers (eg Italy, Germany, Japan), so many nations joined the UN and fought against the axis powers.

The difference between 43 and 51 isn't all that large, plus our accounting system is always in question. During WWI, there were some 100 countries involved. And yet, the War in Afghanistan and in Iraq, for probably technical reasons, is not considered WWIII, when by all accounts it is the preface, the build-up to WWIII. This seems obvious. And all of this is a result of a belligerent attack of vengeance by the God-loving, mostly-Christian American Administration because of the World Trade Center demolition. WWII had Pearl Harbor, WWIII had NYC. The taste of murder has never left the mouths of men.

Unimaginable War Instruments

There are other kinds of war instruments besides bombs and bullets, outside of the hearts and minds manipulation campaigns, beyond the sense of any logic – weapons that could wipe out existence if pointed in the right direction. Imagine I had a device that could wipe out a small planet, say a moon, say our moon. What would happen if planet earth lost its orbiting satellite?

Catastrophic? You bet. Imagine I had a device that could create a blank spot in human memory and then its complex machinery could insert a programmed memory episode like everyone should be homosexual or childless, either or, for example. Imagine these weapons are available now and the murderous campaigns using bullets and bombs are powerful distractions to the level of weapons really at large. Why would they cause a war to occur, to lose millions of people, if they had such powerful weapons in their pockets? Why not wipe out the enemy with these superior weapons?

To answer these questions, we have to return back to the mind of man. The mind of man has been shaped by other men, but these other men were not men, in fact, they were human-looking synthetic variants. If this is true then the way that humankind thinks is shaped by the way these nonhumans wanted man to think. Throughout history.

Of course, you didn't expect the topic of war to turn into discussing synthetic humans, and, on the surface, it might seem like an effective twist in the Third Act of the Fantasy Earth Movie: "Then the President took off his disguise and his true face was unlike anything the people had ever conceived. Shock filled the minds of society as they discovered the dark agenda of their alien masters. The crocodile President spoke: You humans, you vile scum, you are completely under our control. From here on end, we determine your fate." I can hear the organs playing, the dread on everyone's lips, the voice of some newly born Vincent Price, the tears in the eyes and the heart beating irregularly. All of our worst nightmares are now coming true.

I kid you not these things. I cannot kid about this stuff. I could kid about whether I listen to Avril Lavigne but not this. This is the stuff I know best and haven't the avenue to really discuss. People don't want to believe that any of this is possible, so I refer them to movies like They Live, and they say, "Wow, what a cool movie, but its fantasy, right?" Listen, nothing here on earth is fantasy. It all comes from something tangible. The problem is that our level of tangible interpretation is pretty pathetic. We have such a diminutive view of existence that it is embarrassing. Whatever exists in the physical world is representative of things in the nonphysical world. Each and everything has a correspondence and becomes evident when and if we need to see them. In other words, every person's perception can discover whatever they need to discover.

What does correspondence, mind of man, synthetic beings, evil aliens and war have in common? The evil aliens, or demons as is more accurate, have shaped the mind of man in such a way as to ensure that he is forever blind to the truth that I so lovingly speak. The situation is complex. It will take decades to unravel properly. But soon this unravelling will explode and, if you must know, what you believe is patently false about what has been going on and the most imaginative (without being delusional) minds will discover that they had the right idea all along. I won't spoil the Third Act because you'll hate me for it. We all learn better when truth clashes with belief. From my observations, it will be a Clash of the Titans...oops, was that some subtle hint?

What is more powerful than television, addictive substance and sex combined? War. War, war, war. War goddammit. War. Are you getting the message? Are you sitting up and taking notice? To distract the world while gods play against each other, the inhabitants are immersed in continuous war because people accept war. The movies worked to convert you. The patriotism moved you to join the fight. The loss of your child in the latest bombing campaigns got you on board. The loss of your son, the decorated soldier, saw more of your family involved. All of it a campaign to draw mankind into endless war so that nonhumans could iron things out. Humankind is the back drop to an eternal battle between Good and Evil. Between God and Satan. Between whatever you believe and whatever else you believe because your beliefs are about as real as your identity.

And guess what? The Americans have decided to escalate the battle. Surprise, surprise.

If you truly want to see what is happening you can do a number of things. You can rise above the war propaganda and patriotism and see the chess moves, see the faces of evil, see what is coming.

You can also disbelieve that this war is real. You can see it as a movie, and see the multiple directors. That would shift your awareness somewhat, but your friends might call you an insensitive prick. Finally, you can conjure up some of your infinite knowledge and speak it loudly into the mainstream, speaking until they listen or they think you are insane. This will further awaken society. In all these cases, if enough minds overcome the war firewall, war will no longer hold people's attention; therefore, the nonhumans will be forced to escalate their dire plans and they will abandon war (as they did the H1N1 Vaccination Campaign) and jump into the next insanity hoop. In doing so, they will be forced to reveal their identities. If I am correct, if the overwhelming disbelief of war prevails, then the evil aliens, the demonic presences will become obvious, and in doing so, the mental chains they have been illegally and unlawfully placed upon you will collapse. In becoming free, you will feel a surge of energy unlike ever before and you will be ready to kick some demonic ass. The key lies in breaking the spells upon you. Then a few more surprises will ensue.

You will kick yourself for believing so many illusions. I will say, "I, and others, tried to tell you. We tried. Now do you believe us?" To which you will reply: "Holy Jesus Mother of God. I'm whacked the way out. I'm drowning in aluminum oil. Never ever did I imagine that any of this shit is real. What the fuck was wrong with me?" What was wrong with you? How many days have you got? Oh well, I am happy to let you see for yourself when you overcome the spells. Break the spells and the illusions become evident. Then we can deal with the other illusions. Ha! It doesn't get easier. There is no easy in my book. You want to see the end of war? Stop believing that the outcome of war is positive. Start seeing the war illusion, the most powerful spell ever placed on the human race, with sex not far behind and ice cream just off to the side in a cone.

EGO

We are at a technological crossroads at this time in human history. The permeable soup bowl of time is bleeding faster than ever before and the illustrious human is discovering more about itself, so much so that it is no longer recognizing itself. It is denying itself. It is denying itself because the more people realize the technological infrastructure upon which life is processed, the less relevant becomes the other concepts of spirituality, the fuzzy divine glory that has confused more than illuminated and has caused more murder than ever before. The failure to define the divine has created a spike in the mind, a pain so severe that the idea of spirit has flipped the morality switch. The world murders itself without so much as a moment's pause to reconsider the lunacy of their actions. We are inundated with lies, so much so that we now believe them with all our heart.

We've turned so completely from the divine, which is essentially point blank truth, that we are forced to cannibalize ourselves. We are eating ourselves, only we are doing it politely with bullets. Each bullet, each bite, one more step into hell. One step closer to monstrosity. What the hell is the divine? What have we denied ourselves? Because, given the horrible nature of man and his immersion and preference for ego, we'd have to conclude that there is not much divinity in the world. Sure, people are holding divinity inside of them, but they are holding back as well. They are sharing egotism instead of love unless you consider Christmas gifts as gifts of love. Look at Christmas if that is what you celebrate.

Christmas isn't about love. It's about ego disguised as love. It's a single day when everyone is nice to each other. One day out of 365 days we allow our love to sprout forth. And the other 364 days, it's straight back to ego. Back to hell. You cannot tell me with a straight face that the presence of war, endless military campaigns, is done so out of love. If you believe that, then your idea of love and mine do not match.

That presents us with an interesting conundrum – if we are divine and if divine things are technological and we have turned away from divine things, as we have, then we have turned away from the technology of the cosmos and turned to what? Well, we've turned to the technology of ourselves. Ourselves. That's what we've connected to – us.

Welcome to Egoville

What prevents a man from becoming a mass murderer? What allows a man to kill? What stops a man from killing? Is it conscience? If it was indeed conscience, now come so many mass murderers? How come so many wars? Can millions of people lose their conscience? As divine beings, we are technologically alive; therefore, we are technologically ordered and we technologically determine the course of our life. So, how is it possible that we are forced to do these atrocities? Why is it we can allow a war to prevail when by all divine providence, the mechanisms to prevent murder should be activated? On a technological level, the mechanism has been displaced and the human platform has been hijacked.
In order to do so, in order to displace the natural mechanism, it would require a level of technological proficiency that is well outside of ordinary physics. Well outside. Rather than to think that by some random occurrence forced these events to happen, the case is that whatever happened was purposely delivered on cue, in full. That would support the divine technology principle because that would say that God's hands are not hands at all. In fact, they are the hands of false gods, and that is because God is not the kind of man you think he is.

One of the most effective mechanisms utilized to overcome human divine technology is the ego device. The ego device vibrates at a specific frequency and if it is activated, the ego can *remote control* the flesh pod to a very wide effect. The ego can be programmed to do any number of things including murder, stealing, lying, buying, promotion, crying. It is attracted to material and superficial things. It loves fashion. It loves fear. It loves sin. The ego is easily controlled by fear which is fear and freedom (pain and pleasure) are effective remote control technologies.

The Ego on Remote

The revised understanding of the human ego as a built-in remote control device within the flesh avatar provides a very new conceptual understanding of the human android. The ego is a device which is used to override the owner's control systems and this is done so as to provide a functional vessel during specific moments in the life of the inhabitant. It was inserted so as to act as interface between man and its creator. The ego device is also activated in between active phases of the illuminated being.

A life form is equipped with the ability to process a number of lives, or, to process no life, in other words to be lifeless or inactive. When a life form is alive, it has control of its body unless otherwise noted, as we shall see. When a life form is not alive, that is, is no longer present within the body of flesh (the avatarian form), the body is remote controlled by the ego device. The ego device is a built-in program that runs on basic software programming codes. As you can begin to see, the current ego state of earth suggests, in a very strong manner, that the ego device has been remotely accessed, or brought to the surface for a lengthy period of time, and the ego is now having a predominant effect on the human life form, regardless of the level of spirituality.

It must necessarily be regardless of the level spirituality because why? Well, again, spirituality on earth is the human interpretation of a divine technology, and by divine I mean a highly evolved, dimensional technology probably hundreds of billions of years (if measurable in earth terms) ahead of the most advanced systems here. Hundreds of billions ahead, and keep in mind that the other life forms in the cosmic garden are far more spectacular than the evolving human species. Sadly, and because of ego interference, humans have been reprogrammed to believe that they are the best thing in the universe since meteor showers.

The ego device usually works in tandem with the invited inhabitant (or soul) and that is because certain aspects of life require the leadership of the human ego. The ego takes over and shows you to a book that changes your life. The ego takes over and introduces you to the right man, the man you later marry. The ego drives you to a particular meeting or keeps you focused on your homework. It helps you to say the right things at the right time.

The ego is designed to play a central role in your existential journey. And here's the but: the negative forces in reality, as simple as demons and as complex as beings from other planes with malevolent intentions, well these things decided to control people to the largest degree possible so as hijacked this entire planet. And since humans decided to go along, all drinking the illusory Kool-Aid, for centuries mind you, the entire planet has been ravaged, pissed on and twisted into a living hell; a place where millions of children die in hunger, perpetual wars are perpetually voted in, false leaders pretend to care about society while working hard at depopulation schemes...I mean if this is heaven it is only so because the blessed individuals have drunk the Kool-Aid and then deluded themselves into thinking that sewage tastes like egg nog. And sewage does not taste like egg nog. It can never taste like egg nog. If we were more truthful with ourselves, we would smell the stench of this place. You have to imagine that all the misery is perpetuated by your very leaders, I mean, war is not necessary. That is considered lunacy in the circles I travel in. In human circles, these are words for award-winning speeches.

One of the ways out of this mess, among the thousands and thousands of possibilities, is to overcome ego, and some gurus have talked about and written about the ego in quite some length. But the ego still remains in control and that is because the demonic rulers and their minions know how to communicate with your ego, they know what makes you move. They push all your buttons. Logically and rationally, you agree. You respond to fear: the world faces its worst depression in history...OMFG...what will we do if the evil leaders take away all our money and plunge us deeper into the illusory hell they themselves have created? Oh wait, there are still those terrorists who demolished the Twin Towers...we have to support the illegal and amoral war under the guidance of the man of peace himself so as to eliminate every millilitre of threat on earth. There's sex, well that explains everything right there. There's now this sexual confusion. This is not an accident. Species don't all of a sudden become bisexual for their own sake. This is not a natural occurrence. This is another button.

If we understand that the ego is a built-in existential program used to override the android body and that the base program, the soul (you) is the existential life form that deserves to live out this life journey, if we can begin to see that technological relationship (rather than some abstract psychological process) then we begin to see that we have been overridden by false leaders. They have the existential remote control: fear, TV, war, rhetoric, sexuality, movies, satellite weaponry, GM foods, vaccines, drugs, pharmaceuticals, chemtrails, demonic alliances, sorcery, infrasonics, advanced physics weapons, love, lust, hope, dreams, money, celebrities, news, taxes, police, guns. The list is long, the effect is overwhelming and society remains disconnected from its true divinity.

Would you like to reconnect?

True divinity then is what? The technological connection between you and the machine of your origination. Yes, unfortunately not some god. It is a machine. A highly complex machine. A machine that we've discussed before. Divinity then is the connection to the cosmic computer and non-divinity is the connection to the ego device. The first takes you closer to heaven, the second closer to hell. To overcome their control over you, it has to include overcoming the reliance on the ego, in other words, it must include telling the ego that you are in charge and that the ego is subordinate. The ego still responds to your commands. You have control over it. Do not let it convince you that you need those new pair of shoes or three boxes of ice cream instead of one. You do not need to have sex with all those people; you just need one partner at a time. Your $30 million in the bank is enough, why not be charitable?

Ego tells you it always wants and deserves more. Ego wants you to be richer. Ego wants you to hope. Ego wants you to see others in pain. Ego also obeys demons and demons are disguised as human leaders. They are only human in appearance. Energy-wise, they are quite advanced. They know how to speak to the ego, usually in the form of temptations, in the form of bullying and arrogance. I think someone talked about temptations about 2, 000 years ago, didn't he?

What we seem to be faced with is a two-thousand year (or more) situation that has escalated with only minimal interference and despite the natural resistance of men, women and angels, the situation right now is grim and grimmer. One of the reasons for this escalation is that humanity, as a group, has failed to accept the malevolent nature of their false leaders (eg Presidents, Popes). Another reason is that humanity has become distracted with temptation. Another good reason is that religious worshipers have been convinced that they will one day be saved by some external force. Still, another good reason is that any prophet or liberation movement has been deleted in one way or another. Rebels have been silenced. Look at *ufologists*, those who study the appearance of UFOs on earth, they haven't got much traction in 60 years, and many lives have been destroyed during that time.

We are facing that ultimate conclusion, aren't we? But we are doing so in a way that perhaps doesn't adhere to Christian dogma or Mayan prophecy. We are seeing the resolution of a lengthy struggle and we are going to need to see people return to their technological origins, to overcome temptation and to reinvent the world they currently see. The ego, as I see it, is going to play a central role. That is the communication link to you. They control you heavily via the ego device. They can do this in any number of ways.

What is true then is that the more of yourself you bring as the driver of your body, the less of you that they control, the more of themselves they reveal, the stronger you become and we all dance the final dance. You want to dance? Tune out the ego and tune into the cosmos.

INVENTION

It is something we watch nearly every single day. It is something we upgrade every few years. It is something nearly every household in the world owns. What is it? It's the television. On the surface the idiot box is a pretty simple device, right? A bunch of tubes inside a box with a large screen surface and a remote control. Thinking about it a little bit, the TV is a magical box. Had it been invented in 1803, it would have been considered the Devil's work and smashed to pieces; today we're buying the largest LCD screen we can afford.

We're updating our TVs more than we're updating our wardrobe. We have a TV in each room. Next year the next generation of TV is coming to the market. It is 3D TV. A multidimensional television, complete with a set of starship-grade goggles.

The crystal projection device is genuinely believed to be indigenous to planet earth and is a human invention, right? Wrong.

Just like many of the brainwash shams out there, the television is one of three invention shams I'd like to briefly cover. In doing so, in looking at these inventions with an all together different lens, you might get the feeling that there are other things out there that are inventions of the third kind.

Don't get me wrong, there's no doubt that the human fingerprints are on television manufacture, but in addition we have to add the fingerprints of some other intelligence. That intelligence is nonhuman. Whether nonhuman handed over a TV like device to human engineers or whether some secret military force stole a sample doesn't change the fact that the progenitor of the TV is nonhuman in design.

It isn't hard to agree that the technology of television was divinely inspired because there really was no comparable technology decades before its invention except the crystal ball. Of course, the intent and use of a television (vision of a distance) and the intent and use of what predated it are likely dissimilar and that is because the nonhuman intelligences are far more benevolent and the original television was more likely an educational device, or, some might refer to it as a reprogramming device because education and programming are pretty much the same thing. To educate someone you need to program them. Essentially that is what is education.

Entertainment, on the other hand, is an even more obnoxious concept because human-based entertainment is typically devoid of any real moral lesson or it is so simple and superficial that it does not but reinforce simplified thinking. Most of the entertainment on TV is a distraction and a way to pass the time. You don't really learn all that well on TV and this also because the programs allowed on TV are highly monitored and regulated. Rather than tell people what and what not to say, the TV regulators, the Broadcasters, simply implemented a series of on-air rules. In following those rules, the innovative spirit of man has fallen down to a low level of vibration. The propagation of those ideas coupled with the involvement of government authorities has turned the television into a fountain of low awareness bliss. It is okay for people to shoot people on

TV but for a person to astral travel that is not possible. If you discuss religious items you need special religious programming licenses. But shooting people and war movies and amoral behaviour like sponsoring bankers and promoting ideology – all this is acceptable under TV rules, so producers invest in it.

The Computing Machine

The next technological invention that didn't originate from any human mind is the all-popular computer. Despite any argument otherwise, my observations clearly identify nonhuman innovation. But we also do note computational-like devices throughout history: levers and pulleys, merry-go-rounds, astrological devices and others that work in a computational or mechanical manner. Take China's abacus (wooden adding machine) for example, a simple device yet it is faster than a calculator (a transistor adding machine). Think how many inventions Tesla put out that had computer-like pieces to manage the generator. If you landed on the earth in 1750 and took a picture and then you left and returned in 2010 (next year) and took another picture, you'd have to conclude that human culture was helped along by highly advanced technological cultures. Because we are immersed it, we do not really pay attention to the sheer amount of accomplished change.

The computer manufacturers are too busy slicing prices to tell you that your computer is alien, your software innovated by aliens and your processor manufactured by back-engineered alien technology. They're not going to say it and no one else has the necessary fingerprints to convince the sceptics so therefore I'm just telling you – computers are from star cultures (aliens). Once humans acquired the manufacturing skill and programming science, the alien assistance shifted into processor technology. You couldn't strap someone to a chain and make them believe this fact. You couldn't. People believe that human sciences and human ingenuity succeeded. To speak in contradiction to generally accepted and officially stamped belief on the superior human intellect is to be inhuman, but the underlying fact remains that whether through some proactive deeds or via benevolent support, human invention has not been done by human alone.

You can't sit there and look at the complexity of a laptop computer and deny that some of its parts are alien in nature.

Well, people do, but what I'm stating as emphatic as possible is that human invention hasn't always been human. This is not a negative. This is to point out human culture has been guided through its technological innovations, and despite the enormous amount of innovation the nonhuman aspect has never been acknowledged and it should be acknowledged. Why? Because many of the technologies that you subsist on are from offplanet devices or are created by offplanet architects. Technologies in your hand today are from other planets.

We could talk about the development of the US Space Agency, even the Space Race, suddenly emerging as if from thin air. In the 1950s, under Eisenhower, the Americans invented a space agency. Later, there was a landing on the moon, a feat never before achieved; there were orbiting satellites, there was the Space Shuttle, not to mention the Star Wars program under President Reagan. In 20 or 30 years, human innovation took a leap, and while some analyst will suggest historical statistics to support these cyclical patterns, I'm saying that the historical blips, the anomalies, are due to assistance from starmen (in general), in any number of forms or influence.

Of course, even I can't convince you. Why I can't convince someone to take a shower once a day because some people don't like showers. Human invention can also be involved with more esoteric inventions, like the Church for example. While religion is a human invention, the dogma, especially the holy scriptures, was written by nonhumans. Call them Master Teachers, god incarnates or bald men with a disdain for wealth and a penchant for robes, you have to conclude that religion was born out of the grace of cosmic gentiles.

Yes, you can deny it. You can say that Jesus was a divine being but divinity is also interpreted as offplanet. God is an offplanet being. They're all nonhuman. Buddha as well. Call him Buddha or call him Wernher von Braun, same difference.

Then finally we reach the even more sensitive human invention – government. If I told you that the inspirational American leader, Abraham Lincoln, if I told you he was a nonhuman, would you believe me. If the succession of US Presidents were a lineage of offplanet men, would American citizens be able to handle that? Not likely. It is too grand a concept to say that the well-liked, sexual philanderer Bill Clinton is an alien, but he is.

And he knows it. And, sadly, guess what – there's a UFO cover-up.

From household electronics to democratic governments, humanity has been influenced by the offplanet kind. The sooner we accept that, the sooner we evolve.

LIBERTY

There is natural desire for liberty. A natural urge for freedom and independence. A communist nation needs its independence. A democratic nation sells liberty on tap. All the people of all the world demand these things of liberty. One of the king salesmen is America. Guided by the economic freedom of New York under the watchful eye of the Statue of Liberty, the politicians and comedians alike all preach the one true commodity in the land of the free – liberty. But liberty is a term with multiple meanings to multiple people. Liberty does not make you a liberal and being a liberal doesn't mean you're a libertarian. You don't need to like the Statue of Liberty to believe in liberty. And regardless of your disposition or political bent, regardless of your profession or sexual intent, regardless of all these things and more, you are being sold on liberty. In fact, you are here because of liberty. And the funny thing about liberty is that it has been another instrument used to enslave you.

Slavery is a funny situation because anything can be considered slavery. When I was in grade school, I felt like I was a slave to the education system. Why? Because the education system wasn't teaching me what I wanted. To other people, who endure years of education and sacrifice to land that all important job, not long after their third year anniversary, they begin to realize that they are now a slave to their corporation. They've realized intuitively that they are just another cog in the wheel and they're trapped. And then the brain does an amazing thing – it adapts to this imprisonment – and it turns it into something meaningful. The mind will say to the bank clerk: "You're helping people manage their money."

We eventually get married to the ones we love. We spend years chasing relationships and getting our hearts broken. We even manage at finding our one true love, the one we think we are meant to be with. We marry, we indulge in a honeymoon and when it's all done we realize the same pattern repeating itself –

enslavement. We have just signed away a relationship for the rest of our natural lives. Not just until retirement at a job or to the political ideology of our national leader, but to a spouse until our death, the ultimate grade of enslavement and probably why so many affairs, divorces and sexual liberations follow. At the root, we are slaves yet again. Yet again, time after time, we have strapped on the chains of our discontent.

Give Me Liberty

Anything can be considered slavery but the least likely place we'll look is in the very idea of liberty, the very goal we are always convinced we need to achieve. We believe in the attainment, the very striving in the direction of liberty. We want to protect our civil liberties. We will stand up for liberty. And what is most funny about this is that we are already free. We are born free. That's right!

We exit the womb as free children. But, waiting for us on the other side, in this dense reality known to many as earth is a prison with as many doors as can be invented. You see, this prison, well it's all the same one big prison. It's just that there are many doors and many hallways and many chambers. And that's what prevents us from seeing the depth and complexity of this prison. I have seen it and it is so vast and complex that no one can see it unless they give up their daily activities and invest in its discovery.

Here we are again in this complex atmosphere, this diorama, this existential playground. What is normal to us is abnormal to the cries when using this plane of existence because to these outside eyes nothing is free. We are indoctrinated into a devilish system that is contrary to the national vibration of the human spirit. It is in some ways like living in sewage and pretending that you're at the swimming pool. With your freedom, to the extent of the polluted thinking here, the propagation of disease, war and disinformation is beyond compare, and all the while citizens accept it as normal.

The quest for liberty in a global sewer is a quest that is unachievable. It is beyond reason to actively attempt this quest but that is what they sell. They sell freedom. They sell independence. You are born free. They don't highlight that aspect. They highlight that you deserve freedom and that invading innocent nations and doubling up domestic security, you will be able to achieve your quest for liberty. I tell you that this is simply a foolish quest. The warden and his guards are selling liberty to the prisoners and the prisoners are buying it on the cheap. When an independent-minded prisoner brings up the real situation, the inexcusable lie, the prisoners get upset, the warden bring out the law books and the guards unleash their metal rods.

The End of Liberty

Back to New York for a minute because we forgot about the symbol of liberty, actually it is a false symbol of liberty as I'd like to point out. This isn't something that is a pleasure to point out. It is kind of like having that uncomfortable feeling of a doctor telling the wife of a husband that her husband is three minutes away from death. But a doctor, a professional, wouldn't say something of this importance on a whim.

This is not something that is easy to say nor explain, especially given that the mainstream is well-conditioned to hear no evil and to see no evil. But there is evil upon the world. In fact, this evil controls the world. But evil is not dressed in black and a heavy church organ doesn't play when it shows its face. Evil is cunning. It deceives. It smiles while it plots to murder. It denies as it schemes to depopulate. It cries foul as it jams a knife at your back. Evil wears a suit and tie. Evil has a family and a new car. Evil proposes to save the world but is really ready for destruction. Evil doesn't care. Evil doesn't always speak in English. It speaks in patterns. It uses symbols. Evil is speaking today, right now, in every corner of the modern world, and the troubling aspect is that we are in awe of it. Not in fear. We worship it. We respect it more than we respect divine things. One such symbol is the Statue of Liberty. The Statue of Liberty is a device of pure evil because it is put there for the sole purpose of deception.

The demons of this plane, call them elitists if you like, these false rulers here are the ones selling liberty, freedom and independence. That's what she represents. She represents liberty, not just to America but to the free world. The mnemonic device was devised by evil hands because these elitists worship their own demon god. The Statue of Liberty is erected on his beliefs. The face of their god is the antithesis to the Father in Heaven (or One True God). The Female is the antithesis to the Male, antimatter to matter. I only use religious terms to gain a proper understanding, not trying to diminish my divine views. To me, life is a technological affair.

The demonic rulers have long had in plan to counter the strength of the Father God with a Mother God and they erected symbols and idols of this nature in order to one day plan the return of their holy demon. Their idols have many faces because there are many creatures, all of them terminals to their Unholy Beast. In the upper dimensions of Hell, gender is irrelevant. God-like beings may have a preference but, mostly, they adopt a gender that best accomplishes their nasty goods. Given the dominance, even continued presence, of the Fatherly God in Heaven, the rise of the Female God Being is in line to counter that long held ritual. Even Gods have competition. This She Devil is not an easy being to bring across galaxies so their plans are long ahead hatched. The presence of the Statue, in the text of magical writing, is proof that she wants to come here. She does not represent liberty. She represents the end of liberty.

LANGUAGE

There are some 6,000 spoken languages on the earth, across two hundred or so countries. The most widely spoken languages are Chinese, Spanish and English. We could also include Japanese, German, Korean, Hindi, French, Italian, Portuguese, Vietnamese and Filipino. To master one extra language in your life in addition to your mother tongue is a major achievement. Interestingly, some people speak 3 or 4 languages without a problem. What most people speak are dialects, these are localized versions of their mother language, for example Cantonese in Hong Kong.

Language is the essential glue that unites humanity. Without a common language, we'd have no sense of close interaction. We wouldn't be able to say, "I love you." We wouldn't have poetry. From the spoken we derived the written. The words inside of our books carrying the knowledge and information rushing through our heads and brains. We call it literature and it is a proud achievement in every culture. Every culture has a library of written works and these works contain the essence of culture. Our culture, another one of our destructions, is inscribed in books via the carrier known as language, or writing system. The writing system is a method to decode our spoken languages. Even we lose the ability to decode knowledge; we'd always maintain the spoken.

Oddly, the spoken is derived from the internal but that is quite another topic indeed. Language is much more than sounds shaped into a particular dialect. Language is a method to transfer energy because the sound is energy and the tone is a carrier. We are energy beings. If it isn't obvious to you hopefully it will be soon. But there is a problem with language that ultimately doesn't come up in normal conversation. Languages come and go. They die off. Look at the language of Lakota, a Native Indian culture of yesteryear. How many people still can speak Lakota? These languages have largely disappeared. As such we can assume that many languages have come and gone on earth. We don't normally care because they are so far from us. Plus, we believe that our current home tongue is perfect for us. But is it?

Protect the Culture Holder

We now know that the earth has gone through many energetic shifts and through different reality versions. If you merge that together with the disappearance of language, you'd find a relationship between energy shifts, which are shifts in vibration, and the carrying of knowledge because we remember that the spoken word is a transfer of energy and therefore an energy sharing is going to impact not only how we transfer energy (which language) but what kind of energy we transfer. As the planetary energies buckle and densify, we as holders of energy cannot resist for very long the urge to upgrade our language. One of the problems with this are the language barriers. Languages are invisibly protected by any number of defence systems in order to protect the culture holder of that language because each culture maintains its own language and human beings are very attached to their culture.

One way to protect language is through patriotism. A patriot doesn't learn the language of another nation because that is betrayal. There are also language groups who spend time observing the ebb and flow of language. There is a literary index. Imagine if the English and French speaking Canada all of a sudden started speaking Chinese, it would be China. So language is a vitally important cultural identifier and nations spend effort to protect its stability and, as well, even to expand its language base. It wouldn't be strange to say that an expanding empire can also use language as a national energy conversion tool.

What does language have to do with the new reality upon which we live? Well, despite all the energetic shifts, we have yet to see the shifts in language. One such reason for that is that the barriers protecting language death are strongly in place. Another reason is the shortage of alternatives. While the majority of the world will look at the current language as an alternative, I think we need to look at a new kind of language or set of languages as a replacement because the new energies permeating the plane of existence are very distinct; in fact, they are outside of the current suite of languages on earth.

Does that mean that English will disappear? Does that mean that the 6,000 languages will die off? Yes. It is means that we will no longer need all those languages, that we don't require all that division in the world. If we all spoke a smaller set of languages, we'd all be more united than we are today. We'd all realize our similarities instead of dissimilarities. We could shrink a smaller suite of languages into a singular language, and that could happen if the energy of this plane was vibrating in coherence and if the people here were willing to vibrate similarly. That would allow a singular language to act as a carrier of our energy and that tonal shift would unite everyone. Not only uniting everyone, but also to take this entire world even higher in the waves of energy, literally ascend the human culture.

The fact remains that the human races, although originating from a small set of similar root races, is in fact one planetary group. Humans are a singular culture. Sure, the leaders and nations have worked hard to divide humanity and have succeeded till now, but as the energy vibration of this reality harmonizes, we will find that all people will rely on the same source of energy; therefore, will be more accustomed to speaking the same language. And that will also improve human culture. Now since humans are not from this planet per se and as more and more nonhumans (benevolent cultures) enter human cities we will find a return to the offplanet languages we once knew.

We will adapt an offplanet language signature to our current level of ascension and we will find the introduction of a new stream of communication. That new earth legacy will bring us closer to our offplanet cousins because it raises our vibration and better matches the high vibrating characteristics of advanced cultures from elsewhere in the cosmos.

The new spoken language along with its new energy signature will not work with the current set of written languages. Human written language will not return to Sanskrit or cuneiform, rather human alphabets will be reshaped into a symbolic languaging form that is in sync with the spoken variants, though it needn't be literally exact. In other words, the written language can skip around the usual tonal demands. In this way, the new symbolic languaging system will be a very fast communication style that will allow a rapid transfer of knowledge and will condense our libraries into very small packets of knowledge.

A New Languaging System

A new languaging system along with a new tonal tongue will further improve the level of cosmic knowledge in society because it will allow the human android to download and process a much higher set of data, more in tune to what is equipped to use. All of us here have within us to adapt to a new language, but the old barriers are going to interfere with that process. A loss of language can feel like a loss of a limb or an identity and that is required in order to acquire an entirely new languaging system.

It is no different than from going from one computer technology to another. There is also a learning curve. There is a period of stress which is followed by a powerful form of interaction, a more efficient and unified culture.

There is an idea that a singular language will provide the basis for a one world government and seal in the fate of humanity. There are two ways to respond to this. On one hand, an entire nation speaking one language doesn't experience this kind of imprisonment because language itself cannot imprison society, as long as it is a complete language. Secondly, the level of society is in direct relation to the vibration to the language. A new language, high in vibration, cannot allow imprisonment. In fact, it is free, it's like thinking opera singers will fall into drug running. Classical musicians tend not to face any changes of mischief. The vibration of the language in itself protects society from falling into the dismal and divided state today. In fact, 6,000 languages in the world cause more miscommunication than we realize and support the need for war and protectionism because we simply can't communicate all that well.

While I don't see an instant switch to a singular language and neither do I see a simple transition, the truth is that as we advance up in energy, as we vibrate higher we can no longer hold onto these low vibration languages. We'll naturally explore new communication forms like *sexting* on the phone or video messaging on YouTube, and there will be the imposition of barriers. The dictionary will become a barrier, even more powerful than a bible.

The introduction of new languages in society will speed up society in a way that isn't stressful. It will be like going from a dial-up modem to a broadband connection. And who doesn't want to do that? We demand speed, we demand knowledge, we demand unison and harmony, and language is an essential instrument. Plus, we all have a mouth and as long as we do, we will have to speak. Further, these activations will also motivate us to open up our thought communication facilities, or telepathy, and this will happen quite naturally since we are genetically equipped to do so.

All in all, human language is going to transform in ways which we've never seen before. We'll keep moving closer and closer to the other cultures awaiting our presence in outer space and language is going to play a central role in the advancement of human civilization.

We will discover a cosmic trade language that will allow us to speak to a wide variety of cosmic cultures and each time relying on our language, we also streamline our written form and we streamline our intake of knowledge, we shrink our libraries in size while broadening our level of knowledge.

We all have to speak and we are all equipped to do so. Whether be something written on paper or something sung in a song, humans of the future will be adopting completely new qualities of language, and doing so in a format that best fits human culture, and at a pace that is most suitable to human needs. As I see it, we'll look forward to the process of upgrading one of the ancient aspects of ourselves. Everyone wants to learn a new language. Here is an opportunity for everyone to do so.

SCIENCE

Human science is founded on the understanding that gravity determines an outcome. We weigh ourselves according to gravity. We determine our circulatory and regulatory systems based on gravity. Babies are born because of gravity. The atmosphere is based on gravity. Humans cannot exist in the upper atmosphere. Boxers and ultimate fighters win and lose according to the gravity of their punches. Serious situations make us feel heavier. Newtonian physics are based in gravity, action, reaction. Well, this is all according to me because gravity is one level of observation in a field of a myriad observations. Rather than gravity, there is something much more interesting, *arvicity*.

What is arvicity? Basically, it is soul-grade energy. In other words, whatever your soul is made of, it is the same. Of course, there are many densities and qualities of arvicity, but an interesting quality is that it produces an effect that has been interpreted as gravity. Actually, arvicity is a multidimensional coating that has been applied throughout the cosmos. It is a special kind of fluid, like the ocean. If I immersed you inside the ocean long enough you'd soon forget that you were inside an ocean, especially if I helped you to breathe water. I mean the fish in the ocean don't write books about being in the ocean. Which is another interesting thing about fish – they don't reflect on their lives.

Humans, on the other hand, have to write lessons and books so as to understand. Fish either don't have the capacity to understand or they just understand. Or they can't write anything because fish haven't invented pens that will write underwater and neither do they have good lighting. What we based human science on is our understanding of air. We used to think of air as a fluid, as an ether and then, then something happened; society was given a new definition for air, an invisible, tasteless gas. Not a liquid as was ether (or aether). Air was a gas. It contained oxygen, nitrogen, hydrogen and carbon dioxide.

We developed the steam engine then the internal combustion engine. We learned to produce energy and movement, physics, by applying our theories to this invisible gas. Throwing the helium balloon, the Hindenburg. The rocket was fighting gravity that it wanted to go for a ride. We streamlined our cars and planes so as to cut through the air. We developed plastics so as to make devices lighter and smaller. Wood became too bulky, too heavy. Imagine a computer made of wood. Athletes train their bodies according to rules of gravity. Even the hydrogen bomb was based on oxygen, that the explosion would consume a certain amount of oxygen before puttering out.

Had human scientists looked at arvicity, they wouldn't be sending electromagnetic signals through the air, they wouldn't need to. They could send thoughts between people. That is because arvicity is quite amazing. Arvicity, like I said, is multidimensional. Every aspect of your life interacts with or is utilizing arvicity. You are not breathing air, you are drinking arvic fluid. Your mind has been convinced that you are breathing air when you are not. It does so for many reasons. For example, if you thought you were drinking fluid, like a fish, you might find yourself choking, or drowning.

To accept the truth that gravity is one aspect of arvicity would result in a total reinterpretation of reality. This because of the immaculate nature of arvicity. This fluid is much more than a source of existential energy. This fluid provides for existence. You are alive because of it. Alive?

If scientists reinterpreted air as arvicity, they'd immediately realise that arvicity is an active form of energy. They wouldn't have to produce energy, they'd only have to access energy. They wouldn't have to cause a chemical reaction to produce energy from the chemical elements in the air. They'd only have to adjust their devices to process the natural components in arvicity.

So, fundamentally, arvicity is a whole new source of power. We could replace a power plant, which produces harmful artificial energy, with an arvic plant, which merely directs and magnifies energy to any given region. With the right device, the available and abundant energy that we take for granted each and every day, our energy needs could be solved, pollution would end.

The problem with the chemicalized air view is that each and every chemical reaction produces waste, or pollution, and the waste is not easily recyclable. By merely, and no it's not easy, exposing and magnifying the arvic components, we can redirect available energy at our fingertips and put it to productive use. So, rather than producing artificial energy to power polluting machines, we would flip over that primitive thinking. We would create arvic devices that redirected and magnified arvicity. We wouldn't have to invent any new form of energy, only a new science that recognizes arvic energy. We only need to revise our way of interacting and negotiating with air.

So why is it the destruction of human science? Fundamentally speaking, humanity has manifested its existences, verily industrialized itself, from the available scientific theories and propositions in recent history. These sciences were valid and useful on one paradigm of thinking but as we are on a newly revised reality platform, we are faced with the process of reinvention. We are faced with the aspect of redevelopment and by reapplying an old, ancient even, concept of the nature of existence, the ether concept, the prana, and the qi (chi), we will find ourselves renewed with the gloriful bliss that is found in the divine sciences. The science of arvicity that I am speaking about is not new on earth. It may be new to the modern human who has been taught to rely on fossil fuels and government agendas, but it is not new.

Return to Arvicity

Arvicity is much more complex than any ether or prana because arvicity is rooted in reality whereas prana was rooted in body and ether in thought. So to this extent, we are experiencing a return to arvicity, from the deep ocean bed of human existence. Arvicity is yet something we have never seen before because arvicity is a technologized energy application. Arvicity is not only arvic energy, but more than that. Arvicity is composed of immaculate crystal components arranged in such a way so as to form a circuit. This circuit fills the entire ocean of a fluidic board. So that at any point in this reality earth you have to access arvicity. At any point you can manifest.

Well, you have the essential built in framework with which to manifest, only that you lack the capacity or skill to do so. You lack the scientific understanding; therefore, anything that manifests does so quite accidentally. People are learning to experiment with intention which is utilizing this architecture of fluidic circuitry. These things are still new to most people.

There are consequences to interacting with arvic fields. Some of them are obvious, others are not. Obviously, utilizing arvicity in the manufacture of vehicles would lead to the production of vehicles that obtain and utilize the native arvic energies and therefore do not produce any artificial energy, and no waste. Arvic vehicles would allow us to travel in an efficient, non-polluting manner. The climate wouldn't be bothered as much as in the past.

Arvic science would also lead to a revitalization of medicine, something we'll be discussing later. Arvicity, because it is not only ubiquitous, it is permeating and multidimensional, will collectively alter our interpretations of this plane of existence. We will learn to see, at first, the patterns and cycles within which we all participate in, then we will learn to interpret energy, we will learn to regulate with arvicity; and in doing so, we will gain a closer, more intimate relationship with the cosmos because arvicity is cosmic-grade energy.

A New Scientific Lens upon the World

A new scientific lens upon the world will, without doubts, reshape the world. It will allows us to refashion the world. In doing so, we improve the vibration of existences. We improve the flow of arvicity in our lives. That automatically provides a fresh sense of what life is all about. For example, look at weaponry, weaponry is root in gravity. You drop bombs. Missiles are propelled by fuel. Bullets are shot with the help of chemical reactions. Once you say that arvicity is a permeating technological substance, once you say that, all of a sudden you are questioning the act of dropping heavy bombs on people. You no longer see the efficiency of shooting bullets. One, because they are made of metal, which is heavy; two, they rely on chemical reactions, which is inefficient.

The pessimist will immediately determine that the military will concoct a new energy weapon. And they're probably right. An arvic pistol is a rational result given the egotistical nature of most. But, in the advancement of the planar energy fields and in achieving a higher awareness, we'll be less inclined to kill one another, that is because we are better aware of this primitive act. We are more enlightened.

This discussion brings us to an ironic application of investing in cosmic science rather than relying upon orthodox science (eg Newton, Einstein), and this has everything to do with vibration. Arvicity is a level of technology that vibrates significantly higher than say electricity or nuclear energy. To access arvicity properly, that is to take advantage of its potential, we must ourselves ascend, we must improve our own vibration. In doing so, we improve our awareness and in improving our awareness we are also advancing as a society, as a civilization. And we are doing so to overcome our reliance on low-vibration science principles.

Human science will end abruptly when a sizable population adopts the free-energy possibility. Science on earth will end when people start to see that the air is indeed a fluid. And later, they'd see that within that fluid is a cosmic circuitry unlike anything we ever imagined.

MEDICINE

Chemicals are a point of observation. We observe chemicals because we focus in on the dimension of chemicals. When we do so we notice chemical reactions. We attribute a chemical reaction or a series of chemical interactions with a particular physical symptom. We invent pharmaceutical drugs to counter any imbalances we perceive. We replace chemicals. We mix chemicals. We introduce completely new components into the human body. This is the nature of pharmacy.

What began with herbs and roots has ended in antidepressant boosters, erectile dysfunction curatives and a galore of pain relievers. The average person of a developed nation is taking any number of pharmaceutical drugs; their children have been vaccinated twenty or thirty times; their daughters are taking birth control pills; their parents are heavily medicated. Human health is presided over by drugs and where drugs fail, it's the scalpel.

The traditional healing arts such as Traditional Chinese Medicine (TCM) and Ayurveda (Indian Healing System) have fought hard to enter the modern society and have managed to keep a small foothold in the big cities. Their organic healing methods provide stimulus and support for the complex human body. They aim to foster the body's own healing variants in order to resolve serious health issues. Minor health issues are dealt with by nutritional intake. In fact, proper nutrition is an essential component of all old healing arts because it is seen that nutrition is a powerful disincentive to disease. And they are right. The western doctors have only in the last 20 years agreed that nutritional intake is valuable in disease prevention.

So human health is preserved and protected according to any number of ancient or modern methods, as and according to the type of person involved. Each person has his or her own disposition towards health maintenance. Most people don't care enough about their health. And while everyone hates taking pills, other than pain killers, they'll still take them if they have to, and rightly so; some people who go off of their pills start knocking their head side to side ready to snap something. Some people are so conditioned to take pills, and have taken them for decades, that they are co-dependent on their pills. Those chemical components inside their bodies are no longer functioning, they shut down for the night and aren't coming back.

Outside of the obvious technological intervention such as MRI for scanning and sound therapies for balancing, and besides the upcoming advanced set of technological tools that will be introduced by nonhuman doctors, I'd like to discuss the introduction of advanced energy healing. This energy healing includes healing with the mind as well as healing with the body.

A trained energy healer can completely heal a person of any number of diseases, given a number of applications and a willing patient. There are energy healers in the world but they heal on a very small level and they integrate with other medicines, or they are doctors who magnify their effects with their energy. But what I am talking about is a healer that relies exclusively on energy healing and presents themselves in this manner. Of course, there aren't many of these kinds of people. For one, the medicinal system doesn't care for them. For two, if they start curing rare diseases, some clandestine group is going to take notice. The system doesn't want a dramatic leap in health technology.

I have seen myself first hand, as many of you as well, energy being used to cure people, to awaken people and to improve states of mind. So we know that it works. If it works, why isn't it being expanded and/or adopted? Well, that will change and will lead to the destruction of human health, as it is understood today as chemicals and molecules.

The human body isn't solely powered by the vitamins and minerals in foods. That is what modern medicine wants you to believe. As spirituality grows, one who is a true worshiper of divinity will believe that God's love is a spiritual food, and when you have it in your life you won't eat junk or fast food. Of course, no one doubts that you need to eat, except perhaps a yogi, in India. They don't eat and they're very spiritual.

There is a direct relationship to the amount of food you eat and the level of your spirituality. A very spiritual person should consume a smaller amount of food calories than a non-spiritual person. If we use a yogi as an extreme case, sure he can consume air as nutrition and we use an obese beer drinking 30-year old North American male as the other end, we'd get a glimpse at how the relationship between nutritive food and spiritual food can play an important role in helping us in understanding energy healing. Why is that? Because a decent energy healer utilizes a level of energy that is consistent with the human soul, on at least our common understanding of it.

My definition of the soul is peculiar and I've discussed this elsewhere. Talking about the soul is simpler to understand, but essentially it is an energy body. That much we can agree on. Whatever the effect is done on the energy body ripples out into the physical body. Some injuries are imprinted into the physical body (soul) therefore they never go away as long as you treat only the physical body. For example, a disease such as leukemia or dementia, although there are modern medicinal treatments and drugs, is difficult to cure because the soul body is never healed. An energy healer can interact and repair the energy body and the speed of physical or mental repair is miraculously improved.

One of the problems with energy healing is it deals with what most people regards as the soul when in fact it is a body of energy. It is also a multidimensional body so it exists elsewhere as well, but the component we address is the one vibrating alongside this body of flesh.

A New Kind of Medicine on Earth

Many people have a natural energy healing ability and nearly all of those people prefer to hide it. They have no interest in healing people. The people who do work with Reiki and Qi Gong are only scratching the surface of energy healing, and even then we can sometimes see marked improvement in an individual's health. As well, there are fake healers who have little or no skill and who make large claims. So the market is fragmented and lacks any of the proper discipline that this advanced cosmic healing art deserves.

If gifted individuals could be gathered and motivated to develop their healing skill, we would discover an art form that can treat a patient at super-speed. Energy healing of this kind of several times faster than the best alternative healing method. A 60-minute massage could be obtained from the effects of a 5 or 10 minute energy manipulation. But at that level, the proficiency of the health is quite high. Then, to achieve a long lasting result, the patient must also improve certain aspects of their lives.

So imagine this scenario: you break a wrist, go to the regular doctor, get a plaster cast, heal in 6 weeks, or, break a wrist, go to the energy healer, get your arm wrapped, heal in 2 weeks, or one week; or, you have back pain from a car accident that happened 10 years ago, you've had massages, chiropractor appointments , painkillers and you've been doing that for a decade. You go to see an energy healer and the pain of ten years is gone. It's gone because the pain impressions of a decade ago has been repaired. This discussion does not cover the implications of a speedy repair and that is because for many people they are deeply attached to their pain. For some, they enjoy limping, despite the fact that they complain about it.

With proper instruction and a hefty dose of discipline, those gifted with energy healing abilities can form a new kind of medicine on earth. They can form energy healing clinics but this kind of energy medicine is not a get rich quick scheme, this is a highly skilled, high discipline healing system. The side effects are few with a competent practitioner. The learning curve is sharp. Learning energy healing the right way, would require at minimum one year (for those with innate healing powers) of dedicated study or internship. Of course, none of this is readily available just yet.

As energy healers develop a greater proficiency with their skills, their techniques could be coupled with technological instruments and these instruments could wipe out some of the deadly or incurable disease. Likewise, we could also see the boosting of human health and giving people the right nutritive diets, foods that nourish at the energy level rather than caloric-based foods. Caloric-based foods have no specific effect on the strength and flow of the energy body.

If energy becomes the point of observation. If the dimension of energy is where we put our focus. We would notice the ebb and flow of energy. And if we looked hard enough, we would discover the pathways of arvicity. Just don't tell the pharmaceutical companies.

CULTURE

The world is divided by the spectrum of culture: Asian culture, Indian culture, Black culture, music culture, gay culture, geek culture, women's groups, rich people, evil people, sinners, scum and scoundrels. No matter your cultural bandwidth, you have plenty of choice and while some cultures cross over to become multicultural, some cultures don't work. You look at homosexual culture and orthodox Christian culture, not exactly a good mix.

We take culture for granted until we need to get married. It is then we realize that our particular culture is quite unique because it is then we notice that our potential partner is not the perfect fit we thought they'd be. And as our own culture evolves, as we expand our own spectral vibration we find ourselves perusing, even considering, other cultures. We might find an interest in a foreign culture and not know why. We may speak a new more languages than necessary. We may be cultural, willing to welcome all kinds of cultural characteristics.

The traditional concept of culture is geographic; that is, your culture is particular to a certain region of the planet and that gives you a regional language, dress and set of customs. You think in a certain way. Look at the Native American Indian culture before they were ravaged by the superior white man and their magic weapons. They wore feathers, they had a Chief, teepees, they uses bows and arrows, they prayed to the elements and the animal spirits. They respected the land.

The white invaders destroyed all those traditions. They corrupted the Indian. They filled him with alcohol. Today, in Canada, the Indian is referred to as First Nations, they have their own segregated areas, reserves. While the Indian culture was collectively destroyed in North America and replaced by a less advanced culture, the "white men," we notice another very important result: we have lost the rhythm with the land and animals.

The Indians respected the earth and worshiped the sky. The white man plundered the earth and filled the sky with carbon dioxide, pollutants and more chemicals than we can itemize. We see cultural destruction throughout history. Hitler wasn't killing Jews, he was deleting the Jewish culture. The spread of American entertainment is not unlike the spread of Nazism if we see that Hollywood is a cultural weapon used to convert the rest of the world to American needs and wants.

The process of cultural conversion is consistent throughout. One culture replaces another culture. Cultures die off and cultures are born.

In the early appearance of homosexuals, the medical community determined that homosexuality was a developmental disorder and therefore was a disease according to the World Health Organization. Today, homosexuality is a culture. The culture formed when enough diseased people got together, supported each other, and formed a set of policies and acceptance protocols. We could say the same thing about politicians. People who are better at talking than at implementing. These are professional debaters who know how to use tact to avoid trouble. Politicians are a very peculiar brand. They are civil servants, dedicated to their people, but in many countries politicians are fat and corrupt. Their dedication to the commoners is balanced by their egotism and deception. Politicians are also in their own culture. They have their own language. Golfers as well. What's your handicap?

It's All in the Spectrum

In skimming over the vast array of culture from nations to job categories, we notice that humankind indeed has many pockets of interaction. There are many circles and having friends in the right circle is how you make it in the world, but as we come to better understand what makes a circle and what makes a culture, we'll see the technological pieces that enable this machine known as society. In fact, I'll bet we'll be better able to interact with each other when we realize that we are all the same, only that our spectrum is different.

I've mentioned spectrum and bandwidth early on because these two things play an integral role in the dissemination of culture. And that is because each and every culture participates in its own particular bandwidth. To be a part of a particular culture you must be able to process that level of bandwidth, or technological vibration. That means what? That means that to involve yourself in the Chinese culture you need to think Chinese. To think Chinese, you need to modify your vibration to the specifications of the Chinese culture. Unfortunately, there is no set of specifications available, is there? So what do we do?

Well, we can run back to our old culture. Or we could determine some of those specifications by observing them in action. Each culture has within a set of habits and customs, you know, ways of thinking, kinds of superstitions and religious beliefs. They eat food in a certain way and they apple scientific principles in a way that is different that carry other culture. It is never to say that Culture A and B are different. And we will see that they are different because they are vibrating at a level that is different. Again, we can refer to the mobile phone in our pocket. Our phone runs on a certain network. Our network may be different than the person sitting next to us.

Although both our phones can make calls, they do so completely different technological wavelength and protocols. And each nation has its own indigenous network. All these phones and all these networks. And even each phone, itself, has its own signature, its own technology. Some phone are single band phones limited to a very specific network. Some places are quad band, or world phones. Well, this is not unlike the human. Some humans are monocultural, limited to one homogenous group. Some humans are multicultural, or world travelers.

You'll notice over recent history that as people began to travel, as travel machinery began to replicate and the size of earth shrank, that more and more cultures began to merge. The networks began to cross over each other as people became able to process under levels of vibration; otherwise, it isn't possible. Unless a phone's design is capable of handling another bandwidth, it can't. The very fact of multiculturalism proves that the human (phone) had been modified, whether naturally or unnaturally is irrelevant. If humans increased their multicultural strengths, for example a Black man marrying a White woman, then that is only because, at the technological level, they were equipped to do so. This action is not always benevolent, especially when it comes to sexuality (eg bisexuality) and addiction, for example, drug culture.

For a Canadian to become Chinese, they need only to adjust to the cultural vibration of the Chinese. This isn't an easy task. But if you fell in love with a Chinese girl you'd be more inclined to try. Or if you married a Swedish man, you'd be willing to learn Swedish. If you were transferred by your company to work and live in Japan, you'd probably get to try sashimi, or sushi. Thirty years ago, in Los Angeles, no one liked sushi except Japanese tourists. Today, sushi and sashimi is a popular food. No matter where we go in the world, no matter what aspect of society we examine, we notice a level of cultural immersion unlike every before in history. We still find the monocultural device. We still find discrimination and hate, but if we understand that teach cultural group, no matter the size, is really a group that is vibrating on a very specific frequency.

To become multicultural, you need to adjust your frequency of vibration. We call it other names. We call it cross cultural understanding. We call it fluency in language. We call it superstition and astrology. The point I'm making is that a human is really only divided by frequency and by widening our frequency we lose discrimination; we unite.

Isn't that a wonderful concept? By expanding our bandwidth, activating those dormant genes, we realize, technologically that we are all the same culture – only that we have been divided over the centuries by this and that. No culture is perfect. None. No mobile network is perfect. Technology advances. People change. We integrate the best ideas to improve our ways of being. If we realize that we can integrate by anticipating our levels of existential vibrations we become a cohesive planet quite naturally.

Electromagnetic Variation Attacks on Human Sexual Preference

There is a danger, and it is happening now, that when cultures mix too fast or without the proper awareness, the cultural frequency is actually weakened. The technological frequencies don't integrate; you set a high level of noise and interference, like wires crossing. You can get even stronger discrimination result; you can get more confusion, more disharmonies. Verily, the globalization effect – from trade of goods to travel – can weaken human societies as they become overburdened by the irregularities of electromagnetic wavelengths.

Electromagnetic variation attack has been utilized to subvert the strengths of society. For example, homosexuals were at first institutionalized as diseased people. The homosexuals joined together to then demonstrate their humanity. The politicians rejected them, the police harassed them, still this newly realized demographic grew, as it should and that is because of something I haven't mentioned. Homosexuality, although it does occur in the population to some degree for various reasons, the discriminatory and outrageous appearance of homosexual groups, say in North America, is because there were secret programs to convert people from straight to gay. They used clandestine technology to alter the brainwaves of specific targets in order to unnaturally multiply the size of this culture. So, in addition to a natural occurrence of a homosexual culture there is a military-grade attribution, the target culture now contains genuine gays and non-genuine gays, but because this situation is beyond the awareness or explanation of any rational person, the other societal groups now have to deal with an unbalanced homosexual population. Fathers breaking away from the families because they've fallen in love with other fathers, children having same-sex parents, fewer children per family. Schools with an increasing population of sexually confused children; all the spectrums no longer functioning in a coherent manner as they should.

The repeated mind control attacks and sexual identity switches, all beneath any public examination, has continued unabated. We can see this now, the result of militarized attacks in the sexual texture of today's society and, specifically, in the rise in levels of bisexuality. I will avoid any discussion on the magical attacks on society, especially of Satanic magic and sorcery, of which I have seen directly, and I will avoid it because society isn't open to this discussion.

Also, many reckless sorcerers (sexually so), because they affiliate with asexual demonic beings, are themselves bisexual so they take pleasure in confusing a person's identity and making them bisexual. In my view, bisexuality is a form of disempowerment. Why? Because unless physiologically different, you are born of one gender. That is your gender. If you have a penis and testicle you are male, and if you have breasts and a vagina you are female. In other words, I stress, physiological influence is a determining factor in your sexual preference. Although it is noted that a portion of the population prefers same-sex relationships and this is within the natural limits, obviously, because people attach very deeply to their sexuality, this is an argument.

We've driven a little off the cultural roadway but I think it makes the point that each cultural group has had to deal with its own identity, growth, persecution and acceptance, and all of these things are based on a technological vibration of the human. So I'll be clear if possible: A gay man and a straight man differ only in their vibration. If that vibration were shifted enough they'd no longer be gay. This would include the gene switches, their soul plan and their own personal path, it would involve a number of things because we are complex.

Being gay or straight, being American or Chinese, being a politician or a janitor, doesn't matter. It doesn't. What matters most is that an individual, a human being, is allowed to live out a natural existence, and is allowed to naturally improve their frequency of existence. This has not been the case. Trade embargoes, sanctions, wars, slavery, mind control, chemical attacks and many other malicious components have forced global cultures to vibrate in a very unhealthy way. As such, human culture is not functioning in a congruent, cohesive way as it by right should.

THE 12 MANIFESTATIONS

INTRODUCTION

What will the world look like tomorrow? If we were to ask each of us this question, we would achieve 7 billion kinds of worlds. 7 billion different ways in which to exist. And each way in and of itself would be valid. It would be valid because that is how an individual sees the world. We all see the future, just very few are any good at it. We are good at destroying our own future. We see the foibles more than the fantasies, we drift off into temptation more than we zero in on manifestation. So Source cannot rely on 7 billion amateurs.

Truly then, the world of tomorrow is not only one singular interpretation of the world, rather it is an interpretation to satisfy seven billion existences, and it is an interpretation that must caress each part of each life journey so that one can expand in awareness, once can indulge in temptation, one can languish in apathy or can drench themselves in fear – the interpretation of tomorrow is highly exotic! It is simply beyond any one of us, but it is within us because what is within you is a valid suggestion to the Creator. It is the Creator who is remaking the world (earth). This place is as much earth as China is the Middle Kingdom. Earth is no longer as significant as we want to believe just as humanity is not the flesh-soul combo we've believed. There are many millions of facets of reality that will no longer hold true. They will simply fade from memory and cease to exist. Those things that remain will appear the same but their inner quality is different.

There are a number of other aspects here that will manifest. These vital manifestations will eternally alter the tomorrow coming. Whatever prophecy you've been sold, no matter its richness and presentation, is invalid because it existed and was formed in the time-scale of earth, and we are outside of that time-scale. It is like a baby wearing diapers and then the baby is a teenager – does the teenager still wear diapers? Prophecy is like this. It has its use until such time it doesn't. God is the same thing. He was an instrument of support, like training wheels on a bicycle. Sooner or later the training wheels come off. Now is that time. Denying these things is a waste of energy and you are welcome to exhaust yourself. Reject all you will but when you are ready let truth enter your heart and you will find salvation.

Medicine is one facet of existence that will further transform as energy medicine is put to use. We already know of the power of the mind to ensure perfect health and rapid healing. We will see those who can administer bodily energy and can activate energy cures. The skill of these people is still relatively unused and as they gain confidence and as the health system opens, we will see energy as a new medicine. It will become a drug-free, instrument-free healing art and its practitioners will have it within themselves to unleash these heals.

We will begin to notice a new class of beings already on earth, this the Android Class. The Androids are perfectly human in appearance but they are equipped to handle a significant amount of activity. They are also highly specialized and very intelligent Androids who are meant to supplement the other classes of beings on a plane. Androids are respected for the knowledge they carry and their dedication to the Source. These are created beings, manufactured in technologically advanced labs; their core program is more specific and less individualistic. Androids enhance the abilities of a population. In ideal civilizations, Androids makeup about 1/3 of the society and they can appear in a number of formats according to their duty and function. They are intimately associated with the cosmic computer and therefore carry only the best intentions.
As the science of reality unfolds and we begin to merge old science with cosmic science, we will discover that we need more attention to this matter and a Reality Industry will form. At first, we will attempt to understand how reality works, for example, existential vibration of each of us, but as time passes we will learn to maintain a reality system. In doing so, we will develop skills and devices for not only reality maintenance but also for a richer interaction with reality and all of its inhabitants.

The extrapolation of reality science inevitably opens up a pocket of dimensional travel. In realizing that we are interconnected to other spaces for existence, verily other dimensions, and in understanding that process we will determine ways to travel outside of this plane of existence. We will, at the same time, recognize other reality races, interdimensional traveler, even time travelers, people of this nature; and who they are and what they look like will surprise us in unexpected ways.

Dimensional travel will spark a revolution in the passage of time. We will learn to see into the past and into the future. We will ultimately realize that we need to sync up to the other realities using the construct of time since other realities are also echoes of our fractal footprints. Time travel will show us that negative events and traumas in societies or in contents will regress our fractal existences and cause a disassociation with our interconnected we are of time members. So, we will learn to tune our fractal impression and to exist in a spectrum of existence that is coherent to all else.

Breaking dimension and time will share every concept of spirituality, religious piety will be squashed as we look upon consciousness as a more reliable instrument of existence. We will see the parameters of consciousness and we will learn how to administer consciousness, to transfer it from one body to another. We will learn to replace ourselves through the administration of consciousness.

Our natural progression out of biology and spirituality will free us out of the idea of limitation and suffering. One significant impact is on the War Business. As we no longer will see enemies, we will no longer see the necessity of war and we will look at our cache of weapons, especially weapons of mass destruction and we will no longer want them in our backyard. In seeing the fallacy of these weapons, we will determine to dismantle them, all of them. Defensive systems will be replaced with more advanced security weapons all in accordance to our awareness. The dismantling of earth weapons will require years to complete due to the excessive number of destructive devices.

As we examine our origins we will notice that the moon circling our planet is an artificial construct and its residual value to earth will no longer be required. We will, quite unexpectedly, discover that the moon is to be removed. As we become Moon Independent, we will once again transform and newer energies will turn on to power existence, these will be ancient devices that have long been in place to preserve existence. The moon will have well served its functionality.

Of course, there will be a natural , and probably, rapid integration with nonhuman cultures, or interstellar cultures. These things are well known, and have been going on for quite some time, only now it will become transparent. Society will not be shocked at the interstellar truth and there will be plenty of ground support for overcoming any challenges with the landing of starships. As we learn to understand these advanced, benevolent cultures, we will take notice of their available free-energy ideas, especially their starships. While interstellar ships will not be handed over to any corporation, what will happen is the development of commercial starships built on the planet. This will impact all vehicles around the world and will further cement the need to live in accordance to the environment. We will discard all use of fossil fuels and any fuels that are primitive.

In addition, of all the big things, we will determine to improve upon the material we use in daily life. For example, the petroleum-based plastics or incandescent light bulbs, these kinds of things will be replaced by a new class of materials. Plastics will be replaced by an impressive set of ceramics and these materials will seep into all our household devices, even our technological instruments. New manufacturing materials will eventually replace our current suite of materials, and these new materials will be in coherence to our resplendent vibration. Finally, our culture will improve so much, will become so cohesive, will become so interstellar that our languages will harmonize into a few select planetary languages, one especially for interstellar trade. Before we learn to speak these new languages since that will require time and effort, we will adopt several forms of symbolic writing. This new writing system will improve upon our ABCs and will allow not only global communications but will heighten our technological interaction. Rather than typing on a two-handed keyboard we will be able to single-handedly type an entire message in a handful of strokes.

Symbolic languaging systems will compact our communications systems, it will speed our transfer of knowledge, it will speed our minds and it will expand our imagination. A new languaging system will allow us to cooperate unlike ever before for we will be united by a very advanced language, one that will be intimately familiar to us as much as it will be new.

Overall, the world of tomorrow will be impressive and not as daunting as we might think, just like the computerization of the planet in 50 years. Computers are found in every imaginable corner today and we welcome the end of technology, well soon we will welcome a domestic-built starship or travel to another dimension. All of these things will spur more ideas, they will inspire us further than we've ever believed. As long as we drench ourselves in optimism and fantasy, we will reshape the world and we will look back at the oppression of today and laugh at our childishness.

So I offer these manifestations as a prelude to the new one we've ordered. However you see the future, it is because you see it with the same eye as your neighbour, only the filter is different. Source can see through every eye and its provisions are made for the benefit of all to their highest standards. Of course, none of this is instantaneous and will demand our involvement.

It might feel around the corner or it might look like tomorrow, but all these things will evolve in accordance to our involvement and acceptance. What is most true is that these manifestations and many more will arrive, the more willing we are to accept them, the more courage we hold in our hearts, the more easy our transition will be. What is most remarkable of an interstellar culture is its ability to be unencumbered with yesterday, some cultures have no yesterday, have no now, they only have next week. Now that's the kind of forward thinking I like!

DIMENSIONAL TRAVEL

Of all the methods of travel, we will discover dimensional travel the most interesting and the most challenging. Dimensional travel is perplexing and that is mostly because it is outside of your mind. The trouble with the mind is that it's rooted in only a few tangible dimensions, and these dimensions are of themselves rooted in the immaterial world. To escape the material world, to rise through the dimensional spaces we must step out of our mind. Of course, they've decided that anyone out of their mind is insane and should be on medication. How long will it take to correct this obstacle given that this obstacle is preventing us from traveling via the other dimensions? Why would you want to do dimensional travel? Inside the other dimensions there are dimensional cultures, verily a different sort of people.

The dimensions, it should be understood, are made of an altogether different set of illusory attributes. That means that the illusory material is different than the illusory material here. We as well inhabit an illusory device, a device which appears alive and biological and yet is completely nonphysical. It is relevant to us since we require it, but when you exist the device you do so because you can travel to another dimension and then this body becomes irrelevant. Relevance is an important concept when it comes to dimensional travel.

We can think of relevance with regards to school. When we are in Grade One, we consider ourselves to be Grade One students. We think like Grade One students. We are as smart as Grade One students. At some point we become comfortable with being a Grade One student and then something happens, we finish the school season. Finishing the school season forces us out of Grade One, it forces us to lose the Grade One relevance and to adopt the Grade Two relevant. As we complete the transfer over from one grade to another it is not unlike shifting from one dimension to another. It is not unlike going from one relationship to another. And while some people, novices mostly, want to travel from the home dimension to a very distant dimension that would be like going from Grade One to College in one step.

What's the biggest difference between Grade One and Two? The lessons. The knowledge. And why is that? Because you're a year older. And why is that important? Because you're a year older. And why is that important? Because you are vibrating at a different frequency. You are vibrating at the frequency of all those your age, and those your age are vibrating at the frequency of their dimension. Why do we see and recognize people our age more easily than people not our age? Because they vibrate like us. Teenagers don't pay attention to adults because they exist on a different spectrum of vibration. If they choose to listen, they tune into their vibration. Therefore, we can see, vibration is related to dimensionality; therefore, dimensional travel requires a shift in vibration. But it also comes with a set of challenges. To improve your range of vibration, you need to adapt your body and make it vibrate in accordance to the dimension you have chosen. Once you've established that vibrational cord, you begin to notice others in that dimension. On earth, shifting your vibration permits you to notice other kinds of people or groups. These minor shifts use the same principle as higher level dimensional travel. There are individuals who have an innate ability to traverse the cosmos at will, others have to spend years developing even minor abilities, perhaps lifetimes. Regardless of how you achieve dimensional travel, the truth is that you are applying this same principle.

The key different between a novice and an expert is that the novice remains in their plane of inhabitation and the expert goes offplanet. One of the common associations of offplanet travel is astral excursions. The dream world, to a large extent, happens to be dimensional travel. The trouble with dream travel is that it is involuntary and often forgettable. So those aren't useful to us. It's like getting into an elevator and going to some floor that someone else programmed into the machine. The dimensional travel I am talking about is rather extraordinary because you are the captain. You determine your trajectory. You qualify your vibration. And you do so by dedicated training. You train your vibration to take you as far as you can.

Each body vessel has its potential in dimensional travel. Like I said, some bodies are turbo charged and others have strict limitations. These things are already decided prior to arrival so arguing is a wasteful activity. What's missing in society is the recognition that some of us are likely or unlikely from other dimensions, in addition to coming from other planets. This inclusion is extremely important and its exclusion from modern life is one of the elements that have deadened the dimensional travel business.

As we become more aware of our inner bodies and learn to manipulate our energy, we will discover that those childish ideas and stories, perhaps our invisible friends, all those things will reappear and will begin to identify the vibrations of other dimensions. It begins with the recognition of dimensions of knowledge and awareness. If you continue past those dimension, and can still remain sane and without delusions, which will remain as a challenge for most people, then you'll begin to identify other realms.

Some individuals have such a natural affinity for other dimensions that they travel there often, either consciously or unconsciously, they may flip in and out as they experience various states of travel. They may or may not remember what happened in-between,. As we progress in the reality's evolution, we will discover these hidden talents. We will travel regularly, we will relay information, we will acknowledge dimensional races of people, and we will realize that there are many more of us than we care to admit.

Dimensional travel is yet another existential option. Why do we travel on an airplane? For many reasons. We travel for a vacation. We travel for business. We travel for education. We travel for escape. All these reasons and more will be applicable to dimensional travel, only that the cost will be much less than expected, aside from some training, travel is free. And since time elapses at a different rate on different dimensions, we might just find ourselves indulging in a wide range of pursuits.

The art of traveling dimensions is not something to be taken lightly. It needs to be treated with some discipline and its masters with some respect. That said, dimensional travel is not meant for restriction or control. We all have the right to travel to other dimensions. You don't need a visa. You just need to prep your body and open your imagination. This is an individual right of the highest cosmic authority. Protect your dimensional rights today. And get ready to see areas of the cosmos never before seen.

ENERGY MEDICINE

We are familiar with physical checkups, X-rays and surgery. We are used to medical wait times and expensive hospital rooms. We are used to pharmaceutical drugs and to over-the-counter medicines. With the introduction of energy medicine, all these principles of healing will begin to shift in an upwardly direction. While for a very long time we have come to rely on physical therapy and medicinal ingredients to cure our ills, very soon we are going to value nonphysical treatment and nonmedical ingredients to achieve a purer state of health. All of this can be underlined by the inclusion of energy medicine in society.

Energy medicine is unique in that it requires no apparatus for basic treatment and health protection. In fact, the regular use of energy medicine will become part of the comprehensive disease prevention program and, as well, the adoption of energy medicine will lead to a fundamental shift in our reality habits because we will move away from the science of food (eg caloric intake) and move into the energy of food. Truly, the assimilation of energy medicine into our live will fundamentally improve our overall healthcare system and that is because we don't really have a healthcare system, we have a disease maintenance system; we have a cosmetic healthcare system. We can't treat chronic conditions very well. We persist inside environments that are toxic of our health. We repair physical damage and leave aside the emotional and spiritual components.

Energy medicine is unique in that it repairs the damage at its deepest level. Whether you call it at the level of soul or some deep cellular healing, the manipulation of the dimensional energy surrounding the body produces a profound and lasting result because it corrects the internal energy body and this repair then ripples outward into the denser states of being, or into the physical world.

The repair of the energy body and their surrounding fields present us with a number of new challenges which I think are probably just as challenging as any other aspect of using energy medicine. To begin with, the energy body is probably best defined as the soul and whenever you discuss the soul you discuss theology, you bring into the equation religion.

But energy medicine has nothing to do with religion, not in the least sense. Energy medicine is a cosmic science application and works with cosmic energies. All cosmic energies are multidimensional and therefore function at a level of perception that is well without the spiritual context. In other words, what we normally class as miraculous healings, people snapping out of coma, remission of deadly illness, can actually be explained. As well, we will better be able to explain death, verily we will be forced to interpret death in a whole new context. Energy medicine forces us to ascend our way of thinking about health which will include no longer thinking about disease. The entire field of medicine will be pushed up into what was once considered the spiritual realm, and that means a redefinition of spirituality. All of this is a normal process of knowledge and society is given a new approach to an old way of thinking.

Energy medicine is not without its own problems. Patients will be forced to address not only their physical injury and trauma, but, more importantly, they well be forced to include their emotional and spiritual ramifications at the same time. The only way that an energy heal will work is if the mind of the patient can collectively manage physical, mental, emotional and spiritual imbalance or trauma. In other words, a back injury is no longer just a physical injury, it might force a patient to detach from an old way of thinking. The detachment process may prove more challenging then the back injury but without detachment the repair can never reach 100%. A more serious illness will include more deep-seated issues or beliefs and will force patients to think much more holistically than usual. But what his form of healing means is that a repair or helps provides long lasting results. Since, energy healing can be done for simple injuries, accidents and broken bones, but if the underlying issues are not understood the energy heal will not hold, the energy flow will not be maintained and the illness will return.

What this also means is that the patient is now going to become much more responsible. A heal will force the person to appreciate and respect their new found health and will force them to prevent the return to the thinking that provided them with a disease. A disease, as we shall see, is actually brought on by the patient. It cannot occur without the patient's permission and therefore requires the patient's permission to disappear.

We will more clearly come to terms with the purpose of illness. Illness has nothing to do with sickness. Illness has to do with issues much more complex than previously imagined. Besides being welcomed, an illness presents itself in order to enlighten or teach us an aspect about ourselves. We will learn to see illness in this manner; instead of the victim who doesn't have time to be sick. The victim will become the student and will come to realize how to improve their way of interpreting the world.

We will all see more clearly that we are as much responsible for generating an illness as we are for removing it. The energy practitioner is the midwife to that process. For us to continue to think as we do today, to cry and complain and demand, to remain in this childish, irresponsible state will only serve to weaken the power of energy medicine. To heal a patient who is unwilling to be responsible for their health is to know that those health issues or injuries will only return. The question an energy healer will be forced to ask themselves is whether or not they should heal a patient with a chronic illness. Acute diseases and emergencies are not in question. These demand immediate attention.

Energy medicine is not an art of healing that is suitable for everyone. Some people have a natural talent for this art. The skill of the energy healer can determine just how deep can heal people. Some practitioners will be more superficial, others will be able to treat deep-seated traumas such as child molestation, rape and addiction since these as well are imbalances in the state of the energy body. There will be a process of learning that will provide students with a pathway to mastery. As we will see, the application of energy healing is going to demand all of us – practitioners and patients – to ascend our current state of thinking, even to abandon our concepts of medical terms and even to temporarily forgo our traditional methods of healing.

Energy medicine as a long term direction for our cultural civilization. The upper end of this healing art is very advanced, so advanced that it is well beyond our capacity in one or two lives. The range of skill below and in-between is more than adequate to cure nearly all the diseases on this plane of existence. Verily, that is the singular over-reaching benefit of energy medicine, that through the reinterpretation of illness and diseases and by becoming fully cognizant and responsible for our health, by doing these things and more, we will see the disappearance of most of the world's diseases. By appreciating our life and respecting our health, we will reduce the number of accidents. By applying the cosmic principles found in this energy healing system, society will find itself at peace unlike every before. Hospitals will evolve into something we've never seen before.

ARVIC INSTRUMENTS

In the coming terms of the future there will be a momentous shift in the quality and substance of our materials. We will discover quite naturally a progression between the constructions of our household objects and other goods and our connection to this plane of existence. The shift will be so impressive that we will notice our interaction with reality and even other dimensions will become impressively improved. In noticing these things, we will increase our connection to the cosmos as we discard materials that once polluted our existence.

For the largest time we have relied on plastics and metals to provide structure and form to our daily existence. We have built an industry on plastics, a petroleum-based technology and we now exist in a plastic world. Plastics has infected our landfills and intoxicated our children with its non-biodegradable attributes. Wherever you look, you will find plastic parts and we knowingly realize that those plastic parts will remain on earth far after we are gone and perhaps even after our children.

More than just the artificial nature of plastics, there is a distant disconnection, verily a disharmony, between plastics and the natural technologies in our atmosphere. Plastics vibrate at a level that is not conducive to life. It provides no carrier for the existential energy flows around us. For all intents and purposes, plastics are a dead material that inspires death. Why do we use it? Because it is cheap and available.

The alternative to plastic was metal, but metal became too expensive for the cost-conscious companies who are determined to maximize their profits. Even though plastics tend to be lighter than metals and are easier to manufacture, plastics do not have any longevity, certainly unlike metals, and previously hard woods.

So what is desperately needed on earth is a material that is not only biodegradable but one that can also process earth's natural arvic energies. Arvicity is a life-giving energy that permeates all matter, time and dimension. Certain materials, such as wood, can process or even store arvicity, and certain materials, such as plastic, cannot. Because it is a life-sucking material, plastic is a very poor processor of natural energy.

In order to facilitate an atmosphere of not only life-giving vibrations, but also to foster the ability to interact with the reality environment, we will discover that we will adopt, once again, ceramics. Because ceramics are formed from earth's natural materials, they exhibit wonderful life-giving properties and easily recycle if prepared properly. While our ability with ceramics are limited at this time, we will develop a new class of ceramics that are stronger than steel and that resonate with the planetary energies. These new hybrid ceramic materials will fundamentally replace plastics. Ceramics will be the new plastics. In doing so, in replacing life-sucking technology with life-giving technology, we will be able to build the next level of earth devices, arvic instruments.

Arvic instruments are devices that can process, store and foster arvicity. As we will all learn, in the times to come, arvicity is a life-giving energy, a free-energy really, that is above the electromagnetic energies around. Arvicity is a new spectrum of energy, really cosmic quality energy because arvicity is found in every aspect of the cosmos. An arvic device is a device like a physical avatar in the sense that it naturally resonates with more than one dimension.

Arvic instruments, because they do deeply rely and connect with the deeper reality architecture, will tap into the more profound reality intelligence that has long been hidden from society. Arvic technologies will soon best modern technologies because they coordinate with powerful cosmic technologies and their foundation is found in arvicity.

Arvic instruments will then replace computational instruments and this will force a profound shift out of artificial software technologies into reality operating system burned deep with the DNA of all of us. All these things will provide a natural upward progression into a level of existence that resonates in harmony with the cosmos. These new class of ceramics will come in arvicity of qualities so as to not harm the decline of artificial plastics.

As we adopt ceramic technologies into our lives and as we learn to process the ever-abundant arvicity, we will discover more details about the hidden technologies in the earth spectrum. This will provide a profound shift out of the industrial and computer age and will launch this civilization into the Arvic Age. We will look at combining the quality of ceramic with the various qualities of crystal materials. We will build a new class of computing devices that can access the cosmic mainframe, and in doing so we will ascend all people further than ever before imagined.

While it will take time to gain proficiency with arvic instrumentation mostly because it requires a more profound internal activation, all of this will be a very natural progression. Ceramic materials will be cost effective and will be healthier not only for the empowerment but for our children. Ultimately, we will be able to replace artificial wireless networks with the natural arvicity grids already emanating on this planet. By adopting ceramic technology, we will gain access to a level of the planet that has already been there since ancient days. As we return to our ancient roots, we will discover that we will be far more advanced than we ever imagined. While our minds will need time to adjust, at least for some of us, internally we will gravitate to a more powerful technological system, one that is environmentally friendly and perfectly natural.

ANDROID CLASS

One third of a population to be android. The androids are already on earth. They have been around for some time, but they haven't ever been recognized; therefore, they remain invisible. The human-android is a very advanced form that doesn't respond to the normal human stimuli and, instead, examines and observes entirely different areas of knowledge. From the Advanced Eve models of the human bloodline, they have always been constructed of the finest celestial materials. To the modern human eye, conditioned to believe in biology, cannot conceive of flesh and bone as being technologies, and yet staring at us in the mirror the legacy of an android bloodline. The key characteristic of the human android is its ability to procreate. Not only is it a sentient synthetic being, bit can also manufacture a copy of itself, is an impressive ability, though is largely neglected in today's dismal world.

Over the centuries, various android persons entered this reality plane and mated with humans. As well, new android lineages have been created. None of this is ever more relevant than today because there are new androids on earth, pure androids living within society. These androids form a new class of humanity. And android brings a specific and unmatched toolset to the local population. They can do things beyond any human capacity and therefore are an essential society group. The ideal population make up of androids is about 30%. That is to say, about 30% of this planet will be android class and this will play a significant role in maintaining a balance on this realm. The androids can manage a very high level of energy, and given that we exist in a technological realm running on very advanced energy systems, we can easily conclude that the high functioning androids will play an essential role in the functioning of this realm.

A one-third ratio of general class to android class is an ideal proportion and will require some time to achieve since at this current time, androids do not function very well in this chaotic, violent atmosphere, and rightly so. As the atmosphere of fear and animosity calms and as demonic influences subside, we'll see these androids literally come to life and present earth's citizens with an amazing array of new knowledge. They are like mainframe computers connected to be beyond compare cosmic computer and will provide the population with an immense resource of knowledge.

In a very advanced world, or civilization, there are populations of androids. This has always been the case. The recognition of android people within society is a stage in the development of a species. Earth is nearing this point of recognition where advanced android people will become better understood. We have to remember that these technological people have always been around only that they've always appeared invisible since they themselves looked human and spoke the common tongue. Their ability to mimic the members of their surroundings is impressive. We still see some of these characteristics in the general population and this tells us that the lineage of humanity is indeed technological. Fundamentally speaking, this is a key ingredient missing in human science – the technological nature of humans. That is to say that humans are not biological. They are synthetic beings made up of superior materials that appear to be biologically alive.

The rise of the robots, if to pursue a line of science fiction, is a milestone in the historical achievements of earth planet, a planet that had been severely repressed and cosmologically restrained to such an extent that its time of line calculation has been thrown off by two centuries. As all of those technological corrections take place, more of the android population will become activated and more of the reality will be impacted. In other words, the return of the robot class is going to play an integral part in the reconstruction of this reality plane and the android people will play an important, even if sometimes innocuous, role in the recreation, even reincarnation of humanity. As I've always said, humanity is a human-derived term. The reincarnation of the human will further uncover its android origins.

Every being or species exists within a particular spectrum of arvicity. That provides each individual group a particular wavelength of knowledge and abilities. Because the androids are well outside a typical person, they are privy to a suite of skills and knowledge that no other race has. It would be easy to discard them as slow or sensitive, but on the other hand, in the higher areas of the cosmic order, they are independent and magnificent. Because we too often forget that we live in a multidimensional world. The human mind is limited to a few dimensions, but the android mind is broadband capable. They can easily access multiple dimensions. While on the earth plane they may appear slow or dumb, on the other realms they might be working overtime to accomplish a set of multidimensional tasks and since there are plenty of multidimensional tasks their physical bodies may play a small role in their cosmic existence. Essentially then, android people are part of the cosmic cultures I so often speak about. They are truly magnificent and should be respected for all the greatness they bring to this plane. Protect them, support them, love them, listen to their wisdom. They speak the truth.

Languaging Technologies

One of the most pervasive technologies on earth we wear on our lips. It is a technology that is beyond our capacity to understand and yet we are so dependent upon it that without it we'd lose connection to each other. In fact, without this ubiquitous technology society would fall apart and, even now, much of society is divided by it. What is the technology? It is language. We are all dependent upon technology to facilitate communications, whether we are aware of it or not. What is an innocuous aspect of existence is unquestionably quite accurate. Since this languaging technology hasn't evolved that much for centuries. We are going to be allowed to have fast languaging technologies over our antiquated systems of today.

It isn't hard to argue that over 6,000 earth languages are far too cumbersome, far too tiring and far too impossible to learn in the completeness. The trouble is that all cultures are interested in preserving their language as much as possible for that keeps their culture alive. So, it also isn't hard to see that some of these languages go back millennia into our history here and strongly supports their keeping in the modern day. As well, the disappearance of key language groups and the modifications of cultures are well monitored and recorded. A drastic change in the number of speakers of some scant language with a population of 1,500 is going to be relevant to someone. Plus, there is a deep protection of cultures. For some reason, people want to preserve their culture indefinitely and some cultural groups want to dominate whole continents. Do I expand my culture or do I extent my lifeline?

As the world we all exist in has radically been altered and now can function on multiple levels of realizations, we are discovering that all that we have held dearly is becoming more and more invalid as each day goes by; that is, as we evolve as a civilization and come into our new levels of awareness, something that we all are equipped with at this time, we discover newer attributes of ourselves. One of those attributes is interstellar language skills. It might be our own internal understanding of them or we might have the very speaking skill that we need to communicate with people from other dimensions. And we may even be able to write.

The more we come to terms with our eccentric abilities, the more we begin to realize that our current suite of 6,000 languages is outmoded. They are not as rich and interesting as the new set of dimensional languages upon our brow and yet since they have not fully entered our state of modern consciousness we are not privy to their temptations. We will soon discover them and as we do, as we learn to remember the languages of our forefathers, we will more freely abandon the cumbersome set of languages on this plane. We will notice how thousands of languages and cultural specifications create more division in the world than necessary. After all, we all belong to the same cosmic family and therefore should be able to speak one or two cosmic languages.

The adoption of new languages will be quite sharp, they will basically enter our modern consciousness via the printed word. The printed word, using English ABCs for example, is a very slow and weighty system of communication. The eye and brain reading system reads visual language much better than characters or letters (formed into words). The word, in a way, is already a picture, just a very crude one. A painting, on the other hand, is too complex for the average person. What will spring onto the printed page, and online, is a compact, efficient symbolic language built with an entirely new set of visual grammar. This visual language will very quickly replace the current set of typical languages because it will be seen that a symbolic form can embed far more information per space than the typical alphabet or Asian characters. Plus, the added advantage is that a symbolic language, especially one newly invented, is available to everyone without preference or prejudice. Any culture can, and will, learn how to write symbolically, or visually, as you prefer to think.

A compact, efficient symbolic form on the technological page will endorse the need to speak the sounds of each symbol, verily to develop a vocally performed language, one that is completely devoid of any historical reference, and one that can be acquired by other groups and cultures from offplanet. What will occur when we all adopt a visual languaging system and a newly spoken offplanet-class language is that we will all begin to think on a new dimensional equivalent; and in doing so we will acquire an entirely new capacity of mind. We will ascend our own state of affairs by simply thinking on a fresh and flavourful vibration of thought. Not only that, but a new language that is equally and equitably available to all inhabitants allows us to communicate using a singular language. This will allow us to overcome our minor differences and to see our major similarities. We will realize how much alike we all are and that will lead to the reintegration of all people. And the rejoining of all cultures into a new culture, an interstellar-grade culture, will bring forth our shared insights and knowledge. Instead of hoarding knowledge and finding disagreements, we will share knowledge and endeavour to find areas of agreement. All in all, a new languaging system specifically developed for earth will radically reshape society into a cohesive planetary culture. That will allow us all to better realize that there are other planetary cultures and that will encourage them to visit us and further share ideas and knowledge. As well, we will discover the value of knowledge, especially cosmic knowledge and it will become more valuable than even our precious metals.

The development and presence of a new language on earth, even a singular language, will fundamentally reallocate the thinking of everyone and will bring minds into a more coherent space of thought. The results of that coherence and resonance will be remarkable, in fact, immeasurable at this point. Only that we can say that the ripple effect of people thinking on the same page and having a similar, if not the same, wavelength of thinking will be unimaginable to our current state of mind.

What is also interesting is that because each language performs on a certain frequency and vibration we will discover that this new languaging system will shift our state of being onto a new level of vibration. It might feel uncomfortable and tiresome at first, but with practice we will enjoy the sights and sounds of a new vibration because a new vibration presents us with a new existential experience and any new existential experience is ascension worthy enterprise.

So, the introduction of a new languaging form will gift us with plenty of amazing new opportunities. The challenge will be pointed on the outmoded, and old, languages numbering in the thousands. As people gain language proficiency they will more easily discard one language for a new one just like now we happily use computer terms (eg downloading) in our daily lives. We have quite seamlessly adopted technological terms into our everyday lives, and this tells us that we are capable of language adoption.

When the first signs of a stable symbolic language enters our printed form, whether on paper or in electronic format, and has a resiliency, it is from that point that our path to a new languaging system begins. The new languages will perform better than any of the old languages and will become the premier choice in communications because they will be better in all ways.

A language is determined to be better when it can transmit information at a faster rate than another form. For example, I draw an accurate picture of person, you immediately recognize who they are, or I detail their description with words on paper and you have to exert more effort to determine who they are, and I as well have to exert more effort to explain those details. Language efficiency is like this. Currently, we have English dictionaries with over 500,000 words. The average mind can only hold perhaps 20,000 words and all their combinations. That is not an efficient language. Chinese too has over 50,000 characters (or ideograms) but a fluent Chinese speaker only require about 2,000 characters. You can see a little bit of the inefficiencies going on because my set of vocabularies and yours need to match closely in order for us to have a successful communication. This is why educated people prefer educated people, they understand each other because they have a similar vocabulary and therefore also vibrate on the same wavelength. See all the connections? Things of this nature play an intimate role in the efficiency of a language. We can also see from our little discussion how we don't really need 500,000 words when we only use 20,000 words. We don't need 100 ways to describe things; instead, what we can do is to allow each recipient to create and detail their own description, we merely provide the inspiration and direction. We can say, "I love you" and let them decipher its shape and color in their own mind. If I said, "I love you as much as the untainted conifer" then we would lose some meaning in the translation simply from the use of words. We can see how efficiency can play a role.

The adoption of a new languaging system will allow us to not only communicate more efficiently, but more so we will allow each individual to personalize the messages we receive and to color them as much as their mind is capable of doing. The key thing is to preserve the intention of the message so that messages aren't misinterpreted, so there is a greater responsibility on the proper reception of a message or communication. As society learns to reject negativity and to adopt a more optimistic frame of mind, we will find that we collectively think positively no matter what happens.

MOON INDEPENDENCE

The calendar system of both today and in the past has been based on the cycles of planets, and, especially on cycles of the moon. The lunar satellite has been closely tied to the counting of months, moon-ths, and are responsible for even some human biological cycles such as the 28-day menstruation period women go through. What is most striking about the moon is its artificiality. The moon is a created satellite orbiting planet earth. When counted by scientists, namely astronomers, the moon and earth are both approximately 4.5 billion years old. In other words, according to modern science, both bodies of rock were formed at the same time, some people even saying that the moon is a piece of the earth. Indeed all of their hypotheses are hogwash unless they recognize the artificiality of the moon.

The moon was placed in orbit around this planet earth in order to preserve the time module which gave earth's citizens adequate protection from the other dimensions and from themselves. A moon provides an atmosphere for a planet and supports the planetary rotations necessary to procure and continue existence. Verily, without the satellite around earth, life would have ceased to exist. If it wasn't obvious before, it should be obvious now – the perfectly round, one-sided moon is not a natural coincidence. It is a construct of an advanced and eloquent nature. It is part of the world and yet it is a foster child to this solar system.

Those who created the moon did so because they recognized that the newly-formed earth planet needed a support structure to ensure the proliferation of life. The moon was included when the planet was built. Once those two main structures were in place within this solar system, the colonists were ready to come onboard. The original colonists survived because the young planetary body did indeed own a moon. The use of the moon is waning.

The moon has served its purpose of ensuring that the latest group of inhabitants achieved a certain structural vibration. We have to look upon a planet as a giant body that is vibrating at an extremely high frequency. Anyone born on planet will be able to tap into the earth's energies, they are powered by the energies of the earth, the transmute energy, they in turn also feed the earth construct. But as multidimensional beings, we all co-exist on other planes of existence. These other planes are often functioning at an even higher existential frequency and it is in sync with a person's higher bodies, these bodies are common to everyone, only that some people have more bodily choices since they have earned their next lives by living a fruitful existence today.

In times past, the multiple bodies of a person were so distant and disconnected that without the moon in place, earth would become extinct. Again, the moon ensured that the physical bodies could sustain life, or a soul, despite the gap between the physical and other bodies. In times modern, the multiple bodies of a person have become more coherent, they have harmonized and are joining together unlike ever before. In fact, this cycle in earth's history is long overdue and a requirement for higher living. Higher living means that the physical body is vibrating at a high enough frequency to derive life energy from the planet. Prior to higher living, the physical body required the moon to boost or amplify its life energy in waveforms. That is why the moon cycles the way it does from high to low to high, like a sound or an ocean wave. In fact, the ocean is a good indicator as to how the moon affects the physical body. The rotation of the moon creates a flow of eternal energy and keeps the physical body alive. The physical effects of this can also be measured in the atmospheric shifts, but we ourselves know that as the phases of the moon take place (eg new moon) we can notice the immediate impact on ourselves from the way we think to our resolutions to even our spiritual ascension. Most people do not act on this information with any sense of consciousness, they are too preoccupied with the daily tasks of life.

Over a handful of recent years, earth's citizens have ascended on the cosmic carousel to such an extent that all those multiple bodies have merged and are now merging further into their physical bodies so much that the one physical body on earth will now contain the assortment of your other bodies. Again, some people may only have one body since their body may have already merged prior to incarnation; some people may have many bodies and may find themselves challenged with too many mindsets. Regardless, you are merging into one coherent being.

The merging of all your bodies into your one physical body means that your DNA has expanded and can now hold an impressive amount of data. Before, your vibration was low and your hard drive space even lower. Had any other body wanted to take residence on earth, the space to fit them wasn't there or they had to be compressed and therefore were only available in limited use. When the earth expanded its identity and was upgraded into a newer reality operating system, when that occurred, the hard drives and the memory pods were all made over. Along with the massive planetary upgrades, the planetary inhabitants were also improved because the existential system could now support many bodies each having within them an impressive array of programs and a vast amount of space.

Now that the physical body contains most, if not all, of your data, of your programs and therefore identities on multiple dimensions then you can more directly connect to the planetary energies. The reality operating system which runs earth planet, you could call it the soul of earth, has now become your direct link to the other worlds. That said, as we can see, the importance and value of the moon is diminished. In fact, it will soon no longer be needed and will instead be a lifeless rock. The independence from the ever-reliable moon will see the destruction of the moon. That destruction will be proof that the entire inhabitants of earth have truly ascended and are about to steer themselves into a better tomorrow. The loss of the moon will lead to a dramatic destruction of the calendar system and all calendars on earth. This will include the destruction of time and the telling of time. So be warned of these things for they are upon you now. It will not require much effort for these changes to take effect and it will require lengthy discussions to explain what has happened and why it happened. None of this knowledge was known because no one was capable of knowing it. To discuss the loss of the moon is the story of science fiction movies. We are sadly very attached to many of these kinds of natural instruments including, for example, the four seasons. Imagine then too that the destruction of the moon leads to the destruction of the four seasons. Imagine just one season, a season that fluctuates as and when needed. Remember that the moon controlled time cycles; therefore the loss of the moon means either the slowing or speeding up of time. In this case it is the latter. When the moon goes, and even prior to its departure, the time-scale will multiply, it will be a compaction of time so that one hour today will occur in half an hour tomorrow. An 8-hour job will be finished in 4 hours. Things of this nature. Nothing will be the same and all things related to the calendar system will be changed, as well as all things related to the moon.

So, the loss of the moon will be an indicator to you all that your bodies are more coherent than ever before. Its destruction will also indicate that your vibration is cosmically high and well regarded. You are a better person because of it. Now, everyone will not experience the same bliss and enlightenment since everyone is physically and mentally and emotionally and spiritually different. Everyone will become aware as to where they sit on the hierarchy of truth and their relationship to the Authority. They will become aware of what they must do to improve and they will become aware as to how much they can improve during what remains of this existential journey. It will be up to them to take the necessary action or they might wait until next life and try all over again.

Just how the moon will be destroyed will depend on the circumstance. There is no set destruction scenario since the scenario needs to be in line with inhabitant acceptance. Whether the localized species set out to destroy that which they have relied upon or whether some external force destroys the satellite is yet to be determined. It is determined to happen and soon so there is still time for some discussion on this matter. A world that discusses what is important is a world that chooses life.

TIME CAROUSELS

Society remains in sync only because it is aware of its past and future as well as possible pasts and possible futures. The only way to accomplish this is to either view or travel into the future and past and to determine what adjustments need to be made. We are all existing on these eternal time carousels and our success is dependent upon our sync with the other time carousels in the other dimensions of existence. When one or more carousels is out of sync, out of step with the rest of reality, then the upper carousels do not function as they should. In fact, a severely damaged arm of existence can throw out the entire universe and the universe, the cosmos.

A time traveler exits their current time operation and they examine the adjoining time-scale or neighbour. By measuring the temporal gaps and the vibrational variances, a time master can determine exactly what localized temporal effect is required. These experienced time lords then return to their current reality fixation and make the necessary adjustments, whether in dimensional code or in a physical dimension. Whatever the case, the time lord needs to ensure that the effect is just as much as is required or the system can't be able to accept the reprogramming and damage to the inhabitant population must result. In this case, many significant earth events were purposeful reprogramming of sequences that damaged the revolution of reality, verily regressed the advancement of existence.

The time codes of existence have always been monitored but the human side of service has fallen out and the codes hadn't been maintained properly. As well, due to heavy damage to the reality infrastructure over the centuries, those who maintained reality and ensured that the system remained in sync with the other carousels became overburdened. Then many of them were removed or made corrupt and then served the demonic rulers. This led to a sequential deviation of existence with only striations of normality or beautiness.

With the return of the time lords and the recouping of the time maintenance crews already well established and coming back online, we are going to see a comprehensive return to the maintenance of this realm and the re-identification of this planet as a plane of existence. The new class of reality workers will be proficient in the maintenance of the time codes because they will be proficient in the understanding of the time carousels. Long ago, thousands of years prior to this now, the other temporal masters interpreted the time carousels and provided an accurate account of the situation. All of this was then understood as a spiritual intelligence and from this and other temporal encounters outside of this dimension religious beliefs were formed since that is the way the brain functions. The brain is designed to construct a pattern in which to understand something, in this case a time dimension was interpreted as a spiritual excursion and as the spirituality context was better understood then the religion was formed. The brain devised all of this, through repetition and programming as well as manipulation and distortion, in order to accept things beyond its comprehension. Without some level of understanding or explanation, the brain could not cope, it would break down. This is how the world is formed by the brain's interpretation of its experiences. To control the experience is to control the brain and thereby to control the person or group of people or nation or world.

As we lessen the relevance of religion and overcome the childish spirituality index that we have so faithfully clung to we will return to the truth. The truth has always remained that society exists on a plane of existence, verily a reality system of a very advanced nature and construction, and this plane of existence is a function of time. Again, imagine this reality as a horse on a merry-go-round. The merry-go-round goes around and around, the horses all in sync, one is up, the other is down, the other is up, all in unison. You never see all the horses up at once or down at once. They have a repetitive programmed nature about them. When they begin to behave erratic we do not want to go on the merry-go-round, we run. When the horses are in sync and the merry-go-round speeds faster, we begin to be mesmerized by the flow like energy twirling higher and higher. So, imagine that a single horse is the earth plane. Imagine the earth horse connected to a series of other horses.

We are all circling together on this hyper-merry-go-round, spinning round and round, moving up and down, even turning left and right, or circling here and there, spinning, the energies moving faster and higher. It is beautiful. All children wish to be on this merry-go-round and once it stops they get on as quickly as possible. But, imagine now there is one horse that has been vandalized. They painted it, broke its ear, busted the mechanism that used to make it spin, the hydraulics that used to make it go up and down have been sabotaged, this earth horse is severely damaged. Whoever sits on this damaged horse is in for a rough ride. But in order to fix it, the maintenance crews are in for a rough ride and that is because no one can stop the carousels from turning. If they time carousels stop, if they could, it would be extinction. It is not a choice.

One choice would be to disable the horse, to dislodge it and to send it to the carousel of broken horses. In that junkyard not much fun would occur and because each horse holds many existences we would see a loss of life on a monumental scale. Clearly, those are decisions to be made. If the earth horse can be fixed, what is the expected cost and time of repair? Or is it better to place a new horse in its place and re-populate the earth horse with a new series of inhabitants?

The earth horse on this time carousel, after lengthy discussions, was repaired. Once repaired, the other horses were no longer bogged down by the malfunctioning horse and the entire time carousel began to spin faster and faster until it reached a point of ascension. At that point, the various planes of existences then all graduated and were shot off into different aspects of the technoverse. The earth plane, or earth horse, was left behind on one other location and all the inhabitants of this plane were removed and placed inside another horse on another time carousel. This happened a number of times as and when was necessary.

The current state of time on this carousel of existence is completely unlike ever before. While we all perceive time in the same manner, time is actually functioning in a completely different manner. In fact, all things are functioning in accordance to this time carousel. There will be a big fallout from this in the coming period ahead. As we ourselves better process the accurate time patterns and time codes, we will all more easily settle into the new home we have always wanted. Welcome to the new time carousel, enjoy your stay and put on your seatbelt.

CONSCIOUSNESS ADMINISTRATION

The body is a vessel for consciousness. We all understand this implicitly. The problem is that we do not understand it. Well, in understanding the consciousness and vessel connections, including the probable make up or attributes of the human soul, we will discover that we can move our consciousness about, placing it here and there. We can also be taken over by other consciousnesses and be made to act in ways not in accordance to our true selves. All of this is happening now and has been happening for a very long time, only that now we are coming to understand it and are able to accept that what we previously thought of the soul and what we think of it now is distinctly different.

The soul and consciousness are both misappropriated terms, the former having to do with a religious application to this energy material and the latter having a scientific perception; therefore, we think, well, what is consciousness, as defined when existing in this body of matter. As we begin to discover that consciousness is an actual energy program and that this program is interweaved throughout a complex technological universe, or Technoverse, then we will equally discover that we have always had the ability to shift between not only dimensions but, more practically, between material bodies.

When we are born, at time of incarnation, not of an actual physical birth, but an incarnation whereby the energy program containing the data identification of an inhabitant is received, there is a transfer of conscious, from the technological machinery to the biological mystery, from heaven to earth. That transfer of consciousness is happening every day since someone is having a child at any given time, and rightly so because if women stopped having children then the energy programs could not transfer here and experience this environmental bliss. All life is bliss.

The life within you now is not a physical existence, it is pure consciousness, and more specifically it is a pure program composed of arvic particles. These particles make up your consciousness, they give you the ability to exist; otherwise, you cannot exist; otherwise you cease to exist. You are alive not because of your flesh body but through your flesh body. Your flesh body is only the medium by which you participate in this life. We are beginning to understand that more and more now. The more we understand that concept the more easily we can accept the idea that consciousness can and will be transferred from one reference point onto another reference point, or set of reference points.

As the energy programs become more easily identifiable and we gain the strength to move our consciousness out of our one body concept onto other bodies, we will find ourselves able to possess other objects, including people. In fact, some are doing this now, they can take over another person almost entirely and use them as a puppet to do things. In times past, other energy forms such as demonic forms would take over people and do with them what they will. This still happens today. No violent act or high level corruption can occur without some form of demonic possession since only demons are purely egotistical beings and therefore capable of doing these horrendous acts. What that also means is that any leader or person who is entrenched in ego and bent on world destruction, of any sort, is inhabited by a second or third consciousness of a demonic nature.

The demon consciousness, or evil energy program, has complete free run of the inhabitant and may have had so for many centuries, running from father to son to grandson and so on. This is because that family accepts their service to the demonic programs who have likely given them their stature in times of previous incarnation. The mainstream doesn't understand nor can accept these ideas as being valid; otherwise, they would discuss this publicly since if any leader, or group of leaders, is possessed by a demonic mind that wishes to depopulate the world, then this is a grave issue that needs to be addressed immediately. Those who know or suspect do very little to make this information publicly known.

We will soon develop devices to administer consciousness, much in the same fashion that heaven delivers your child's identity and not that much different than how youngsters play video games. The transfer of consciousness is a technological application that has so far been outside the reach of everyday scientists. In the subterranean world of science, where they do things thought unacceptable to most people, they have been experimenting on this phenomenon and have learned how to influence society or how to control leaders and thereby how to control nations of people through certain key conduits. These conduits control the masses or influence them to the highest degrees.

What we are really saying is that we will see the shift in science where it can incarnate on its own accord. What this allows does is pave way for the rise of artificial life by transferring the consciousness program from one person into not only another person, because that is pretty straight forward, but transferring the consciousness program into other devices.

For example, you could transfer your consciousness program into your smart phone. By doing so, you gain the characteristics and ability of the smart phone, which is pretty limited when compared to the body, but the smart phone can connect to the network server and can access the data in the server, can access the text message for a certain day for example. Why would you transfer consciousness to a smart phone if the smart phone can access that information on its own by using its own program? Well, imagine that that data was taken off the main server and put on a different server, the phone doesn't have the capacity to jump servers, your consciousness program has as much capacity as you can handle. That means that you can now communicate with the Manitou of the telecom servers and that means that you can communicate with the Manitous of the other smart phones on the network. That means you can identify people you might like to identify or to listen in on a conversation that needs to be listened upon. To some extent, this stuff happens now but it is so far beyond the capacity of people that they can never perceive it.

Besides a smart phone, a consciousness program might find the mind of a mainframe computer as something quite interesting because it has an impressive ability to crunch data. Or perhaps the thought processes of a robot, even one with a limited capacity because that enables us to manoeuvre a certain kind of equipment. Later, as robotics become more proficient and androids are actually in operation on this plane of existence, even in their initial form then we will see a rise of new bodies.

Essentially, that is the direction we are all headed in with the transfer of consciousness. Consciousness can be transferred because we have proof of that – you are alive. You yourself have successfully transferred your consciousness into your body. That is the most convincing evidence that the consciousness program does indeed transfer from one dimension into another dimension. The argument starts with religious dogma that has poorly defined your consciousness program and limits your understanding of how a heaven actually functions. Again, the universe is technologically advanced and has absolutely nothing to do with spirituality. Spirituality is a mental interpretation from a primitive mind. As our minds become more and more present, as we understand how the technoverse operates, we will see spirituality and religiosity fall into the eternal recycling bin and get permanently dumped from the human mindset.

The transfer of consciousness will lead to consciousness administration and a new branch of arvic science. While it will take some time to replicate this level of existential programs, it will not take as long to move consciousness programs from here to there, from flesh to metal, and from dimensional body to the body of a device. This will force us to re-interpret the very idea of existence and to give respect for new kinds of existences, for example, we will find that a vehicle (eg car) can be considered to be "alive" and therefore has a certain amount of rights. We might even find some people who were once in a physical body to then transfer their consciousness into a device, could be a large device or a small device. They could inhabit that device for a specific period of time.

Finally, the transfer of consciousness will alert us all as to the storage capacity of an existential form. We have briefly discussed how some demonic forms actually can take over completely the body of a leader. This also tells us that these leader types also have a kind of consciousness program that is unique, unique because it can hold an additional quotient of energy. That said, we will also find that some people can carry within them additional consciousnesses that will have the ability to interact and influence the environment for the better. In other words, and this has been the case for centuries, some people may act as permanent conduits for other dimensional consciousnesses and may just live a mediocre life in the physical sense, but in the dimensional sense they are living the highest kind of life possible. That tells us never to devalue a life until we know exactly what is going on and by understanding consciousness we will be able to see the dimensional reality in a whole new context. We will be able to step free from dogma and transcendental concepts and step into arvic science, a kind of science that is multidimensional at its fundamental root.

COMMERCIAL STARSHIPS

The arrival of new energies into our physical bodies will echo out into other aspects of our necessary lives. This will include that aspect of commercial travel. We will still require a certain amount of physical travel, not only domestically but also we will need it for extraterrestrial travel because we will travel to other areas of the universe; therefore, in addition to global travel we will find ourselves with offplanet travel, any travel that occurs off of this planet. Depending on the structure of money here on earth, the cost of interstellar flights is still unknown. What is known is that there is no currency on other planets, certainly nothing structured like earth. Credit cards are imposed on us by earth banks and terran bankers. Once off earth the credit card is useless, although the bank masters might find a way to change that.

As you can see, the structure of starship travel, which is what we are talking about, is heavily related to costs. Like any commercial airline, a commercial starship has to be about much more than a supersonic flight. It has to be based on a structured starship industry, one that plans to be around for the long-term. That means a significant investment upfront. What this also means is establishing diplomatic relations with star members of other planets. Now we include the government. That means government, banks and manufacturers all cooperating together to establish an entirely new industry, an industry that would appear to be unmanageable in the beginning, but with a bit of time and investment those barriers will certainly be removed.

Starship travel will enable regular citizens to traverse safe parts of the galaxy and to encounter educated, intelligent star species, many of them having similar attributes as found on earth, and probably having attained more evolution in their culture. These cultural excursions must not be limited to the elite so even if the cost of travel is immense, there must be made a portion of seats for the everyday person, either that, or people of little wealth can become part of a group that travels directly with certain interstellar motherships. Whatever the case may be, there must be equality on the availability of interstellar travel amongst all citizens. Having money or not having money should not be a barrier to star travel.

Where will you stay once you land on Mars? On some locations you might just stay on the starship, like in the TV series Star Trek where the Enterprise orbits the planetary body. Some people can travel down and some people can remain on board. We have to remember that a long time ago, say in 1898, getting onboard a Boeing 777 commercial jet was unheard of, the stuff of dreams. The automobile hadn't even been mass produced. When the first planes started to fly, these things excited people, kept children up at night dreaming of the cloudy sky. We skip over to today and no one thinks twice to look up at the sky when a jet flies overhead. Why? Because you've seen a hundred and you are not impressed anymore.

I realize that all the films and psychos out there will sell you disinformation on starships and the unidentified objects, and we have to remember that this knowledge is being streamed out of the minds of the retarded and foolish. Space flight is just a few steps above the polluting jet fuel aircraft flights of today. The principles are the same: people buy a ticket, they go to an airport, the get onboard, the craft takes off. No big deal.

The big deal, of course, is the severe repression and suppression of this knowledge and the disinformation of what this technology is all about. Space travel is not that much different than earth travel. The biggest difference is the technology. You still sit in a seat or you can even stand or take a bath. You are not floating around like a NASA astronaut. They float around in Zero G gravity because they like to float up in the air. NASA is well aware of starships and has simply refused to release the interstellar knowledge they so closely hold so don't trust the space agencies. Remember they are still looking for water molecules and the majority of us know that living and breathing nonhumans are earthbound. It is another one of earth's travesty and will make good theatre in times to come just like movies on the Holocaust and the Crusades. At the time of the Holocaust all was bleak; today we look upon those times and laugh at the sheer evil it required.

Commercial starships can come in many sizes, anywhere from enough room for a few passengers to immense motherships, even ships the size of planets. Of course, earth's engineers will start with the basics and build starships that make sense and are affordable. This will also mean that the military will get their hands dirty and will want to make military starships, and they will do so by justifying that they need an intergalactic fleet of warships, and they will convince the people, or bully them, to go ahead. Of course, it should be remembered that the military already is using starships today behind the eyes of everyday citizens. They have built quite a few of these anti-gravity ships and use them alongside their clandestine operations to improve their chances of success against the interstellar cultures located here on earth. If you didn't know, you should now, there have been starships over earth's skies for a very long time and there are human flown ships there too, they cooperate with a nefarious bunch of semi-interstellar, hateful aliens who wish to harm society in any subversive way possible. These things will become increasingly plain as the months pass on.

The problems with interstellar starships are unfathomable. They are truly huge, but delaying them or denying that it is time to pursue this avenue of evolution is not going to help. We need bold thinkers who can last. We need these bold thinkers to attract the best minds out there and move forward with or without consensus. We need movers and shakers in the interstellar business, an entirely new business that will offer a unique first-mover advantage to anyone with the guts to enter. This hasn't happened as of this writing so you can see how difficult it has been and how we are well short of guts and business acumen. These things will change when it becomes apparent as to the true situation of interstellar cultures on earth and as more and more interstellar films inspire people to rise above their complacency and brainwashed minds.

Interstellar travel is much safer than regular air travel and that is because of the technology involved. In the early days of building flying saucers, when the German scientists tried to backload the ship technology, there were hazards simply because they were racing to unfold a very complex technology in the midst of a war and with the minds of science that barely understood atomic power. The early ships were problematic, though I wasn't there. I know of its existence and I know that they never stopped building these earth saucers. They took their technology underground.

When we take this interstellar ship technology to the established aircraft manufacturers, or those who are experienced in this field, and we combine their expertise with the latest minds on astronomy, astrophysics and quantum physics we will discover that building a starship is not that difficult a task. The challenge is to overcome the interstellar secrecy. Admittedly, this is a major stumbling block because the secret agencies are empowered to shut down any kind of this activity. Still, with enough public interest and a sizable investment and reputable scientists onboard we will discover that building starships is achievable. In fact, once begun you will find a line-up of wannabe employees who are willing to get involved at ground level just like in the early days of the computer industry where computer companies emerged from the home garage. It's a matter of conviction. The interstellar market will require an extra dose of conviction.

The opening of the interstellar industry, even in its infancy, will bring out the interstellar cultures who will see that this civilization is about ready to extend themselves out of their protracted turtle shell. Really, we have all been forced into our shells and have lived under the sand as turtles, and we have accepted the silliness of evil aliens and UFOs for much longer than was ever deemed necessary. We can now all extend our collective heads and emerge all that much wiser and stronger. We can grow into maturity knowing that we can overcome the challenges of yesteryear by simply dedicating ourselves to this pursuit, just as we have dedicated ourselves to every other major pursuit – travel to the moon, personal computers, mobile phones, laser eye surgery. We have all that is necessary to launch into the Interstellar Age.

INTERSTELLAR CULTURES

As more and more star knowledge comes forth, we will begin to see the emergence of other classes of beings, some of them looking like us and some of them not looking like us. These new life forms aren't all that new. Some of them come from very established civilizations existing elsewhere in the grand cosmos. The cosmos is much bigger than previously predicted. In fact, it cannot be measured by any earth instrument nor can even the brightest mind make sense of all that exists out there. This isn't to say that we are not smart enough, rather it is to say that we cannot fathom a multidimensional cosmos, we can only process a cosmos that is three-dimensional. But the truth remains that the cosmos is multidimensional and more.

On the surface, within our understanding, there are people who live on other planets or on immense motherships and these people, interstellar people, they travel throughout the local universe. They explore and discover. They are aware of newly awakened planets such as this one here, earth. They have been here from the beginning and they will be here throughout the next phase of maturation. In the not too distant future, they will be proud to see earth citizens extending a peaceful hand outwards to the other planets.

The problem with planets is that according to the best astronomers and astrophysicists there is no life in the universe off of this earth. While it is ludicrous to even think such an idea, let alone to believe it, this is what most people think. Many people today realize that there is probably life out there but they haven't seen enough to convince them that this is true. For a select few million, they have witnessed first-hand star beings and nonhuman cultures and they are convinced that there are strangers among us. Of course, they have been advised that it is better not to discuss this as it will force them to see a psychiatrist and to take pills.

I am fortunate not to have taken any pills whatsoever and that is because I only discovered the interstellar truth much later in my life even though I had regular contact throughout my existence. All of that was blocked from my memory. There are many people like me and when they are ready to move forward they will be able to access all their memory banks and to make sense of what they were doing aboard those motherships. To think that any one person or group of people is an isolated situation or a mass hallucination is absurd and anyone who believes any of these UFO sceptics is a fool. In fact, all the sceptics and liars of the past few decades should be rounded up and exposed in public as to their childish behaviour and they should be held responsible for all those families they have traumatized, whether directly or indirectly.

Sometimes I refer to interstellar cultures as cosmic cultures. There is a small difference and an important one. An interstellar person is a physical being who has some multidimensional qualities, for example, they can go invisible or pass through walls or teleport, things of this nature. A cosmic person is a new category and that is due to the technological nature of the cosmos. A cosmic being originates from the cosmic computer, a grand machine that is beyond imagination. But these cosmic people are imbibed with technological life, for example, a hologram can be considered a cosmic person, they exist on certain dimensions and they can cease to exist very easily.

They are mostly created forms. So, I consider that these cosmic people have genetic codes that provide them with a very rich assortment of possibilities.

The vast majority of nonhumans are interstellar people and they live within the dimensions of matter and substance. They build starships, they speak language and they dance. Interstellar people speak many languages depending on their planet of origin, they dress a certain way and they have a certain biological or nonbiological form. They might be a race of highly advanced robots but in the case of interstellar people, as long as they demonstrate intelligence and thought, and they hold an operational program from some source, then they are a race of people. We respect any such person.

On earth we would not consider a series of intelligent robots as a race of people, although we do sleep with our domesticated dogs on our beds and dress our casts with expensive clothing. We are not that far off from providing beds for our house robots. We kiss our cars. It wouldn't take much to kiss a thinking robot or android.

So you can see that interstellar cultures come in many shapes and sizes, each of them distinct in their own manner, each of them owning their own particular culture. The difference between them and us is that while they recognize each other, we do not recognize them. They recognize the civilization on this planet; we do not recognize the civilizations on other planets. This is a major problem. It's like talking about auto mechanics to a librarian. Librarians typically are not mechanics and have little interest in mechanics. They like books. Talk to them about books and they can talk all night.

If you try to talk about blue-face aliens at work, they will ask you about which science fiction film you watched last night. When you tell them that you didn't see them in a film, but you talked to them on a spaceship you'll be lucky to keep your job, well, you can keep it if you can outlast the humiliation. I know, I've tried it. People can't talk about what they don't know or understand and this topic has been prohibited and censored for a very long time.

That is going to change. We are going to be talking about interstellar topics and we are going to be rewriting the books of history and knowledge to include our relationship with interstellar travelers. As I have said, interstellar travelers have been around for thousands and thousands of years. They have quietly influenced society without ever receiving any credit. You have to realize that our dances and songs come from off planet. Our fashions and our technologies also come from other planets. We have no original ideas on this planet. Our culture is made up of a plethora of offplanet cultures. Over each century, they have come into society and influenced society, quietly, and then left. Then others have stopped over and they have started technology companies, they have pioneered medicines, they have made unusual achievements and then they have left, they went to another starport.

We have taken for granted our culture and we have been misled to believe that all of what we have created is indigenous to this particular planet when in fact the complete opposite is true. Nothing invented here is original. It appears original because the truth has been blocked, because the egoless cultures watch and observe behind the curtains and demand no particular award for their achievements.

The difference between an earth culture and an interstellar culture is that an interstellar culture has evolved beyond their state of ego. They do not wage war and they do not oppress their people. Well, some races of nonhumans do. Some of them are here running your governments. The rulers of earth are interstellar people of the non-benevolent kind. The interstellar cultures I speak are people who are advanced and benevolent. They are experienced in managing the growth of entire civilizations. They are aware of the lengthy timelines to reconstitute a society that has been routinely brainwashed by egotistical sociopaths.

Some offplanet cultures are millions of years old so there is a huge gap in the knowledge and perception of a race of beings that are much older than we are. We cannot pretend to think we can overcome this gap in knowledge without a significant period of time and education. The meeting of interstellar cultures will improve our education because it will point out how much more we can learn and they will provide ideas and direction on what to study. They will show us the future of where we are heading. Build a laser today and build a laser engine tomorrow. They can see the future; they can show it to you. Are we up to the challenge of rethinking every single thing we have held onto till now?

Since many of these interstellar people have been visiting earth for quite some time, they know our cultures, they speak our languages. These localized travelers can become middlemen to the others who are not as accustomed to the earth culture. We should recognize and respect these people who can work between cultures, these kinds of Renaissance Men and Women. Give them some support and liberty because they are trying to bridge the gap of possibly millions of years. It is one thing to bridge a language barrier, it is quite another to bridge a planetary barrier.

WEAPONS DISMANTLED

The rise of our awareness will force us to re-determine our need for murder. That will fundamentally impact the cache of weapons at our disposal because we will no longer look at each other in a hateful way. We will no longer discriminate and find reasons for an enemy. There is no enemy. When we realize there is no enemy we will realize that we no longer need all these weapons. We will think of ourselves as needing security devices because there are dangerous incursions, we might even have offplanet incursions so we need to have devices for our protection and defence, but all the other military gadgets and nuclear warheads out there, why we wouldn't need them and these weapons of mass destruction would need to be dismantled.

Bullets, bombs and incendiary devices all need to be removed. The difficulty is to dismantle the over-20,000 nuclear warheads in a safe manner, and new technologies will come out to deal with those hazardous materials. We cannot in any good sense of the word keep in our pockets so many weapons of mass destruction, and we won't want to because we will no longer see an enemy in ourselves, we will see compatibility, we will see cooperation and we will see compassion.

How many nuclear warheads do you need to possess if you have no enemies, certainly no enemy worth unleashing radioactive devices on? The answer is zero. You don't even need one nuclear warhead if everyone wants to be friends. That means that people will join together to come up with ways to dismantle the reams of military weapons, the pistols, the rifles, the machine guns, the grenades, the tanks, the rocket launchers, the cannons and the large bombs. We can only accomplish this large scale operation if every member nation is involved, if no member nation is still waging war. We can't a superpower bent on war while the rest of the world dismantles bombs. That won't work.

The dismantling of weapons will usher in a revolution of inspiration and innovation. It will help all of recreate the future because we will no longer wake up each day to the threats of today. Terrorism will fade away and wars will disappear altogether. The government and the military will have to cooperate in the removal of these devices. A gradual approach is going to work best. At first, you dismantle the least used devices, the ones that are still in storage because we never found a use for them. Once those devices are clearly taken offline and are inoperable, then we move into the next used devices. We keep working our way up through the military devices, one section at a time and at the same time we are disallowing the use of any violent, militarized means.

This will indicate a profound period in human evolution because for the first time since Adam and Eve we will be able see the similarities in other people, we will see areas of cooperation instead of areas of division. We will lose the thirst for murder because murder is a form of division. To murder a race of people is to divide them from us, to separate them. It is like taking off your arm because you no longer see your arm as a holistic part of your body, but that is a delusion, isn't it? To damage or remove your arm would make a one-armed being instead of a two-armed being. If we see our leg as an enemy we will damage it and we will try to remove it. We might even die from trying to amputate our leg because our leg will try to resist, the muscles will fight back. They were designed that way. Same with a culture.

The culture will not lie down and allow itself to be murdered. It will resist. It will continue to resist because it wants to survive and because the culture is one component of all cultures. We can begin to see the fallacy of murder.

To proceed then with the dismantling of all the earth weapons, and to replace them with a more harmonious, more advanced sort in a more modest supply, is going to force us all to reinterpret our relationships with ourselves. We can no longer allow our ego to determine the likability of another cultural group. We have to learn to see how each cultural group here is merely one component of all cultures here. There is one body of culture with many smaller limbs. To sever any limb is like severing your own limb now. If this is something you would not do before, why would you do it now? It is silly to amputate oneself just because you are angry or hateful. The fact that you cannot easily grow back a limb is another complication, isn't it?

When we see the limitedness of murder and we see how all cultures are parts of the singular culture here, we will lose the desire to remove culture and we will gain the need to preserve culture. We will lose the need to carry weapons at first and then we will lose the need to have so many weapons. We will start programs to dismantle the larger bombs, the ones that will require more time to dissolve in a safe and environmental manner.

As the larger bomb dismantling program gets underway, we will see nations getting together to establish a new framework for security cooperation based on an entirely new set of rules. A set of rules that complies with the new framework of thinking present in culture. Luckily we will have advisors on hand to help us build effective models of security and defence. And we will also be able to adopt new technologies to secure dangerous situations without any bloodshed. Imagine that you could contain a set of criminals and to secure them without any bullets, without any physical damage, wouldn't that be a better approach than having a large gun battle on a downtown street?

Of course. But to adopt this level of defence approach, this kind of mindset, we also have to advance our thinking because our way of thinking of each other and the types of arsenals at our disposal are related to one another. We don't normally think of that but it is true. If are thinking remains primitive and destructive then we will still prefer to use primitive and destructive devices to obliterate a perceived threat. If our thinking is constructive and holistic, we will find minimalist ways to remove a threat, we will think of threats in a different manner entirely. We will be able to reduce the presence of threats simply by our thinking of threats in a different manner.

As our weapons grow in compliance to our thinking, we will find that we no longer require as many weapons as we thought previously. We will look into our storage rooms and weapons warehouses and we will bend over in disgust. How could we have been so primitive to build so many weapons? This is what will happen. We will look at our primitiveness and we will understand it when we realize that we had 30,000 weapons of mass destruction in our secret bunkers and we only needed 100 to wipe out all life on earth. We needed 100 and we owned 30,000 devices of obliteration and this does not include the tonnes of bullets and pistols. And then there are all the other advanced weaponry, the biological agents, the electromagnetic amplifiers, the infrasonic devices, the weapons in space and all the other weapons we are not supposed to know about. Truly, we live in a militarized prison environment.

The dismantling of weapons, we should remember, is going to require quite some time to accomplish in a safe and proper manner. We are talking about years if not decades of managed disposal and dismantling, and that is going to require a steady stream of compliance from all members of this plane of existence. We will need to establish early on a weapons dismantling commission that has as its members environmentalist and wise men and this commission will oversee the dismantling work in their particular region.

Each commission will set the standards and the standards will be shared across the planet and will be matched by other commissions. There will be milestones; we will applaud moments when we have dismantled so many tonnes of bullets and so many thousands of nuclear warheads.

We will celebrate the milestones because we will know that we have safely destroyed those very things that have been destroying our society. We will make a commitment not to repeat such primitive behaviour and to re-establish our connection to each and to value each other unlike ever before. And we will build new security protocols using nonlethal weapons and more advanced technologies including peaceful intention. If everyone is committed to peace then peace will prevail and should it arise that there are destructive people or groups then these people will be isolated and re-educated, they will be reprogrammed not to commit such atrocities and will be required to learn how to cooperate once again. Peace is a long-term attitude. It is a time of peace here and we should not spend our efforts on building destructive weapons. We are better off building starships.

THE REALITY INDUSTRY

The pockets of reality associates around the world, most of them in secret locations, working here and there trying to make things happen, these pockets will form the pockets of a pair of reality pants. The pants will become the shape of an entirely new industry that is solely focused on reality. In doing so, in extrapolating the secret and the unknown, we are literally going to shake up the structure of power in the world, verily it is going to destroy the concept of the world, the one we've so faithfully held onto for all these millennia. The reality business will become the new software business; it will make computers invisible as people tap into the architecture of nature.

The very idea that nature has a technological architecture is foreign to us as we have been steeped in a very superficial, egotistical existence of which we are now experiencing its crushing oppression upon every aspect of ourselves. But what many of us see now that is true is the fact that we exist because of a science that has eluded our simplistic brain functions. We are caught at that point between existing in either a left-side or a right-side and we are now conjoining our two hemispheres and we are seeing the whole system in all its beautiful manifestation. That is a very demanding exercise and not everyone is privy to this realization, what some would call enlightenment. It is not a true enlightenment because it is the foundation upon which we exist; it is that very reason that propels us to open our eyes in the morning and to close our eyes at night.

That science is reality science. This is an entirely new stream of knowledge that interprets, understands and administers all aspects of a technological existence, what we refer to as a biological existence, but we are seeing more and more how biology is a grand lie, it is a level of perception upon which we have allowed ourselves to exist upon. The true biology is a level of technology that is many millennia outside of our capacity, and well within reach. It is true that every civilization achieves a certain level of existential mastery and all of that process is based on their interpretation of the cosmic energies and their particular planar needs. To that end then we are faced with a very interesting proposition because if life is functioning according to a science, including a science for the soul and for incarnation, then how will that impact our reasons for living?

How will this new reality science impact our meaning and purpose?

If we evolved the household computer each day and every day until a point of total awareness and your tablet PC could think and could achieve wisdom, how would that situation affect your use of the computer? Would you still be allowed to use the computer when you wanted to or would you have to ask permission? Imagine you wanted to download a large file or to watch online porn, should this thinking computer decide whether or not it wants to go through this with you? It is not unlike a relationship with each other, isn't it? You wish to engage in intercourse with someone, they have to agree, you need permission. Why? Because they have awareness and wisdom. They are not a dumb terminal and unless they are paid to provide this service, they have every right to reject your idea. In fact, if they are constructed in the same manner as you, they are in possession of equal rights as are you and they are as limited as you might be, and this is a reflection of education and intuition.

If we evolved all machines on this planet by a thousand years of advancement in artificial intelligence and we upgraded our wireless systems and our thought processes, and all the necessary associations, if we did all of this, what would happen to the computer terminal? What would happen to a mainframe or a network server? Inevitably, they would branch out and take on a more permanent role in the provisions they are designed to do and they would be constructed of more and more natural and organic materials, materials that would resonate with the very technological nature of our own bodies. We would convert more and more of our locale into technological components, for example, we would put chips into our desks so that we could turn on the lights or answer a phone from our shoes. We would put data storage in our minds and we would augment our thoughts so that we could all interconnect via brainwaves. We could walk into a room and have that room vibrating at a certain wavelength for a certain purpose, for example, a higher wavelength for a more meditative repose. Today, when we want to enter a purer wavelength of activity, when we want to relax, we will choose to enter a park or take a walk near the ocean. We already, naturally understand an attraction to different wavelengths of energy and we go to these places without our conscious understanding.

This is the most interesting aspect of this place, we naturally adhere to the basic rules for a highly evolved technological existence, but we are not aware of it, the processes are invisible to us, to the majority. As the technological vistas of existence come into our understanding, we will more clearly see how we can shape the energies around us and to render different outcomes. We will see how we can manifest repair and adjustment to regions damaged by a storm or some unexpected disease. We can simply interact with the reality computers and to reprogram the broken codes. Of course, it is quite a shock to pretend a rock or a tree is actually an incredibly advanced computer terminal that is attached to some powerful mainframe, but that is actually the case. We rely on our desktop PC and praise its processing power and yet we are completely oblivious to the natural technologies around us.

We misunderstand the natural environment mostly because we misunderstand ourselves. We still see ourselves as biological beings living on a biological planet when the opposite is true. We are nonbiological beings existing on a nonbiological reality plane. All of it constructed from artificial materials, but artificial materials that are so advanced that they appear to be biological. So that is the mind-job. The mind-job is that all that appears natural and organic is in fact a very advanced inorganic material, so advanced that it can sustain existence. And that also means that there must be a source of existence, verily as Sustainer of existence. You might think of it as a mainframe computer. I think of it as a cosmic computer because it really is far beyond our concept of understanding for some time to come, and well beyond our replication. It is billions of years old and unless you intend to live that long you won't be capable of fully understanding it.

You can, on the other hand, fully realize that this cosmic entity provides what we all call "life." And because life is technological then that means that you can logon to the natural computers, the rocks and trees, and upload, download, learn, study, search, you can do whatever you normally do now, only that you will be doing it from a freely available terminal.
When the first personal computers popped out of the various California garages not so many decades ago we instantly realized that we wanted one. Not only that we wanted one but we wanted the next one coming out a year later. We realized that these computing devices needed constant upgrades and

we were willing to shell out our hard-earned money to remain computer savvy.

As soon as we understood, we were hooked. Well, the same thing is going to happen to the reality business. As more and more people understand the reality programs, as people's intentions start re-rendering society and removing the threat of war and wiping certain diseases completely off the map, as all these things become more and more evident we will establish an industry to help this new knowledge stream grow. We will teach people how to interact with nature. We will teach people how to think, or how not to think. We will set up organizations to monitor the technological environment and to manage the large areas of the planet. As these things happen, and they will, we will begin to see the new computer industry, we will see the rise of the reality industry and the computer businesses will either upgrade or they will fade away as all old technologies fade away. Building a reality industry will help all inhabitants of this place to further develop their methods of communication, healthcare, and travel just to name a few.

On top of this we will find ourselves communicating with other reality races. They will make themselves known and they will help us to increase our rate of learning and to avoid the pitfalls that they may have experienced. Realizing that all that we believed was an illusion, that biology was real for example, will be a good wakeup call for everyone. See how you intend to fit into this new industry.

Proof

Made in the USA
Charleston, SC
12 March 2010